THE LORDS OF WAR

OF WAR

FROM LINCOLN TO
CHURCHILL

By the same author:

The Desert Generals
The Swordbearers: Studies in Supreme Command in the First World War
Britain and Her Army, 1509–1970
The Collapse of British Power
Marlborough
Bonaparte
The Great War
Hitler's Generals (ed)
Engage the Enemy More Closely: The Royal Navy in the Second World War

THE PRIDE AND THE FALL SEQUENCE

The Collapse of British Power
The Audit of War: The Illusion and Reality of Britain as a Great Nation
The Lost Victory: British Dreams, British Realities 1945–1950
The Verdict of Peace: Britain Between Her Yesterday and the Future

THE LORDS
OF WAR

FROM LINCOLN TO
CHURCHILL

Supreme Command
1861–1945

Correlli Barnett

First published in Great Britain in 2012 by
The Praetorian Press
an imprint of
Pen and Sword Books Ltd
47 Church Street
Barnsley
South Yorkshire S70 2AS

Copyright © Correlli Barnett, 2012

ISBN 978 178159 093 5

Printed and bound in England
by CPI Group (UK) Ltd, Croydon, CR0 4YY

Typeset in Times New Roman by
CHIC GRAPHICS

Pen & Sword Books Ltd incorporates the imprints of
Pen & Sword Aviation, Pen & Sword Family History, Pen & Sword Maritime,
Pen & Sword Military, Pen & Sword Discovery, Wharncliffe Local History,
Wharncliffe True Crime, Wharncliffe Transport, Pen & Sword Select,
Pen & Sword Military Classics, Leo Cooper, Remember When,
The Praetorian Press, Seaforth Publishing and Frontline Publishing

For a complete list of Pen and Sword titles please contact
Pen and Sword Books Limited
47 Church Street, Barnsley, South Yorkshire, S70 2AS, England
E-mail: enquiries@pen-and-sword.co.uk
Website: www.pen-and-sword.co.uk

Contents

List of Photographs vii

List of Maps viii

Foreword ix

Author's Acknowledgements xi

Author's Preface xiv

Introduction xv

PART I: *The Nineteenth Century*

1   THE ROMANTIC IDEAL OF LEADERSHIP
    Napoleon Bonaparte...1

2   CRUSADER WITH A BLUNT SWORD
    Abraham Lincoln and the Failing Generals............................9

3   A STUDY IN CONTRAST
    Ulysses S. Grant and Robert E. Lee 24

4   THE CALCULATOR OF VICTORY
    Helmuth, Graf von Moltke and the Wars of Bismarck 41

5   THE PRICE OF INCOMPETENCE
    Napoleon III and his Marshals...56

PART II: *The Great War 1914–1918*

6   NERVE AND LOSS OF NERVE
    General Joffre versus Moltke the Younger 67

7   STALEMATE AND SCAPEGOAT
    General Sir Douglas Haig 82

8   BRILLIANCE AND BETRAYAL
    David Lloyd George as War Premier....................................98

9   THE SAVIOUR OF AN ARMY
Maréchal Pétain and the French Mutinies 109

10 LEADER TO CATASTROPHE
First Quartermaster General Erich Ludendorff 120

11 THE VICTOR OF 1918
Field Marshal Sir Douglas Haig 135

PART III: *The Second World War 1939–1945*

12 LEADER FROM THE FRONT
Generalfeldmarschall Erwin Rommel 143

13 THE RELUCTANT GAMBLER
Admiral Isoruku Yamamoto 161

14 FIRE-RAISER IN CHIEF
Air Chief Marshal Sir Arthur Harris 173

15 FROM DEFEAT INTO VICTORY
General Sir William Slim 187

16 NEPTUNE'S ADMIRAL
Admiral Sir Bertram Ramsay..204

17 COALITION SUPREME COMMANDER
General Dwight D. Eisenhower 219

18 STALIN'S MARSHAL
Marshal Georgi Zhukov..243

19 SPELLBINDER AND FANTASIST
Adolf Hitler 258

20 VICTORY AT ALL COST
Winston Churchill 278

Bibliography 301

Index 304

List of Photographs

1: Napoleon Bonaparte: the romantic ideal of a leader, but in reality a gambler with an unsound system of war and statecraft which condemned him to ultimate failure. (Taylor Library)

2: Abraham Lincoln, President of the United States of America, 1860–65. As supreme leader in the Civil War, he combined political vision and strategic grasp with a resolve to save the Union by destroying the secessionist confederacy of slave-owning states. (Library of Congress)

3: General George B. McClellan, C-in-C of the Union Army in 1861–62. Although an able organizer and trainer of troops, he shrank from conducting a remorseless war of attrition, costly in blood, against the southern Confederacy. (Library of Congress)

4: General Robert E. Lee, commander of the Confederate Army of Northern Virginia 1861–65, and C-in-C of all Confederate forces in 1865. Noble in appearance and personality, the very image of a great leader, he proved an ineffective battlefield commander. (Library of Congress)

5: General Ulysses S. Grant, C-in-C of all the Union armies 1864–65. 'A man of a good deal of rough dignity,' recorded a colleague, 'rather taciturn; quick and decided in speech'. He wore Lee down into defeat by an unrelenting campaign of attrition. (Mathew Brady: Library of Congress)

6: Field Marshal Helmuth Graf von Moltke, Chief of the Prussian (later German) General Staff 1857–88. His personal ascendancy sprang from a mastery both of strategic calculation and the logistical nuts-and-bolts of war in the field. (Public domain: UK)

7: Napoleon III, Emperor of the French, Commander-in-Chief of the French armies in the war with Prussia in 1870, taken prisoner after the catastrophic defeat at Sedan. He was neither an able strategist nor a decisive leader: a Napoleon only in name. (Public domain: UK)

8: Colonel General Helmuth von Moltke, Chief of the German General Staff, 1898–1914. The nephew of the great von Moltke, his nerve cracked under the strain of implementing the over-ambitious 'Schlieffen Plan' to destroy the French army in six weeks. (E. Bieber Atelier, Berlin/Public domain: USA)

9: General (later Marshal) Joseph Joffre, French Chief of the General Staff and C-in-C, 1911–16. Unshaken by initial disasters in 1914, he finally wrecked the Schlieffen Plan by his well-timed counter-stroke on the Marne on 9–12 September 1914. (Public domain: UK)

10: General (later Marshal) Philippe Pétain. In 1916 he defended Verdun against ferocious German assault; and as C-in-C in 1917 restored army morale after widespread mutinies. He advocated 'bite-and-hold' offensives instead of attempts at breakthroughs. (Library of Congress)

11: David Lloyd George, Minister of Munitions 1915–16 and Prime Minister 1916–23. He looked for an easier way to defeat the German Empire than fighting her main army on the Western Front. His deviousness destroyed all trust between him and Haig. (Library of Congress)

12: Erich Ludendorff, First Quarter-Master General, and Germany's *de facto* supreme warlord from 1916 to 1918. Being a disastrous director of a war economy and a grand-strategic muddler, he was a major factor in his country's defeat in the Great War. (Library of Congress)

13: General (later Field Marshal) Sir Douglas Haig, C-in-C of the British armies in France, 1916–18. He believed that the war could only be won by defeating Germany's main army – on the Western Front. This he finally achieved in the campaign of 1918. (Library of Congress)

14: General (later Field Marshal) Erwin Rommel, commander of the German/Italian PanzerarmeeAfrika in the Western Desert, 1941–43. His renown as a leader in battle even captivated Winston Churchill, who paid public tribute to him as 'a great general'. (Bundesarchiv)

15: Admiral Isoruku Yamamoto, C-in-C of the Japanese fleet, 1939–43. He planned the air strike on Pearl Harbor on 7 December 1941, but recognized that this could only win time for Japan, and that America's superior national strength must eventually prevail. (US National Archives)

16: Air Chief Marshal (later Marshal of the Royal Air Force) Sir Arthur Harris, AOC-in-C Bomber Command, 1942–5. He relentlessly carried out political directives to cripple German industrial production by destroying the housing of the workforce. (HM Government/Public domain: UK)

17: General Sir William Slim (later Field Marshal Lord Slim). Known affectionately as 'Uncle Bill', he led the British Empire forces in Burma from defeat at the hands of the Japanese invaders in 1942 to the victorious re-conquest of the colony in 1945. (HM Government/Public domain: UK)

18: Admiral Sir Bertram Ramsay, Naval Commander Allied Expeditionary Force. He planned and commanded Operation NEPTUNE, the naval side of the Anglo-American landings in Normandy on D Day, 6 June 1944, the largest and most complex amphibious operation in history. (HM Government/Public domain: UK)

19: Marshal of the Soviet Union Georgi Zhukov. His ruthlessly tough leadership saved Moscow from the German invaders in 1941 and Stalingrad in 1942. His speciality lay in launching a well-timed offensive in massive strength against an overstretched enemy. (US National Archives)

20: General Dwight Eisenhower, Supreme Allied Expeditionary Force. Though written off by Generals Brooke and Montgomery as a mere 'chairman of the board' he was superior to them in strategic judgement and in the conduct of large-scale operations. (US National Archives)

21: Adolf Hitler, *Der Führer* of the most formidable military and industrial power in continental Europe. He combined the personal magnetism of an evangelical preacher, the political ideas of an adolescent dreamer, and the managerial capabilities of a junior clerk. (US National Archives)

22: Winston Spencer Churchill, Prime Minister of the United Kingdom, 1940–45. A fighter by nature, and devoted to the cause of freedom and democracy, he found complete personal fulfilment in waging a victorious war against Hitler and the Nazi tyranny. (Yousuf Karsh/Library and Archives Canada/PA-165806)

List of Maps

1: The American states in 1861: the United States of America, the Confederate States of America, the border states and territories.
2: The Eastern Theatre of the American Civil War: Major battles 1861–1865.
3: Bohemian Battle Area, 1866, showing main railways and the advance of the Prussian Armies.
4: Germany in 1871.
5: The Franco-Prussian War.
6: Axes of advance of German right-wing armies, August–September 1914.
7: Moltke's alteration of the Schlieffen Plan.
8: Battle of the Somme, 1 July 1916. Haig's problem: the dense German trench system, as here along the Fricourt salient.
9: Joffre's Plan for the Battle of the Marne.
10: The Passchendaele Campaign 1917.
11: Pétain's limited offensive at Malmaison, 23 October 1917.
12: German Offensives, March–July 1918.
13: The Allied Offensives, July–November 1918.
14: Gazala Battles. Phase A, 27–28 May 1942.
15: Gazala Battles. Phase B, 31 May–5 June 1942.
16: First Battle of El Alamein July 1942, Phases One and Two.
17: Battle of Alam el Halfa, 31 August–3 September 1942.
18: Battle of El Alamein: Dispositions on 23 October 1942.
19: Battle of El Alamein 23–26 October 1942: Defeat of Montgomery's Breakthrough Plan.
20: D Day, 6 June 1944: Rommel's defence prevents Allies from achieving their planned objective line.
21: Japanese conquests, 1941–1942.
22: Bomber Command Major Targets, 1942–1945.
23: The Burma Campaign 1941–1945.
24: Operation Extended Capital, February–March 1945.
25: Operation Neptune, 6 June 1944.
26: Operation Overlord, 1944–1945: the liberation of Western Europe by the Allied Expeditionary Force under General Dwight Eisenhower, Supreme Allied Commander.
27: German offensives, 1941–1942.
28: Operation Uranus, 19–23 November 1942.
29: Russian Offensives 1942–1945.
30: Berlin surrounded late April 1945.
31: The Hitlerian Empire 1952.
32: The Mediterranean Theatre.

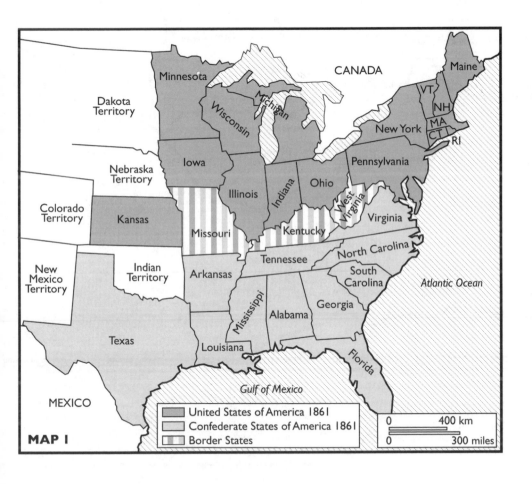

United States of America 1861
Confederate States of America 1861
Border States

MAP I

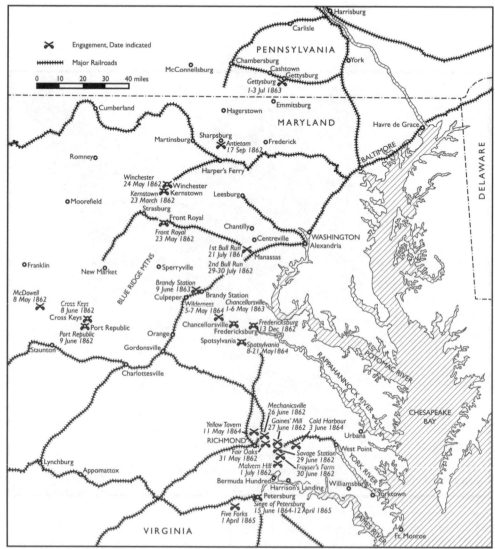

MAP 2 The Eastern Theatre of the American Civil War. Major battles 1861-1865

MAP 3 Bohemian Battle Area, 1866, Showing Main Railways and the Advance of the Prussian Armies

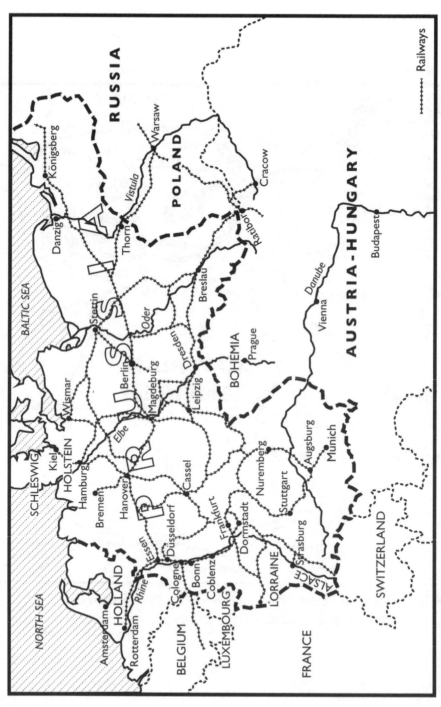

MAP 4 Germany in 1871

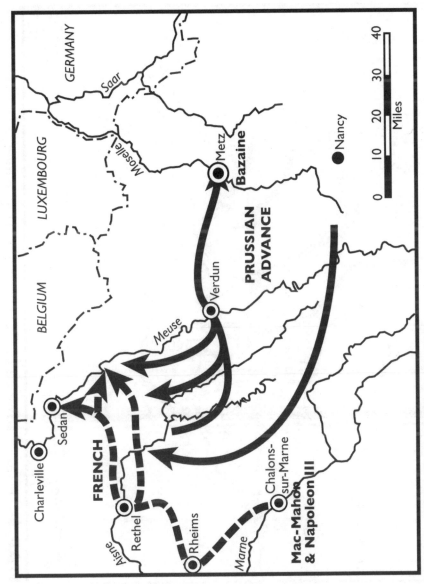

MAP 5 The Franco-Prussian War

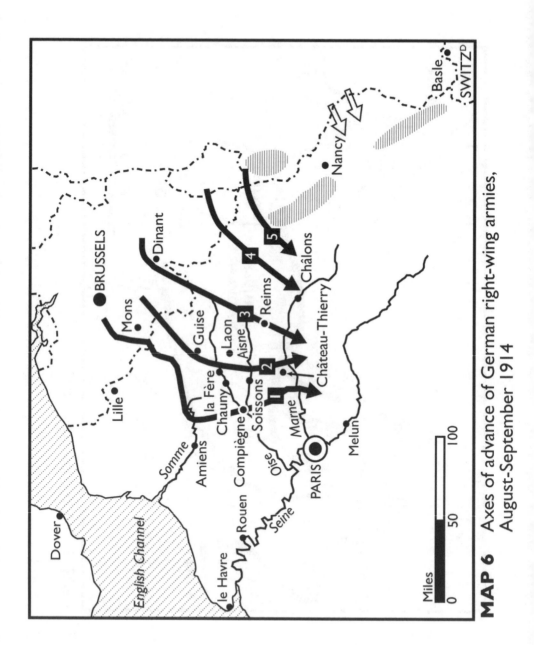

MAP 6 Axes of advance of German right-wing armies, August–September 1914

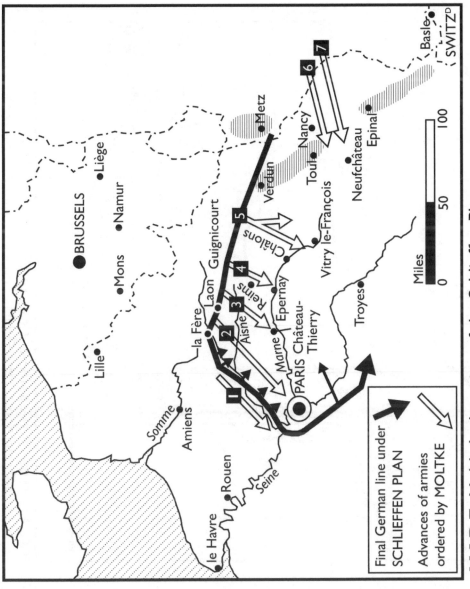

MAP 7 Moltke's alteration of the Schlieffen Plan

Key:
- Final German line under SCHLIEFFEN PLAN
- Advances of armies ordered by MOLTKE

Miles
0 — 50 — 100

Labels on map: le Havre, Rouen, Amiens, Somme, Seine, Lille, Mons, Namur, BRUSSELS, Liège, Metz, Verdun, Nancy, Toul, Neufchâteau, Epinal, Basle, SWITZ^D, PARIS, Château-Thierry, Epernay, Reims, Aisne, Marne, Troyes, Vitry le-François, Châlons, Guignicourt, Laon, la Fère

Army numbers: 1, 2, 3, 4, 5, 6, 7

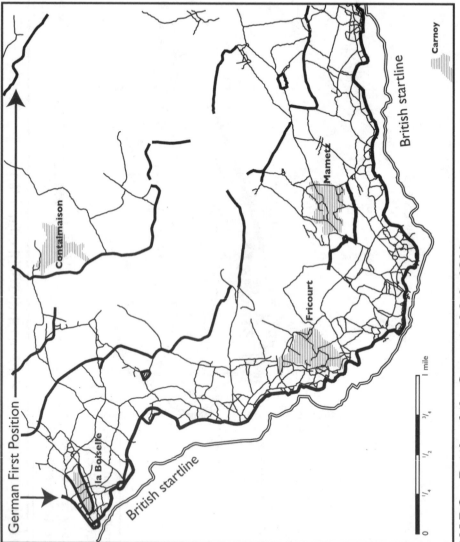

MAP 8   Battle of the Somme, I July 1916
Haig's problem: the dense German system, as here along the Fricourt salient

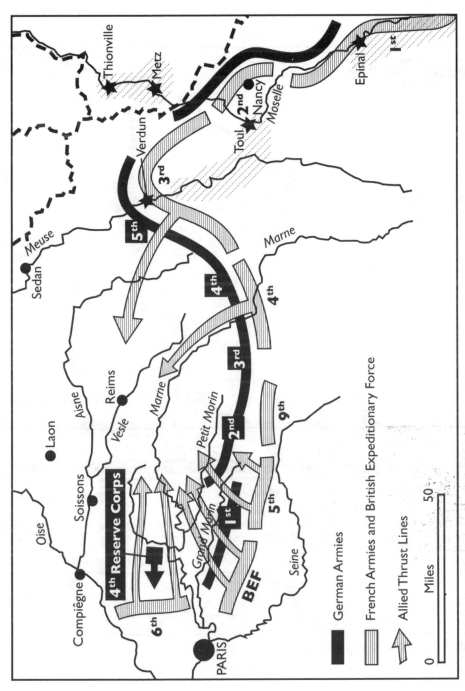

MAP 9 Joffre's Plan for the Battle of the Marne

Thionville

Metz

Nancy

Toul

Epinal

2nd

1st

Moselle

Verdun

3rd

Meuse

Sedan

5th

Marne

4th

4th

Laon

Aisne

Reims

Vesle

Marne

3rd

Soissons

Petit Morin

2nd

9th

Oise

Compiègne

4th Reserve Corps

Grand Morin

1st

5th

BEF

Seine

6th

PARIS

German Armies

French Armies and British Expeditionary Force

Allied Thrust Lines

Miles

0   50

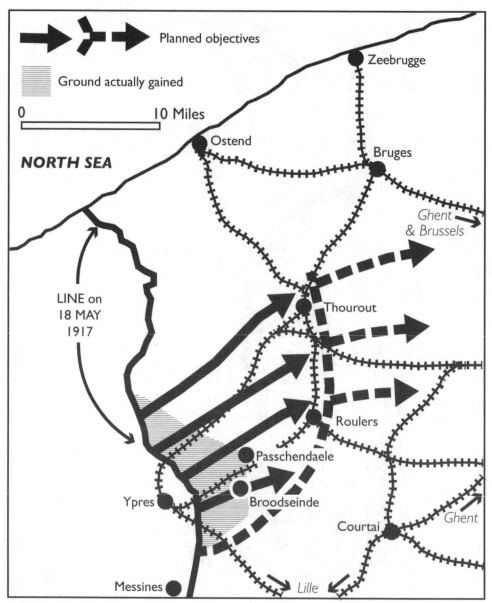

MAP 10 The Passchendaele Campaign 1917

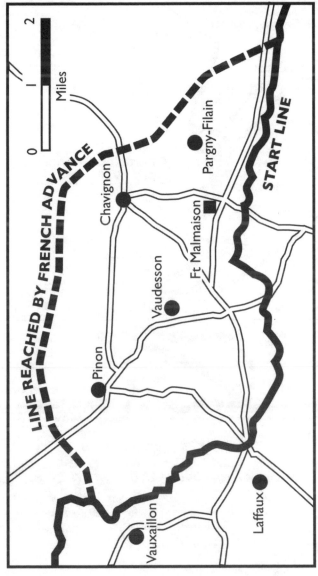

MAP 11 Pétain's limited offensive at Malmaison, 23 October 1917

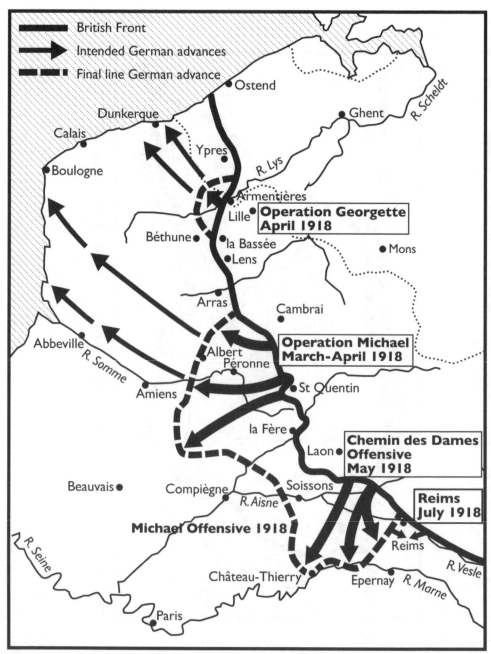

MAP 12 German Offensives, March–July 1918

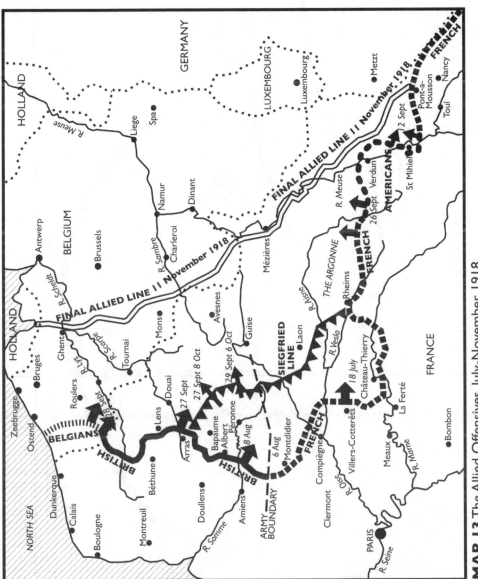

MAP 13 The Allied Offensives, July–November 1918

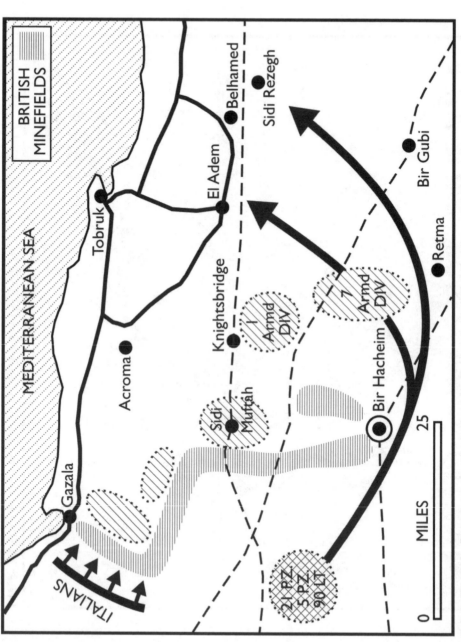

MAP 14 GAZALA BATTLES. Phase A, 27-28 May 1942

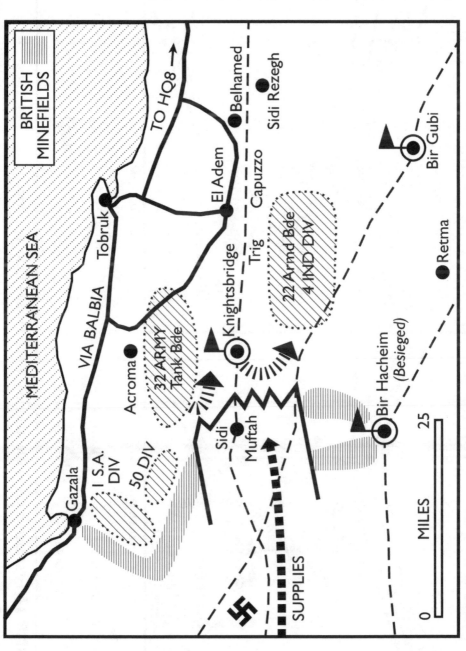

MAP 15 GAZALA BATTLES. Phase B, 31 May - 5 June 1942

MEDITERRANEAN SEA

BRITISH MINEFIELDS

TO HQ8 →

Gazala

Tobruk

VIA BALBIA

Acroma

El Adem

Belhamed

Sidi Rezegh

1 S.A. DIV

50 DIV

32 ARMY Tank Bde

Knightsbridge

Trig Capuzzo

22 Armd Bde 4 IND DIV

Bir Gubi

Sidi Muftah

Bir Hacheim (Besieged)

Retma

SUPPLIES

0   25

MILES

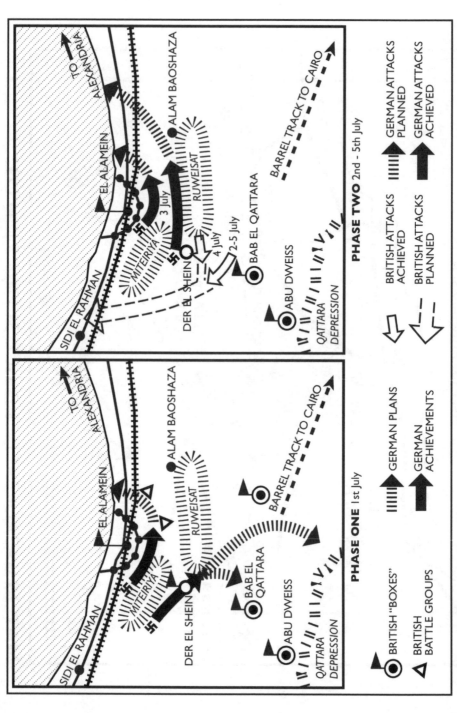

MAP 16 First Battle Of El Alamein July 1942, Phases One and Two

PHASE ONE 1st July

TO ALEXANDRIA

SIDI EL RAHMAN

EL ALAMEIN

MITERIYA

DER EL SHEIN

RUWEISAT

ALAM BAOSHAZA

BAB EL QATTARA

ABU DWEISS

QATTARA DEPRESSION

BARREL TRACK TO CAIRO

◉ BRITISH "BOXES"

▲ BRITISH BATTLE GROUPS

▆ GERMAN PLANS

▲ GERMAN ACHIEVEMENTS

PHASE TWO 2nd – 5th July

TO ALEXANDRIA

SIDI EL RAHMAN

EL ALAMEIN

MITERIYA

3 July

4 July

2-5 July

DER EL SHEIN

RUWEISAT

ALAM BAOSHAZA

BAB EL QATTARA

ABU DWEISS

QATTARA DEPRESSION

BARREL TRACK TO CAIRO

▆ GERMAN ATTACKS PLANNED

▆ GERMAN ATTACKS ACHIEVED

⇨ BRITISH ATTACKS ACHIEVED

⇨ BRITISH ATTACKS PLANNED

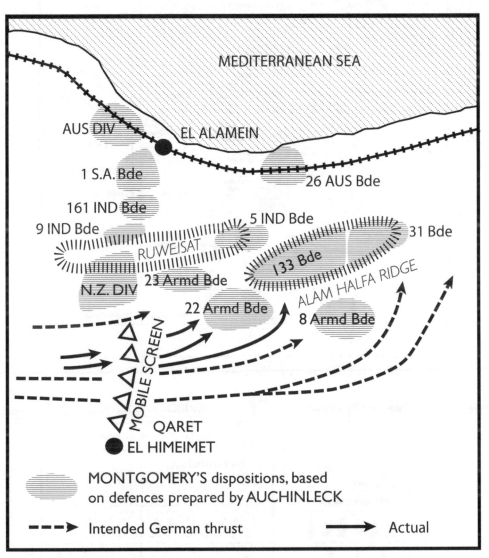

MEDITERRANEAN SEA

AUS DIV

EL ALAMEIN

1 S.A. Bde

26 AUS Bde

161 IND Bde

9 IND Bde

5 IND Bde

31 Bde

RUWEISAT

133 Bde

N.Z. DIV

23 Armd Bde

ALAM HALFA RIDGE

22 Armd Bde

8 Armd Bde

MOBILE SCREEN

QARET
EL HIMEIMET

MONTGOMERY'S dispositions, based
on defences prepared by AUCHINLECK

- - - ▶ Intended German thrust   ───▶ Actual

MAP 17 Battle of Alam el Halfa, 31 August - 3 September 1942

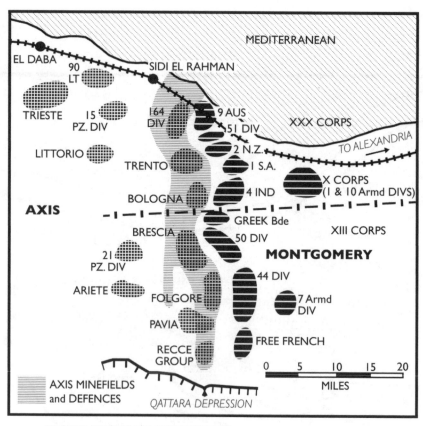

COMPARISON OF STRENGTHS

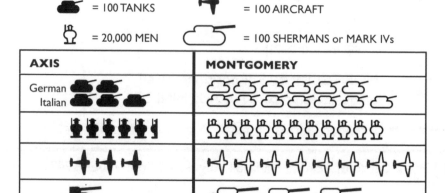

MAP 18 Battle of El Alamein: Dispositions on 23 October 1942

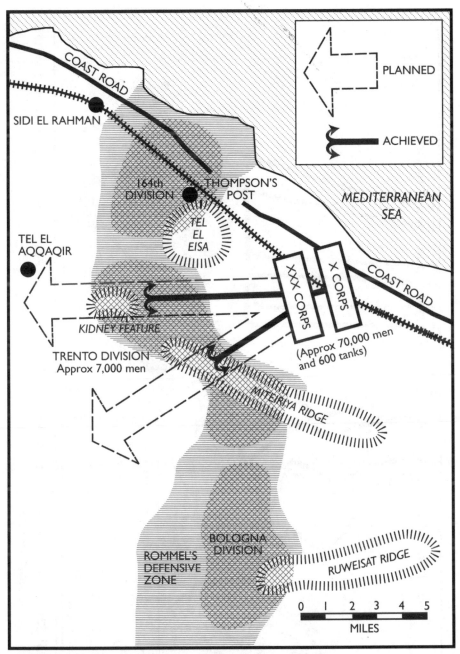

MAP 19 Battle of El Alamein 23-26 October 1942:
Defeat of Montgomery's Breakthrough Plan

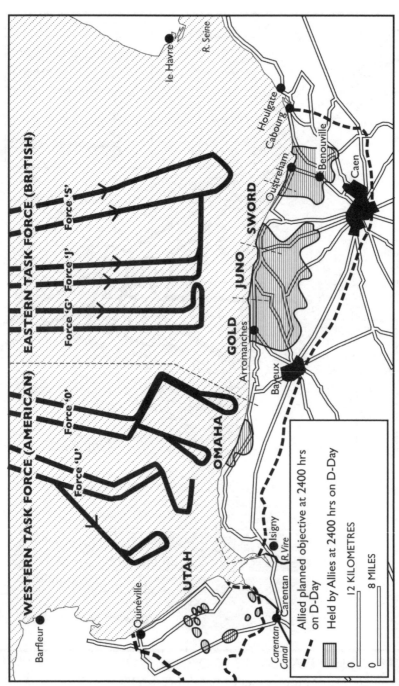

MAP 20 D-Day, 6 June 1944: Rommel's defence prevents Allies from achieving their planned objective line.

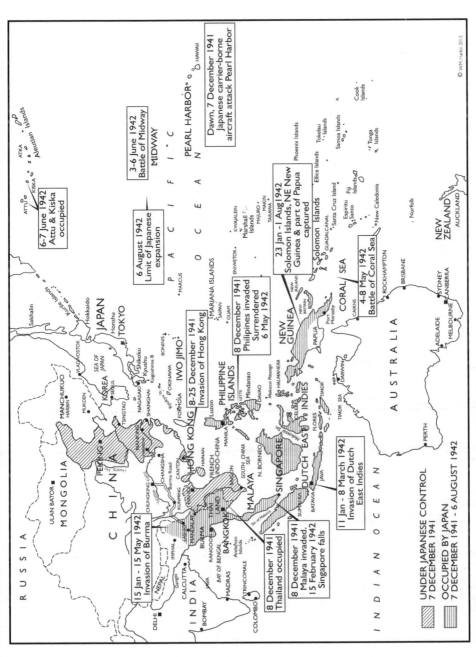

MAP 21 Japanese Conquests 1941-1942

MAP 22 Bomber Command Major Targets 1942-1945

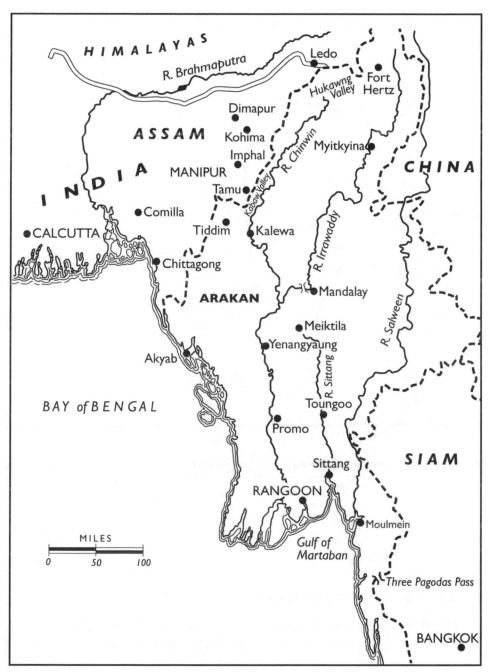

MAP 23 The Burma Campaign 1941 - 1945

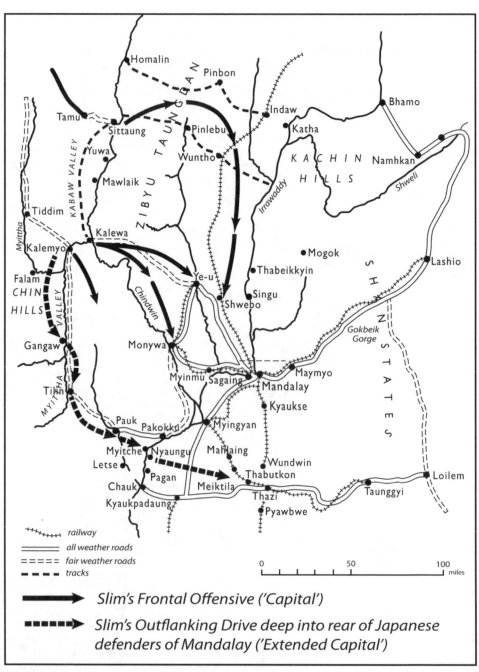

Homalin
Pinbon
Tamu
Sittaung
Pinlebu
Indaw
Bhamo
Yuwa
Wuntho
Katha
K A C H I N
Namhkan
Mawlaik
H I L L S
Shweli
Tiddim
ZIBYU TAUNGDAN
Myittha
Kalewa
Kalemyo
Mogok
Lashio
KABAW VALLEY
Ye-u
Thabeikkyin
Falam
Chindwin
Singu
S
CHIN
Shwebo
H
HILLS
Gangaw
MYITTHA VALLEY
Monywa
Gokbeik
Gorge
N
Tilin
Myinmu Sagaing
Maymyo
Pauk
Mandalay
S
Pakokku
Myingyan
Kyaukse
T
Myitche Nyaungu
Mahlaing
A
Letse
Wundwin
T
Pagan
Thabutkon
Loilem
E
Chauk
Meiktila
Thazi
Taunggyi
S
Kyaukpadaung
Pyawbwe

+++++++   railway
━━━━━   all weather roads
═════   fair weather roads
▪▪▪▪▪   tracks

0   50   100
                        miles

━━━▶ *Slim's Frontal Offensive ('Capital')*

▪▪▪▪▪▶ *Slim's Outflanking Drive deep into rear of Japanese*
        defenders of Mandalay ('Extended Capital')

MAP 24 Operation Extended Capital February - March 1945

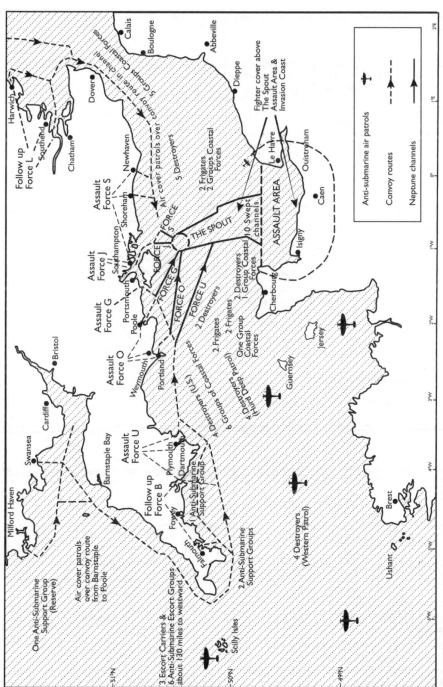

MAP 25 Operation Neptune, 6 June 1944

The following labels appear on the map:

Milford Haven
Swansea
Cardiff
Bristol

One Anti-Submarine Support Group (Reserve)

Air cover patrols over convoy route from Barnstaple to Poole

3. Escort Carriers & 6. Anti-Submarine Escort Groups about 130 miles to westward

Scilly Isles

Barnstaple Bay
Assault Force U
Follow up Force B
Dartmouth
Plymouth
Fowey
Falmouth
Anti-Submarine Support Group
2 Anti-Submarine Support Groups

4 Destroyers (Western Patrol)
Ushant
Brest
Guernsey
Jersey

4 Destroyers Patrol (Hurd Deep)
4 Destroyers (U.S.) Coastal Forces
6 Groups of Coastal Forces
One Group Coastal Forces
2 Frigates
2 Frigates

Assault Force O
Weymouth
Portland
FORCE O
FORCE U
FORCE G
Poole
Portsmouth
Assault Force G

Southampton
Assault Force J
FORCE J
FORCE S
THE SPOUT
10 Swept channels

Shoreham
Assault Force S
Newhaven

Air cover patrols over convoy route
5 Destroyers
2 Frigates
2 Groups Coastal Forces

2 Destroyers
1 Group Coastal Forces
Cherbourg
Isigny
Caen
Ouistreham
Le Havre
ASSAULT AREA
Fighter cover above The Spout Assault Area & Invasion Coast

Dieppe
Abbeville
Boulogne
Calais

Convoy route in Channel
5 Groups Coastal Forces
Dover
Chatham
Southend
Harwich
Follow up Force L

Legend:
Anti-submarine air patrols
Convoy routes
Neptune channels

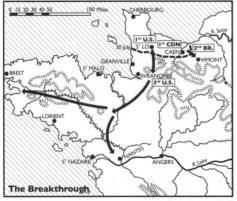

The Breakthrough

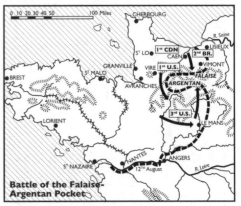

Battle of the Falaise-Argentan Pocket

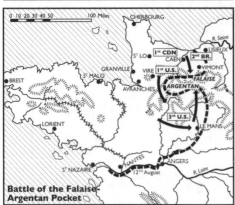

Battle of the Falaise-Argentan Pocket

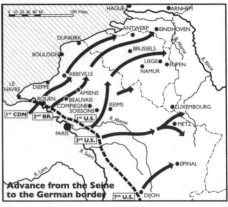

Advance from the Seine to the German border

German Ardennes Offensive

MAP 26
Operation Overlord, 1944-1945:
the liberation of Western Europe by the Allied
Expeditionary Force under General Dwight Eisenhower,
Supreme Allied Commander.

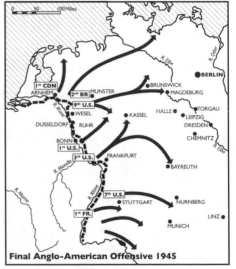

Final Anglo-American Offensive 1945

MAP 27 German Offensives 1941-1942

Legend:
- Furthest German advance 1941
- Furthest German advance 1942
- Startline "Barbarossa' June 1941
- Recaptured by Red Army Winter 1941

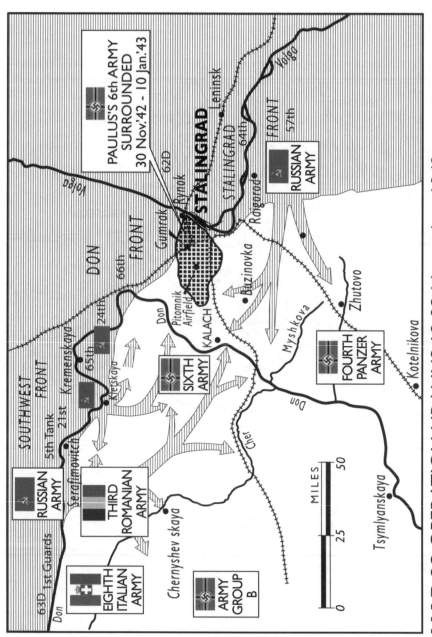

MAP 28 OPERATION URANUS 19-23 November 1942

Within the map:

PAULUS'S 6th ARMY SURROUNDED 30 Nov. '42 – 10 Jan. '43

SOUTHWEST FRONT
5th Tank
21st
Serafimovich
63D 1st Guards
Don
Kremenskaya
Kletskaya
65th
24th
DON FRONT
66th
Volga

RUSSIAN ARMY

THIRD ROMANIAN ARMY

EIGHTH ITALIAN ARMY

ARMY GROUP B

Chernyshev skaya
Chir
Don

SIXTH ARMY

Kalach
Don
Pitomnik Airfield
Gumrak
Rynok
62D
STALINGRAD
STALINGRAD
64th
Leninsk
Volga

Bazinovka
Rasgorod
Myshkova
Zhutovo

FRONT
57th
RUSSIAN ARMY

FOURTH PANZER ARMY
Kotelnikova

Tsymlyanskaya

MILES
0   25   50

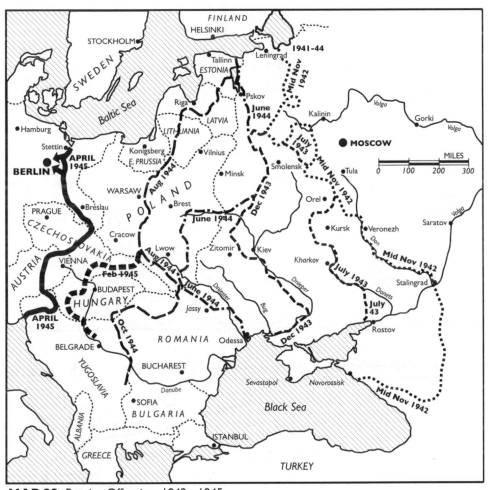

MAP 29 Russian Offensives 1942 - 1945

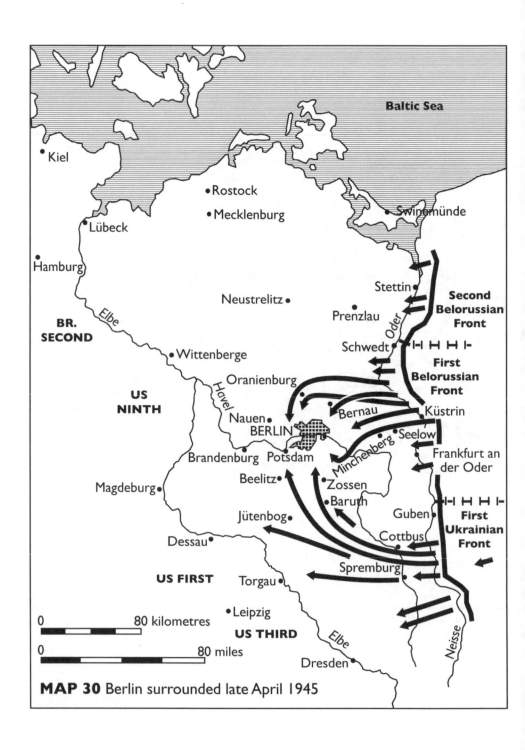

MAP 30 Berlin surrounded late April 1945

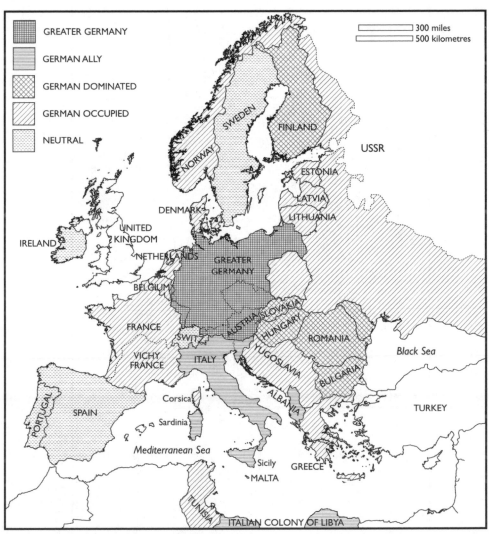

GREATER GERMANY

GERMAN ALLY

GERMAN DOMINATED

GERMAN OCCUPIED

NEUTRAL

300 miles

500 kilometres

USSR

SWEDEN

FINLAND

NORWAY

ESTONIA

LATVIA

LITHUANIA

DENMARK

IRELAND

UNITED KINGDOM

NETHERLANDS

GREATER GERMANY

BELGIUM

FRANCE

SWIT

AUSTRIA SLOVAKIA

HUNGARY

ROMANIA

Black Sea

VICHY FRANCE

ITALY

YUGOSLAVIA

BULGARIA

PORTUGAL

SPAIN

Corsica

Sardinia

ALBANIA

TURKEY

Mediterranean Sea

Sicily

MALTA

GREECE

TUNISIA

ITALIAN COLONY OF LIBYA

MAP 31 The Hitlerian Empire 1942

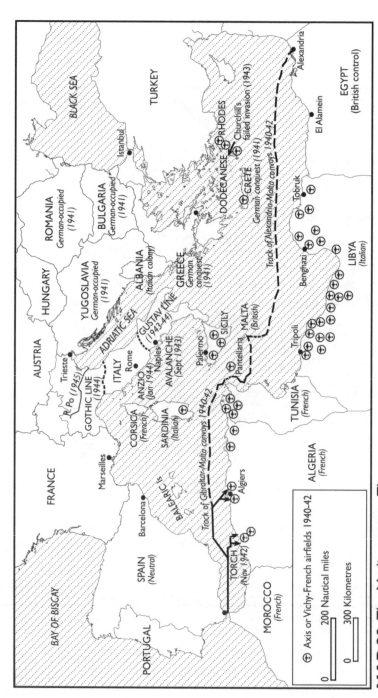

MAP 32 The Mediterranean Theatre

Foreword

General The Lord Dannatt GCB CBE MC DL
Chief of the General Staff 2006–2009
Constable of Her Majesty's Tower of London

After a lifetime as historian and writer Correlli Barnett has produced his most accomplished book to date. *The Lords of War* is no ordinary book on military leadership; it is an extraordinarily privileged examination of command in war at the highest level. The individuals whom Barnett has chosen to illuminate are not all generals, admirals and air marshals but include an emperor, a president, two prime ministers and a dictator. This book is truly about command at the highest level and that essential relationship between those who lead and those who follow – recognition that *leadership* and *'follow-ship'* are the two sides of the same coin. And this examination of command is a privilege for the reader to savour, drawing as it does on Correlli Barnett's lifetime of scholarship.

The brilliance of this book is signposted in the author's introductory essay on the nature of leadership. In the final paragraph of his introduction, Barnett concludes that 'the secret of leadership lies not in managing human resources, but in cherishing human relationships'. In the chapters that follow he tests this thesis in limited war, coalition war and total war, from the perspectives of military and civilian leaders alike. In the twenty chapters that comprise the book, one famous or infamous career after another is distilled with great clarity and skill into a refreshingly focused conclusion that leaves the reader in no doubt about the particular trait of character that Barnett has highlighted to pursue his argument. From Napoleon Bonaparte's realisation that to succeed he had to feed his army with success almost regardless of the strategic consequences, through Lincoln's struggle to find a general with whom he could do business and on to Churchill's determination to achieve victory at all cost, this book is a grand march through the nineteenth and twentieth century experiences of war in all its energy and ferocity. Every chapter adds to the strength of Barnett's original thesis.

Perhaps the apparent surprise is the absence of a concluding essay drawing the threads of the work together. The tidy mind has always sought a beginning, a middle and an end to any enterprise, but Barnett dignifies both himself and the reader by allowing the text to finish at the conclusion of the twenty studies. Although the study of Churchill's leadership to victory is very appropriately the final offering, the penultimate study of Adolf Hitler – 'Spellbinder and Fantasist' – validates Barnett's thesis most vividly. After the easy victories of 1940 the German people would have followed Hitler to hell and back, but when the gates of hell beckoned the German people were abandoned by their leader. As Barnett comments, for Hitler 'the German people's existence was only justified by their usefulness as instruments of his personal ambition'. To paraphrase Winston Churchill, never in the field of human conflict had a people been abused for so long by a leader determined to fulfil his own selfish wishes. With judgements such as that, Correlli Barnett quite properly refrains from a concluding essay leaving the reader the privilege of drawing his or her own conclusions. Such an ending is a tribute to the author's brilliance. This book is a most compelling read for the military historian and the general reader alike. It is Correlli Barnett at his vintage best.

Author's Acknowledgements

Once again I thank my wife Ruth for acting as a first-rate chief of staff and quartermaster, and for reading the draft narrative of the book chapter by chapter with the sharpest eye for errors and stylistic infelicities.

I would also like to express my deep gratitude for the invaluable help given by Mrs Josephine Sykes (my one-time colleague in the Churchill Archives Centre) and by Mrs Kelly Fair.

I wish to thank General The Lord Dannatt for his kindness in reading the typescript of *The Lords of War*, and for his critical comments thereon.

I also wish to thank Mr Lewis Lehrman for his good advice and unstinted help in regard to the chapters on Abraham Lincoln and the Civil War. I am likewise grateful to Professor Richard Behn, Professor Michael Burlingame, Professsor David Reynolds, Professor Brooke Simpson, and Professor Howard Temperley for their kindness in reading draft chapters lying within their specialist expertise, and for offering numerous helpful criticisms and suggestions. The errors of fact or judgement that remain are mine alone.

I would like to express my thanks to my publisher, Mr James Wilson, to my editor, Mr Richard Doherty, and to their colleague, Mrs Laura Lawton, for all their support, to Lucy Sylvia Menzies-Earl for compiling the index, and Tim Webster and Liam Harkin for drawing the maps.

I am indebted to the following publishers for permission to quote from copyright works in their control: B.T. Batsford Ltd, *Napoleon as Military Commander* and *Haig as Military Commander*, by Sir James Marshall-Cornwall, *Rommel as Military Commander* by Ronald Lewin; G. Bell and Sons, *The Gamble: Bonaparte in Italy 1796–7* by Guglielmo Ferrero; Cassell Ltd, *Defeat into Victory* by Field Marshal the Viscount Slim, *The Loss of the Bismarck: An Avoidable Disaster*, Graham Rhys Jones, *History of the Second World War*, B.H. Liddell Hart; Eyre Methuen, *Soldiers and Civilians: The Martial Spirit in America 1775–1865* by Marcus Cunliffe, *The Young Lloyd George* by John Grigg; London, Eyre & Spotiswoode, *Two Men Who Saved France* by Major General Sir Edward Spears; Stacpoole Books, Mechanicsburg, *Lincoln at Peoria: The Turning Point* by Lewis E. Lehrman; Knopf, New York, *Abraham Lincoln* by Benjamin Thomas, *Lincoln and His Generals* by T.H. Williams; D. Appleton-Century Company (reprinted by Eric Lundberg, Maryland), *The History of the United States Army* by W. A. Ganoe;

Faber, London, *Strategy: The Indirect Approach* by Basil Liddell Hart; Phoenix Press, London, *The Coming Fury* and *Never Call Retreat* by Bruce Catton, *War Diaries 1939–1945; Field Marshal Lord Alanbrooke*, Alex Danchev and Daniel Todman (Editors); Hodder and Stoughton, London, *The Two Marshals* by Philip Guedalla, *Engage the Enemy More Closely* by Correlli Barnett, *Tug of War: The Battle for Italy, 1943–1945* by Shelford Bidwell and Dominick Graham; Rupert Hart-Davis, London, *The Franco-Prussian War* by Michael Howard, *Ludendorff* by D.J. Goodspeed; Oswald Wolff, London, *The Schlieffen Plan; Critique of a Myth* by Gerhard Ritter; HMSO, London, *Statistics of the Military Effort of the British Empire, History of the Ministry of Munitions, Military Operations France and Belgium 1918* Vol IV by J. E. Edmonds, *The Strategic Air Offensive Against Germany 1939–1945* by Webster and Frankland, *Grand Strategy* by John Ehrman, *British Intelligence in the Second World War: Its Influence on Strategy and Operations*, Vol Three, Part II by H. Hinsley, with E.R. Thomas, C.A.G. Simkins, and C.F.G. Ransome, *Victory in the West*, Vol II by Major L.F. Ellis, *British Foreign Policy in the Second World War* by E.L. Woodward, *Report by the Supreme Commander to the Combined Chiefs of Staff on the Operations in Europe of the Allied Expeditionary Force, 6 June 1944 to 8 May 1945* by General Dwight D. Eisenhower, (and Longmans, Green), *Merchant Shipping and the Demands of War* by C.B.A. Behrens; Collins, London, *Bomber Offensive* by Marshal of the Royal Air Force Sir Arthur Harris, *Churchill and the Admirals, Decision in Normandy: the Unwritten Story of Montgomery and the Allied Campaign* by Carlo D'Este, *The Memoirs of Field-Marshal The Viscount Montgomery of Alamein KG*; Oxford University Press, *The Great War and Modern Memory* by Paul Fussell; Princeton University Press, *Army, Industry, and Labour in Germany 1914–1918* by Gerald D. Feldman; Sidgwick & Jackson, London, *To Win a War: 1918 The Year of Victory, The Smoke and the Fire* and *Trafalgar* by John Terraine; Coronet Books, London, *Hitler* by Norman Stone; Leo Cooper, London, *The Road to Passchendaele: The Flanders Offensive of 1917; A Study in Inevitability*, John Terraine; Hamlyn Paperbacks, London, *The Rommel Papers* by B.H. Liddell Hart (Ed); Michael Joseph, London, *Bomber Command* and *Overlord: D-Day and the Battle for Normandy 1944* by Max Hastings; Sphere Books, London, *Inside the Third Reich* by Albert Speer; Weidenfeld and Nicolson, London, *Hitler's Generals* by Correlli Barnett (Ed), London, Weidenfeld and Nicholson 1964, *Inside Hitler's Headquarters 1939–45*, Walter Warlimont (Deputy Chief of the OKW Operations Staff), *Churchill: A Study in Failure, 1900–1939*, Robert Rhodes James, *Alex: The Life of Field Marshal Earl Alexander of Tunis* by Nigel Nicolson; Viking, London, *Inferno: The Devastation of Hamburg, 1943*, Keith Lowe, *Stalingrad* and *D-Day: the Battle for Normandy* by Antony Beevor; Heineman, London, *Winston S. Churchill* by Martin Gilbert; Greenhill Books, London, *Bomber Harris: His Life and Times* by Webster and Frankland; Pan Books, London, *The Collapse of British*

AUTHOR'S ACKNOWLEDGEMENTS

Power by Correlli Barnett; Pimlico, London, *The Second World War* by John Keegan; Penguin Books, *Origins of the Second World War* by A.J.P. Taylor; The Clarendon Press, Oxford, *The Wartime Alliance and the Zonal Division of Germany* by T. Sharp; Kegan Paul, London, *Paris* by B. H. Liddell Hart; Routledge and Kegan Paul, *Napoleon 1799–1807 and Napoleon 1797–1815* by Georges Lefebvre; The Johns Hopkins Press, Baltimore and London, *The Papers of Dwight David Eisenhower; The War Years: IV* by Alfred D. Chandler; Military Heritage Press, New York, *Stalingrad to Berlin: The German Defeat in the East* by Earl F. Ziemke; Jonathan Cape Ltd, New York, *The Memoirs of Marshal Zhukov* by G.K. Zhukov; Limes Verlag, Berlin, *Der Feldherr Ludendorff in Ungluck* by Colonel Merz von Quirnheim; Berger-Levrault, Paris, *Le Commandement en chef des Armées Françaises du 15 Mai 1917 á l'Armistice* by General Laure and *Le Devoir des Elites dans la Défense Nationale* by Marshal Philippe Pétain; Payot, Paris, *La Bataille de Verdun* by Marshal Philippe Pétain; Plon, Paris, *Trente Ans avec Pétain* by General Serrigny; Editions du Conquistador, Paris, *Les Grandes Heures du Général Pétain* by Lt Col Henri Carré; Charles-Lavauzelle, Paris, *Le Haut Commandement Allemand Pendant La Campagne de la Marne en 1914* by Major General Baumgarten-Crusius; The Reprint Society, *Years of Victory 1802–1812* by Arthur Bryant; John Wiley, London, *Grant and Lee* by J.F.C. Fuller; Printing Office – for the Use of the War Department, *The Command of the Air* by Giulio Douhet; Barnes & Noble, New York, *Death of a Nation: The Confederate Army at Gettysburg,* by Clifford Dowdey; John Murray, London, *Tanks in the Great War* by J.F.C. Fuller; Larrey: *Surgeon to Napoleon's Imperial Guard* by Robert C. Richardson; Odhams, London, *War Memoirs* by David Lloyd George; Weidenfeld and Nicolson, *Wellington: The Years of the Sword* by Elizabeth Longford; Churchill Archives Centre, letter of 27 May 1940. Ramsay Papers, RMSY 8/10; National Archives, Kew, ADM 234/363, BS No. 49, *The Campaign in North-west Europe, June 1944–May 1945.*

Quotes from Admiral Yamamoto's family or former colleagues are taken from interviews conducted by the BBC for the 1973 television series 'The Commanders'. Thanks are also due to the BBC for quotations from interviews conducted for this series.

Note to Reader

I have chosen the civilian and military leaders for portrayal in this book because they offer a rich diversity of national background, individual character, and style of command; and also because their careers, taken together, encompass the conduct of limited war, coalition war, and total war. No doubt other historians would choose differently.

Author's Preface

The theme of the present work is the decisive effect on history exerted by individual human leadership. The background, in sharp contrast, lies in the profound political, social, and technological changes that took place in the world between the outbreak of the American Civil War in 1861 and the conclusion of the Second World War in 1945.

The twenty civilian and military leaders portrayed in this book have been chosen because they offer a rich diversity of personal character, national culture, and style of command; and because their careers encompass limited war, coalition war, and total war, as well as campaigns of brilliant manoeuvre and campaigns of bloody attrition.

For the historian, with his priceless gift of hindsight, it is fascinating to study these men locked in struggle with great events, in moments of clear-sightedness' and self-delusion, of despair or unbreakable resolve. And for the leaders of today, in whatever walk of life, there is much to learn from the examples of the leaders of the past.

Introduction

The Nature of Leadership

In a memorable passage in his book *On War*, Carl von Clausewitz describes the role of a commander in a long, hard battle:

> As long as his men, full of courage, fight with zeal and spirit, it is seldom necessary for the Chief to show great energy of purpose in the pursuit of his object. But as soon as great difficulties arise – and that must always happen when great results are at stake – then things no longer move on of themselves like a well-oiled machine, the machine itself then begins to offer resistance, and to overcome this the Commander must have a great deal of force of will. As the moral forces in one individual after another become prostrated, the whole inertia of the mass gradually rests its weight on the Will of the Commander; by the spark in his breast, by the light of his spirit, the spark of purpose, the light of hope, must be kindled afresh in others.

This is not generalship. This is not the art of command, let alone 'management'. This surely is *leadership* – the communication of moral energy to a human herd that needs it.

Here is another quotation which conveys the essence of leadership, as distinct from mere rank or authority:

> Markmann knew precisely how he stood with his men. To them he was not their commanding officer; he was their Leader! And they were his comrades! They trusted him blindly and would have followed him into hell itself if it were necessary.

The quotation in fact describes a company commander in the German storm-troops on the Western Front in the Great War. Yet it would equally fit Vice Admiral Lord Nelson and the Mediterranean Fleet, or Napoleon Bonaparte and the Grande Armée. It should be noted that the quotation does not speak of blind obedience, but blind *trust*. Unlike formal rank or authority, true leadership is not *imposed* on a human herd, but instead *desired* by it.

It follows that a leader's personality must fit the particular psychology of those he leads. Napoleon's leadership style – rhetorical orders of the dday, the imperial gaze close into each soldier's face, the familiar back-chat with his 'children', the pinch on the cheek – was exactly suited to French conscripts in an era of revolutionary tuurmoil. When Napoleon reviewed the Imperial Guard in 1812 on their way to Russia (recorded an observer, the German poet Heine), 'the old grenadiers glanced up at him with so awesome a devotion, so symppathetic an earnestness, with the pride of death ...'

Napoleon's spell was so powerful that it survived the military catastrophes in Russia in 1812, in Germany in 1813, and in France itseelf in 1814; and in 1815 the whole of the French active army 'the Emperor' to Waterloo.

In stark contrast, the Duke of Wellington was a cool and aloof aristocrat who practised no arts of ingratiation with his long-service soldiers. Yet they placed absolute trust in his as their leader, rightly convinced that if he were at their head on the field of battle the French would be beaten.

When appraising individual leaders, it is therefore important to take into account the collective character of those they led (or lead). For leadership is a two-way relationship.

The Impact of the Industrial Revolution on Leadership

The nineteenth-century industrial revolution transformed the nature of warfare along with almost every other aspect of western society. The impact proved all the greater because technological change and the growth of population accelerated together, proving a fearsome combination of ever more destructive weaponry and ever larger armies.

The growth in sheer scale was indeed astonishing. Whereas Wellington commanded an army of 67,000 men at Waterloo, Field Marshal Sir Douglas Haig on the Western Front 100 years later commanded a force of one and half million men, divided into four armies each much larger than Wellington's. And whereas Wellington could and did command his entire army in person on and off the battlefield (even giving orders to individual battalions at Waterloo), Haig had to exercise leadership through the medium of four subordinate army commanders and a chain of command extending down through army corps, divisions, brigades, and battalions.

This vast increase in scale and complexity, coupled with ever faster technological innovation, resulted in a complete revolution in military affairs – and, above all, in firepower. At Waterloo, Wellington fielded 156 guns, all short-range muzzle-loaders, the propellant being black gunpowder which shrouded the battlefield in acrid smoke. In 1917 just one of Haig's armies in a single attack deployed 1,295 breech-loading guns and howitzers, all with smokeless powder as the propellant, and, for the heaviest calibre, a maximum range of some 14,000 metres. Whereas at Waterloo the enemy had been bombarded over open sights, a century later on the Western Front the practice of gunnery had come to mean complex moving barrages plotted and directed thanks to target-spotting by aircraft or tethered observation balloons, and by precise sound-ranging and flash-spotting of enemy guns. In order to ensure maximum accuracy, the calculations of the gunners now had to take into account such factors as barrel wear, the quality of the propellant, and current meteorological conditions affecting the flight of shell. In short, gunnery had become a science instead of an art.

In logistics, the wagon train of Wellington's day drawn by horses or bullocks at a slow walking pace had given way by the Great War to railway freight trains steam-hauled at speeds ten or even twenty times faster, and with far, far larger loads. In the Great War, moreover, the motor truck made its debut as a means of military logistics, most famously in supplying the beleaguered French fortress of Verdun in 1916. In the Second World War, and thanks to the prodigious output from American assembly lines, the truck moved entire armies and their supplies with an operational flexibility which the railway could not match.

A similar revolution occurred in seaborne logistics, with sailing ships dependant on the vagaries of wind and tide replaced by steam-driven freighters and troopships making their steady 10–12 knots between home ports and far-off theatres of war.

Yet it was the truly astonishing advances in signals technology during the nineteenth and twentieth centuries that made the greatest direct impact on leadership. For, in any era, the key to a leader's power to command and control lies in the then available means of transmitting his orders and receiving back operational reports and intelligence.

In the close-range land battles of the pre-industrial era, commanders on horseback could see for themselves how well or badly an attack was going. They could see for themselves which of their own regiments lay in danger of being overwhelmed by an enemy charge. And in either case they could give timely and appropriate orders to subordinates. But by 1914–18, with millions of men dug in along the Western Front and a multi-layered military hierarchy, such a direct personal response by a commanding general to the ebb and flow of fighting was no longer possible. Instead there had to be reliance on technological means of communication.

Given the static nature of the Western Front, the answer lay in an elaborate telephone net which linked together all units and formations in the British Expeditionary Force, as likewise in the French and German armies.

Yet temporary lines reeled forward over the battlefield during an offensive were all too easily cut by enemy shellfire or otherwise damaged. The telephone simply could not provide reliable up-to-the-minute voice contact between forward units engaged in battle and the commanders who were trying to direct their operations. Morse-code wireless sets could not supply an answer because they were too heavy and cumbersome, and too slow and laborious in transmission.

These limitations in signals technology meant that troops advancing to the attack disappeared into a 'black hole' of isolation once they had left their own trenches. This isolation might last for hours or even days.

In consequence, their leaders, from battalion level all the way up to the Commander-in-Chief, could know little or nothing about the current state of fighting on the front line; and therefore had no chance of giving timely and appropriate tactical orders.

Only in the Second World War was this key operational problem solved by new technology – the 'walkie-talkie' radio. Fitted in tanks, headquarters trucks, tactical aircraft, and even in back-packs carried by the infantry, the walkie-talkie restored the power of direct personal leadership in the field once enjoyed by pre-industrial commanders like Wellington.

The revolution in signals since the eighteenth century had an equally profound impact on strategic leadership. Back in the American War of Independence in 1776–83, communication between the widely-separated British armies in America by means of courier on horseback or river boat could take many days, even weeks, so rendering it virtually impossible to coordinate their offensive operations. Yet less than a century later, in the American Civil War of 1861–65, the Union Commander-in-Chief, General Ulysses S. Grant, could give instant directives to far-off subordinates by means of Morse-code telegraph lines.

By the end of the nineteenth century a network of sub-oceanic and land-based telegraph cabling covered the entire globe. Imperial governments and their admiralties in London, Paris, Berlin, and St Petersburg could now communicate with their distant colonies, naval bases, and fleets with virtually no delay – a striking contrast with the Georgian era when it took a month by sailing ship for a despatch from London to reach America, or six months to reach the governor-general of India in Calcutta. From the 1890s onwards cable telegraph was supplemented by Morse-code radio, which enabled communication with (and between) ships at sea.

By the Second World War Morse-code signalling had been supplemented by trans-oceanic telephone links; by telex machines clacking out instant prints of reports and orders; and by long-distance radio transmissions between continents. Moreover, the combination of radio with electro-mechanical enciphering machines like the German 'Enigma' and the British 'Typex' now permitted constant secret communication between command centres, warships, submarines, aircraft, and army formations.

Yet this led in turn to another remarkable technical development. For the key to penetrating the enemy's operational secrets no longer lay in reports by spies, as in the pre-industrial era, but instead in cracking the enemy's supposedly unbreakable electro-mechanical ciphers. The task demanded teams of brilliant human brains aided by room-sized electric calculating machines like the British 'Colossus'.

The resulting SIGINT [Signals Intelligence] enabled political and military leaderships to eavesdrop on the enemy while he was making his plans and issuing his orders: an amazing advantage unprecedented in the history of warfare.

INTRODUCTION

The Advent of Airpower

A mere fifteen years separated the first 150-feet flight by a powered heavier-than-air machine (by the brothers Wilbur and Orville Wright in 1903) from the colossal panoply of airpower deployed in the final campaign of the Great War. In 1918 the British Royal Air Force alone numbered more than 22,000 aircraft – heavy bombers flying from airfields in Flanders to reach industrial targets as far as the Rhineland; light bombers and fighters strafing enemy infantry, gun batteries and transport along the Western Front; reconnaissance aircraft systematically photo-mapping the enemy's defences and reporting on his troop movements; spotter aircraft guiding the artillery's fall of shot. At sea flying-boats and airships patrolled the convoy routes in search for German U-boats.

During the Second World War all these existing functions of airpower in support of armies and navies were vastly enhanced by developments in the speed, range, and armament of aircraft, as well as by new electronic devices for target-finding and navigation.

In land warfare this enhanced support took the form of the so-called 'tactical air force' assigned to each army or army group, and commanded from a joint air-army headquarters. In the Battle of Normandy, in June and July 1944, the allied tactical air forces acted as flying artillery devastating German defensive positions and relentlessly attacking his troops on the move. By bombing roads, bridges and the rail network, 'tac air' slowed enemy deployments to a crawl.

In the war at sea the airmen and the sailors likewise learned to work together as a team – supremely so during the 1942–43 crisis in the Battle of the Atlantic against the U-boat. The battle was masterminded from a joint headquarters shared by the Royal Air Force's Coastal Command and the Royal Navy's Western Approaches Command, while out in the mid-Atlantic land-based 'Very Long-Range Aircraft' and carrier-borne aircraft formed joint teams with convoy escorts in finding and sinking enemy submarines.

Moreover, the advent of carrier-borne airpower spelt the demise of the big-gun battleship as the key to naval mastery. Now an enemy fleet could be attacked by bombs and torpedoes at ranges of up to 200 miles, compared with the ten to fifteen miles range of 15-inch guns at the Battle of Jutland in 1916. In the decisive Battle of Midway in the Pacific in 1942, the Japanese deployed seven battleships; the Americans none. Yet once the Japanese had lost all four of their aircraft-carriers to air attack launched from the three American carriers, the Japanese admiral ordered his task force to steam back to base rather than risk further American air attacks.

The Battle of Midway, where the opposing surface ships never saw each other, therefore marked not only the turning-point in the conflict between Japan and the United States, but also in the history of naval warfare.

Yet during the Second World War airpower became more than just an extra dimension to campaigns fought on land and sea: it emerged as an arena of war in its own right, complete with its own strategically decisive victories and defeats.

The Battle of Britain in the summer of 1940 constituted the first such victory, when the Royal Air Force's Fighter Command defeated the Luftwaffe in the skies over southern England, so compelling Hitler to abort his planned invasion of Britain. Thus denied German air superiority, neither the Führer nor his admirals and generals would risk sending an unwieldy mass of towed barges full of troops across the English Channel in the face of the Royal Navy.

What is more, by ensuring Britain's survival the Royal Air Force's victory made possible the huge deployment from 1941 onwards of American military power in the United Kingdom. And that deployment in turn made possible the Anglo-American invasion of Hitler's Europe in June 1944, and the allied advance into the heart of Germany in 1945.

Yet Fighter Command's triumph had other huge consequences. Hitler, being robbed of his hoped-for final victory in the West, turned to the East and in June 1941 invaded the Soviet Union. But instead of the expected short and successful campaign, he had begun a conflict in which the Wehrmacht would be gutted in four years of mass battles with the Red Army: a conflict which would end in May 1945 in the streets of his own capital, Berlin.

However, the possibility of such future deliverance was far from the minds of Winston Churchill and his coalition government in the summer of 1940, faced as they were with a grand-strategic problem of daunting immediacy. How could Britain, fighting on alone, strike back against a triumphant Nazi Germany?

An invasion of Hitler's Europe at that time or even in the future was out of the question. Since the British population amounted to little more than half that of Greater Germany, it followed that the British Army (even supplemented by Dominion contingents) could never be large enough to take on the Wehrmacht in mass battles.

So to Winston Churchill and his colleagues in 1940 it seemed that the only answer lay in airpower – and this time meaning the heavy bomber. The bomber would take the war to the heart of Germany, wrecking German industry and devastating German cities. The bomber would break the morale of the German people. In fact, the proponents of airpower even argued that the bomber could win the war without the need to invade Hitler's Europe at all.

So Churchill's war cabinet opted for a colossal expansion of Royal Air Force Bomber Command.

Yet it was not until 1943, two years after the entry of the Soviet Union and the United States into the war had actually put an end to Britain's isolation, that Bomber Command was ready to launch a sustained campaign of night bombing. Only now had the Command enough aircraft; and only now was it adequately equipped with electronic devices for navigation and target-finding.

INTRODUCTION

By this time the United States 8th Air Force based in Britain was also ready for a sustained campaign: in its case, of daylight raids against specific targets like ball-bearing factories and petrol-from-coal plants.

And so, with the full-hearted backing of Winston Churchill, Franklin Roosevelt and the Combined Chiefs of Staff, the two bomber forces undertook a strategic air offensive intended to cripple Germany's war economy and break the morale of the German people.

When the war in Europe ended in May 1945 the allied air forces had dropped a total of nearly two million tons of bombs, reducing Berlin and other great cities to burnt-out hollow hulks of buildings and heaps of rubble.

There is no question that the strategic air offensive made a major contribution to the Anglo-American victory. It had slowed the rate of growth in German war production. It had compelled the enemy to devote huge resources of manpower, guns, and aircraft to the defence of the Fatherland against the bomber, and so created a virtual 'Second Front' a year before the actual Normandy invasion.

Nevertheless, the bomber had not won the war by itself as proponents of the strategic air offensive had believed it could.

Instead, Nazi Germany had been brought down by the defeat of the German land forces by the Soviet, British, and American armies (together with their tactical air support), and their advances from east and west into the heart of the Reich.

Only with the two nuclear bombs dropped on Japan in August 1945 did airpower alone win a war.

Yet it must be remembered that this was a unique case, in that the target country (Japan) had no means of nuclear retaliation. In the 'Cold War' of 1946–90 between the Soviet Union and the United States, the possession of huge nuclear arsenals by both sides (meaning in the phrase of the time 'MAD: Mutually Assured Destruction') was simply to lead to nuclear stalemate.

There was a further consequence: both the American-led North Atlantic Treaty Organisation (NATO) and the Soviet-led Warsaw-Pact alliance were conscious that any direct military confrontation between them would carry the risk of escalation to use of nuclear weapons. In this way, nuclear armouries capable of destroying civilisation became the guarantors of peace between the superpowers and their alliances.

The Impact of Technological Change on Leadership
The very nature and scope of leadership was profoundly altered by the revolution in military affairs – technological and social – from the eighteenth century onwards. This revolution put an end to the effectiveness of the 'practical-man' leader self-taught from experience like Cromwell or Wellington. Even though the basic psychological power of leadership still remained vital, this power now had to be married to professional mastery of complex technical questions. It had to be

married to a highly trained ability to manage organisations of a size unparalleled in contemporary civilian society.

It is therefore little wonder that it was the military – above all, the *Prussian* military in the 1860s and 1870s – who were the first to develop the key concept of a collective brain that could master the new complexities: the general staff.

The role of a general staff lies in studying systematically the strategic and operational problems that confront a top leader, and then presenting alternative solutions for the leader to consider before he makes his final decision. Once that decision has been taken, it falls to the general staff to draw up the detailed operational plans; and to draft, and issue, the necessary complex orders. It also falls to the general staff to organise the logistics for a battle or a campaign or even a war. And it is their role to re-make the operational plans and re-organise the logistics as often as the shifting and unpredictable fortunes of conflict require.

A first-rate general staff has therefore constituted the essential tool of military leadership ever since the mid-nineteenth century. The concept has now been adopted throughout industry and government as well.

But the leader himself must know how to make best use of his staff and their varied expertise. He must know how to enthuse them with his own will and purpose. It is indeed his staff – and his immediately subordinate commanders – who present the modern top leader with his one opportunity for exercising direct personal leadership.

Yet the era of the Industrial Revolution has also witnessed the growth of mass populations and a huge expansion in popular education and the media. The waging of war therefore ceased to be the preserve of a narrow political and military elite, as in Wellington's day, and instead involved the entire nation. In particular, small all-professional armies gave place to mass citizen levies, a process which culminated in the two twentieth-century world wars.

So it became a supreme task of national leadership to sustain the morale of the citizen, whether in uniform or back on the home front. A leader in war, whether he or she be civilian or military, therefore now needed to project their personality to the distant masses – which in turn meant that the media became an essential tool of leadership. In the Great War of 1914–18, 'the media' signified the popular newspaper and the cinema newsreel; in the Second World War it signified radio as well, which for the first time brought live reporting from the Front. And today's neo-imperial campaigns, as in Afghanistan and Iraq, are carried out in the brilliant glare of up-to-the-minute satellite-television coverage.

This relentless exposure poses an unprecedented challenge to military and civilian leadership alike.

The Successful Leader Today and Tomorrow

First and foremost, successful leaders must possess those age-old fundamental strengths to which other people will respond: willpower, character, and personality. They must have an aura of confidence and certainty springing from an inner faith in themselves and their mission. They must be technical masters of their profession in all its complexities. But they must also be blessed with the vision and judgement to enable them to place their own role in a wider context, whether within their own organisation or in regard to the outside social and political environment. They must enjoy the ability to communicate – not just in terms of verbal fluency, but in terms of genuine human warmth and concern. Successful leaders will therefore spend more time among their workforce than at their desk: more time listening than talking.

Above all, they will understand that the secret of leadership lies not in managing 'human resources', but in cherishing human relationships.

PART I:

The Nineteenth Century

CHAPTER 1

The Romantic Ideal
of Leadership

Napoleon Bonaparte

The career and character of Napoleon Bonaparte, the self-crowned 'Emperor Napoleon', supply the essential prelude to the studies of leadership in war in this book. Throughout the nineteenth and twentieth centuries, Bonaparte was to be celebrated by the romantically minded as the very incarnation of martial genius. He was to be admired by those military historians (such as Basil Liddell Hart and David Chandler) who treat campaigns and battles as if they were games of skill played for their own sakes; and who discuss the performance of military commanders as one might discuss the stroke-play of cricketers or tennis-players.

Yet these approaches are fundamentally wrong-headed. War is not a romantic stage-play in which to play the hero; nor is it a game or a duel. And nor is it, as some Western liberal thinkers would have it, a violent and meaningless breakdown in a natural order of 'peace'. War is simply an available political instrument, as Clausewitz acutely pointed out in his book *On War*, and Lenin and Mao Tse Tung well understood.

War may serve as a last resort when all attempts at resolving a political dispute by negotiation and compromise have failed – no matter whether the dispute is between sovereign states or within a state, as in the run-up to the American Civil War. It may be willingly chosen as the instrument of policy of a sovereign state seeking either territorial expansion or control over foreign markets and sources of raw materials. Or it may serve the purpose of a revolutionary movement seeking to overturn an existing political and social order. And it may even supply the bloodied cutting edge of religious zeal, as in Europe during the sixteenth and seventeenth centuries or with Islamist militancy today.

Nonetheless, it is war regarded as an instrument of state policy that has constituted the norm in Western society for more than four centuries. The utility of this instrument in any particular case can only be measured by the war's political and economic consequences. The wisdom of a national leader in resorting to this instrument can only be judged in the light of his own prior assessment of what those consequences are likely to be.

The consequences of Napoleon Bonaparte's wars, entirely unforeseen by him, are easily stated: the destruction of his self-build empire, and the lasting reduction of France from the superpower of Europe to a country in long-term decline, while he himself ended his career not as Emperor of the French but as a prisoner of England on St Helena, a remote island in the South Atlantic.

How could all this be, given that (as myth would have it) he was a political and military genius? His admirers have done their best to explain the paradox. They say that there was a 'turning-point' in his career after which his political and military judgement deteriorated, although opinions differ as to exactly when this supposed turning-point occurred. Medical explanations have proved popular too: it is alleged that had it not been for painful piles in the anus or incipient cancer, Bonaparte must certainly have won the Battle of Waterloo. Then also it is argued that he was again and again let down by his subordinates. For example, it is alleged that it was all Marshal Ney's fault that the day of Quatre-Bras and Ligny in 1815 did not end in the total destruction of the Prussian Army under Blücher; and Ney's and Marshal Grouchy's joint fault that Bonaparte lost the climactic battle of his career at Waterloo two days later.

But there is a simpler explanation as to why Bonaparte's career ended in such utter ruin. It is this: he was not a political and military genius at all, but an over-confident gambler pursuing from start to finish a fundamentally unsound system of war and statecraft.

It must always be remembered that Bonaparte was no mere soldier obediently implementing decisions already made by politicians in government. Even before his first campaign in 1796 as commander-in-chief in Italy, he had been closely involved in policy-making and strategic planning by the revolutionary regime in Paris. After he became 'First Consul' in 1799, he *was* the government, and remained so for the next fifteen years. So he alone was the author of his ultimate ruin.

The calamitous process of launching France into military adventures that were against her true long-term interest began with Bonaparte's renowned Italian campaign of 1796–97. By 1795 France was bankrupt after six years of revolutionary turmoil and war against much of Europe. Her plight really demanded a compromise peace, whereby the existing regime, the so-called Directory, gave up its annexationist demand for the 'natural frontier' of the Rhine from Basle to the sea. Such a peace could have made possible much-needed retrenchment and reconstruction at home; and perhaps even opened the way to a deal with the exiled King Louis XVIII in order to heal the deep rift in French society since the Revolution.

But the loss of prestige entailed by a compromise peace would spell political doom for the Directory. And so, on the advice of General Bonaparte, the Directory instead decided to gamble on being able to dictate 'a glorious peace' to their principal enemy, Austria. The gamble would involve, firstly, the conquest of northern Italy, and thereafter the invasion of Austria itself via the Tyrol. The pillage of Italy en route would not only pay for the campaign and supply the army, but also rescue the French state from bankruptcy.

So just like a modern capitalist seeking to avert a cash-flow crisis by stripping and selling assets, the Directory and its general set out on their ambitious march.

*   *   *

It is this Italian campaign of 1796–97 which above all others has been praised ever since by Bonaparte's admirers as a marvel of strategic invention, daring, and leadership. Bonaparte, so the legend goes, threw off the shackles of eighteenth-century warfare, with its elaborate supply trains and consequently slow advances, and its preoccupation with besieging fortresses. Instead he inaugurated a new era of warfare – fast-moving manoeuvre leading to decisive battles with all forces united, to victory and a triumphant peace. But in reality the Italian campaign displays a different model; and one which was to recur in every campaign Bonaparte fought.

In the first place, Bonaparte's method of providing cash-flow and supplies for his army by stripping the assets of Italian states soon led to unexpected and potentially disastrous results, for the outraged population rose in widespread revolt, so forcing Bonaparte to disperse much of his strength in protecting his own communications and putting down the insurrections with fire and sword. The Bonapartian shortcut solution to the problem of supply in fact led him straight into a morass of political and social complication, and just at the time when he was desperately fending off Austrian counter-offensives. Far from Bonaparte going effortlessly from success to success in 1796, he was writing in November: 'Perhaps we are on the verge of losing Italy.'[1] And the pattern was to repeat itself in Egypt in 1798, in southern Italy in 1806, in Spain in 1808, in Russia in 1812 and finally in Germany in 1813. In each case the forcible extortion of money and goods, coupled with his high-handed interference with local institutions, led to popular uprisings, with all their serious political and military consequences. In Spain, a country so large and so barren, but inhabited by a uniquely proud and ferocious people, Bonaparte's favourite methods of repression – shootings and burnings of villages – failed for the first time to quell the trouble. Hence his system of supply by pillage failed to work; and the Duke of Wellington and the Spanish *guerrilleros* between them brought the French armies to ultimate disaster.

A second basic flaw in Bonapartian warfare also manifested itself in that inaugural campaign in Italy in 1796–97. Because Bonaparte advanced without adequate supplies or transport, it was absolutely vital that he won a quick decisive victory. To an army living from hand to mouth by pillage, any unexpected hold-up, any unexpectedly prolonged march, carried with it the danger of starvation and the collapse of the campaign. Within a week or so of Bonaparte's first celebrated victory at Montenotte over the Piedmontese, the dearth of food, forage, and ammunition was such that retreat seemed inevitable.

Since every one of Bonaparte's campaigns was similarly an immense gamble on inadequate logistic margins, he again and again was to face supply crises threatening him with imminent catastrophe. In 1799 when Bonaparte's march across the Sinai from Egypt into Palestine was blocked by an unforeseen Turkish fort at El Arish, he wrote that the army was 'in a situation where the least delay could become disastrous for it'.[2] In 1800 when during his crossing of the Great St Bernard into Italy he was blocked by the Austrian-held fort of Bard, he wrote to his chief commissary that the army was 'exposed to dying of starvation'; and he signalled his chief-of-staff that 'the destiny of Italy, and perhaps of the Republic, depends on the taking of Fort Bard!!'[3]

The march in 1805 from the invasion camp at Boulogne to the Danube in order to surround the Austrians at Ulm is often cited as one of Bonaparte's most brilliant exploits. In fact, so inadequate proved the Bonapartian system of subsisting off the country, so ramshackle his supply arrangements, that only the ineptitude of the enemy saved him from disaster. As Bonaparte himself acknowledged at the time, 'had the army suffered some reverse, the lack of magazines would have led us into the greatest difficulties'.[4] And, striking an already familiar note, he told his Intendant-General that delay in sending up supplies 'could have the most disastrous effects on the army and the Empire'.

Even when, in the poverty-stricken countryside of East Prussia and Poland in 1806-7, Bonaparte did revert to the eighteenth-century system of supply depots and wagon trains to bring the supplies up to the troops, he could not bring himself to tailor his strategy to his limited logistic resources. As a consequence, his army once again faced the near prospect of destruction by hunger. Bonaparte wrote to his Intendant-General that 'It is the penury of victuals which shackles all operations', and to a minister that 'Today the destiny of Europe and the grandest calculations depend on supply'.[5]

Yet this campaign, like all his previous ones except the invasion of Palestine, ended in a victory. How was it that so far none of these repeated supply crises had actually brought him to disaster? The answer lies in the mistaken strategies of his enemies. They had almost always been kind enough to come forward to meet him in battle, often in ill-conceived offensives of their own, thus offering him the gift of that early decisive encounter upon which his gambler's system so much depended. And when they lost that initial battle, they gave up the fight and made peace overtures – often thanks to a 'peace party' at court, as was the case with Piedmont in 1796 after the Battle of Montenotte. His enemies failed to adopt the one strategy necessarily fatal to a commander like Bonaparte working on the slenderest of financial and logistic margins – a war of evasion; protracted war.

It was the Russians in 1812 who stumbled on this strategy by accident. In planning his invasion of Russia, Bonaparte certainly recognised that his Grande Armée of 450,000 men and thousands of beasts could not live off so poor a country as Russia, and he therefore made the most elaborate plans – on paper – for stocking depots along the route of advance, and wagon trains to shift supplies forward to the troops. But the reality fell far short of Bonaparte's grandly optimistic orders, while the scarce and mud-bound Russian roads could not in any case carry the necessary volume of traffic.

Within two weeks of the start of the invasion, the Grande Armée was reduced to marching on an empty stomach in true Bonapartian style. As a consequence, Bonaparte himself, again true to form, hungered ever more desperately for the deliverance of a decisive battle. However, squabbles within the Russian high command prevented them from offering this battle. Thus fortunately spared a Bonapartian onslaught, the Russians retreated ever deeper into their vast country, while Bonaparte vainly pursued them. Every mile of road saw his supply crisis sharpen and his army melt away. At Vitebsk he was down to 230,000 men; at Smolensk to 156,000. Nevertheless, in the most dangerous gamble of his career, he still pressed on in search of victory. When he at last entered Moscow the Grande Armée was reduced to only 100,000 men.

He now found himself in a familiar enough situation, though this time on the grand scale: outwardly a picture of successful conquest, but actually one of growing weakness and peril. In all his previous Continental campaigns his enemies had got him off the hook by rashly attacking him or asking for an armistice. The Russians did neither. The weeks passed; the Russian winter approached. At last Bonaparte faced the fact that he had no alternative but to retreat, and on 14 October 1812 issued the preparatory orders.

So finally it had come to pass - that total collapse of his strategy, that destruction of his army, which had very nearly occurred so many times before.

And other nations would learn from the Russian experience. Never again would Bonaparte enjoy the essential prerequisite of his earlier successes – opponents who conveniently played into his hands.

It had taken him sixteen years to rise from command of the Army of Italy to the supreme height of imperial power he enjoyed on the eve of the Russian adventure. But after his return from that adventure, sixteen months sufficed him for him to lose it all. It was not, as some have argued, that his military talents and energies had decayed. His performance as a strategist and commander in the field in 1813–14 was neither better nor worse than in, say 1796–97. His vigour (measured by volume of correspondence and strenuousness of activity) was even greater. However, he failed to perceive that he was now operating in a fundamentally altered political and military environment, and hence he failed to adapt accordingly. Instead he went on stubbornly clinging to his old formula of seeking a great victory in battle and then dictating a peace. He was like a gambler sticking to a favourite system even when the game has swung persistently against him.

It was not Bonaparte who had changed in the years 1812–15, but his enemies: the Austrians, the Russians, and the Prussians. In the German campaign of 1813, they refused to be discouraged by his initial successes at Lützen and Bautzen; and in the second phase of the campaign adopted a strategy of evasion which wore out Bonaparte's troops in ineffective marches and counter-marches. After gradually netting him from north, east and south, they destroyed his tired and outnumbered army in the three-day Battle of Leipzig.

Next year, Bonaparte's attempted defence of France against invasion saw this pattern repeated: delusory initial successes, an army worn out by forced marching, and enemy columns closing relentlessly back towards Paris despite all Bonaparte's frantic thrusts this way and that.

And even if in 1815 Bonaparte had managed to win the Battle of Waterloo itself, the allies would have followed the same strategy of wearing him down into defeat by superior numbers and protracted campaigning.

*   *   *

Yet what of Bonaparte as a fighting commander? What was the secret of that run of victories in battle from Montenotte in 1796 to Ligny in 1815? He has been presented as the inventor of a wonderfully flexible 'Napoleonic' system whereby army corps marched separately from each other but came swiftly together at the decisive moment. He was, so his admirers believe, a master of concentration of all forces on the battlefield. Yet time and again Bonaparte is found waiting for a subordinate corps commander to arrive on the field with desperately needed reinforcements – Desaix at Marengo in 1800, Davout at Austerlitz in 1805, Davout and Ney at Eylau in 1807, Ney at Bautzen in 1813 and at Ligny in 1815, and Grouchy at Waterloo. Lack of orders or muddled orders could lead to major formations failing to take part in a battle at all. This was the case with Bernadotte's corps at Jena and Auerstädt in 1806 and again at Eylau in 1807; the case with Bertrand's corps at Lützen and Souham's at Leipzig in 1813; and d'Erlon's corps on the day of Quatre-Bras and Ligny.

On the morning of the Battle of Waterloo on 18 June 1815, Wellington and Blücher, the Prussian commander, lay near enough for cooperation in a joint battle. Bonaparte, however, had divided his own army by despatching Marshal Grouchy with 20,000 men to pursue the Prussians in retreat after the Battle of Ligny the previous day, but in the wrong direction: eastwards instead of northwards. This mistake landed Bonaparte with the task of fighting against an ever heavier superiority of numbers as the day of Waterloo wore on.

In fact, the early victories to which Bonaparte owes his military fame were, like Rommel's in the Western Desert during the Second World War, really the product of quick-witted opportunism and fast, hard punching; they were product of a ruthless will to win. They were victories for sheer pugilistic skill over ponderous, slow-reacting, conventionally-minded opponents. Yet even this superiority did not last: his enemies learned the lesson, while Bonaparte squandered the lives of his veterans across the face of Europe, re-filling the ranks with green conscripts. By the time of the Wagram campaign of 1809, the French army as a whole could only manage crude tactics in clumsy mass formations; it depended on massed cannon to blast a path for it. By a paradox the very decline in quality of Bonaparte's army was to breed another Napoleonic legend: that of the master of artillery.

But cannon, however numerous, could not redeem false policy and bad strategy. Not one of Bonaparte's wars served as an instrument of policy conceived in the best interests of the French people. Not one of the 'glorious' peace settlements dictated after his victories lasted long.

In 1797 the Treaty of Campoformio consummated an outwardly impressive expansion of French power in Europe at the expense of Austria. However, these humiliating terms exacted at the point of a bayonet led to no stable equilibrium, but instead paved the way for the next war by making France's enemies bent on revenge.

In the event, the 'glorious peace' of 1797 dissolved in 1799, while Bonaparte was absent trying to found a French colony in Egypt. All the famous Italian conquests were lost to the Austrians, and France found herself back in the plight of 1795, bankrupt, riven by disunity at home, the régime tottering, and at war with a great European coalition. When, after the coup d'état of 18 *Brumaire* (9 November) 1799, Bonaparte became First Consul and dictator, he again disdained a compromise European settlement, deciding instead to seek another 'glorious peace' at the head of his army by once again defeating the Austrians in northern Italy. He chose this course partly for reasons similar to those which prompted the Italian campaign of 1796–97, and partly because as a new ruler just illegitimately installed after a coup d'état, he needed a glittering success to consolidate his position. So his much praised Italian campaign of 1800, ending in the victorious Battle of Marengo, was launched more to further Bonaparte's personal career than the good of the French people. After he crowned himself 'Napoleon, Emperor of the French' in 1804, the French state became merely the servile instrument of his own egotism; and the French people became merely the supporting cast in his own romantic drama. And so the cycle of recurrent war, begun in 1796, continued to revolve – renewed war with England in 1803; with Austria and Russia in 1805;

with Prussia in 1806; with Russia again in 1807; war in Spain and Portugal in 1808; a fresh war with Austria in 1809; and with Russia again in 1812; war in Germany in 1813; and in France itself in 1814.

Each conflict essentially sprang from Bonaparte's refusal to live quietly on equal terms with his neighbours – and from the underlying precariousness of his own régime. As he himself confessed to a Councillor of State in 1800: 'A First Consul cannot be likened to these kings-by-the-grace-of-God, who look upon their state as a heritage ... his actions must be dramatic, and for this, war is indispensable.'

In 1812–13, after the destruction of the Grande Armée in Russia, his enemies offered him a generous settlement whereby he would have retained dominions wider than those to which Louis XIV had aspired in vain. Instead he once more chose to gamble on winning a great victory over coalition armies in Germany, and then once again dictating a 'glorious peace'. The consequence, however, was yet another colossal defeat.

Although France itself now lay under threat of invasion by the Russians, Austrians, and Prussians, he still turned down fresh peace terms that in the circumstances were generous enough, opting again for war, even though he could only muster a small and ragged army partly composed of ill-armed boys. This is perhaps the supreme example of his callous irresponsibility as a national leader.

And the pattern repeated itself for the last time in 1815 after his escape from Elba, when, in the face of strong political opposition at home and an enemy coalition abroad, he yet once more sought to perpetuate his personal adventure through victory on the battlefield – only to be beaten at Waterloo by a better general.

In truth, Bonaparte was neither a great statesman nor a military genius, but a colossal failure. Nevertheless, his personal spell was so strong that the Grande Armée from marshals to grenadiers in the ranks believed even in the worst of times that all would come right under his leadership. The whole of the French active army willingly marched with him in the last fatal campaign, dying in their thousands under Wellington's gunfire and musketry, or sabred by Blücher's avenging *uhlans*. That this all-round failure of a leader should have been so long revered as a genius at statecraft and war says much about human credulity and the power of myth.

References

1-5 These are drawn from *Correspondence*: Bonaparte's official papers.

CHAPTER 2

Crusader with a Blunt Sword

Abraham Lincoln and the
Failing Generals

The American Civil War marked the first time in modern history that a democracy waged a great war, because the successive French revolutionary régimes after 1789 can hardly be called democracies in the modern sense. President Abraham Lincoln was in consequence the first democratic politician to bear the unrelenting strains of national leadership in time of war. He had to grapple with the novel problem of bridging the gap between popular hopes of quick victory and sombre military reality, given that, to begin with, the fighting capability on both sides was roughly matched. He had to learn how best to harmonise his own leadership as a civilian President and constitutional commander-in-chief with the leadership of military commanders in the field.

Moreover, he was the first leader of a democracy to have to answer fundamental questions about the conduct of war. How far should the war be handed over to the generals to run? How far should politicians take strategic decisions? And how should military strategy be related to the political objectives of the war? These were questions that would challenge the minds of later statesmen like Woodrow Wilson, Lloyd George, Clémenceau, Roosevelt, and Churchill. But for Lincoln the questions presented a far more daunting challenge – partly because of their sheer novelty at that time, but largely because this was a civil war, and not a conflict with an external enemy. As President of the United States, Lincoln had set himself the supreme task of national re-unification after the secession of the slave-owning states of the South: a task demanding shrewd judgement, rare skill at political manoeuvre, and a steely will to succeed.

Even geography itself rendered the Civil War unique in the history of conflict. Between the existing States of the Union and the Pacific lay the so-called 'territories' in the course of being settled, and otherwise vast spaces only lightly populated by Indian (Native American) tribes. To the north lay Canada, a self-governing part of the British Empire, and a friendly neighbour; to the south lay Mexico, not so reliably friendly but hardly a major military threat. To the east lay the Atlantic Ocean, a 3,000-mile-wide moat safely policed by the Royal Navy.

Thanks to this continental isolation, the United States needed neither alliances, nor an active foreign policy of the European kind. As a result, the state apparatuses long evolved in Europe for promoting national interests – including the planning and conducting of wars – were quite absent in America.

And Lincoln himself mirrored this American mental and institutional unpreparedness for conflict on the grand scale.

*   *   *

A lawyer by profession, he was rooted in small-town life and politics.[1] He had been elected to the Presidency on a supremely domestic issue, that of slavery and the future of the Union. Now this intensely civilian figure found himself the supreme war leader in the first 'modern' war – 'modern' because it was the first to combine ideological passion with mass military manpower and the products of the Industrial Revolution like the railway, the steamship, and the telegraph.

As Clausewitz points out, the scope and intensity of a war is proportionate to the cause for which it is fought. A European so-called 'Cabinet War', like the Prussian and Austrian quarrel in 1866 over predominance within Germany, means a limited war; limited both in time and in scope. Once the armies have fought a battle or two and one side has lost, there follows a conference, a deal, and a peace treaty. But the blazing fire of the American Civil War was fuelled by two irreconcilable but passionately held views of America's future; two irreconcilable economic interests; and two irreconcilable convictions about constitutional right and wrong. The key question at issue lay in the possible extension of the Southern institution of slavery to the so-called 'territories' well to the west of the Mississippi: areas of new settlement which in time were sure to become fully fledged states. To the existing northern states of the Union, such an extension of slavery was abhorrent; and, worse, a potential bridgehead for the extension of slavery into *all* states. To the Southern slave-owning states, it would be a breach of the Constitution to deny the western territories the option to become slave states if they so wished. Moreover, such a denial could pave the way for a general attack on slavery as an institution. In other words, southerners believed that their plantation economy, worth $4 billion of investment, and their way of life lay under threat from the Yankees of the industrialising states of the north.

In 1858 Lincoln himself had starkly summed up the issue at stake:

'A House divided against itself cannot stand.' I believe this government cannot endure permanently half *slave* and half free. I do not expect the Union to be dissolved - I do not expect the house to *fall* - but I do expect it will cease to be divided. It will become *all* one thing, or *all* the other. Either the *opponents* of slavery will arrest the further spread of it, and place it where the public mind shall rest in the belief that it is in the course of ultimate extinction; or its *advocates* will push it forward, till it shall become alike lawful in *all* the States, *old* as well as *new*, *North* as well as *South*.[2]

When in 1861 the Southern states finally seceded and formed themselves into the Confederate States of America, it created yet another fundamental conflict of interest, this time constitutional, since the survival of the Union necessitated the complete obliteration of the Confederacy as a political entity. When was added to all these factors Lincoln's own wartime oratory, which transformed the conflict into a moral cause embraced with almost religious fervour by the people of the North, the result was indeed a 'total war'.

But this only gradually became apparent to the belligerents, who, in a mood of patriotic euphoria, entered the conflict believing that it would soon be victoriously over. Under existing law, Lincoln at first could only call for 75,000 volunteers, and then merely for three months' service.

What qualities did Lincoln bring to the task of conducting the first modern war? Unlike Churchill in 1940, he had no previous experience as a member of a wartime administration. Unlike Churchill again, he had never taken a deep interest in military and naval history. His background was wholly civilian except for brief service as a young man in the Illinois militia against the Indians.

Nonetheless, Lincoln had been formed by the pioneering spirit of the American frontier; he had been schooled in a hard early life where what counted was the commonsensical ability to sort out practical problems. The rough-and-tumble of small-town lawyering and local politics had further matured his natural sagacity and good judgement. Though his formal education had been limited, he was well-read, mining from books the material that would be useful to him. He was physically and mentally tough, and blessed with an earthy sense of humour that could help to lighten the grimmest moments of setback.

Above all, he possessed that weight of character, that strength of will which are absolutely essential to a supreme commander, as Clausewitz explains:

> As long as his men, full of courage, fight with zeal and spirit, it is seldom necessary for the Chief to show great energy of purpose in the pursuit of his object. But as soon as difficulties arise; and that must always happen when great results are at stake - then things no longer move on of themselves like a well-oiled machine, the machine itself then begins to offer resistance, and to overcome this the Commander must have a great deal of force of will. As the moral forces in one individual after another become prostrated, the whole inertia of the mass gradually rests its weight on the Will of the Commander; by the spark in his breast, by the light of his spirit; the spark of purpose, the light of hope, must be kindled afresh in others.

11

This quotation perfectly applies to Lincoln during the disappointments and disasters to the Union cause in the first two years of the Civil War.

Yet if Lincoln as President was militarily ignorant in 1861, the United States Army and its leadership were little better, being in no way the equivalent of European professional armies and their high commands; and in no way ready to wage a mass industrialised war.

The enlisted strength of the Army on the eve of secession was only 16,000 men, the majority of the ranks being immigrants. It was scattered across the country in small garrisons and on local construction jobs. A formed battalion was rare; even companies were often divided up into detachments. The human quality in the ranks was not much better than in the British army of the time, which was notoriously recruited from the dregs of society. In the US Army, many had enlisted to escape personal problems. Drunkenness was rife. Because the rank-and-file were employed so much in civil engineering work, 'Their existence was at once too military and not military enough'.[3]

Apart from the regulars, there were the militia (an ancient English institution) and the volunteers. After long years of peace, the militia was of uneven military quality. At its nadir, a muster could have broken a regular sergeant-major's heart:

> There were forty warriors, very miscellaneous indeed. Three of them were not serviceable, having sticks instead of guns, and several more were supremely drunk. The gallant captain wore a sword like a scythe blade, and his heroes looked like Sir J. Falstaff's ragged regiment. The line was very crooked; there was an astonishing curvature towards a certain beer room.[4]

Although by the outbreak of the Civil War the militia had somewhat revived, its readiness for war depended on the degree of zeal shown by its officers in the different states of the Union. In any case, civilian zest for the military life now found outlet in the independently raised regiments of local volunteers, an early example of the American love of joining a group. Their zest was much inspired by the Napoleonic glamour of fanciful uniforms and splendid parades. Although the volunteers could, and did, attract men with genuine martial instincts, it was the social and sartorial aspect that prevailed. According to an account of the 7th New York Volunteers, 'During the whole history of the Regiment no subject ... has ever provoked so fierce and bitter a controversy as the proposed change in the uniform hat ...'[5]

Neither the militia nor the volunteers were prepared to serve more than the traditional militia stint of ninety days.

The officer corps of the regular army was dominated by graduates of the US Military Academy at West Point. Yet even at West Point the tone was half-civilian by European standards and its training was not such that its alumni could make

Lincoln look a hopeless military amateur. For West Point was primarily a school of engineering. Strategy formed only a minor part of its curriculum, and its cadets mostly regarded it as a good foundation for a civilian career. Several Civil War senior commanders had been previously following such civilian careers. George McClellan, appointed Federal General-in-Chief in 1861, had been an engineer and managing director of a railroad; Ambrose Burnside had been an armaments maker. Joseph Hooker and William Sherman had been trying to make their fortunes in California. Ulysses Grant had been working in his brother's hardware store. Henry Halleck, appointed Federal General-in-Chief in 1862, had, before the war, been practising law as well as silver-mining.

Even those West Pointers who had stayed on in the Army, like Robert Lee (now to command the Confederate Army of Northern Virginia on the key front in the war, and eventually become the Confederate General-in-Chief) were mere colonels at the outbreak of the Civil war. As Irvin McDowell, who lost the first battle of the war for the Union at Bull Run (west-south-west of Washington) in July 1861, plaintively observed afterwards: 'There was not a man there who had ever manoeuvred troops in large bodies. There was not one in the Army. I did not believe there was one in the whole country.'[6]

Nor was there any kind of high command organisation or general staff in Washington: just the General-in-Chief since 1841, the seventy-five-year-old and now infirm General Winfield Scott (nicknamed 'Old Fuss and Feathers'), who had served with distinction in the Mexican War of 1846. No contingency plans for war, either strategic or logistic, existed. There were not even available maps of the main battle area of Northern Virginia.

It would therefore be wrong to think that in military competence there existed sharp contrasts between regular soldiers and the volunteers, or between newly-minted generals and President Lincoln. All had to learn as they went: and Lincoln, with his excellent practical judgement, was to show that he could learn better than the supposed professionals.

The grand-strategic problem that confronted Lincoln was indeed daunting. In order to achieve its war aim of independence, the Confederacy only needed to remain in being. But for 'the North' to restore the Union would demand the total defeat and political extinction of the Confederacy. Lincoln had no alternative but to adopt an *offensive* grand strategy.

Yet the problems of bringing the South to the point of unconditional surrender were enormous. In the first place, while it was true that the North had a superiority in white military-age manpower of over four million to the South's 1,140,000, the institution of slavery could enable a higher proportion of Southern whites to go to war. From first to last, some 900,000 men served in the Confederate forces, as against some two million in the Union army. Secondly, although the North heavily outweighed the Confederacy in industrial resources, with nearly 100,000 industrial establishments of one kind or another to 16,000, the Confederacy could draw on imports from Europe.

The superior overall weight of the North could therefore only tell over the long term, and then only if effectively applied.

Moreover, the Confederacy enjoyed a major advantage in a defensive war because of the sheer size of the territory to be fought over. From the Potomac to Atlanta in Georgia was sixty days' march – as long as from the English Channel coast to Vienna. And this territory, like the Russia which Bonaparte invaded in 1812, was for the most part sparsely populated and poorly-roaded. The essential lifeline for armies engaged in long-distance operations lay in the railways. Taking all in all, then, it would be an immense undertaking to conquer the Confederacy and its resolute defenders.

In order to succeed in this undertaking, Lincoln, as the Union's Commander-in-Chief and supreme war leader, must first of all find competent generals he could trust, and then achieve a harmonious relationship with them. He must create a machinery of command in Washington for running the war under his direction. And he must personally evolve from country-bred politician into a grand-strategist of the highest calibre.

*   *   *

The Confederacy established its capital at Richmond, Virginia, which lay only 106 miles by road south of Washington, the Federal capital. This decision was largely political, although Richmond was also the site of the Tredegar Iron Works and other important industrial assets. Yet, by choosing Richmond as capital the Confederacy went far to throw away the defensive advantages conferred by the vast extent of its territory. The area between, and around, the two capital cities became the cockpit of the war, because politics and prestige alike demanded that each must be denied to the enemy.

The other decisive theatre lay along the Mississippi, which divided the western states of the Confederacy – Texas, Louisiana and Arkansas – from the rest. Between these two theatres lay a third theatre straddling the Southern border state of Tennessee and the northern border state of Kentucky, a scene characterised by largely unrelated local struggles between rival groups of bushwhackers.

Naturally enough, it was the Eastern theatre, embracing Washington and Richmond, that attracted the closest attention alike of Lincoln and his opponent, Jefferson Davis, the President of the Confederate States of America. In regard to campaigning in this theatre, they could readily debate plans with their commanding generals in person instead of relying on long-distance exchanges of telegraphed signals.

In July 1861 Lincoln ordered his first offensive against the Confederates in

Northern Virginia. Off went the volunteers garbed as zouaves, dragoon guards and whatever else took their fancy; ladies in carriages went along to see the spectacle, and everyone knew that Richmond would fall in a week or so. In the First Battle of Manassas or Bull Run (Bull Run is a stream) this motley and green array was beaten by no less green and motley Confederates, thanks more to luck than leadership; and the Union forces retreated in haste to Washington.

This encounter marked the beginning of the real war fought with mass armies. Even before the battle, Lincoln had appealed for 42,000 volunteers to serve for three years. Now Congress voted to raise a volunteer army of half a million – not by a national appeal like Kitchener's 'New Army' in Britain in 1914–15 but by individual regiments, who would do their own recruiting. Yet the realities of war had by no means dawned on these regiments. One recruiting poster stated: 'As this regiment is to be constantly garrisoned in the forts round Washington, those anxious to enter the military service will find in it the inestimable advantage of exemption from the hardships and privations incidental to camp life.'[7]

Lincoln now sacked McDowell, the unfortunate loser at Bull Run, and appointed George McClellan as Commander of the Army of the Potomac. It appeared a sensible choice at the time. McClellan had just conducted a successful minor campaign in West Virginia; had served with distinction on the staff during the Mexican War; been sent to Europe to report on the organisation of European armies; and later had run a railroad. He was thirty-five, good-looking, immensely vain, his head further swollen by his sudden elevation to command of the Union's principal field army. Yet he was also hard-working, an able organiser, and, as an excellent trainer of troops, he enjoyed the devotion of his soldiers. The press dubbed him 'the young Napoleon'.

McClellan vindicated Lincoln's choice by organising the newly-raised volunteers into an army and training them effectively. But now the real problem began: having trained his army, McClellan showed extreme reluctance to venture it in an offensive.

The relationship between Lincoln and McClellan now fell into a pattern that lasted until Lincoln finally sacked him in November 1862. The pattern was this: Lincoln, the civilian, had grasped that the only way to defeat the Confederacy was to engage its armies – and especially Lee's Army of Northern Virginia – in remorseless battles that would bleed their strength away. But McClellan, the soldier, shrank from so grim a course, pleading again and again that he was not ready to take the offensive; that he was outnumbered; that he must have reinforcements; that he would move as soon as he had reinforcements. Instead of the direct invasion of Virginia via the town of Manassas urged on him by Lincoln, McClellan wanted to adopt a strategy of the indirect approach (to use the term beloved of Basil Liddell Hart, a plausible charlatan of a military writer). He proposed to embark the Army of the Potomac, land it at the tip of the Peninsula that lies between the James River and the York River, and take Richmond, the Confederate capital, by the side door.

Despite his misgivings, Lincoln agreed. The landings duly took place; and slowly, cautiously, and laboriously McClellan moved up the Peninsula, whining all the time about his difficulties. In a highly revealing remark, he said that his capture of two towns without fighting – in fact evacuated by the enemy – would be regarded by history as his 'brightest chaplets' because the towns were won without loss of life. Meanwhile, the Confederate forces simply re-grouped to block his route to Richmond.

Lincoln himself sent McClellan a devastating indictment of this strategy of evasion: an indictment which indeed applies today to the whole concept of 'the indirect approach', or 'manoeuvre warfare'. This is what he wrote:

> ... let me tell you, it is indispensable to *you* that you strike a blow. I am powerless to help you. You will do me the justice to remember I always insisted, that going down the Bay in search of a field instead of fighting at or near Manassas [in northern Virginia], was only shifting, and not surmounting, a difficulty – that we should find the same enemy, and the same, or equal entrenchments, at either place. The country will not fail to note – is now noting – that the present hesitation to move upon an entrenched enemy is but the story of Manassas repeated.

But he added a characteristic word of support for a worried general:

> I beg to assure you I have never written you or spoken to you in greater kindness of feeling than now, or with a fuller purpose to sustain you, so far as in my most anxious judgement, I consistently can. But you must act.[8]

Nevertheless, Lincoln confided to a colleague a more homely comment. He said that sending reinforcements to McClellan was like shovelling fleas across a barnyard – few seemed to get there.

It is worth noting the contrast between Lincoln prodding McClellan to fight a great battle, and Lloyd George in 1917 during the Great War trying to stop Haig doing that very thing. It is also worth noting that Lincoln's prodding of McClellan cannot be compared to Churchill's prodding of Auchinleck and Wavell, the British Cs-in-C Middle-East in the Second World War. Whereas McClellan's army was equal in military quality to Lee's and by 1862 almost double in size, the British forces in the Western Desert under Wavell and Auchinleck were seriously inferior to Rommel's Panzerarmee Afrika in professional skill and in the quality of tanks and anti-tank guns.

And so while Lincoln's interventions with McClellan in 1862 were fully justified by the military realities, Churchill's interventions in 1940–42 were not. There is a further contrast between the two war leaders; whereas Lincoln was patient and supportive with McClellan, as indeed with other generals, Churchill was too often a relentless harasser of commanders already under stress.

As for McClellan himself, his fundamental shortcoming lay in that he was not a fighter by temperament: and war is at bottom about fighting – as Lincoln understood. Having advanced to within eight miles of Richmond, McClellan halted before the outnumbered but strongly posted Confederate defence while he extended his right flank northward to link up with reinforcements which never turned up. It was this extended flank that took the full brunt of a Confederate counter-offensive conducted by Lee. In the so-called 'Seven Days' battles (26 June-1 July 1862), McClellan again and again repulsed Lee's assaults, but each time then resumed a step-by-step retreat. The last of the Seven Days' battles, at Malvern Hill on 1 July 1862, ended in Lee's outright defeat with heavy loss after a vain attack on an entrenched Union position. Moreover, in the course of the week's fighting, Lee had lost 20,000 killed, wounded, and missing to McClellan's 15,000. A hard-punching counterstroke against Lee at this point might well have led to a decisive victory. Instead McClellan retreated to a new base at Harrison's Landing on the James River, whence he uttered brave talk about taking the offensive once he received reinforcements. A signal from him to Edwin Stanton, the Secretary of War, provides an unwitting but vivid psychological self-portrait of him at this time:

> I have seen too many dead and wounded comrades to feel otherwise than that the government has not sustained this army ... If I save this army now, I tell you plainly that I owe no thanks to you or to any other persons in Washington.[9]

Although Lincoln (with his cabinet) was by now convinced that McClellan ought to be sacked, he failed to do so; a rare sign of irresolution, and a serious mistake.

While the supine McClellan was nursing his grievances at Harris's Landing, there took place on 29-30 August 1862 the Second Battle of Bull Run (or Manassas) between the Confederate Army of Northern Virginia commanded by Robert Lee and a newly-formed Federal 'Army of Virginia' commanded by Major General John Pope. Pope, having won public acclaim by winning two actions – not important enough to be dubbed battles – in the Mississippi theatre, now became Lincoln's latest choice in his quest for a general who would serve as his effective military instrument. But Pope proved incompetent at manoeuvring large formations and unable to provide a clear strategic or tactical direction. On the first day of the Second Battle of Bull Run on 29 August 1862, he wrongly believed he had won a muddled but savage encounter, and that Lee was retreating. But next day Lee, far from retreating, ordered a general attack on the Federal position. As darkness fell at the end of another savage day's fighting, Pope fell back in retreat. Clearly not the first-rate leader hoped for by the President, he was now induced to resign his command, to be replaced on 5 September by McClellan, whose Army of the Potomac had now been brought back from Harrison's Landing to the main eastern theatre of war between Washington and Richmond.

It therefore fell to McClellan to cope with Lee's first raid into the North, which began on 4 September 1862. When on 17 September, Lee paused during his retirement back into Virginia and offered battle at Sharpsburg (also called Antietam after the creek of that name), McClellan with a two-to-one superiority in numbers, and with the benefit of Lee's captured marching orders, actually did venture to attack him. It was a day of chaotic fighting in which McClellan failed to exercise firm tactical control or display strong personal leadership. After the battle, he made no attempt to pursue Lee's army and destroy it.

Lincoln now pressed for a ruthless offensive into the Confederate heartland of Virginia, but McClellan, true to form, pleaded every kind of difficulty as a reason for inaction. Confronted again with this familiar pattern, Lincoln's patience finally ran out. He telegraphed McClellan: 'I have just read your despatches about sore-tongued and fatigued horses. Will you pardon me for asking what the horses of your army have done since the battle of Antietam that fatigues anything?'[10]

On 7 November 1862, he at long last sacked McClellan. Lincoln is credited with this valedictory comment on the man: McClellan 'is an admirable engineer, but he seems to have a special talent for a stationary engine.'[11]

McClellan had lasted a year. The next twelve months saw three successive commanders of the Army of the Potomac. The first was General Ambrose Burnside, a man adorned with enormous mutton-chop whiskers; hence the slang word 'sideburns'. Burnside, being an able fighting divisional commander but without the capacity for army command, suffered a crushing defeat at the Battle of Fredericksburg on 13 December. In January 1863 he was succeeded by Joseph Hooker, an able corps commander but above his ceiling at the head of an army. Hooker was outmanoeuvred and defeated by Lee at the Battle of Chancellorsville in May 1863, and then replaced by George Meade, a fighting soldier who certainly won the tactically defensive Battle of Gettysburg against Lee on 1-3 July. Sadly, however, Meade then emulated McClellan by refusing to hound Lee's shattered army to total destruction. Lincoln described Meade's pursuit as like an old woman trying to shoo her geese across a creek.

And Lincoln had little better luck with his generals in the Mississippi and Tennessee theatres. Politician-generals, appointed in the grand American tradition of 'political' appointments to high state offices in order to rally important constituencies behind the President, did as badly as the professionals. Nathaniel P. Banks, nicknamed from his initials 'Nothing Positive Banks', got beaten by Stonewall Jackson in the Shenandoah Valley campaign in 1862. McClernand, another politician in uniform favoured by Lincoln, was fired by Grant as incompetent and insubordinate. Don Carlos Buell, in the Kentucky-Tennessee theatre, suffered like McClellan from what Lincoln described as 'the slows'. Again, Lincoln did his best to prod his general into action, while the general pleaded problems of every kind. Buell was told: 'he [the President] does not understand why we cannot march as the enemy marches, lives as he lives, and fight as he fights ...'[12] Buell got the push in October 1862, replaced by General Rosecrans. Rosecrans in his turn was badly beaten at Chickamauga in September 1863 and thereafter was, in Lincoln's vivid phrase, 'confused and stunned like a duck hit on the head'. Rosecrans was sacked by Grant with Lincoln's sanction in October.

The point about this procession of sacked commanders is that none of them was a capable leader sacrificed as a political scapegoat, like some of Churchill's victims in the Second World War; they were each in their own way just not up to the job. And that there should have been so many of these failures indicates the paucity of available talent for army or theatre command, where strategic grasp has to be combined with organisational and tactical ability and with the sheer ruthless urge to destroy the enemy.

No wonder Lincoln intervened and prodded, and put forward his own ideas for offensive action. He was trying to fill a vacuum. As he wrote to Hooker after Chancellorsville:

> Have you already in your mind a plan wholly or partially formed? If you have, prosecute it without interference from me. If you have not, please inform me, so that I, incompetent as I may be, can try and assist in the formation of some plan for the army.[13]

And Lincoln faced a similar dilemma over the formulation of a grand strategic design for winning the war.

* * *

To this novel question he had applied his practical mind as soon as the war began. His first plan had been to secure Washington from attack, blockade the ports of the Confederacy, and then attack Charleston, South Carolina. This really was cigar-butt strategy, because there were neither armies nor shipping, nor warships in enough quantity to carry it out. What was more, he left out the Western theatre astride the Mississippi. Winfield Scott responded with what became known as the 'Anaconda Plan': blockade the Atlantic coast of the Confederacy while moving an army of 60,000 men down the Mississippi to the Gulf of Mexico, so sealing off the South and killing it by the slow economic squeeze.

Lincoln however wanted a quicker, more active, method of crushing the rebellion; so invasion and battle it had to be. But he picked up one major concept from Winfield Scott and never let it go – the concept of clearing the line of the Mississippi, so cutting the Confederacy in two.

THE LORDS OF WAR: FROM LINCOLN TO CHURCHILL

Lincoln's next immediate operational plan was for a direct drive on Richmond via the railway junction of Manassas. He hoped that the fall of their capital might induce the Confederacy to pack it in. But here too he was being naive; the Confederacy, having gone to war for causes desperately dear to it, was not going to surrender after one lost campaign. Anyway, McDowell's defeat at First Bull Run put an end to the plan, at least for another two years.

After First Bull Run, Lincoln came up with a fresh strategic concept: one which showed how fast his practical mind could learn. This time the concept encompassed the whole war rather than just one theatre. In the Eastern theatre (that is, Virginia), there would be a major drive on Richmond via Manassas with fresh armies now to be raised. In the theatre west of the Alleghanies, there would be twin offensives, from Cairo on the Mississippi south towards Memphis, and from Cincinnati south into Tennessee. Meanwhile the Confederacy would be economically weakened by blockade.

Here was foreshadowed the grand strategy that finally won the war in 1864-5.

In the meantime, however, Lincoln had looked to his generals for strategic answers, starting with McClellan when in command of the Army of the Potomac. McClellan proposed a fantastic scheme by which an army of 273,000 men would land on the Virginian coast and take Richmond from the rear (the germ of his disastrous Peninsular campaign of 1862), while local strokes took place in Missouri, Tennessee, and on the Mississippi. After the capture of Richmond, all the Confederate ports would be taken by similar seaborne operations. Unfortunately, McClellan failed to take note that the Union in 1861-2 could not have raised and fielded a single army of 273,000, or supplied it, or provided the shipping lift.

After McClellan became General-in-Chief in November 1861, Lincoln tried to persuade him of the importance of the Mississippi, suggesting that, first of all, New Orleans should be taken and then Vicksburg, the fortress which in his view was the key to the Confederacy: 'The war can never be brought to a close until that key is in our pocket.' McClellan disdained this presumptuous civilian advice, partly because his mental horizon was really limited to his own current campaign in the Eastern theatre, and he therefore saw all other operations as subsidiary or a diversion. In any case, in March 1862 he was demoted back from General-in-Chief to commander of the Army of the Potomac only. So in this period of the war Lincoln was really acting as his own strategic adviser, indeed his own chief of staff. He personally directed by telegraph the Union efforts to outwit Stonewall Jackson in the Shenandoah Valley campaign. That it was Jackson who continued to do the outwitting may be blamed on the sluggishness and stupidity of the Union field commanders rather than on Lincoln.

Nevertheless, it is clearly wrong that a national war leader should have been trying to run a regional campaign in detail. Lincoln himself was well aware that he needed an able soldier who could design a coherent grand strategy and direct its implementation; and in July 1862 he appointed Henry Halleck, who had been commanding in the Western theatre, to 'command the whole land forces of the United States, as General-in-Chief'.

Halleck was nicknamed 'Old Brains' because he was the Union's most renowned 'intellectual' soldier, having written one weighty book on military theory, and translated another from the French.[14] As a staff officer and administrator, Halleck was able enough; as a strategist and director of operations, he was pedantic and formalistic, and lacked the essential force of character and willpower that such a post required. When Lincoln's trust in his strategic ability faded away, Halleck dwindled more and more into a super chief-clerk, transmitting the President's orders and running the administrative machine.

In particular, Lincoln was irritated by Halleck's ducking of responsibility or, in the President's words, 'habitual attitude of demur'.[15] And Halleck never came up with a clear grand-strategic plan for the whole war.

In November of that year, Lincoln once more reverted to his idea of clearing the Mississippi. In the spring, a seaborne Union force had occupied New Orleans. Now he wanted that force to be reinforced and sent up the river, while another army marched down it, with Vicksburg as the joint objective. It was only after bitter quarrels between generals in the West as to who of them ought to be in command over whom that Lincoln's concept finally bore fruit in Ulysses Grant's siege and capture of Vicksburg in July 1863. Now the Confederacy was cut in half, marking the turning-point of the war.

In the Eastern theatre, Meade, after the victory at Gettysburg, proposed making Richmond the focus of a methodical advance through Virginia. Once again Lincoln showed that he had learned faster about strategy than his generals, writing to Halleck about Meade's proposal:

> My last attempt upon Richmond was to get McClellan, when he was nearer there than the enemy was, to run in ahead of him. Since then I have constantly desired the Army of the Potomac to make Lee's army and not Richmond, its object point.[16]

This was a strategic insight of the first importance. Lee's Army of Northern Virginia was the military engine of the war. Its destruction would finish the Confederacy. Yet Richmond, being the Confederate capital, would still remain the 'object point' of first instance because Lee would be compelled to give battle in its defence.

Now it was Grant's turn as the new Union General-in-Chief to come up with a plan of war. Even before he left his command on the Mississippi he had suggested an advance from New Orleans along an eastern axis through Mobile in Alabama and then northwards up into Georgia towards Atlanta. The weakness of the plan lay in that, to the north of this axis, Tennessee would be protected only by the Army of the Cumberland, a weak covering force. Lincoln thought Grant's plan too dangerous and turned it down, partly because he wished to secure Louisiana and invade Texas. Grant then proposed dual advances into Georgia, one from New Orleans, the other from Chattanooga (in Tennessee) eastwards. But Lincoln turned this down too, because it would split up the Union forces west of the Alleghenies instead of concentrating them. So Grant suggested that the Army of the Potomac would be landed by sea in North Carolina, whence it would march up northwards into the rear of Lee's Army of Northern Virginia. The drawback with this plan, like McClellan's and Meade's similar ideas, was that it did not make Lee's army the primary objective. It would also remove the Army of the Potomac too far from Washington, which in consequence would then need its own separate protection.

On being appointed General-in-Chief in March 1864, Grant had discussed the Union's future strategy with Lincoln, and afterwards drafted the plan on which the war was finally won. No documentary evidence exists to establish how far the plan should be credited to Grant or how far to Lincoln. Nonetheless, its architecture has more in common with Lincoln's thinking than with Grant's own earlier ideas.

The plan was based on the concept of concurrent interrelated offensives pressing concentrically on the Confederacy, so as to pin down and destroy the outnumbered Confederate armies.

In the East, Meade, in command of the Army of the Potomac, was to make Lee's army his one objective. He was instructed: 'Wherever Lee goes, there you will go also.' In the West, General William Sherman was to launch an offensive from Chattanooga eastwards to Atlanta in Georgia. However, his true objective, like Grant's, was to engage the Confederate army opposite him and destroy it. Sherman was further directed to lay waste the war resources of the country along his line of advance. A third offensive starting from New Orleans was to take Mobile and perhaps later link up with Sherman.

The Union at last had a war-winning strategy. Just before Grant was appointed General-in-Chief, the longstanding problem of the organisation of the high command in Washington had also been solved. Previously, there had been no clear division of responsibility between Lincoln as President, Halleck as General-in-Chief and the various commanders in the field: no clear chain of command and communication. Now a new post of Chief of Staff was created and Halleck appointed to it. It was his role to act as the channel of command and communication between the President and Grant, as General-in-Chief of all Union armies; and between Grant and his theatre commanders.

Grant himself wished to be near Washington (and the President), but not located within it: he also wished to be close to the Army of the Potomac, his principal army and on the principal front of the war. He therefore rode with Meade, who remained executive commander of that Army.

At last the Union had a clear plan, a clear command organisation, and, in Grant, a general-in-chief of proven capability. And Lincoln at last had a commander he could trust to get on with it. In return, Grant comprehended Lincoln's political problems better than his predecessors.

In May 1864, just as Grant was preparing to launch the first of a series of bloody battles of attrition in Virginia, he received the following letter from the President:

> The particulars of your plans I neither know nor seek to know. You are vigilant and self-reliant, and pleased with this, I wish not to obtrude any constraints or restraints upon you. While I am very anxious that any great disaster or capture of our men in great numbers shall be avoided, I know these points are less likely to escape your attention than they would be mine. If there is anything wanting which is within my power to give, do not fail to let me know it. And now, with a brave army and a just cause, may God sustain you.[17]

References

1. For Lincoln's background and early career, see Lehrman, *Lincoln at Peoria: The Turning Point.*
2. Thomas, p.117
3. Cunliffe, *Soldiers and Civilians: The Martial Spirit in America 1775–1865*, p.125
4. Ibid, p.186
5. Ibid, p.235
6. Ganoe, W. A., *The History of the United States Army*, pp.256–7
7. Ibid, p.249
8. Williams, T. H., *Lincoln and His Generals*, pp.83–4
9. Ibid, p. 126. Lincoln and Stanton never saw the self-pitying last line because the telegraph operator omitted it. I am grateful to Professor Michael Burlingame for pointing this out.
10. Ibid, p.176
11. Ibid, p.178
12. Ibid, p.184
13. Ibid, p.244
14. *Elements of Military Art and Science*, Henri Jomini
15. Williams, op cit., p.140
16. Ibid, pp.286–7
17. Ibid, p. 315

CHAPTER 3

A Study in Contrast

Ulysses Grant and Robert Lee

Grant and Lee practised high command at a time when the battlefield was being transformed by advances in military technology. Although the infantry were still equipped with muzzle-loading muskets fired by percussion caps, the hollow expanding bullet meant that there was no longer a need to ram the round down the rifling. Therefore each infantryman could fire up to three rounds a minute, perhaps two as a combat average, with precise accuracy up to a range of two hundred yards, and even hit a target up to eight-foot square at a thousand yards. At that range, the round would still penetrate four inches of soft pinewood. This meant that attacking formations would be within a lethal fire zone from 1,000 yards distant from the enemy positions, whereas the defenders would enjoy the advantage of firing while static, or even from the cover of trenches.

Rifled cannon and explosive shell similarly extended the range and destructive power of artillery compared with the Napoleonic era. This, too, strongly favoured the defence against the attack, especially against headlong assaults in mass formation such as the charge at the Battle of Gettysburg[1] of Pickett's division in Lee's Army of Northern Virginia. In that one charge, Pickett's division of 4,500 men lost two-thirds of its strength in dead and wounded.

In fact, battle casualties in the Civil War were fully as high in terms of percentages of forces engaged as in Western-Front offensives in 1914-18. Lee lost 20.7 per cent of his army in 'the Seven Days' Battles in 1862[2]; 30 per cent of his army in just three days' fighting at Gettysburg in 1863. Grant lost 29 per cent in the Wilderness and Spottsylvania offensive in May 1864.[3] The overall loss in dead and wounded in battle for the whole war worked out at around 11 per cent for the Union and over 12 per cent for the Confederates.[4] It was no wonder that Lincoln, who had been so keen to prod McClellan into a relentless offensive, would flinch at the human cost of Grant's attacks. Given the then state of surgery and medicine, and taking into account the diseases incidental to mass life in the field, it is not surprising that deaths in action amounted to only half the total death rate. One estimate gives that total for the Union side alone at 350,000 dead, while another puts the tally of dead for both sides together at a million. In relation to a total

American population of 32 million, these figures represent proportionate losses higher than the British nation suffered in the First World War.

* * *

In their characters and in their methods of leadership, Lieutenant General Ulysses Grant (General-in-Chief of all the Union forces from March 1864) and General Robert Lee (General-in Chief of the Confederate armies in 1865) embody the military, social, and cultural contrasts between 'the North' and 'the South'.

Robert Lee – tall, handsome, courtly – was a member of the Virginian land-owning gentry. One English observer actually referred to him as the best type of *'English* gentleman'. The son of 'Light-Horse Harry' Lee (who had fought in the War of Independence), he was born and spent his early childhood at Stratford Hall, the family seat in northern Virginia, a modest red-brick Georgian mansion of the kind that abundantly grace the English shires. And just as the life and loyalties of a Victorian English country gentleman were rooted in the soil of his native shire, so too were Lee's life and loyalties rooted in the soil of Virginia. Both as a man and as a military leader he was inspired by a powerful sense of *territory.*

Lee further resembled the English gentry of his time in his strongly-held Episcopalian Low-Church faith. He was a moralist to the core, seeing the strivings of men as completely subordinate to God's will. Defeat, loss, and suffering were for him a punishment for sin. Yet Lee's belief in the supremacy of the will of God bred in him a kind of fatalism or acceptance: passivity even. Thus, although he personally judged that slavery was 'a moral and political evil in any country', he believed that in regard to its abolition 'we must leave the progress as well as the result in his [i.e. God's] hands, who sees the end and who chooses to work by slow things, and with whom a thousand years are but a single day'.

All witnesses testify to his aura of nobility. The British Colonel (later Field Marshal) Garnet Wolseley wrote:

> I have met many of the great men of my time, but Lee alone impressed me with the feeling that I was in the presence of a man who was cast in a grander mould, and made of different and finer metal than all other men ...[5]

When Lee at the end of the Battle of Chancellorsville in 1863 rode into a clearing full of soldiers, it was the signal, according to an eyewitness:

> for one of those uncontrollable outbursts of enthusiasms which none can appreciate who have not witnessed them. The fierce soldiers, with their faces blackened with the smoke of the battle, the wounded, crawling with feeble limbs ... all seemed to be possessed with a common impulse. One long unbroken cheer ... rose high above the roar of battle ... As I looked on him in the complete fruition of the success which his genius, courage, and

confidence in his army had won, I thought that it must have been from some such scene that men in the ancient days ascended to the dignity of the gods.[6]

Such language reveals that Robert Lee had now become a mythical hero whose shining sword would miraculously save his people. It was this faith of his soldiers in him as their commander that enabled him to hold the Army of Northern Virginia together through all its later tribulations and defeats.

*   *   *

In every way except sheer power of leadership, Ulysses Grant presents the starkest imaginable contrast to Robert Lee. His father was a tanner. He spent his early years working on the land, just like Lincoln: ploughing, hauling logs, and acting as teamster. Though he was educated at West Point like Lee (where he distinguished himself in mathematics and horsemanship), he did not follow Lee's example and long pursue a military career, although he proved a very capable line officer in the Mexican war as a quartermaster and commissary officer. Since then he had tried and failed in various business ventures. In 1860 he was just a clerk in the Grant Brothers' leather store in Galena. A friend described him as he was in 1858:

> He had no exalted opinion of himself at any time, but in those days he was almost in despair. He walked the street looking for something to do. He was actually the most obscure man [in town]. Nobody took any notice of him.[7]

Grant hardly made a better impression when, at the age of thirty-nine, he took command of the 21st Illinois Volunteers just before the outbreak of the Civil War. An eyewitness recounts:

> I went with him to camp, and shall never forget the scene when his men first saw him. Grant was dressed in citizen's clothes, an old coat worn out at the elbows, and a badly damaged hat. His men, though ragged and barefoot themselves, had formed a high estimate of what a colonel should be, and when Grant walked in among them, they began making fun of him ...[8]

An officer said to Grant nervously: 'They're an unruly lot. Do you think you can manage them?' 'Oh, yes, I think I can manage them,' replied Grant. The troops called on him for a speech. So he gave them one: 'Go to your quarters!' When a soldier got drunk and disorderly, Grant knocked him down, bound him and had him thrown into the guardroom. Other men who were insolent were tied to posts; late risers got no rations all day.

Three years later, when Grant was appointed to command all the Union armies, one sophisticated Washingtonian described him as an 'ordinary scrubby-looking man with a slightly seedy look'.[9] But the key to Grant's character and his eventual strength as a leader lies in the blend of that ordinariness with sheer toughness. He was very much an American of his time, a product of a wide-open and egalitarian society. An eyewitness recorded his first impression of Grant in 1864 after Grant had arrived in Washington to take command of the Union armies:

> He is rather under middle-height, of a spare strong build; light-brown hair, and short, light-brown beard. His eyes of a clear blue; forehead high; jaw squarely set, but not sensual. His face has three expressions: deep thought; extreme determination; and great simplicity and calmness.[10]

And after another meeting with him:

> Grant is a man of a good deal of rough dignity; rather taciturn; quick and decided in speech. He habitually wears an expression as if he had determined to drive his head through a brick wall, and was about to do it.

And again:

> He is a man of a natural, severe simplicity in all things – the very way he wears his high-crowned felt hat shows this: he neither puts it on behind his ears, nor draws it over his eyes; much less does he cock it on one side, but sets it straight and very hard on his head ...

One last quote from this same witness:

> He is an odd combination; there is one good thing, at any rate - he is the concentration of all that is American. He talks bad grammar, but he talks it naturally, as much as to say, 'I was so brought up and, if I try fine phrases, I shall only appear silly.' Then his writing, though very terse and well expressed, is full of horrible spelling.[11]

Certainly Grant's correspondence with Sherman, for instance, is almost colloquial in its laconic and even homely language, whereas Lee's letters are formal and stilted in a high-Victorian wordy style. So in all sorts of ways Grant seems a very *modern* man, with the problem-solving approach of a practical engineer. He can be imagined in charge of developing an oilfield; or sorting out a loss-making major industry. That cannot be said of Lee any more than of Washington or Wellington.

The contrast between Grant and Lee does not only lie in upbringing and personality; it embraces their conduct of campaigns and their methods of command; it embraces their thinking about grand strategy.

This contrast even extends to their perceptions of the very nature of the civil war. Robert Lee for his part failed to grasp that this was a total war between two entire societies, and instead remained faithful to the traditional belief that war should be limited to a duel between armed forces. During the Gettysburg campaign in 1863 he issued the following General Order in order to restrain ill-behaviour that would anger the North and render it all the more determined not to conclude a compromise peace:

> The commanding general considers that no greater disgrace could befall the army, and through it our whole people, than the perpetration of the barbarous outrages upon the unarmed and the defenceless, and the wanton destruction of private property that have marked the course of the enemy in our own country ... It must be remembered that we make war only upon armed men ...[12]

This chivalric attitude may be compared with Grant's instructions to Sherman in 1864:

> You I propose to move against Johnston's army, to break it up, and to get into the interior of the enemy's country as far as you can, inflicting all the damage you can against their war resources.[13]

If Lee failed to comprehend that this was a war between societies, not just armies, his grasp of grand strategy was little better. To the end of the war, his mental horizon remained essentially restricted to the operations of the Army of Northern Virginia. He never saw the war as a whole; never perceived that all the fronts from Virginia through Tennessee to the Mississippi were essentially interlinked. He never understood the strategic importance of those theatres of war lying to the west of the Alleghenies, and treated them as secondary to his own operations. Even when Sherman had taken Atlanta in Georgia on 2 September, 1864, unlocking the back door to the heartland of the Confederacy, Lee could write to his wife: 'The fall of Atlanta is a blow to us, which is not very grievous and which I hope we will recover from.'[14]

Why was Lee so poor a thinker about grand strategy? Part of the answer lies in his own personal motive for fighting. He had not drawn his sword to defend secession, let alone slavery. He was not fighting for the Confederacy as such. He was fighting for Virginia. On resigning his commission in the United States Army in 1861 (or, as some might say, breaking his soldier's oath of allegiance to the Constitution of the United States), he wrote to the Commander-in-Chief, Winfield Scott, that 'Save in defence of my native State, I never desire to again draw my sword'. Five days later, Virginia appointed him commander of her state forces. In accepting the appointment, Lee repeated, 'I devote myself to the service of my native State, in whose behalf alone will I ever again draw my sword.'[15]

To Lee, therefore, it was a secondary issue that Virginia was part of a confederacy of states fighting for a common cause. When Richmond, Virginia, was chosen as the Confederate capital this only served to reinforce Lee's obsession with defending his native soil. At a meeting under President Jefferson Davis in 1862 to discuss the possible evacuation of Richmond in the face of McClellan's peninsular offensive, Lee's renowned calm and self-control left him. According to an eyewitness, he proclaimed in a voice loud with passion: 'But Richmond *must* be defended.'[16]   Yet in fairness to Lee it must be remembered that (except for a very brief period in 1861) he was not appointed General in Chief of all the Confederate forces until the beginning of 1865, when the war was already hopelessly lost. Until June 1862 he had largely served as Jefferson Davis's military adviser or trouble-shooter, and after that as commander of the Army of Northern Virginia.

Grant for his part had already turned his mind to the wider grand-strategic picture even while an army commander in the Mississippi theatre in 1861-3, keeping himself as closely informed as possible about events in the theatres beyond his own. After his capture of Vicksburg in July 1863, he submitted a complete war plan to Halleck which chimed in certain respects with Lincoln's own grand-strategic thinking. After Grant was appointed General in Chief in 1864, he and Lincoln jointly agreed on the grand strategy that won the war for the Union – to hold Lee fast by the throat in Virginia while General William Sherman swung from Tennessee south-eastwards through Georgia into the Confederate heartland. In a letter of April 1864, Grant explained to Sherman:

> It is my design, if the enemy keep quiet and allow me to take the initiative in the spring campaign, to work all parts of the army together and somewhat towards a common centre.

In a later letter to Sherman, Grant considers the danger that

> if the two main attacks, yours and the one from here, should promise great success, the enemy may, in a fit of desperation, abandon one part of their line of defence, and throw their whole weight upon the other ...

If so:

> My directions, then, would be, if the enemy in your front show signs of joining Lee, follow him up to the full extent of your ability. I will prevent the concentration of Lee upon your front, if it is in the power of this army to do it.

Sherman himself perfectly comprehended Grant's unitary approach to strategy, writing 'That we are now all to act on a common plan, converging on a common center, looks like enlightened war.'[17] Where responsibility for grand strategy and political considerations overlap, Grant and Lincoln achieved an excellent working relationship. Because Lincoln reposed every confidence in Grant as general in chief, he largely (though never entirely) left him free to execute that strategy. Grant for his part was perfectly willing to take that weight on to his own shoulders. As Lincoln put it:

> Grant is the first general I have had. You know how it has been with all the rest. As soon as I put a man in command of the army, he'd come to me with a plan of campaign and about as much as to say, 'Now, I don't believe I can do it, but if you say so, I'll try it on', and so put the responsibility of success or failure on me. They all wanted me to be the General. Now it isn't so with Grant.[18]

Here too Lee makes a sharp contrast. For all his personal courage and his moral fervour, he would not assume the responsibility for grand strategy in the face of President Jefferson Davis's clear desire to hold on to that role. Again and again Lee would refer grand-strategic decisions to Davis, rather in the manner of the deferential servant. 'The President', wrote Lee on one occasion, 'from his position being able to survey all the scenes of action, can better decide than anyone else.' On another occasion he wrote to Davis: 'Should you think it proper to concentrate the troops near Richmond, I should be glad if you would advise me.' He asks Davis to visit him in the field: 'I need not say how glad I should be if your convenience would permit you to visit the army, that I might have the benefit of your advice and direction.'[19] Even when Lee was finally made General-in-Chief of all Confederate forces in February 1865, he assured Davis that their relationship would remain the same: 'I must beg you to continue these same feelings for me in the future and allow me to refer you at all times for counsel and advice.'[20] Yet before his 1862 invasion of the North, Lee wrote to Davis that he might well embark on this strategy, only to march his army off before Davis could respond. Now it is true that whereas Grant was co-operating with a Confederate President of great good sense and immense strength of character, Lee had to deal with a President who was brittle and touchy, and, moreover, one who (as himself an ex-West Pointer) sought to interfere in operations in the field.

Lee's customary deference towards Davis also meant that he did little to combat the blatant corruption and gross inefficiency of the Confederate war administration. This deference, coupled with his reluctance to assume responsibility for framing grand strategy must put into question Lee's calibre as a supreme commander.

However, his reputation really rests on his performance in command of a single army: the Army of Northern Virginia.

There was little in Lee's past career to prepare him for the role of manoeuvring a mass of troops in the field. He had served as an engineer officer modernising various forts. During the Mexican War of 1846, he had been mentioned in despatches for daring and intelligent reconnaissance and for leadership in action. Thereafter he had spent some dreary years commanding a small post in West Texas.

In October 1859 he commanded the scratch Federal force which recaptured the arsenal at Harper's Ferry, Virginia, from John Brown, the anti-slavery zealot; and by 1861 was reputed the outstanding soldier in the country. As America slid into civil war in April of that year, Lee had therefore seemed a natural choice for the post of General commanding the army to be formed round Washington, only for him to resign his commission and take command of the secessionist Virginia state forces instead.

Lee's first operation in the field in the Civil War ended in failure, and very much owing to the bent of his own character. In summer 1861 he had been despatched to a mountainous region of Western Virginia in order to 'co-ordinate' the Confederate forces there. Coordination was certainly needed: two of the three local commanders were furiously quarrelling, while the troops had lapsed into an appalling state of filth and indiscipline. It may be imagined with what a quiet but ruthless exercise of authority Ulysses Grant would have sorted out such a mess. Lee, however, refused to bang the commanders' heads together or enforce discipline in their camps. Nor did he seek authorisation from President Davis to deal firmly with the quarrellers and their disorderly troops. Instead he relied on tactful persuasion, appealing to them to 'permit no division of sentiment to disturb its [the command's] harmony'. Yet tactful persuasion failed to sort out the quarrelling commanders or their unsoldierly rank-and-file, with the result that they suffered a local defeat by Federal troops, whereupon Lee found himself temporarily posted to command coast defences in South Carolina, Georgia, and Florida. In March 1862 he was hauled back to Richmond to serve once again as Davis's military factotum. On 1 June, with McClellan's Army of the Potomac now closing on the Confederate capital, Davis appointed Lee to command the 'Armies in Eastern Virginia and North Carolina', soon to be re-dubbed the 'Army of Northern Virginia'.

So, at long last, at the age of fifty-four and with little campaigning experience, Lee found himself for the first time commanding an army in the field, and, what is more, an army already committed by his predecessor, Joe Johnston, to a counter-offensive against McClellan.

In the following 'Seven Days Battle', Lee's operational strategy was clear and clever enough. With only 30,000 men well posted in field defences, he would block the advance south of the Chickahominy river on Richmond by McClellan's powerful left flank, 75,000 men strong. North of the Chickahominy, Lee would deploy 50,000 men against McClellan's right wing (only 25,000 men), outflank it, and drive it back. He would then swing across McClellan's communications, cutting him off from his coastal base and destroying him. He ordered General 'Stonewall' Jackson,[21] fresh from a campaign of agile and cunning manoeuvre in the Shenandoah Valley, to join him in the attack on McClellan's right flank. But Jackson was slow to come up, too late for the first battle of the 'Seven Days' campaign, and thereafter was held up by destroyed bridges along the Chickahominy. This was not the Jackson of the Shenandoah: perhaps he was tired; his soldiers certainly were.

As a whole, the execution of Lee's offensive during the Seven Days' battles was muddled and tactically ill-led, costing the Confederates just under 20,000 men killed and wounded, as against the Federal loss of only 15,000.

The reasons for this botched performance lay firstly in inadequate prior reconnaissance of Union positions, leading to attacks being directed at the wrong tactical objectives; and, secondly, it lay in poor battlefield cooperation between Lee's divisional commanders, with the effect that Confederate attacks were often launched piecemeal, so weakening their impact. These were all failings for which Lee's chosen permissive method of leadership was in large part responsible. Once a battle was joined, it would always be his custom to entrust its tactical conduct to his frontline commanders. Such orders as Lee issued on a battlefield were often verbal rather than written, and hence open to misinterpretation.

This habit of permissive leadership curiously foreshadows the doctrine of 'mission command' now prevailing in today's Western armies, whereby the general sets the operational objective, but then leaves it to his subordinates to choose the best way of achieving it.

Yet manoeuvring troops in a nineteenth-century battle as large in scale as 'the Seven Days', with bugle calls or gallopers as the only means of communication, really demanded direct personal leadership by the commander in chief, like Wellington during the war in the Iberian Peninsula and again on the day of Waterloo. Lee, however, would again and again fail to practise such leadership.

Nonetheless, Lee had won a famous victory in the 'Seven Days' battles, driving McClellan back from Richmond, forcing him to switch to a new coastal base, and reducing McClellan himself to whining defeatism.

In July 1862, Lee further enhanced his reputation by skilfully outmanoeuvring the Federal 'Army of Virginia' under Major General Pope,[22] and whipping it in the Second Battle of Bull Run (or Manassas). In May 1863 he won his most celebrated victory, the Battle of Chancellorsville. The battle exemplifies Lee's skill in exploiting any mistake made by a clumsy foe, in this case Joseph Hooker, the latest commander of the Army of the Potomac and a man given to an outward show of aggressiveness. Hooker was advancing towards Richmond when he lost his nerve, hesitated, and pulled back a little. Lee, divining Hooker's state of indecision, split his own army into two wings even though he was outnumbered. While he himself frontally attacked Hooker, he sent Stonewall Jackson on a wide march round Hooker's right flank, there to deliver a devastating surprise onslaught which led to Hooker's crushing defeat. This bold manoeuvre marks Lee's crowning achievement as a field commander.

* * *

For Lee as a strategist, the conundrum to be solved lay in the huge superiority of the North's resources, human and material. It followed that to stand on the defensive must inevitably lead to defeat through sheer attrition. So in 1862 after his success in the Seven Days' campaign, he opted for a bold offensive into the Northern state of Maryland. It would enable him to feed his men and beasts on Maryland's rich farmlands, relieving the strain on Virginia's own resources. His operational objective was to seek out McClellan and the Army of the Potomac (now returned from Harrison's Landing) and bring him to battle, sure that he could beat him. Yet Lee also cherished a far grander vision. By invading the North and defeating the Army of the Potomac, he hoped to cause such panic and defeatism in the North as to compel Lincoln to accept a compromise peace. In his own words in a letter to Jefferson Davis on the day after his army crossed the Potomac northbound on 5 September 1862,

> The present position of affairs, in my opinion, places it in the power of the Confederate States to propose with propriety to that of the United States the recognition of our independence.[23]

For once, Lee was venturing advice on high policy. Yet his advice rested on a complete misjudgement of Lincoln and the people of the North. For they were not going to succumb to a mere raid, even by an army led by Robert Lee. And a mere raid was what this invasion of Maryland in 1862, and the similar invasion the following year, really were. It was beyond Lee's strength to occupy Northern territory in the way that Union armies were later to occupy the South. At best, he could only cause a passing panic by winning a battle against the Army of the Potomac on its own soil and thereby posing a threat to Washington.

But in the event Lee disastrously botched both his invasions of the North, in 1862 and 1863.

* * *

His plan of campaign was much the same in both years: a northward march by the Army of Northern Virginia well to the west of Washington, so outflanking the Army of the Potomac, threatening the Federal capital's communications with the rest of the Union, and spreading alarm as far north as possible.

In both campaigns again, Lee's operation orders divided his forces on the march, partly for foraging purposes, partly because he seems to have held his opponents in contempt, having each year recently defeated them – Pope at Bull Run in 1862; Hooker at Chancellorsville in 1863.

Towards the end of his 1862 raid, Lee decided to offer battle at Sharpsburg on Antietam Creek rather than tamely continue his retreat back into Virginia. Although he held his ground against McClellan, the battle cost him over 13,000 men. But such was his contempt for McClellan that he stood his ground next day, daring McClellan to attack him: a vain hope. Only then did he withdraw his army intact across the Potomac, to Lincoln's frustration and fury. Yet this was hardly the outright victory needed to crown his raid into the North with strategic success.

His 1863 raid fared far worse. A portion of his divided forces blundered into an action with Federal troops at Gettysburg, Pennsylvania, whereupon the main bodies on both sides converged on the town. Even though Lee could only field 75,000 men and 272 guns against the Union enemy's 83,000 men and 357 guns, he now chose to fight a battle; and, moreover, a battle in which he would attack the Army of the Potomac and its batteries well posted by its present general in chief, George Meade, along a low north-south ridge giving an excellent field of fire. In his report on the campaign, Lee contends that it was not out of choice that he sought battle:

> but, finding ourselves unexpectedly confronted by the Federal Army, it became a matter of difficulty to withdraw through the mountains with our large trains. At the same time, the country was unfavourable for collecting supplies while in the presence of the enemy's main body ... a battle thus became, in a measure, unavoidable.[24]

Lee's conduct on the battlefield at Gettysburg, the encounter which passed into legend, displays his leadership at its worst. His orders were ambiguous: a critical lapse in a confused and fast-changing situation. Yet a far greater lapse, indeed a fatal lapse, lay in his failure to exert firm personal control over his army, and especially over the timing and execution of major attacks on the Union line. In fact, Lee displayed an extraordinary passivity that stands in the sharpest contrast to, say, Wellington at Waterloo or Marlborough at Blenheim. The British Colonel Fremantle, who was with Lee throughout the battle, writes of Lee during the doomed Confederate attack on the second day of Gettysburg:

> What I remarked especially was, that during the whole time the firing continued, he only sent one message, and only received one report. It is evidently his system to arrange the plan thoroughly with the three corps commanders, and then leave to them the duty of modifying and carrying it out to the best of their abilities.[25]

This is really an abdication of leadership. Is it to be explained by that curious fatalism which ran deep in Lee's character? Nonetheless, in that abdication of leadership lay the main cause of the shattering defeat of the Army of Northern Virginia at Gettysburg.

* * *

A STUDY IN CONTRAST

Despite the weaknesses in Lee's methods of command, despite his failure to win a decisive strategic victory over the North, his record as an army commander in the field in 1862–63 remains impressive enough. He had defeated four Union generals at the head of the Army of the Potomac: McClellan, Pope, Burnside, and Hooker. He had twice brought panic to Washington and fear to the North. With an army sometimes as little as half the size as that of his enemy, he had gained and held the operational initiative, dominating the minds of his opponents by the power of his own personality.

*   *   *

Since neither army succeeded in destroying the other, the Gettysburg campaign only confirmed the stalemate between the Union and the Confederacy in the principal theatre of operations. It was clear that what lay ahead was war to the bitterest of ends: and yet a war which at the beginning of 1864 Lee and Lincoln alike thought the Confederacy might yet survive unbeaten. In May that year Robert Lee with an army of some 50,000 found himself facing a new Federal enemy, Ulysses Grant, commanding an army some 90,000 strong.

*   *   *

Grant's wartime career had been very different from Lee's. Instead of being plunged into army command in the midst of battle after largely staff duties like Lee, he had climbed the ladder of promotion step by step, gaining experience all the time – experience of battle, of organisation, of logistics. His maturing professional judgement formidably complemented his native fighting spirit and the granite strength of his character.

He had made his fighting debut on 7 November 1861 as a brigadier general in a small action on the Mississippi; green troops and a green commander. In February 1862, in command of three divisions, Grant launched an offensive against Fort Henry and Fort Donelson, on the Tennessee and Cumberland Rivers, protecting vital Confederate communications. Though sanctioned by his superiors, the offensive was his own idea. Fort Henry fell quickly: a major boost to Northern morale. But Fort Donelson proved tougher. After Grant had invested the fort, the Confederate garrison launched a surprise sortie in an attempt to cut their way out, whereupon the besiegers fell back in confusion. At the time, Grant was some miles away conferring with a colleague, and he had failed to leave a deputy in temporary command.

On hastily returning, he found the battle hanging in the balance. His answer was to launch his one unscathed division into attack against the opposite section of the fort's perimeter; then, with the enemy thrown off-balance, he rallied his other divisions and personally led them forward into action. Here was a cool nerve and clear thinking in a crisis. But now Grant showed his toughness of character: when Simon Buckner, the Confederate commander, asked to negotiate terms, Grant told him that he would only accept unconditional surrender. On 16 February 1862, Fort Donelson duly surrendered, along with a bag of 11,500 prisoners and forty guns. This was a major milestone in Grant's career.

Yet in April he was taken by surprise by a Confederate counter-stroke against an advanced division under William Sherman at Shiloh on the Tennessee River. Grant had under-estimated his enemy: a mistake from which he learned an important lesson. He now redeemed his error with a display of energetic personal leadership, rallying and re-deploying his shaken forces, and denying the Confederates their hoped-for major strategic success.

In July 1862 he was appointed general in command of the Armies of the Tennessee and the Mississippi, and in the autumn two of his subordinate generals won engagements at Iuka and Corinth. Then in spring 1863 he embarked on the campaign that displayed him as a fully-fledged commander of large formations, and finally made his reputation.

His objective was the Confederate fortress of Vicksburg on the Mississippi which he had failed to take in the autumn of 1862. His strategic purpose was to cut the Confederate states west of that river off from the heartland of the Confederacy to the east. Grant fielded some 50,000 men to the 40,000 commanded by his opponent, Lieutenant General John Pemberton, and the 24,000 reinforcements under General Joe Johnston. An earlier attempt to march on Vicksburg from the north along the east bank of the Mississippi had been blocked by the enemy defence, while a Confederate raid on a Union supply depot had shown how vulnerable were the communications of any army taking this route down the Mississippi. So Grant decided to attack Vicksburg from the south. He marched his army down the west bank, then crossed to the east bank south of Vicksburg, and there set up an advanced base which was supplied by a naval squadron running the gauntlet of the Vicksburg batteries.

Now came Grant's boldest move of all. He decided to cut free from his base by carrying his own supplies with him and for a time living off the country. This enabled him to march north-east and capture the key railway junction of Jackson, so cutting Vicksburg's own communications. Pemberton sought in vain to find and sever Grant's non-existent supply-line, then fell back into Vicksburg, where Grant put him under siege. On 4 July 1863 Vicksburg surrendered. This victory persuaded Lincoln of Grant's high ability. It also marked a strategic turning-point: the Confederacy was now cut in two, with its principal (or eastern) segment exposed to a flanking strategic offensive from the west as well as direct attack from the north.

Along with Meade's virtually simultaneous defensive success against Lee at Gettysburg, the capture of Vicksburg restored Northern morale at a time of deep discouragement – with the profound political consequence that, in the autumn elections to Congress, candidates in favour of a compromise peace were routed.

After Vicksburg, Grant was appointed by Lincoln to command all the armies in the region from the Appalachians to the Mississippi. In this capacity, Grant won fresh distinction – especially in Lincoln's eyes – by routing a Confederate army in the Battle of Chattanooga on 24–25 November 1863, so securing East Tennessee for the Union, as long desired by the President. Grant's fresh success came at a time when Lincoln was coming to recognise that Meade, commanding the Army of the Potomac, though able enough at defensive operations in the field, was not up to the higher strategic task of bringing Lee and the Army of Northern Virginia to complete and final defeat.

So Grant, the proven victorious leader of large formations and equally proven organiser and quartermaster, was the man. On 9 March 1864 came his formal appointment as general in chief of all the Union armies in every theatre, but with special responsibility for masterminding Meade's operations in Virginia. According to the grand strategy agreed between him and Lincoln, it was now up to him to engage Lee in battle in Northern Virginia while Sherman sliced into Georgia.

Clausewitz has an interesting concept in his book *On War* which he calls 'polarity'. In brief, this means that if one side wishes to play things a certain way, it must be in the other side's interest to play it the opposite way. It was clear that Lee, outnumbered two to one, would wish to fight the kind of a campaign of manoeuvre that had been so successful against previous Union commanders. However, Grant had no intention of presenting Lee with any opportunity for manoeuvre. Instead he meant to engage Lee frontally in remorseless in-fighting that would grip Lee fast. His directive to George Meade, field commander of the Army of the Potomac, could not have been more succinct: 'Lee's army will be your objective point. Wherever Lee goes, there you will go also.'[26]

On 4 May 1864, the Army of the Potomac began to advance through the Wilderness of Virginia, a tangled area of second-growth woodland, on the direct route to Richmond, the Confederate capital – not for the sake of taking Richmond itself, but because Lee would have to offer battle in its defence. The so-called Battle of the Wilderness, 5–6 May 1864, was as confused and bloody a frontal collision as any battle on the Western Front in the Great War: Grant lost 17,000 in killed, wounded, and missing, while the result on the ground was a tactical draw. But strategically the Battle of the Wilderness *was* decisive. Whereas earlier Federal commanders would have fallen back after such an indecisive and bloody battle, Grant ordered Meade to push on. Already Lee had been deprived of all freedom of action, compelling this supreme manoeuvrist to resort to a Western Front-style defence in a system of trenches.

On 10 May 1864, Grant assaulted Lee's positions in the Battle of Spotsylvania, its bloody climax coming two days later: another drawn battle; more colossal losses on both sides. Yet there was to be no let-up in the relentless pressure on Lee. In Grant's words in a letter to Lincoln: 'I propose to fight it out on this line if it takes all summer.' On 1–3 June he attacked Lee's strongly held new position north of the Chickahominy river. The Battle of Cold Harbor (so named after a nearby settlement) proved even bloodier still, with Federal casualties amounting to some 10,000 killed and wounded (estimates vary); and yet ending in another draw. This is the battle cited above all by those who would accuse Grant of sending soldiers to a needless death.

Grant had indeed inaugurated a new era in the history of warfare: *continuous* fighting contact between armies that lasted for month after month, and swelled from time to time into major collisions given the title of 'battles'. As for Lee, he conducted a tactical defensive within his trench systems with skill and determination. In contrast, Grant and Meade's own attacks were often tactically clumsy and sometimes botched in execution. It did not matter, for Grant never loosened his grip on his opponent and never gave him an opening. As early as June 1864 we find Lee writing to Jefferson Davis:

> I hope your Excellency will put no reliance in what I can do individually, for I feel that will be very little ... [the enemy] is so situated that I cannot attack him.[27]

As Grant edged steadily round Lee's right towards Richmond, Lee had no alternative but to conform to Grant's movements, while all the time the much smaller Confederate army was gradually bleeding away through attrition. In the next stage of the campaign Grant moved even farther leftwards round Richmond and round Lee's army, crossing the James river and threatening the town of Petersburg. The winter campaign of 1864–65, with its mud, trench warfare, and heavy bombardments, serves as a preview of the Western Front in 1916–17. Yet all through that dreadful winter, Grant steadily tightened his grip round Petersburg, and gradually extended his front towards Lee's last railway links to the south. And the Army of Northern Virginia, forced by Grant to accept a form of warfare that it could not sustain, was wasting away in body and in spirit. As Lee himself had written back in the summer: 'We must destroy this army of Grant's before he gets to the James River. If he gets there, it will become a siege, and then it will be a mere question of time.'[28]

And while Grant held Lee fast in Virginia, Sherman drove from Tennessee south-eastwards to take Atlanta in Georgia on 2 September 1864; and then, freeing himself from his supply train of wagons and living off the country, marched on to the sea at Savannah. Sherman's march, later to be famous in the annals of war, had cut a swathe of despair through the heart of the Confederacy; and Lee's own soldiers in the Army of Northern Virginia began to drift away to join their endangered families back home. Moreover, Sherman's 'March to the Sea' exerted a decisive political influence by enabling Lincoln to rout McClellan, the Democratic candidate, in the Presidential election in November 1864.

At the turn of the year 1864–65, Grant and Sherman co-ordinated the final concentric squeeze on Lee. Grant ordered Sherman to march north through the Carolinas into Virginia, while he, Grant, continued to hold Lee by the throat, sidling across his last free lines of communication. By the beginning of 1865, Lee was down to some 50,000 men against Grant's 90,000. The end for the Confederacy was very near.

On 2 April 1865, Lee finally abandoned Richmond and Petersburg and retreated westwards. His army was now reduced to some 25,000 starving soldiers. An eyewitness described him at this time of utter defeat and failure:

> His face was still calm, as it always was, but his carriage was no longer erect, as his soldiers had been used to see it. The troubles of those last days had already ploughed great furrows in his forehead. His eyes were red as if with weeping; his cheeks sunken and haggard; his face colourless. No one who looked upon him then, as he stood there in full view of the disastrous end, can ever forget the intense agony written upon his features.[29]

On 9 April 1865, Lee, finally hemmed in, surrendered to Grant in a farmhouse at Appomattox, so effectively ending the four-year struggle between North and South. Grant later wrote of this moment:

> What General Lee's feelings were I do not know. But my own ... were sad and depressed. I felt like anything rather than rejoicing at the downfall of a foe who had fought so long and so valiantly, and who had suffered so much for a cause.[30]

*   *   *

The Union's victory in the Civil War secured America's future as a single political entity and a single multi-racial nation. Furthermore, that victory made possible the rise of the United States to the rank of great power and then of superpower; and by so doing made possible the triumph of democracy in the two twentieth-century world wars and the Cold War. Here, in the partnership between Lincoln and Grant, is a remarkable example of the decisive influence of personal leadership on history.

References

1. See below, p.34.

2. See below, pp.31–2.

3. See below pp.37–8.

4. See Fuller, *Grant and Lee*.

5. Quoted in Dowdey, *Death of a Nation*, p.322.

6. Ibid, p.354,

7. Quoted in Fuller, op cit, p.59.

8. Ibid, p.71.

9. Ibid, op cit, p. 82.

10. Ibid, op cit, p.83.

11. All quotes from Fuller, pp.82–3.

12. Dowdey, op cit, p.363.

13. Ibid.

14. Dowdey, op cit, p.502.

15. Ibid, p.143.

16. Ibid, p.202.

17. Liddell Hart in his book *Strategy: The Indirect Approach*, pp.143–54, seems to think that in 1864–5 Grant and Sherman were pursuing two separate, almost rival, strategies, with Sherman getting all the credit from Liddell Hart because of his 'indirect approach'.

18. Fuller, op cit, p.89.

19. Ibid, p.115.

20. Dowdey, op cit, pp.519–20.

21. During the First Battle of Bull Run, a Confederate officer trying to rally shaken and wavering troops, shouted: 'Look! There is Jackson standing like a stone wall. Rally behind the Virginians!' Cited in Catton, *The Coming Fury*, pp.445–6.

22. See above, p.17.

23. Fuller, op cit, p.167.

24. Ibid, p.197.

25. Ibid, p.198.

26. Quoted in Catton, *Never Call Retreat*, p.304.

27. Ibid, p.228.

28. Quoted in Dowdey, op cit, p.485.

29. Ibid, p.549.

30. Quoted in Fuller, op cit, p.62.

CHAPTER 4

The Calculator of Victory

Field Marshal Graf von Moltke
and the Wars of Bismarck

Since the waning of the Middle Ages, war had been accepted in Europe as a normal adjunct of diplomacy and nation-state rivalry, while armies and their professional officer corps had played a major role in the life and politics of most states. Although by the 1860s internationalists and humanitarians were beginning to challenge the legitimacy of collective violence as a means of resolving disputes between nation-states, they had thus far made no impact on cabinets, general staffs, or public sentiment. War remained an accepted instrument of policy: one step beyond the sending of stiff diplomatic notes.

In Otto von Bismarck and Helmuth von Moltke, 'cabinet' war found its joint maestros: Bismarck, a supreme political opportunist, and Moltke, a supremely intellectual soldier, a chess-player with real men.

In personality, Moltke leaned more to the Robert Lee model of aloof dignity and tremendous presence than to the informal yet ruthlessly tough style of Grant or Sherman. His ascetic appearance accurately expressed an austere and reserved nature. He demanded, and exacted, meticulous professional standards and rigorous hard work from his subordinates, as he did from himself. But much of his personal ascendancy sprang from his sheer intellectual power, his evident professional mastery: qualities later reinforced by the prestige of success. His was the dominance of a formidable Victorian headmaster.

The Moltkes were an old German noble family of the kind that traditionally furnished recruits for the Prussian officer corps. Moltke's father was a soldier, retiring after thirteen years' service as a lieutenant. Moltke himself first joined the Danish army because his father had become a naturalised Danish citizen in 1806 when he bought an estate in Holstein. It was the sight of Bonaparte's soldiers plundering the family home that gave Moltke a lifelong detestation of France and the French that ran like a hot spring beneath the ice of his surface reserve and professionalism.

In 1819 he passed out of the Danish Military Academy fourth from the top, but, surprisingly enough, with 'Tactics' and the 'Art of War' as his weakest subjects. Three years later he entered the Prussian officer corps after passing the stiff entrance examination. In 1823-6 he studied at the *Kriegsakademie* in Berlin under Clausewitz as commandant. The course was both daunting and comprehensive – maths, military geography, general history, statistics, gunnery, surveying, horsemastership, spherical trigonometry, mechanics, fortification, natural science, military history, tactics and strategy; staff duties. Moltke also became an excellent linguist, eventually mastering German, Danish, English, French, Turkish, Russian, and Italian. Between the *Kriegsakademie* and becoming Chief of the General Staff at the age of fifty-seven, he enjoyed a wide mixture of experience – regimental soldier; special missions to Denmark and Italy; topographical survey work in Germany and Turkey; military adviser to the Turkish government; active service against Mehemet Ali in Syria; visits to England, France, and Russia as First Adjutant to Prince Frederick William of Prussia; and ever more senior staff appointments. Moltke also wrote a short story, published various pamphlets on strategic topics, and managed to translate Volumes I and II of Gibbon's *Decline and Fall* into German. Here really was a soldier equal in intellect to a university professor or a scientist.

As Chief of the Great General Staff, he was directly responsible to the King of Prussia for the training and equipment of the army for war, for contingency war plans, and for the actual conduct of war. His influence in the counsels of the State became second only to that of the Chancellorship in Bismarck's hands. Yet there was even more to his peacetime achievement. He created the first modern general staff of the kind today possessed by every advanced country. To him is owed the basic concept of the systematic analysis of strategic problems, coupled with the working and re-working of possible solutions by means of the 'war game'. Modern industry and commerce – the syllabi in today's business schools – also ultimately owe their conceptions of management to Moltke and his prototype general staff. In the words of a French general, Moltke perceived war as *une affaire industrielle aux règles précises de calcul.*

As early as 1844, he grasped the supreme importance of railways in deploying and moving armies in the future. He wrote to his brother:

> While the French Chambers are still engaged in discussing the matter, we have laid down three hundred miles of railway, and are working at two hundred more.[1]

In fact, he judged that in some cases it was of more military value to spend money on railways than on fortresses. On average, troop trains travelled at 15-20 miles per hour compared with twelve miles per day by old-style road marches. Moltke grasped that the speed and carrying capacity of railways, plus the huge size of conscript armies, demanded that plans for mobilisation must be evolved long in advance and in detail: corps by corps, division by division, brigade by brigade, train by train, route by route. The better the plans and schedules were worked out, the faster the army could be mobilised and deployed ready for an offensive. And whoever emerged as the winner in the race between two opponents to complete their mobilisations would start a war with the advantage of a heavy, if short-lived, numerical superiority in the field. Hence Moltke's papers are full of calculation and re-calculation of his own and his potential foes' rates of build-up.

Meanwhile, Moltke set about creating a common professional way of thinking in all Prussian staff officers. He did so by means of staff studies of recent wars, or staff rides where fictional campaigns would be played out. Moreover, every general in command would be advised by a chief of staff trained in the Moltke system: through him alone would the general receive the results of operational studies by the staff.

Moltke has some sagacious thoughts to offer on the nature of leadership in this new system:

> In the great majority of cases the head of an army cannot dispense with advice. This advice may in many cases be the outcome of the deliberations of a small number of men qualified by abilities and experience to be sound judges of the situation. But in this small number, one, and only one opinion must prevail. The organisation of the military hierarchy should be such as to ... give the right and the duty of presenting a single opinion for the critical examination of the general-in-chief to one man and only to one. Though the advice given may not always be unconditionally the best, yet, if the action taken be consistent, and the leading idea, once adopted, be steadfastly adhered to, the affair may always be brought to a satisfactory issue. The commander-in-chief will always have, as compared with his advisers, the infinitely weightier merit of having assumed the responsibility of executing the advice given.

And Moltke warns against collective command by council of war as often seen in earlier periods of history, and as to be seen again in the British Eighth Army in the Western Desert in 1942. He writes:

> But surround a commander with a number of independent men – the more numerous, the more distinguished, the abler they are, the worse it will be – let him have the advice now of one, now of another; let him carry out up to a certain point a measure judicious in itself, then adopt a plan still more judicious but differing in detail, and then be convinced by the plausible objections of a third adviser and the suggestions of yet a fourth - then it is a hundred to one that, however excellent be the reasons he can assign to each measure, he will lose the war.[2]

Moltke was very far from being a remote theorist of the Basil Liddell-Hart kind, enamoured of some particular strategic concept. His writings show him to have been a highly practical soldier, concerned with the state of roads, with the effects of weather, with horsemastership. Above all, he had absorbed Clausewitz's profound dictum that 'In war, only the simple succeeds' – or put another way, also by Clausewitz, that in war everything is affected by 'friction', meaning those inevitable hold-ups or breakdowns in movement or supply which can sabotage a carefully-framed plan. Clauswitzian 'friction' equates to 'Sod's Law' (in the modern colloquialism), according to which everything that *can* go wrong *will* go wrong.

So what emerge from Moltke's endless chess-like ponderings of some future war are not elegant and complex blueprints, not sweeping arrows on the map, but broadly simple schemes by which a heavy preponderance of strength may be brought to bear on the key front. This preponderance, together with the sheer fighting effectiveness of Prussian troops in the field, would ensure a victory despite the worst effects of 'Sod's Law'.

In evolving broad strategies for possible future wars, Moltke's mind worked like that of a chess grandmaster pondering the possible consequences of alternative moves: a total contrast with, say, Bonaparte's penchant for instant opportunism.

Thus Moltke began to study the problem of a war with Austria in 1860, six years before it actually broke out. In his Memorandum No 1, Moltke assumes that it would be a defensive war, given that Austria was then the dominant Germanic military power, and that only ten years earlier, in a quarrel over German affairs, Prussia had acknowledged this Austrian upper-hand by backing down politically rather than go to war. In his memorandum, Moltke works out step by step how best to fend off an Austrian invasion of Prussia from Bohemia. He argues that if the Prussians were beaten while trying to cover Berlin frontally, they would lose their capital city, and because Prussia as a theatre of war lacked operational depth, the defenders could be driven back on Stettin on the Baltic cost. This would sever the country in two. So he came to the conclusion that it would be better to concentrate the army behind the Elbe, so threatening the flank and communications of an advancing Austrian army. Moltke had a predilection for flank positions in a defensive war.

In 1862 Moltke again considered the problems of a war against Austria, this time reckoning that Austria would have France and Bavaria as allies. But now, more confident in the fighting power of the Prussian army, he contemplated an offensive stroke against Austria while standing on the defensive with minimum force against France and Bavaria. And finally, in the winter of 1865–66, he produced a complete war plan for a conflict with Austria. This time the planning was for real, because Bismarck was preparing to supplant Austria by Prussia as the dominant power in the German Confederation: an essential first step in the ultimate unification of Germany as a nation-state under Prussian leadership.

Bismarck's political tactics were much like Hitler's sixty years later – stir up a crisis, put his opponent in the wrong, scrape his nerves with menaces, and be always ready to take advantage of whatever opportunity thereby comes about. The point of diplomatic pressure lay in the duchies of Schleswig and Holstein taken from Denmark in 1864 and now jointly occupied and administered by Prussia and Austria. 'Popular' agitations were got up in the duchies against the Austrians; protests were made to the Austrian authorities by the local Prussian authorities.

Bismarck also worked to manoeuvre Austria into war with as few allies on her side as possible, because otherwise Moltke's military sums would not add up. As Moltke wrote when drawing up his war plan in the winter of 1865–66:

> Prussia will not voluntarily bring about a war in which two or three of the Great Powers attack her simultaneously. It must therefore be assumed that we shall not declare war against Austria until we have some guarantees that we shall not, at least not at the beginning, be disturbed by France or Russia. If we had only to leave two army corps on the Rhine, and two on the Vistula in observation, we should not have force enough for a vigorous offensive towards the south [i.e. into Bohemia].

In fact Russia had her own reasons for not springing to the aid of the Austrians. But Bismarck secured the neutrality of Napoleon III, Emperor of the French, with vague but alluring hints of territorial 'compensations' round France's frontiers. That was one major step. But Moltke also needed Italy to be a Prussian ally, in order that the Austrians would be compelled to deploy an important portion of their army south of the Alps to defend the then Austrian territory of Venetia. After long negotiations Bismarck secured this alliance with Italy on 8 April 1866, if only for three months' duration. Except for Saxony and Hanover as feeble allies, Austria would fight alone against Prussia and Italy. That was Bismarck's contribution.

Concurrently Moltke had been elaborating and polishing his strategic plan for defeating Austria. He reckoned that although the Austrians could mobilise a total of 544,000 men, they would have to divert 170,000 against the Italians. Allowing for other diversions such as internal security, he calculated that the Austrians could field 240,000 men in the Bohemiam theatre of war. Their Saxon allies would add another 25,000. As for Bavaria and other south German states, Moltke calculated that they could field 80,000 men, but judged that they were unlikely to go to war so long as Prussia left two defensive corps on the Rhine – which proved to be the case. Totting up the numbers on both sides after necessary deductions, and providing that Austria had to detach 92,000 men as protection against the Italians, Moltke reckoned that Prussia and Austria could each deploy armies of around 240,000 men on the main Bohemian front. Events were to bear out his calculations.

But another vital factor lay in the comparative speeds of Austrian and Prussian mobilisation and *aufmarsch*. From February 1866 forward, as the diplomatic crisis deepened, Moltke's memoranda and notes for crown councils concentrate on this topic, always citing what was known, from week to week, of the state of Austrian preparations. He was deeply anxious lest Prussia lost the advantage of her capacity for faster mobilisation by delaying too late in starting it. He wrote to the War Minister at the beginning of April 1866, that by the twenty-eighth day of mobilisation, Prussia could field 285,000 men to Austria's 179,000, but on the forty-second day, 285,000 to 239,000. Again and again Moltke reminds his government colleagues that time, not total numbers, is the vital point. A memorandum on 2 April gives a clear picture of how Moltke's mind was working:

> The war against Austria, its probability or inevitability as a political question, is outside my judgement. But from my point of view, I think I ought to express the conviction that success or failure in this war essentially depends upon our determination to fight being reached sooner than that of the Austrians, and, if possible, now.
>
> Our advantage, which we cannot value too highly, consists in being able by the use of five railway lines to bring up our Army and have it in all essentials concentrated on the Bohemian-Saxon frontier in 25 days.
>
> Austria has only one railway to Bohemia, and allowing for the troops she already has in Bohemia and Galicia, and assuming her cavalry is already on the march, she requires 45 days to get together 200,000 men.
>
> If Bavaria joins Austria, the disadvantage to us is not so much the Bavarian army, as the probability that Bavaria will lend the Austrians her railway Regensberg-Pilsen-Prague, which will shorten the Austrian concentration by 15 days.

What we see here is a foreshadowing of the July crisis in 1914 when, as A.J.P. Taylor puts it, railway timetables forced Europe into the Great War; that is, the enormous pressure on governments to pre-empt their opponents' mobilisation, even though their own mobilisation effectively meant a decision to go to war. In fact in 1866 the pressure of military timetables was outweighed by other factors: the Prussian King's reluctance to launch an aggressive war on a Germanic 'brother'; hopes of a compromise settlement; and the reluctance of the Prussian people to fight. Not until 3 May 1866 did Prussia order partial mobilisation, and general mobilisation not until the 12th – a fortnight later than Austria. The result was that instead of Prussia completing her *aufmarsch* well ahead of Austria, there was more or less a dead heat.

At this point, Moltke won back for Prussia her time-advantage by a characteristically simple but brilliant idea. Instead of the Prussian armies concentrating on Prussian soil before advancing into Bohemia, they would complete their concentration forward in Bohemia itself.

Making full use of the five railway lines available to him, Moltke had assembled the Prussian field forces along a 280-mile front in three main groups – the Army of the Elbe, round Torgau; the First Army round Gorlitz under Prince Frederick Charles, and the Second Army round Schweidnitz-Neisse under the Prussian Crown Prince. The Austrian army, for its part, had concentrated round Olmütz, and on 18 June 1866 began to advance towards Josefstadt. On 22 June Moltke issued a directive to his army commanders: 'His Majesty orders both armies to enter Bohemia and to seek their union in the direction of Gitschin ... '

Moltke explained to the commander of the Second Army that he had chosen Gitschin 'because the distances, the communications by road and the railways make it seem suitable.' But he added a typical note of pragmatism: 'Of course this does not mean that Gitschin must be reached in any circumstances; that depends on the course of events.'

The forward concentration at Gitschin not only saved time but made operational sense even before the armies could unite, because if the Austrians sought to concentrate against one army, the other would be near enough to close in and strike the Austrians in the flank.

Yet in the event, 'friction' marred this admirably simple concept. The Second Army was held up in two hard-fought actions as it sought to advance through passes in the Bohemian mountains, while the First Army's advance was far less energetic and enterprising than Moltke wished. On 29 June he signalled the First Army that His Majesty expects 'that the First Army by a quickened advance will disengage the Second Army which ... is still for the moment in a difficult situation.' As it happened, that very day the First Army succeeded in defeating an Austrian corps at Gitschin, whereupon the Austrian Commander-in-Chief, Benedek, decided to fall back to make a final stand at Olmütz on the Elbe. So far, then, Moltke's offensive strategy had been working well.

Now came another of his stunningly simple strategic ideas. Instead of uniting his three armies round Gitschin as originally intended, he now ordered them to preserve their existing distances from each other. As he explained it later:

This arrangement, strategically safe, was also tactically very advantageous. If the army were united in one mass, and the enemy were then to be met with in a position whence he could not be dislodged by a frontal attack, it would be necessary again to be divided in order to make a flank attack. On the other hand, in keeping the two armies a short march apart, no risk was run if the enemy should attack, for then the other would take him in flank.

In the Battle of Königgrätz, 3 July 1866, this strategy reached fruition in a decisive Prussian victory. While the First Army held the Austrians locked in a frontal battle, the Second Army marched into the Austrian right flank. To complete the Austrian rout, the Prussian Army of the Elbe came into action later on the Austrian left flank.

In contrast to Bonaparte's repeated failure to forewarn detached formations in good time to rendezvous on an intended battlefield and to make sure that they actually received his directive, Moltke despatched his instructions to the Second Army in duplicate by separate gallopers. The order itself was a masterpiece of brevity and clarity. First, it gave the exact position, by reference to villages, where the First Army would be posted for battle with the Austrians; and then stated:

> Your Royal Highness [the Crown Prince, commanding Second Army] will be good enough immediately to make the necessary arrangements to be able to advance ... in support of the 1st Army against the right flank of the enemy's probable advance, and in so doing to come into action as soon as possible.

Thus Moltke made no attempt to lay down in detail *how* the Second Army was carry out his orders, nor what routes it should take, but left it to the army commander to decide for himself: 'mission command' indeed. During the battle of Königgrätz he issued only that one order.

Yet his method of 'mission command' is open to question, since his army commanders more than once compromised his operational strategy by their own errors or disobedience. It may be argued that he should have travelled with the headquarters of the army charged with the most crucial task, rather as Grant travelled with the Army of the Potomac, which would have enabled him to keep a tighter grip on operations.

Of Moltke's cool nerves at moments of supreme crisis there is no doubt. At Königgrätz, when the Prussian First Army was desperately engaged with the Austrians and there was still no sign of the Second Army turning up on the flank, the King and Bismarck badly got the jitters. But an eyewitness recalled that when the chain-smoking Bismarck offered Moltke a cigar, Moltke selected one with particular deliberation as if he had nothing else on his mind. When the King nervously asked him what he thought of the situation, Moltke replied: 'Your Majesty will win today not only a battle but a campaign.'[3]

Moltke's success in *de facto* command of armies (the King of Prussia remained the titular C-in-C) is the more remarkable when it is remembered that when he launched 250,000 men into Bohemia in 1866, he had never before commanded so much as a company in action.

Now that Moltke had delivered a decisive victory over the Austrian army, it was up to Bismarck to clinch the political objective of the war: the expelling of Austria from the dominant position within the German Federation. Yet he also wished to win her back eventually as a friendly power. These considerations meant wrapping up the conflict as swiftly as possible, and with a minimum of rancour.

He therefore wished to offer a generous peace which Austria would find it easy to accept.

Here his judgement differed starkly from that of the Prussian King (who thought that as a victor he was entitled to grab territory from the vanquished) and also from that of Moltke (who now wanted to emulate Bonaparte by marching on Vienna, and there dictating peace to the Austrians). Moltke's proposal indicates either that his mind, normally so cool, had been momentarily turned by winning a war; or that his powers of analysis did not extend from things military to the wider field of national policy. For a direct threat to their capital city would surely have been the very thing needed to spur the Austrians to fight on.

Only after much agonising argument did Bismarck manage to override Moltke and the military lobby, and persuade the King to agree to an offer of moderate peace terms.

It should be said that the performance of the Prussian army in the war was marred by a great deal of Clausewitzian 'friction'. Despite Moltke's careful pre-planning of railway movements, there were some gigantic traffic jams, with loaded wagons blocking tracks for want of adequate space to unload them. Army commanders misinterpreted or even disobeyed orders, so causing some nerve-scraping moments of crisis. Moreover, Prussian intelligence services and cavalry reconnaissance were abysmal, leaving Moltke to grope for an enemy of whose whereabouts he was largely ignorant.

Nonetheless, Moltke's fundamental calculations and his grand strategic architecture proved sound enough to give him his victory despite all the incidental hold-ups and mishaps. And his achievement made now possible Bismarck's achievement: the end of Austrian dominance within Germany, and the creation of a North German Federation north of the Main under Prussian leadership: a major step towards the creation of a united Germany.

Now it was time to deal with France: the country which had again and again marched across Germany in the past; which had crushed Prussia in a single day at Jena and Auerstädt in 1806; which at present under the Emperor Napoleon III appeared to have revived Bonaparte's military glories; France which took itself, and was taken by other nations, to be the pre-eminent power of Europe.

The evolution of plans for a war with France supremely displays Moltke's talent for rigorous strategic analysis. In 1860 he drew up a memorandum on a possible invasion of German lands by Napoleon III, then at his zenith after French victories against the Austrians in Italy had led to the creation of an Italian national state. Moltke's memorandum began with the diplomatic background, and he judged that France could count on no allies. He reckoned that a direct French invasion of the Prussian territory of the Rhineland would suffer from having too narrow an operational base, and that therefore the French would probably advance from Strasbourg into the south German states. The

Prussian army should therefore concentrate behind the Rhine and the Main. Wrote Moltke:

> No matter if the French advance from Strasbourg to Würzburg, Nürnberg or even to Ulm: as long as we hold the Rhine, our advance from the Main will threaten his communications; each battle will threaten their flank. Before the enemy has gained a larger victory it is impossible for him to penetrate into Franconia or into Suabia. He is absolutely attracted by our flank position on the Main and he must attack it. The right flank of that position is impregnable on account of the fortress of Mainz, and, to gain that position farther up the Main, the opponent must endanger all of his communications.

In November 1861 Moltke again pondered a war with France, this time considering the possibility of a French advance through neutral Belgium into the Rhineland – the reverse of the later Schlieffen Plan. He reckoned that such an advance would weaken the French army by the need to protect its communications and also to find 40,000 men to mask the fortress of Antwerp. This weakened army would, at the end of its long advance, come up against a strong Prussian defence on the Rhine. It was on this basis that Moltke decided his deployment: three corps on the Rhine, three on the Main and three in central reserve to reinforce either front as necessary.

This would be a deployment far to the rear of the frontier between France and the German states. But Moltke based his choice not only on the strength of the Rhine-Main position but also on a calculation of the opposing armies' comparative speeds of *aufmarsch*. These made an early battle undesirable. And once again, he emphasised the strategic advantage of the flanking position behind the Main and Mainz both as a deterrent to a French advance in southern Germany, and as a springboard for a counter-offensive.

The same elements – rearward deployment, the strength of the Rhine-Main position, the delaying of a decisive battle – appear in later memos of 1863 and 1866. But from 1867 onwards, after the victory over Austria, Moltke began to evolve an *offensive* strategy against France. In successive memos, the problems and timings of different deployments were worked out in detail in relation to possible French concentrations and advances. The final version was drawn up in the winter of 1868–69, but even then he refined this version several times before the actual outbreak of war in July 1870.

First he had to consider what to do if Austria were to fight alongside France in a war of revenge. He opted for a defensive against Austria with three out of the thirteen available Prussian corps, deploying them in his old favourite flank position behind the Elbe to deter an Austrian advance on Berlin. The remaining ten corps were to seek an early victorious battle with the French.

Moltke then turned to the question of a plan of operations against France. This, he wrote, 'consists mainly in seeking out the enemy's main force and to attack it where found. The only difficulty lies in executing this simple plan with very large masses.' Nevertheless, Moltke clearly perceived the inherent difficulties confronting the French: an inefficient military system and the unhelpful geography of France's eastern frontier region. He writes:

If the French would fully utilise their railroad system for quick concentration of all their fighting forces, they are compelled to detrain in two main groups, at Strasbourg and Metz, separated by the Vosges Mountains.

In the Palatinate we stand on the inner line of operations between both hostile groups. We can turn against the one or the other and, provided we are strong enough, against both at the same time.

Moltke calculated that, with six railway lines available, he could concentrate the forces of the Prussia-dominated North-German Confederation in the Palatinate by the twenty-fourth day of mobilisation. He counted on an early superiority of 360,000 men to 250,000, thanks to Prussian efficiency in mobilisation, but later sinking to only 386,000 to 343,000.

How would Moltke utilise his strategic and numerical advantage? It would not be by some grandiose scheme of encircling arrows on the map, but, and I quote him,

simply of our advancing, closed up as much as possible, a few marches into French territory until we meet the enemy and give battle. The general direction of this advance is Paris, because in that direction we are most certain to find our objective – the hostile army.

How did Moltke's calculations work out in practice? For a start, Bismarck once again provided the perfect diplomatic launching platform for Moltke's strategy. Bismarck's skill and timing as a tactical opportunist in politics brought France into war without a friend, indeed as the apparent aggressor. Moltke was therefore free to bring Germany's combined and undivided strength against her: a field army of 484,000 against a 343,000 maximum if France embodied all reservists, but more likely 250,000. In view of the railway confusions during the mobilisation for the Austrian war, Moltke had taken fresh steps to ensure that all should run smoothly this time. And despite the occasional blockage, it did: within eighteen days more than a million men had been called up, passed through the barracks and sent to the field or reserve army, while 460,000 men had been railed forward to the concentration areas of the armies.

By contrast, the French mobilisation and *aufmarsch* were straight out of the pre-Moltke era of military affairs – a quite unutterable shambles of improvisation which led to wide paralysis on the railways, to starving recruits and their units all in the wrong places. Whereas the French had reckoned on having 385,000 men on the frontier by the fourteenth day of mobilisation, the actual figure was 200,000. Moreover, as Moltke had long foreseen, the Vosges barrier plus the shortage of available railway lines meant that the French had to concentrate in two major groups divided by the Vosges: one round Forbach facing Saarbrucken, and the other north of Strasbourg, with a smaller force in between at Bitche.

According to Moltke's conception of leadership, it was proper to delegate the direct responsibility for conducting operations in the field to his army commanders, who were so much nearer events than himself, necessarily stationed back at royal headquarters with the King and the Chancellor. He saw his role as that of coordinator of his armies' movements in accordance with his broad campaign strategy. He would only intervene if and when subordinate commanders disobeyed his directives, strayed from their allotted routes of advance, or were moving too slowly or too impetuously. In this permissive style of top leadership Moltke again stands as the prototype of a twentieth-century supreme commander like Dwight Eisenhower or Harold Alexander. Moltke was relying – as had Nelson – on his subordinates being thoroughly indoctrinated with his way of thinking.

Unfortunately, this reliance was by no means always justified. Time and again the errors of his generals in the field threatened to derail his broad strategy. In particular, the Prussian cavalry commanders failed throughout to fulfil their primary role of efficient reconnaissance, and clung instead to the glamorous tradition of massed shock action on the day of battle. The result was that, just as in 1866, Moltke lost his enemy more than once. Nevertheless, despite such incidental 'friction', Moltke's basic and simple strategy, that of advancing towards Paris with an overall superiority of numbers, *did* succeed. The French found themselves overlapped and flanked both strategically and, on the battlefields, tactically.

In the first phase of the campaign, Moltke shepherded the French main body back towards the fortress of Metz and began to flank it from the south. In the decisive battle of St Privat/Gravelotte on 18 August 1870, 188,000 Germans defeated 112,000 Frenchmen, and induced the French Army of the Rhine to lock itself up in the fortress of Metz. During the second phase of the invasion, Moltke's armies advanced like beaters at a shoot, moving forward on a wide front towards Paris, the left flank echeloned forward. When Moltke received firm intelligence that the French Army of Châlons was no longer lying between him and Paris, but marching by a north-easterly route in order to slip by his right flank and relieve Metz, Moltke ordered his own armies to wheel from westwards to northwards. As a final result of this simple movement, he trapped the Army of Châlons (together with Napoleon III, Emperor of the French) at Sedan, and on 1 September 1870 destroyed it.

With the exception of isolated fortresses and the decaying and inactive Army of the Rhine shut up in Metz, the French Empire had now been utterly defeated. The French Emperor was a German prisoner, and the Imperial régime itself had been overturned by a revolt in Paris. Moltke had won a sensational victory; sensational in its speed of only six weeks from the start of the war; sensational too in its apparent completeness.

And yet although Moltke had won this classic 'cabinet' war, a short-lived contest of professionals in pursuance of a diplomatic quarrel between a king and an emperor, a new war of a very different kind was just starting: one fuelled on the French side by popular hatred of the invader. In Paris the Government of National Defence began to organise a people's struggle, raising new armies from citizen volunteers – echoes here of the early days of the American Civil War.

Moltke and Bismarck therefore faced awkward decisions after the apparent climactic success at Sedan. First of all, with whom could they negotiate a peace? The legitimate French monarch might now be their captive, but he had been deposed and disowned. As for the new Government of National Defence, it had publically pledged itself not to surrender an inch of French territory. So should Prussia use its immense military strength to impose a peace on the new French government?

Moltke, the soldier, wanted to march on Paris, just as he had wanted to march on Vienna after Königgrätz; just as the allies had marched on Paris in 1815. Bismarck, a politically far wiser head, was not so sure. He wrote to his son:

> My wish would be to let these people stew in their own juice, and to install ourselves comfortably in the conquered provinces before advancing further. If we advance too soon, that would prevent them falling out among themselves.[4]

Nonetheless, for whatever reasons, Bismarck did not object when Moltke ordered the armies forward on Paris on 7 September.

Moltke, a man who by professional nature was usually so cool and reflective, had fallen into the same trap as Bonaparte: that of seeing military force as a political short-cut. But by marching on Paris he had launched his armies into a different kind of war altogether, one whose formlessness and savagery evoked in him a matching anger and brutality. Above all, this new war took him by surprise.

For the hastily raised and ill-trained new French armies proved able to sustain the conflict against the most formidable army in Europe from September 1870 to February 1871 – far longer than the imperial French army itself. At the peak of this French national resistance, Moltke's forces were stretched to the very limit, what with besieging Paris, fending off French counter-offensives, and protecting long and vulnerable lines of communication. Indeed, if the French leadership had been more strategically cunning, and directed their offensives against those communications, they might have achieved a decisive success. Instead their misguided attempts to challenge the enemy in open battle finally proved in vain and, in May 1871, the French Government had to sign the Treaty of Frankfurt, whereby France had to cede Alsace and Lorraine to the new German Empire.

*   *   *

The relationship between Moltke and Bismarck raises the perennially important questions of where the boundaries should lie between political and military responsibilities; and of how best to dovetail high policy and its servant, strategy. It must be remembered that Bismarck's original objective in wrong-footing France into war in 1870 was simply to rally the southern German states behind the Prussian-dominated North German Confederation in a popular war against an ancestral enemy, so opening the way for the unification of all Germany under Prussian leadership. Linked to this was the secondary aim of toppling France off her perch of prestige as the predominant power in Europe. Once the war had been apparently won at Sedan, Bismarck therefore wanted to conclude a quick, and hence lenient, peace – preferably with Napoleon III as a safely monarchical ruler. Bismarck did not wish to annex Alsace and Lorraine and thereby stir up abiding French desire for revenge; for him, the fortresses of Metz and Strasbourg would do as trophies and military safeguards.

But the 'people's war' in France that followed, with all the shootings and burnings and mutual reprisals between occupying troops and *franc-tireurs* ('resistance fighters'), blew his hope of lenient peace terms. The Prussian King, the French-hating Moltke, and German public opinion all demanded that France cede the provinces of Alsace and Lorraine and pay a heavy indemnity. And neither Bismarck's arguments nor his influence could avert such a peace.

The tension between Moltke and Bismarck had been brewing all the time that the Prussian court was quartered at Versailles in the winter of 1870–71 during the siege of Paris. Moltke reckoned that Bismarck was interfering in purely military matters, while Bismarck believed, first, that as Chancellor he had a perfect right to so interfere, and, secondly, that Moltke himself had too much to say about high policy than was proper for a soldier.

It was certainly Moltke's conviction that once a war had started, the military ought to be solely responsible for its conduct and decisions, even including the terms of surrender of enemy armies. This conviction has been shared by other military leaders since then – by Ludendorff and MacArthur, for instance. But Moltke's old teacher Clausewitz points out that war is a political activity throughout:

> It is wholly the political leaders' business, and can only be, to determine what events and what shifts in the course of negotiations properly express the purpose of the war. ... It is a senseless proceeding to consult the

soldiers concerning plans of war in such a way as to permit them to pass purely military judgements on what the ministers have to do; and even more senseless is the demand of theoreticians that the accumulated war material should simply be handed over to the field commander so that he draw up a purely military plan for the war or for a campaign.

Bismarck was wholly of Clausewitz's opinion, so explaining his anger when Moltke tried to exclude him from high military decision-making, such as over surrender terms for one of the French citizen armies. But on the other hand, Bismarck, like Lincoln in the early years of the Civil War, did take political predominance to the point of interfering in purely technical military questions, such as when he advocated bombarding Paris during the siege. He carried the day, much to Moltke's chagrin; and the bombardment, far from frightening the Parisians into surrender, simply solidified their morale.

*　　*　　*

In the forty years that followed the Franco-Prussian war, the soldiers and politicians of Europe tragically drew all the wrong lessons from it. They assumed that the swift and decisive campaign up to Sedan was the norm to be repeated in any future conflict. They correspondingly assumed that the people's war that followed Sedan was a mere exception, and, as such, to be ignored – just as European leaders (and soldiers in particular) took the American Civil War to be an exception and an irrelevance.

From 1871 to the outbreak of the Great War in 1914 it therefore remained the received opinion in cabinet rooms and military headquarters that the *next* war would be limited in its political object, and, after a brief and decisive campaign, would end in a new Sedan and a peace. General staffs therefore emulated Moltke in working out ever faster and more efficient plans of mobilisation, ever more elegant strategic plans for outmanoeuvring the enemy and winning a quick victory. The minds of politicians and soldiers alike failed to encompass the possibility of a conflict between entire peoples fuelled by mass nationalist passion – and equally failed to encompass the possibility of a long-protracted war, costly in blood and treasure.

References

1. Whitton, *Moltke*, p. 54
2. Ibid, p.74–5
3. Ibid, p.157
4. Howard, *The Franco-Prussian War*, p.229

CHAPTER 5

The Price of Incompetence

Napoleon III and his Marshals

To turn from the formidable politico-military duo of Bismarck and Moltke to the Emperor Napoleon III, his ministers, and his marshals is to enter a theatre where a national tragedy is played out as farce.

Whereas Bismarck never became involved in a war that he himself had not planned and that Moltke was not ready to fight, Napoleon III and his foreign minister, de Grammont, opted to declare war on Prussia in 1870 merely out of concern for France's prestige; and by doing so fell into a trap cunningly baited by Bismarck. Bismarck's opportunity arose from diplomatic rivalry over who should succeed to the vacant throne of Spain, with Bismarck backing a Hohenzollern princeling for the job, and Napoleon III trying to block the candidature. When the Prussian King, taking the waters at Ems, sent Bismarck a telegram reporting on an interview with Benedetti, the French Ambassador, Bismarck cunningly edited the text so that the published version of the telegram read as if the King had administered a colossal snub to the French ambassador and to France. The French people and the politicians of Paris reacted just as Bismarck had intended, demanding a war to avenge this national humiliation. Napoleon III, with his own prestige and that of his Napoleonic Empire at stake, with France's claimed political predominance in Europe under challenge, duly declared war.

Apart from unsubstantiated hopes that Austria and Italy might in time come in on France's side, France had no allies and, by appearing as the aggressor, no friends either. The political framework of the war could not have been more rickety.

It therefore fell to the French military system to attempt to redeem an impulsive political folly. But, being then in the midst of half-hearted reforms, it was quite unready for war against such an opponent as Moltke's new-model military machine.

As it was, the French system, and indeed the very French concept of war, belonged to a previous era. Instead of universal conscription with mass reserves ready for call-up in an emergency (as in Prussia), France relied on a long-service army limited in size. This standing army met the needs of empire-building and imperial policing in North Africa, Indo-China, or wherever else a French government might wish to intervene. It was the French equivalent of the nineteenth-century British regular army, professionally pre-occupied with small wars in hot places, each expedition being improvised at the last moment, and brilliantly-uniformed troops routing ill-armed enemies with a well-timed charge or volley. 'Le systeme D' ['D' standing for *'se debrouiller'*, to sort things out] was the norm, while leadership was seen in terms of bravely flourishing a sword at the head of your troops.

Even when the Second Empire had become involved in European conflicts, such as the Crimean war in 1854 and the war of Italian unification in 1859, administrative chaos was coupled with glamorous dash and bravery on the battlefield: a perpetuation of an obsolete Bonapartian model. And it was from the experience of these wars and colonial campaigning that emerged the new Napoleonic marshals like Pelissier, Canrobert, Mac-Mahon, and Bazaine.

After the Prussian defeat of Austria in 1866, the French leadership took a critical look at their own military system. In the first place, the French long-service army could only mobilise a total of fewer than 300,000 men against an estimated Prussian total of 1,200,000. Napoleon III and a reform party therefore urged that France should adopt the Prussian system – a short-service army raised by universal conscription, and providing a mass mobilisable reserve. This was bitterly resisted by the traditionalists, who argued that only long-service men with the colours would count in war.

To reform a military system always demands reformers of ruthless will and high professional talent. Yet it demands even more – a favourable political climate. None of these factors was present in the Second Empire. Napoleon III's personal authority carried far less weight than the King of Prussia's, while there existed no French equivalent of Moltke capable of overcoming the resistance of the military conservatives. All the argument finally ended in a complicated compromise passed into law in 1868. This would give a total mobilised strength of 800,000 men by 1875, plus another 500,000 in the Garde Mobile, a body subject to two weeks' training a year.

Yet by the time the war with Prussia broke out, the Garde Mobile had neither been organised, nor trained, nor equipped, while the total mobilisable strength of the army was still under half a million.

Thanks again to the stubborn opposition of military conservatives, France still lacked a modern staff organisation on the Moltke model, capable of the thorough planning of mobilisation and railway movements. When an intelligent and able officer, General Trochu, published a reforming tract entitled *L'Armée Française en 1867*, which attacked the whole prevailing military culture, one military conservative pronounced:

> The man who destroys the legend destroys faith, and whoever destroys faith destroys an immeasurable force in which every race, one after the other, has sought victory.[1]

So in 1870 France still possessed no true general staff, but merely a collection of departments and clerks. She still had no long-matured strategic plan complete with fully worked-out mobilisation schedules. In consequence, she was catapulted into this politically misconceived war with a military instrument flawed and unready in all respects except the admirable Chassepot breech-loading rifle.

So whereas in Berlin it merely took an order from Moltke to start the machine running, Sod's Law reigned supreme in Paris. Mobilisation orders were first issued on the basis of a plan drawn up unofficially by the Military Governor to Napoleon III's young heir. This was for three armies: one barring the road to Metz, one lying on the flank of a German advance on Strasbourg, and a reserve army at Châlons. Then, in a classic example of the wrong kind of political interference in military matters, Napoleon III ordered a fresh deployment – one large army under his personal command divided into three corps.

Now came a quite fantastic attempt at colonial-style improvisation on the grand scale. The French Minister of War, Leboeuf, well understood that, because of France's overall inferiority of numbers, everything depended on getting her available troops into action before Prussia could complete her *aufmarsch*. What a hope! The Prussian army was organised in peacetime as it would fight in war – quartered in corps areas whence the corps reservists would join up, and already furnished with transport and administrative services. The French army was scattered in small garrisons all over the country and North Africa, its units frequently changing location. How then could France hope to mobilise more swiftly, when units would have first to return to their depots in order to equip themselves and take in their reservists, and *then* get in trains for the frontier?

Leboeuf had the answer. Units already with the colours would go straight to designated corps areas on the frontiers, where the corps would then assemble along with their ancillary services: called-up reservists would go first to their regimental depots and then be sent in batches of 100 men to join their regiments in the corps areas.

The result was chaos beyond imagination, with overloaded railways crammed with units and soldiers all going in opposite directions. Reservists in the Zouaves for example had to report to the regimental depot in Oran, Algeria, before proceeding to join the regiment in Alsace. Virtually no arrangements had been made to feed and shelter the troops involved in these nightmare mass movements. Meantime, the rail movement of supplies and horses jammed solid. The French army began the war with half the numbers originally hoped for, desperately short of supplies, and its morale already damaged by the evident incompetence of the system.

It is a signal mark of the endemic hopelessness of the French military 'system' that the high command did not even frame an operational plan for the campaign until after the armies had assembled in the field. Moltke himself expressed his professional amazement that a government could declare war weeks before they would be ready to wage it.

Now came the awkward question of who should command operations. It would have been best if Napoleon III, like the King of Prussia, had limited himself to the strictly titular role of commander-in-chief, and entrusted control of operations to the most able soldier available. But he was a Bonaparte; the Imperial traditions were too strong; he, the Emperor, must command in person (or so his Empress insisted). Although Napoleon III was an intelligent man with some military experience, he was certainly not a great soldier, and, worse still, he was in agony from a bladder stone. In no way was he fit to lead a national army in war. Instead of providing the kind of firm overall control exercised by Moltke, he left things some of the time to the professionals on each corps sector, and some of the time directly intervened when he felt like it.

The most prominent of the professional soldiers were Marshal Edme-Patrice-Maurice Mac-Mahon (duc de Magenta) in command in Alsace, and Marshal Achille Bazaine in Lorraine. Mac-Mahon was a thick-headed fighter in the best tradition of Bonaparte's marshals, an 'African' soldier, a man who had stormed Fort Malakoff at Sevastopol, and led his troops in battle at Magenta in Italy in 1859. Bazaine too was a commander formed in the same tradition of colonial expeditions and the personal leadership of desperate assaults.

It is true that the Prussian army also had its old-style pugilistic generals, whose blunders more than once provided the 'friction' threatening Moltke's careful strategy. But Moltke and his King could always bring the thick-heads to heel. On the French side there was no equivalent strong leadership at the top. When on 28 July 1870 Napoleon III arrived at the front in Alsace, there was an expectation that the French army would now launch a major Bonaparte-style offensive towards the Rhineland. Instead there only took place a limp local attack near Saarbrucken. Already the realisation was dawning that French numbers were quite insufficient for an offensive against the huge Teutonic masses gathering across the frontier. Thereafter, no coherent French operational strategies were ever to exist; only orders and counter-orders; march and counter-march; argument and counter-argument.

Into these disunited and overextended French formations smashed Moltke's formidable array. Although at Spicheren and Wörth, the French managed to defend strong positions with tactical success, they then had to retire because of Prussian outflanking movements.

These early retirements from the frontier inflicted a moral blow from which the French command and the Imperial régime never recovered. Henceforward the initiative lay firmly in Prussian hands; the curve of defeat turned inexorably downwards.

What the French army needed, as it stumbled back, was a clear plan for concentrating its entire strength, and then launching a counter-stroke against a portion of the advancing enemy; best of all in the sector round St Avold. This was what Moltke thought they ought to do. 'But', he added, 'such a vigorous decision is hardly in keeping with the attitude they have shown up till now.'[2] In fact, further news about enemy advances broke Napoleon III's fragile nerve, and he ordered his army to fall back on Châlons-sur-Marne. As Professor Sir Michael Howard writes,

> By [this] decision Napoleon acknowledged defeat. Thereafter he abandoned himself to his private agonies; and this abandonment was felt in the Army, not as a personal abdication of command to others more resolute and competent, but as a decision about the conduct of the campaign. It was the nemesis of a dictatorship. There was nobody at Metz to take up the reins which Napoleon had let fall; even Bazaine, when they were put into his hands, could not believe that he was entrusted with effective control; and this vacuum of command created in the French army a defeatism which military events had done little to justify.[3]

Bazaine himself suggested that the French left wing in Lorraine should fall back southwards to Langres, there link up the right wing under Mac-Mahon retreating from Alsace, and then together threaten, perhaps attack, the left flank of the German invader on his westerly march towards Paris. Napoleon III refused to agree: he believed that the route to Paris, the political key to any French régime, must be directly barred. For a week the French leadership havered between a retreat all the way to Châlons or just as far as Metz; and finally settled for Metz. Meanwhile, commanders and staff officers accustomed to the marches of small columns in the wastes of North Africa wholly failed to solve the problems of organising the retreat of a large army. One unit found that its allotted camping area at night

> was like a lake, with five centimetres of water everywhere. The men, overwhelmed with fatigue, put down their haversacks, sat on them, and many just went to sleep there, soaked to the skin ... no guard was arranged, no sentries were placed; the regiments were piled up on top of one another.[4]

In fact, the retreat all too closely resembled one of Bonaparte's marches, with units dispersing in order to forage round the countryside for food. And while Bazaine fell back on Metz, Mac-Mahon retreated to Lunéville and thence to Châlons, so irrevocably splitting the French army in two.

The primary cause of this disarray lay in Napoleon III himself, still the leader to whom all major military decisions had to be referred; still the political head of government. Sick and indecisive, he now became the focus for the kind of competing military advice that Moltke considered inherently disastrous; a focus too for political advice from his Empress and the Council of Regency in Paris. This latter advice did not express a wise long-term view of the interests of France, but merely a short-term concern for the domestic survival of the régime. In particular, the Empress argued that the Emperor *must* stay with the army, and not return to Paris while defeat hung round his neck.

So Napoleon III hit on a compromise: he would go back to Châlons and there personally organise a new army, while handing over command of the army in front of Metz to a professional soldier. His choice fell on Achille Bazaine. Nevertheless, the Emperor still stayed on in Metz for another three days; no longer giving orders, but proffering advice, which, as Bazaine wrote, 'was the same thing in different words'. Bazaine himself therefore continued to act as if the Emperor were still in command. When the Emperor at last departed for Châlons, he encouragingly told Bazaine that he was confiding to him *'la dernière armée de la France'*. As it happened, Bazaine was not glad at all to see the back of his sovereign, because, as he wrote to his wife, 'the responsibility [of army command] would be too heavy, the more so as all that has been done up to now has gone on quite apart from me – I have only been consulted as a matter of form.'[5]

On Bazaine had now been dumped a campaign already strategically compromised, plus the heavy task of leading an outnumbered and morally shaken army against Moltke and a Prussian army riding a tide of success. The situation called for supreme qualities of leadership. Bazaine did not possess them.

In an era when many senior French officers (like their German opposite numbers) were members of the noblesse or enjoyed connections with the court, Bazaine was not a gentleman, and had risen all the way up from the ranks to Marshal of the Empire. He therefore nourished an abiding resentment against his social betters in the officer corps, writing to his sister:

> My entire plebeian origin and because I come from the ranks of the people
> and the soldiery explains without doubt why jealousy has been unleashed
> towards me, above all since my promotion to the dignity of Marshal.[6]

Bazaine also had his psychological tongue stuck into a second hollow tooth of resentment; he had failed the entrance examination to the *École Polytechnique*, and so was not an educated soldier. Nor had he had gone to staff college, for the simple reason that such an institution did not yet exist in France.

His military experience consisted of small-scale campaigning in North Africa; serving in Spain during the Carlist wars; and acting as Viceroy and C-in-C in Mexico during the brief French-sponsored reign of the Emperor Maximilian. He was accustomed to a warfare of lightly-armed columns, of improvised supply arrangements, *ad hoc* march organisation, and of ferocious local encounters in which he had shown courage and coolness under fire. Thus no man could have been more remote than Bazaine from Moltke's new conception of mass industrialised war and the highly trained leaders and staffs needed to wage it.

Yet Bazaine now found himself directly responsible for the operations of the

170,000 men round Metz and also nominally responsible for the entire 250,000 that France had deployed in the field. The figure of 170,000 was twenty times larger than the biggest body of troops he had ever before commanded on active service. This huge mass he had now to manoeuvre in close proximity to a formidable enemy. He therefore desperately needed a first-class staff headed by a first-class chief. In fact he was given a certain General Jarras, a military pedant with a love of paper, whom he immediately ignored. So Bazaine meant to lead the Army of the Rhine in the same personal *ad-hoc* fashion in which he had led colonial columns.

The ensuing lamentable course of the campaign is easily explained: Bazaine was completely out of his depth; and as a result of this, he was psychologically drowned by a tide of inner hopelessness and helplessness. But outwardly he wore a mask of inscrutability and imperturbability. Big and burly, with little eyes in a heavy face, he communicated little of his thoughts or intentions.

Straightaway he faced a problem that might have baffled the Prussian General Staff itself; how to pass his army of 170,000 men through the bottleneck of Metz and on to Verdun and Châlons. He already knew that the enemy was lapping him to the south, and he feared that the enemy was lapping him to the north as well. On 16 August 1870, the leading elements of this clumsy and slow-moving mass, strung out along the Metz-Verdun road, were attacked from the south by two German corps. Because of errors and confusions on the German side, these two corps had to fight the entire French Army of Lorraine all day in the Battle of Rezonville. A well-timed French counter-stroke at the end of the encounter could have swept these corps away and given France a major success.

How did Bazaine actually conduct the battle? In the first place, he was far more concerned about being cut off from Metz than with having his road to Verdun and Châlons blocked. So this was where he piled up his reinforcements. Secondly, he faced the greatest possible test of generalship in the field – an unexpected encounter battle calling for the agile manoeuvring of a large army. This test Bazaine dismally failed. Instead, he acted like the commander of a column in Africa, galloping hither and thither to post a battery, rally a regiment, even draw his sword when charged by Prussian hussars. He never thought in terms of bringing about a Prussian defeat; only of surviving the enemy attack. Although a total of some 135,000 Frenchmen joined the battle during the day, they achieved only a draw against 65,000 Prussians.

Bazaine had now to decide whether to press on to Verdun, or fall back into Metz. He opted for Metz. 'After all', said he, 'we must save the army, and for that we must go back to Metz.'[7] The army therefore marched back in the direction whence it had come, in even greater confusion, and with understandably sagging morale.

Bazaine now ordered it to pause and to deploy in a defensive position between the villages of St Privat and Gravelotte. It may be guessed that he really had no idea what to do, or how to do it. Jarras, his neglected Chief of Staff, wrote later:

> Not knowing how to draw up an operational plan, he had no clear and precise aim, he fumbled and wished to risk nothing while waiting for events to open up new horizons which he might hope would permit him to disengage his ... army by means of more or less unlikely expedients ...[8]

Sadly, the event that opened up a 'new horizon' took the form of an onslaught by two Prussian armies, 188,000 strong, on the 112,000 Frenchmen deployed in the St Privat-Gravelotte position. This time Bazaine stayed in his rearward headquarters in a mood of virtual abdication of command. He made no attempt to reinforce the critically threatened French right flank; no attempt to exploit the bloody repulse of Prussian attacks on his left flank by launching a counter-stroke. The French conduct of the battle was entirely passive, and for that Bazaine must be blamed. It is Sir Michael Howard's judgement that Bazaine 'was morally if not physically exhausted; that the weight of responsibility had paralysed him, annihilating all power of action and independence of will.'[9]

But so strong tactically was the French position at St Privat-Gravelotte, so destructive was modern firepower, that with firm leadership France could have won a decisive victory. And such a victory might have swung the course of the war and hence of modern European history. It is an illustration of how poor leadership can by default have a major influence on events. As it was, the heavily attacked and unreinforced French right wing finally gave way; and the army fell back into the fortress of Metz. Even though the Prussians had suffered 20,000 casualties compared with some 12,000 French, their will had prevailed; and France's strongest army was now cut off in Metz. Bazaine communicated his reading of the situation to Napoleon III by letter:

> The troops are tired with these endless battles which do not allow them to recover; they must be allowed to rest for two or three days ... I still reckon to move northwards and fight my way out ...[10]

It was a missive redolent with passivity and uncertainty; with a fatal wasting of time and opportunity.

Although it was Bazaine's declared policy to attempt a breakout from Metz as soon as possible in order to unite with Mac-Mahon's Army of Châlons, it may be doubted whether he ever really believed in it, for his actual conduct, or rather lack of it, indicates a willingness to sit back comfortably behind the guns and walls of the fortress.

The defence of strong places under siege offers a stern test of leadership because the townsfolk and garrison constitute an isolated herd in danger: apprehensive, perhaps bewildered. It is therefore the fortress commander's task to dispel doubts, give direction to the herd and mobilise all its energies in the common defence. Cut off from the help of main forces, under the increasing weight of bombardment, suffering from hunger - even famine - and disease, the inhabitants will rest their entire moral weight on the commander. His will, his cheerfulness, his energy and optimism alone can ward off despair. Massena's defence of Genoa in 1800 or Sidney Smith's defence of Acre in 1799 are examples of such epic determination. They were not emulated by Bazaine in Metz.

He lived in aloof isolation in a villa in a suburb, discussing his intentions with nobody, not even his own corps commanders, not even with his Chief of Staff. He planned a limited operation for 26 August directed towards the *east*, merely to divert Prussian attention from the west, whence he hoped Mac-Mahon would be coming to his rescue. With his troops already on the move, Bazaine called a council of officers – that procedure which Moltke denounced as fatal to the conduct of war because the commander would receive a babble of conflicting advice. This is exactly what Bazaine received. During the conference, Bazaine said little. After it, he cancelled the breakout. His troops, drenched with mud and rain, fell into the familiar confusion as they turned back along crowded roads. They finally got back to their quarters after twenty-six hours of useless marching.

On 31 August, Bazaine attempted another breakout with the aim of linking up with Mac-Mahon, who had signalled that he was on his way on a northabout route via Montmédy. When, at the end of that day, Bazaine's troops had achieved a promising initial success against a weak Prussian sector, he himself was already in bed. Next morning he issued the following inspiring order:

> If the dispositions which the enemy may have been able to make opposite you permit, we should carry on the operation undertaken yesterday ... In the contrary case, we must hold on to our positions, consolidate them, and this evening we shall then retire ...[11]

Meanwhile, Mac-Mahon and the Army of Châlons had been marching to the rescue. Consisting of a mixture of human wreckage from earlier defeats and hastily assembled new units, this army was quite unfit to undertake a long and hazardous march in the face of Moltke's line of 'beaters'. Mac-Mahon himself had wanted to fall back under the guns of Paris where his Army of Châlons could serve a rallying point for a national war effort. Two factors aborted this strategy. The first was military: misleadingly confident messages from Bazaine about his proposed breakout. The second factor consisted in a panicky short-term political consideration: the imperial régime could not survive the rage of the Parisian population if Bazaine were left to his fate.

Mac-Mahon's march proved to be another of those disorderly Bonapartian hikes without food or forage, and when Moltke wheeled his armies from westward to northward (see above, p.000) Mac-Mahon was finally herded into the Prussian trap at Sedan and destroyed. In the poignant words of a French general, 'Nous sommes dans un pot de chambre, et nous y serons emmerdés.'[12]

Now Bazaine was left with France's strongest remaining regular army, but holed up in Metz. Throughout September 1870, while the Second Empire régime fell, while Gambetta began to organise the forces of the new French Republic for a 'people's war',Bazaine's army lived the life almost of a peacetime garrison, hardly firing a shot. Far from Bazaine inspiring the townsfolk of Metz, they tried to inspire him, handing him a petition which read: 'We believe the army assembled beneath our walls is capable of great things, but we also think it is time it did them.'[13] On 6 October, Bazaine summoned another of those disastrous councils of war, in which the croakers satisfactorily proved that a breakout was impossible. Now the garrison and townsfolk were reduced to eating the horses of the cavalry and artillery, and sickness was rife. At the end of the month, Metz capitulated – without assault, without bombardment. On the day of the surrender, Bazaine skulked in that villa where he had spent most of the siege out of the sight of his soldiers and the citizens. Then he crept off secretly to a Prussian outpost to surrender himself: an appropriately dim professional finale.

* * *

It was the shortcomings of the French military system and its army commanders that enabled Moltke's new-model system to win a war in just a couple of months, just as it was French political blundering that facilitated Bismarck's diplomatic triumphs. This double ineptitude made possible the emergence of a united Germany as the superpower of the Continent, with all that this boded for the future.

References

1. Howard, *The Franco-Prussian War*, op cit, p.37.
2. Ibid, p.123.
3. Ibid, p.124.
4. Ibid, p.126.
5. Guedalla, *The Two Marshals*, p.177.
6. Ibid, p.15.
7. Ibid, p.186.
8. Howard, op cit, p.164, Footnote 3.
9. Ibid, p.173.
10. Ibid, p.181.
11. Ibid, *p.265.*
12. Cited in ibid, p.208.
13. Cited in ibid, p.246.

PART II:

The Great War 1914–1918

CHAPTER 6

Nerve and Loss of Nerve

General Joffre and Moltke the Younger

The opening campaign on the Western Front during the Great War of 1914-1918 demonstrates that the course of history can turn as much on individual human character as on mass social and economic forces (as Marxists would have it).

Certainly such long-term forces had shaped the Europe of 1914 and propelled it towards potential crisis – forces such as the enormous increase of German industrial and political power since 1871; the rise of Slav nationalism within the Habsburg (Austro-Hungarian) Empire; the bitter political tensions between Left and Right inside the Third French Republic; the challenge of Irish nationalism to British rule over all Ireland. Moreover, deeper forces still had also been at work: industrialisation and the huge growth in urban populations; the imperialist rivalry between European powers in Africa and Asia; the volatile mass psychologies of half-educated city-dwellers fed on nationalistic and militaristic myths.

Nevertheless, it was the decisions – or lack of decisions – by specific individuals occupying specific positions of power in 1914 that steered the immediate course of events. This was particularly true of the national supreme commanders who were to conduct the opening offensives intended to bring a war to an early and victorious end.

In the West, the leadership of these offensives fell to Colonel General Helmuth von Moltke, Chief of the Great General Staff (and de facto supreme commander of Germany's armies), and General Joseph Joffre, Commander-in-Chief of the French Armies.

*   *   *

Back in 1866 and 1870 (and thanks to Bismarck's cunning diplomatic manoeuvres) Moltke's uncle, the great Field Marshal Graf von Moltke, had only had to fight a single, and diplomatically isolated, opponent. But in 1914 the German Empire, with only geriatric Austria-Hungary as an ally, was confronting the Triple Entente, an alliance of France, Russia, and Italy. In the event of a European conflict,

Germany would have to fight on two major fronts, against France and Russia. This grim national predicament had been largely brought about by clumsy and over-assertive German foreign policy after Kaiser Wilhelm II dismissed Bismarck in 1892. It had therefore fallen to the Chief of the General Staff to devise a military solution to the predicament. But this meant that whereas under Bismarck military planning had been subordinated to foreign policy the reverse became true during the crisis of August 1914: now the urgent demands of military timetables drove the conduct of foreign policy.

To make matters worse, the supreme German political and military leadership in 1914 was lamentably inferior to that of 1870. Instead of King William I of Prussia, a man robust, soldierly, and sensible, there was Kaiser Wilhelm II, an unstable neurotic compound of kindness and aggression, sense and impetuousness, arrogant bluster and self-pity. Instead of Bismarck as Chancellor, there was Bethmann-Hollweg, a well-meaning but second-rate bureaucrat. And instead of Field Marshal Graf von Moltke as chief of the Great General Staff, there was his nephew, Helmuth von Moltke the younger.

Moltke was sixty-six years old. His career before succeeding Graf von Schlieffen as Chief of the General Staff in 1906 had been respectable enough, and yet nothing had marked him out as fit for such a key post except his name: the Kaiser too must have his Moltke. However, Moltke himself mistrusted his personal capacity for the role, telling a colleague:

> I lack the power of rapid decision, I am too reflective, too scrupulous, and, if you like, too conscientious for such a post. I lack the capacity for risking all on a single throw, that capacity which made the greatness of such born commanders as Napoleon, or own Frederick II, or my uncle.[1]

Moltke was really a romantic intellectual of the time inappropriately garbed in a *pickelhaube*, a man prone to high-minded but hazy ideas. Influenced by social-Darwinism, he regarded the outbreak of war in 1914 as 'an unavoidable part of world evolution'. He was deeply read in philosophy, especially Nietzsche. He played the cello, and was much moved by the music of Mendelsohn and Bach, linking the emotional experience of music with vaguely religious sentiments. And so, although highly intelligent, Moltke lacked that toughness of mind and character which a leader in war must have. In the judgement of a senior subordinate, 'General von Moltke was a highly cultured, clever man of unimpeachable character. In spite of outward coldness, he was a man of strong feelings, perhaps too much so.'[2] Moreover, he was not fit, being a sufferer from a heart murmur as well as other ailments.

To this untypical German soldier, to this soft and sensitive man, fell in August 1914 the responsibility of directing the largest army in history in a desperate military gamble to extricate Germany from the plight of a two-front war.

His grand strategy was in its essentials an inheritance from his predecessor, Count Schlieffen, who at the end of 1905 had drawn up the final revision of a plan for a war against France and Russia. This revise later became notorious as 'the Schlieffen Plan'. According to the plan, sixty-two out of seventy-two available German divisions were to take the offensive against France while Russia was still slowly mobilising; smash the French army in a six-week campaign; then switch to the eastern front and defeat the Russian army in turn.

In its broad outline, Schlieffen's plan did not essentially differ from the elder Moltke's own strategic concept for a two-front war against France and Russia. The difference lay in their operational thinking. Whereas the elder Moltke never planned a campaign further than the initial deployment of the armies and their broad direction of advance, Schlieffen had laid down a complete blueprint for an offensive against France, stating the linear objectives to be reached by certain days, and designating the final advances that would encircle and destroy the French army.

According to Schlieffen's strategic design, thirty-six out of the forty-one German army corps to be deployed in the West were to act like a gigantic gate pivoting on Metz. The gate would swing through the Dutch Maastricht appendix, across Belgium and then southwards, with its tip passing through Abbeville on the Channel coast. Thereafter, the gate would swing round to the south and east of Paris, and finally corral the French armies against the rear of their own frontier defences in the Vosges. In Schlieffen's words,

> By attacks on their left flank we must try at all costs to drive the French eastward against their Moselle fortresses, against the Jura and Switzerland. The French army must be annihilated.
>
> It is essential to form a strong right wing, to win the battle with its help, to pursue the enemy relentlessly with this strong wing, forcing him to retreat again and again.[3]

The younger Moltke did not, however, share Schlieffen's faith in such pre-designed strategic clockwork. He was indeed one of the few soldiers of any nation to glimpse what the next war might really be like, telling the Kaiser even before his appointment:

> It will become a war between peoples, which is not to be concluded with a single battle but which will be a long, weary struggle with a country that will not acknowledge defeat until the whole strength of its people are broken ...[4]

Despite his doubts, Moltke did not discard Schlieffen's strategy altogether, but merely amended it – perhaps because, given Germany's circumstances, he could think of no better answer. In order to avoid violating Dutch neutrality as well as

Belgian, he scrapped the march of the two outer right-wing German armies through the Maastricht appendix, in favour of an advance through the Liège bottleneck in Belgium. This advance, successful in the event, required meticulous preparatory staffwork. To his left flank, in Lorraine, Moltke assigned newly-formed extra corps, out of fear that a French offensive into Lorraine would cut German communications before his own offensive through Belgium could swing into the French rear. Nevertheless, the German right wing (the swinging gate) still remained at the strength specified by Schlieffen. This strength was in any case the maximum that could be deployed, supplied, and moved by available transport over available road and rail communications.

True to his uncle's opportunism, Moltke also pondered the possibility of striking into the northern flank of any French offensive in Lorraine, in which case he judged that the sweep through Belgium would become pointless.

Yet Moltke's decision to direct the masses of his two right-wing armies through the Liège bottleneck necessarily entailed that the fortress of Liège be seized by surprise attack immediately after a declaration of war. And that in turn entailed a very great political penalty, for it was the news that German troops were already on the soil of neutral Belgium and Luxembourg that, on 3–4 August 1914, finally tipped Britain's Liberal government into declaring war on Germany.

Here was the supreme example of how Wilhelmine Germany had reversed that dominance of policy over purely military considerations which Clausewitz had preached and Bismarck had practised.

The German grand strategy for a two-front war demanded that Germany must mobilise not a day later than Russia or France. Yet to order general mobilisation meant in effect a decision to go to war. It was therefore the combination of the plan to attack France and the imperative need to mobilise without delay that turned a Balkan quarrel involving Russia and Austria into a general European war.

Yet at the very last moment the Kaiser and Bethmann-Hollweg wanted to junk the offensive against France, and instead deploy the bulk of the army in the East against Russia. They were motivated by a false report from the German ambassador in London that Britain was prepared to guarantee that France would remain neutral in the event of war merely between Germany and Russia. Moltke was appalled by the Kaiser's blithe proposal. As he wrote later,

> I answered His Majesty that this was impossible. The deployment of an army a million strong was not a thing to be improvised, it was the product of a whole year's hard work and once planned could not be changed. If His Majesty were to insist on directing the whole army to the east, he would not have an army prepared for the attack but a barren heap of armed men disorganised and without supplies.[5]

At this, the Kaiser woundingly said, 'Your uncle would have given me a different answer.' The Kaiser was wrong: the Elder Moltke would certainly have given the same answer, as his record of deployments long planned in advance goes to prove. There now followed a rambling discussion with the Kaiser, Bethmann-Hollweg, and other bigwigs. In Moltke's words:

> I stood there quite alone ... Of the fact that it was bound to lead to catastrophe for us if we were to march into Russia with a mobilised France at our backs, of this no one seemed to think. Even assuming good will on her part, how could England ever have prevented France from stabbing us in the back?[6]

This interview reduced Moltke to a 'mood of almost complete despair'. He was far from restored when in a second interview that day the Kaiser explained that the German ambassador had quite misunderstood the British Foreign Secretary, and that Moltke was now free to carry out the long-matured plan for a western *aufmarsch* after all.

This imbroglio with the Kaiser and his entourage casts a lurid light on the nature of German government at a time of European crisis. To Moltke's own morale it inflicted a serious wound even before mobilisation had begun, let alone the actual campaign. As Moltke himself was to write in 1915,

> I have not been able to overcome the impressions made by this experience; something was destroyed in me that was not to be rebuilt; faith and confidence were shattered.[7]

*   *   *

In striking contrast to Moltke, his French opponent, General Joseph Joffre, resembled in appearance and in character a stolid old peasant farmer: photographs show him stout and square, trudging along as if following a herd of cattle home. His thought was slow and cautious; his language the basic French of the market place. He slept soundly, ate enormously. If crossed, he could put down the would-be crosser with a flash of intimidating anger. Peasant-like too were his stubbornness and tenacity: his shrewdness in judging men and situations. Joffre had no interest in any topic outside his profession, and would have preferred to read a menu than the works of Nietzsche. It may be that he was not even very intelligent, in the sense in which universities and politicians interpret intelligence – that is, the ability to think fast, and then fluently verbalise the clever result.

Joffre was the son of a cooper from Rousillon who had built up a successful business. At school he had been a diligent swot with a flair for maths, carrying off prizes year after year. At seventeen he passed the entrance examination for the *École Militaire* fourteenth out of 132: proof of application and mental competence.

Like many American Civil War generals, his military career had begun in the engineers, and thereafter he had climbed up professionally by building bridges, laying railways, and erecting fortifications in the French colonies. In 1893 he had commanded an expedition to restore order in Timbuktu after Tuaregs had wiped out a previous French expedition. In 1905 he became Director of the Engineer Corps, and after that a commander of a division. His contemporaries in the army now judged him to be a man calm and reserved in personality, uncontentious, but capable in terms of practical thinking and action. In 1908 he was given a corps, and in 1910 he became a member of the Supreme War Council, which signified that he was earmarked for command of an army in war. As Director of Rear Services, he learned at first hand all about the logistics on which operations in the field must depend.

In 1911, the War Minister chose Joffre to be Vice President of the Supreme War Council, and Chief of the General Staff; posts that meant that he would be C-in-C in time of war. The one other candidate for this post failed partly because his politics were suspect. It must be remembered that under the Third Republic, the French Army was something of a social and political anomaly, its officer corps being thick with Roman Catholic *petite noblesse*, and hence suspected by the anti-catholic lay politicians who formed the 'Establishment' of the Third Republic. Joffre was neither *noblesse* nor a rabid Catholic; nor on the other hand was he rabidly Republican either. He was just a competent, uncontroversial professional. In accepting the job, Joffre wrote:

> I have qualities that have been recognised. I'm hard-working, methodical and, I venture to assert, acquainted with the organization of the army. I fancy I have clear and concise ideas on a number of problems. But I know little about staff work ...[8]

Between 1911 and 1914 this colonial engineer methodically set about studying the staff side of mass European warfare.

Yet as Chief of the General Staff he now found himself surrounded by brilliant stars of French military thought, including Colonel de Grandmaison, head of the Operations Section, who in his highly influential writings had preached that headlong attack could overcome modern firepower by sheer moral effect. Complementary to this tactical doctrine was the belief that the defeats of 1870 had been caused by a mistakenly passive and defensive strategy. So it was urged that France should return to the supposed Bonapartian formula of the pre-emptive offensive with all forces united. For two decades the French plan for a war with Germany had consisted in an onslaught by a group of five armies into German-occupied Lorraine, and ultimately aimed at reaching the Rhine.

In 1913 Joffre and his staff adopted Plan 17, the seventeenth annual revision of this plan; and it was Plan 17 which he attempted to execute in August 1914.

Although the French general staff was aware of the existence of the 'Schlieffen Plan' (to use convenient shorthand), they refused to believe the Germans would carry it out, or even that they would be strong enough to do so. Discounting German reserve formations as unfit for the line, the French staff calculated that the Germans could not field sufficient numbers to enable them to extend their right wing in Belgium to the west of the Meuse. The French also calculated that their own intended offensive in Lorraine would have cut across the communications of the enemy right-wing armies before those armies could reach into the French rear – this being exactly Moltke's own apprehension.

But what would a modern battle really be like? Since the French and German armies had last fought each other in 1870, they had been equipped with quick-firing field artillery and bolt-action magazine rifles, all with smokeless powder. The telephone land-line now supplemented the telegraph. There was now even primitive radio, though needing repeater stations at intervals not much more distant than semaphore telegraphs. And flying machines provided an extra dimension to reconnaissance. Nonetheless, despite the presence of small quantities of motor transport, the armies of 1914 remained beyond their rail-heads just as much hippomobile as in the 1860s or 1800s.

Peacetime military leaderships could only make educated guesses as to how these developments would shape the battle of the future. The German general staff guessed better than the French: according to German tactical doctrine, attackers were to make use of ground and cover; they were to advance by short rushes; and they were to entrench when necessary with the tools issued to each soldier. Moreover, the German army took 5.9-inch howitzers along with the infantry in the field. The French army, thanks to Grandmaison and his fellow prophets of the ascendancy of the moral over the material, placed too much faith in headlong dash and pluck. Its heaviest field piece was the 75mm field gun, which, though an excellent weapon, was not effective against troops in trenches or behind solid cover because of its flat trajectory of fire. In any case, according to French regulations the guns did not *prepare* infantry attacks, but *supported* them. When tactical doctrine, the quality of training, and the calibre of regimental leadership are all taken into account, it may be surmised that the French army of 1914 was inferior to its German opponent in front-line combat effectiveness. It would also be heavily outnumbered by nearly one and a half million Germans to just over a million Frenchmen, thanks to the Schlieffen Plan's allotment of the bulk of Germany's field army to the attack on France. However, the disparity would be somewhat redressed by the Belgian army of 117,000 and the British Expeditionary Force of 100,000.

Unlike in 1870 the French mobilisation and *aufmarsch* were well planned and carried out. On 14 August the French armies began to execute Plan 17 by advancing into Lorraine. Two days later the last of Liège's forts fell, so opening the way for the German right wing to sweep across the Belgian plain. Now nearly three million men were on the march, presenting a scene of war and a problem of command unprecedented in history.

* * *

In the coming days and weeks, all was to go well for Moltke; disastrously for Joffre. In Lorraine the French offensive ran into a tactically clever German defensive based on the woods and rolling hills of the region. After six days the French had struggled as far as the line Morhange-Sarrebourg, the German stop position. French infantry attacks with a minimum of prior reconnaissance or artillery preparation were broken up by German firepower, followed by the first examples of that German speciality in two world wars, the launching of prompt counter-strokes against disorganised attackers. With heavy losses the French armies fell back in disorder even to the rear of their own start-lines. Plan 17 was now a write-off. So for France, another war against Germany had begun with heavy defeats.

Meanwhile the German right wing, with Kluck's First Army of 320,000 men at the head of its swinging gate, was marching west of the Meuse through Belgium. On 20 August, while Plan 17 was collapsing in Lorraine, Kluck's troops passed through Brussels and swung south towards the Franco-Belgian frontier. Neither the French general staff nor the unimaginative Joffre had foreseen such a bold manoeuvre, even despite the German attack on the fortress of Liège and the evident concentration of enemy divisions along this sector. Now the entire French left wing, with the British Expeditionary Force on its extreme left, was in desperate danger of being outflanked and overwhelmed by superior numbers – just as Schlieffen and Moltke had planned.

Yet neither the failure of the French offensive in Lorraine, nor the German threat to the French left wing in Belgium, had shaken Joffre's equanimity. He reasoned that since the Germans had shown themselves strong on both flanks, in Lorraine and in Belgium, then they must be weak in their centre, in the Ardennes. He therefore ordered the French Third and Fourth Armies to attack there and hew the German swinging gate near its hinge. But his calculations were incorrect; by deploying reserve corps in the line, the Germans had managed to be strong everywhere. On 22 August, the hastily planned and impetuous French attacks in the Ardennes were smashed by German firepower, just as in Lorraine earlier.

Meanwhile, Joffre's left wing was giving way under the weight of the German offensive. On 21 August his Fifth Army under an intelligent but pessimistic general, Lanrezac, lost the battle of Charleroi and began a full retreat. On 23 August, the British Expeditionary Force fought off an attack by von Kluck's First Army in the Battle of Mons, but, outnumbered one to three, then had to retire parallel to Lanrezac to avoid being enveloped and destroyed.

The French armies along the entire front west of Verdun were now retreating, their morale shaken. For Joffre everything had gone wrong. Yet his confidence in himself, in his soldiers, and in a successful outcome to the campaign remained intact. It hardly mattered whether this unflustered state of mind might be owing to sheer lack of imagination, or even to slow-wittedness. What mattered was that Joffre was still standing four-square and solid amid the tides of defeat. What mattered even more was that, like a good engineer, he was calmly fashioning an emergency plan to save France.

On 25 August, he issued General Instruction No. 2, containing the germ of his later victory on the Marne. While his Third, Fourth, and Fifth Armies were to continue an orderly withdrawal, a new army, the Sixth, was to be formed on the extreme left of his line (to the west of the BEF), and capable, in Joffre's words, 'of taking up the offensive again while the other armies contained the enemy's effort for the requisite period'.[9]

To create this new army demanded a prodigious feat of staff work and re-deployment – the railing of 300 trainloads of troops from the quiescent Vosges front right across the rear of the struggling French line, and their formation into a properly equipped army, complete with rations and supply services. It would take time; but how much time would the enemy give him?

Joffre not only faced here a strategic problem of the first magnitude; he also faced the supreme test of personal military leadership as defined by Clausewitz:

> As long as his men, full of courage, fight with zeal and spirit, it is seldom necessary for the Chief to show great energy of purpose in the pursuit of his object. But as soon as difficulties arise - and that must always happen when great results are at stake - then things no longer move on of themselves like a well-oiled machine, the machine itself then begins to offer resistance, and to overcome this the Commander must have a great deal of force of will. As the moral forces in one individual after another become prostrated, the whole inertia of the mass gradually rests its weight on the Will of the Commander; by the spark in his breast, by the light of his spirit, the spark of purpose, the light of hope, must be kindled afresh in others.

In Joffre's case, he had to kindle afresh the spark of purpose in his British ally as well as in his own croaking army commanders like Lanrezac. For Field Marshal Sir John French, the C-in-C of the British Expeditionary Force, had lost his nerve under the stress of the retreat from Mons; and by the end of August was wishing to take the BEF right out of the allied line into repose somewhere south-west of Paris. He was only prevented from doing so by the direct intervention of Lord Kitchener, the Secretary of State for War. It also fell to Joffre to kindle afresh the light of hope in the politicians of Paris, who, just as in 1870, had begun to panic at the news of the first defeats. As August turned to September, the whole inertia of the mass [to paraphrase Clausewitz again] was resting its weight on the will of Joseph Joffre.

That will did not buckle. Joffre's method of leadership in the crisis was the reverse of the passivity and invisibility of Bazaine in 1870. He took the pulse of men and events in person by visits to his armies and their commanders: he encouraged, admonished, sometimes sacked.

Yet still the allied armies were tramping back and back towards Paris, with soldiers becoming ever more desperately weary, their morale beginning to sag. On 2 September the French government left the capital. Joffre's own headquarters were now back at Bar-sur-Aube. But still Joffre kept his cool. Every day he ate an enormous lunch at 12 noon prompt, and went off afterwards for an hour's sleep, during which time nobody dared disturb him for anything. In the words of the owner of the chateau where Joffre was billeted, 'One would have thought it was only a question of large-scale [peacetime] manoeuvres.'[10]

In fact, Joffre was calmly preparing his counter-stroke, and patiently awaiting the right moment to launch it.

* * *

In conducting the grandest offensive so far in history, the younger Moltke was challenged by unprecedented problems of command and control: seven armies to direct instead of the three under his uncle in 1870; three times the total number of troops; and a maximum advance of over 500 kilometres from the start-line on the German-Belgian frontier. Schlieffen himself had imagined that the modern C-in-C would sit in an operations room directing his far-flung armies via a vast battery of telephones. But telephone landlines posed a much bigger problem for an army advancing into enemy territory than for Joffre, who could rely on the French civilian net. Wireless communication by Morse code provided no solution because a signal from one of the armies in the field could take up to twenty-four hours to reach GHQ via relay stations.

Moltke had therefore opted to follow his uncle's pattern of 'mission command' – having launched his armies along the chosen axes of advance, he would leave it to the army commanders to use their own operational judgement and initiative, and lend each other mutual support as necessary. But such permissive leadership at the top soon proved inadequate in practice. From the moment the German right wing began its vast wheeling movement, its three army commanders simply reacted to their own opportunities and fears, real or imagined. Thus, for want of firm direction from Moltke to Kluck's First Army and Bülow's Second, a splendid opportunity was lost on 24 August for cutting off and destroying Lanrezac's Fifth French Army in the Sambres-Meuse salient. Five days later, Bülow was knocked off balance by a sudden French flank-attack by Lanrezac ordered by Joffre, so temporarily dislocating the advance of the German right wing, and upsetting the strategic clockwork of the Schlieffen Plan.

From now on during the long pursuit of the French and British armies from the frontier to the Marne, Kluck and Bülow plunged this way and that: sometimes crowding up against each other, sometimes opening up gaps between them. The neat alignment of armies in Schlieffen's blueprint degenerated into a ragged array in the field.

Nevertheless, Moltke made no attempt to grip his campaign by visiting his army commanders in the field as did Joffre, and thereby directly imposing his will. He remained in imperial headquarters, first at Coblenz and later in Luxembourg, and always subject to the Kaiser's demoralising presence: demoralising because the Kaiser reacted to the early German successes with all the sobriety and balance of a football fan when his team scores the first goal. This was not the best psychological atmosphere for a commander anyway prone to nerviness.

And to nerviness Moltke all too soon showed himself very prone. As the reports came in on 5 August that the first German assault at Liège had been repulsed, Moltke's face, according to an eyewitness, 'wore a look of heavy care'. When General von Prittwitz (commanding the defence of far-off East Prussia) wanted to fall back behind the Vistula in the face of a Russian offensive, Moltke tamely accepted this defeatist decision. It was his own staff and Prittwitz's staff who together devised a solution by which the army in East Prussia stood firm and, under the new leadership of Hindenburg and Ludendorff, crushed the Russians in the Battle of Tannenberg.

And Moltke had yet to face the supreme crisis of the French campaign. In the last week of August and the first week of September 1914, the attempt to carry out the amended Schlieffen Plan finally broke down, partly because of Moltke's own decisions, partly because of sheer lack of enough troops. Immediately after the successes along the Franco-Belgian frontier, Moltke had ordered all his armies west of Verdun to pursue the French *southwestwards*, with Kluck reaching the Seine west of Paris. This marked the abandoning of the Schlieffen Plan's wheeling movement round the west and south of Paris. In any case, Moltke's right-wing army commanders, Kluck and Bülow, simply went their own way. Kluck kept trying to hook round the left flank of the allied line, and failing. These abortive hooks helped to turn the direction of advance of the German right wing towards the south-east – a direction which would take it *east* of the Paris fortress zone instead of *west* as under the Schlieffen Plan. Yet in any case there were just not enough troops to maintain the width of front demanded by the Schlieffen Plan; and no more troops could have been fielded anyway, given the capacity of the available railways and the effects of allied demolition of vital tunnels and bridges.

In consequence, the German right-wing armies ineluctably closed on each other to the left in order to avoid gaps being opened up between them – gaps that the enemy might exploit, as at Guise, by well-timed counter-strokes. This shortened front absolutely dictated that the right wing must now wheel to the *east* of Paris instead to the west.

The first days of September found the German armies still marching on, even if in increasingly ragged alignment, and with soldiers and beasts desperately tired, while the allies, equally exhausted, were still falling back in apparently hopeless retreat. But both Moltke in Luxembourg and Joffre at Bar-sur-Aube could recognise from the map that it was now the German right wing that lay in potential danger of being outflanked, and not the allied left wing. Thanks to reports from British and French reconnaissance aircraft, Joffre knew for certain that the direction of the German advance now lay east of Paris. This meant that the German right flank was vulnerable to attack by his newly-formed Sixth Army based on the Paris fortress zone.

Before launching his counter-stroke on 6 September 1914, Joffre either visited his army commanders or fully discussed his plans with them by telephone. He sacked the defeatist Lanrezac and replaced him in command of the Fifth Army with Franchet d'Esperey, a man full of fiery aggression. He pleaded in person with Sir John French for his cooperation; and Sir John promised that all that men could do, the British army would do.

Joffre, then, was a living, massive presence. And his own nerve held on so well that he delayed his counter-stroke for two or three days in order to allow the Germans to advance even farther into the trap and to give his own forces further time to prepare.

Already on 4 September, his opponent had issued a new directive which effectively admitted the bankruptcy of the Schlieffen Plan. Moltke signalled by radio that the advance of his right-wing armies, the First and Second, must be halted, and called on them instead to re-deploy in order to parry a potential threat from Paris. He now looked for victory in a different strategy altogether: a double envelopment of the French forces astride the fortress of Verdun.

The signal to Kluck and Bülow demonstrates that Moltke was so totally out of touch that he did not even know the present locations of his First and Second Armies. In order to deploy where Moltke had ordered, the First Army would not merely have to halt, but carry out a two-day or three-day retreat. In any case, by halting the advance, Moltke handed the strategic initiative to Joffre; he threw away the huge moral advantage of relentlessly pursuing a despondent enemy in retreat. And he made his decision even before battle had been joined on the ground. He simply read the map and came up with a peacetime war-game solution – one which relegated his two strongest armies to a defensive role.

In any case, his signal arrived after Kluck and Bülow had sent out their own orders for the day. Although Moltke had slammed on the brakes, his armies rolled on for another twenty-four hours. Kluck in particular objected bitterly to Moltke's directive: he wanted to keep the initiative and drive onwards to the River Seine. If he had been able to reach Melun, only forty-five kilometres distant from his advanced guard, he would have cut the last main railway link between Paris and the mass of the French armies.

On 6 September 1914, Joffre launched his counterstroke: the BEF and four French armies were to attack concentrically the enemy salient hanging down between Verdun and Paris, with the newly formed Sixth Army striking eastwards into the exposed German right flank. But what followed in the next three days was not so much a smashing onslaught as a sluggish, fumbling, and confused forward movement, repulsed in places by German armies displaying formidable fighting powers and skilled staff work. Joffre's Ninth Army was outflanked and driven back; his Fifth Army simply dug itself in after a short advance; and the BEF was very hesitantly advancing into a gap between the German First and Second armies covered only by a thin screen of infantry, cavalry and guns. In particular, the Sixth Army under General Maunoury, charged by Joffre with driving into Kluck's exposed right flank, could make little headway against Kluck's flank guard, IV Reserve Corps. This gave time for Kluck and his staff to redeploy the First Army's front in a rearward swing from south to west, which successfully blocked Maunoury's offensive.

So the issue of the Battle of the Marne now hung in the balance. In the coming days, that balance would not be tipped on the battlefield, where the German armies might well have prevailed over their opponents. It would be tipped instead at the level of supreme command, where Joffre was displaying calmly resolute leadership and Moltke was suffering a nervous collapse. On 7 September Moltke wrote to his wife:

> Today our armies are fighting all the way from Paris to upper Alsace. I would give my life, as thousands have done, for victory. How much blood has been spilled and how much misery has come upon numberless innocent people whose houses have been burned and razed to the ground.
>
> Terror often overcomes me when I think about this, and the feeling I have is that I must answer for this horror, and yet I could not act otherwise than I have done.[11]

Next day, when his far-off troops were fighting valiantly and with considerable success against Joffre's attacking forces, Moltke wrote again to his wife:

> The weight of responsibility has borne me down in the last few days. For still our army is struggling on and there has been no decision. It would be frightful if there is nothing to show for the blood that has been spilt. The suspense, with the absence of news from the far distant armies, almost goes beyond what human strength can stand, when one knows the issues involved.

And he went on: 'The terrible difficulty of our situation often stands like a black wall in front of me, seemingly quite impenetrable.'[12]

The focus of his anxiety was the twenty-mile gap between the First and Second Armies opened up by Kluck's rearward redeployment of First Army in order to confront Maunoury. Supposing Kluck was entirely cut off and destroyed by allied forces advancing into the gap? Moltke believed that the gap must be closed without delay, if need be by a converging retreat of both armies to the River Vesle or even the Aisne. He would not wait to see if Kluck could first defeat Maunoury and then revert to his original place in the German line. Yet given all the uncertainty, given the apparent peril, this was surely the moment for Moltke go forward and visit his armies and their commanders, read the situation on the spot for himself, give orders accordingly, and then enforce them by his personal authority.

He did not do these things. Instead, on 9 September, he despatched a staff officer, Colonel Hentsch, to the front with full plenipotentiary powers to take major strategic decisions after discussion with the army commanders.

Hentsch was an able officer, but a pessimistic man; he had to endure a depressing and difficult drive through choked roads behind the German front as he visited each army headquarters in turn. Bülow (Second Army), elderly and cautious, told him that retreat was inevitable because the gap between Second Army and First Army was now being penetrated by enemy troops (in fact, the BEF). Finally Hentsch reached the First Army and spoke to Kluck's Chief of Staff, von Kuhl. For Hentsch, the key question was this: could the First Army be in a position to support the Second Army *tomorrow*, 10 September? Kuhl had to admit that there would not be time first to defeat Maunoury and then be back alongside Bülow by the morrow.

This clinched the matter for Hentsch. In his own words:

> As there was no possibility of giving immediate help to the 2nd Army, I therefore gave the 1st Army the order to retreat, basing my action in the full powers given me, because it was only in this way one could bring it once more into co-operation with the 2nd Army.[13]

And he marked in crayon on Kuhl's battle-map the stop-line to be reached, back behind the Aisne.

That crayon mark signified that Joffre had won the Battle of the Marne, one of the great decisive battles of history. Yet it was one thing to thwart the German attempt to end the war with France in a single victorious campaign as in 1870, and quite another to drive the invading army off French soil. That would not be achieved until after four years of bloody attrition battles along a stalemated Western Front.

In the meantime, the European conflict as a whole became, in the words of Moltke's peacetime worst-case scenario, 'a war between peoples ... a long, weary struggle'.

References

1. Von Bülow, *Memoirs*, Vol. II, p.176, cited in Barnett, *The Swordbearers: Studies in Supreme Command in the First World War*, p.16.

2. Bauer, *Der Grosse Krieg im Feld und Heimat*, 1921) pp.33–5, cited in Barnett, op cit, p.45.

3. Schlieffen, Text B, quoted in Ritter, *The Schlieffen Plan; Critique of a Myth*, p.145.

4. As recounted to his wife. Cited in Barnett, op. cit., p.22.

5. Moltke, op.cit, pp.18–19, cited in Barnett, op. cit., p.18.

6. Ibid.

7. Moltke, p.21, cited in Barnett, op. cit., p.21.

8. Isserlin, p.21.

9. Isserlin, p.37.

10. Ibid, p.70.

11. Moltke, p.384, cited in Barnett, op. cit., p.86.

12. Ibid.

13. Baumgarten-Crusius, *Le Haut Commandement Allemand Pendant La Campagne de la Marne en 1914*

CHAPTER 7

Stalemate and Scapegoat

General Sir Douglas Haig

Douglas Haig's leadership of the armies of the British Empire on the Western Front from 1915 to 1918 has provoked sharper and longer-lasting controversy than the leadership of any other British top commander in the two world wars. He has been condemned by his critics as a professionally hidebound general who, with a callous disregard for appalling casualties, launched his soldiers into foredoomed frontal attacks against an immensely strong German defence system.

The blaming of Haig began with a spate of war novels and trench memoirs at the end of the 1920s and the beginning of the 1930s – Blunden's *Undertones of War*, Sassoon's *Sherston* novels, Sherriff's play *Journey's End*, Aldington's *Death of a Hero*, Graves' *Goodbye to All That*; Manning's *Her Privates We*. All became bestsellers, thanks to enthusiastic reviews by critics in the intelligentsia and by the popular press alike. The picture of the Western Front, indeed of the War as a whole, that emerged from these books was of the futility of the fighting, of useless slaughter, and of the squalor of life in the trenches. The British war writers also conveyed a special sense of *outrage*: a moral indignation (not shared by French or German authors) that the Western Front should be happening to them at all.

Close behind this personal and emotional trench literature came the memoirs of wartime political leaders eager to proclaim their own strategic wisdom, and blame the high command for the fact that the German Empire – the most powerful military-industrial state in Europe – took so long to defeat and at such cost in British lives. In 1931 was published Winston Churchill's best-selling account of the war, *The World Crisis*. At that time, Churchill's political career lay in eclipse, for he had been excluded from the new National Government under Ramsay Macdonald and Stanley Baldwin. Moreover, it still nagged away at him that back in 1916 he had been compelled to resign his post as First Lord of the Admiralty following the disastrous failure of the Dardanelles expedition, very much his idea. *The World Crisis* is therefore a verbose attempt to justify his strategy of trying to defeat Germany by fringe campaigns against her allies in the Mediterranean theatre[1] rather than fight the main body of the German Army. Hence he condemns the First Battle of the Somme in 1916 in his ripest prose:

If two lives or ten lives were required by their Commanders to kill one German, no word of complaint ever rose from the fighting troops. No attack, however forlorn, however fatal, found them without ardour ... Martyrs not less than soldiers, they fulfilled the high purpose of duty with which they were imbued. The battlefields of the Somme were the graveyards of Kitchener's Army.[2]

In 1933 and 1934 followed the two fat volumes of Lloyd George's *War Memoirs*. By this time, George's political career too lay in the shadows, for he had been out of office since ceasing to be Prime Minister in 1923 when the wartime coalition government finally disintegrated. Unsurprisingly, his *War Memoirs* abound with mendacious self-justification coupled with unscrupulous slandering of Britain's wartime military leadership. He characterised the First Battle of the Somme as 'this bull-headed fight', as 'horrible and futile carnage', as one of 'the most gigantic, tenacious, grim and futile and bloody fights ever waged in the history of war'. He wrote of the British high command in France:

they knew nothing except by hearsay about the actual fighting of a battle under modern conditions. Haig ordered many bloody battles in this War. He only took part in two ... He never even saw the ground on which his greatest battles were fought ... In the most crucial matters relating to their own profession our leading soldiers had to be helped out by the politician.

Every one of these statements is factually false.

In the wake of these two self-justifiying fallen politicians came the fashionable military commentators of the 1930s – Major General J.F.C. ('Boney') Fuller and Captain Basil Liddell Hart. Liddell Hart in particular was the equivalent of George Bernard Shaw as a pundit of immense personal vanity, but unlike Bernard Shaw a pundit heeded with respect even by cabinet ministers. It is worth remembering that Lloyd George's war memoirs owed much to Liddell Hart's collaboration. As a subaltern on the Western Front, Hart had once admired Haig and the high command. Now in the 1930s he caricatured Haig as mentally hidebound, resistant to the large-scale introduction of the tank, and culpable of prolonging the stalemate on the Western Front. Liddell Hart's new interpretation was, however, a self-serving attempt to make a historical case for his current public advocacy that, firstly, the British army must become a small elite mechanised force spearheaded by tanks; and, secondly, that Britain must never again be drawn into a new Western Front.

By the late 1930s, the politicians, the intelligentsia, and the mass media had all come to accept this version of British generalship on the Western Front as peddled by Churchill, Lloyd George, Liddell Hart, and the trench literati. It remained the received 'truth' long after the Second World War. Political historians like Professor A.J.P. Taylor in *English History 1914–45* (published in 1965), and Sir Llewelyn Woodward in *Great Britain and the War of 1914–18* (published in

1967), repeated the old charges about the callous stupidity of the high command, and the 'futility' of the battles on the Western Front. So too did bestselling popular histories such as Leon Wolff's *In Flanders Fields*[3] and Alan Clark's *The Donkeys*[4] – to say nothing of the musical *Oh, What a Lovely War*, hugely successful on stage and screen.

As late as 1975, Professor Paul Fussell (an American literary academic, not a military historian) asserted in his widely acclaimed book, *The Great War and Modern Memory*[5] that Haig was 'stubborn, self-righteous, inflexible, intolerant ... and quite humourless.' He was also 'provincial'. Furthermore, opines Fussell:

> Bullheaded as he was, he was the perfect commander for an enterprise committed to endless abortive assaulting. Indeed, one powerful legacy of Haig's performance is the conviction among the imaginative and the intelligent today of the unredeemable defectiveness of all civil and military leaders.[6]

The counter-offensive against Haig's critics was launched in 1963 by the late John Terraine with his solidly documented and cogently argued biography *Douglas Haig: the Educated Soldier*.[7] Since then, detailed research by academic historians[8] into every aspect of the British Expeditionary Force (arm by arm, division by division, general by general, battle by battle) have built on Terraine's pioneering work to portray a truth utterly at variance with the facile calumnies of the past. Nonetheless, it has to be said that this truth has yet to overcome the prejudice about Haig and the Western Front still being peddled by the media.

How is this prejudice to be accounted for? Why has Haig been cumulatively denigrated since the early 1930s? The short answer to both questions is that Haig has served as a convenient scapegoat for the British experience in the Great War, when for the first time Britain had to commit a citizen army to mass battles on the European continent, and suffer the killing of her young men on a commensurate scale (though losing only half as many as France with a comparable national population).

The fact is that the scapegoaters of Haig were, and are, intellectual cowards who shrink from confronting the intractable political and strategic dilemmas posed by the war.

The fundamental such dilemma for the Allies lay in the German occupation of almost all Belgium plus eleven northern French departments. This was the legacy of the Marne campaign in 1914, which had ended in a strategic draw when the German Army failed to win the war outright according to the Schlieffen Plan, but the French Army then failed to drive the enemy out of France again. By the winter of 1914–15, this broad zone of German occupation was defended by a deeply-dug trench system, strong in artillery and machine guns, and extending from the North Sea coast in Belgium to the Swiss frontier.

It inevitably followed that Germany now held the strategic upper hand (and if it ever came to peace talks, the political upper hand as well). No French government could do other than strive again and again to evict the enemy from their soil. To acquiesce in the German occupation by simply standing on the defensive was unthinkable. 'The Germans are at Noyon', as Clemenceau kept reminding his countrymen. The British equivalent would have been the German army entrenched at Canterbury. *This* was why from 1914 through to the end of 1917 the allies kept on launching one offensive after another on the Western Front.

It further constrained the freedom of Britain's own strategic choice that until 1917 France was the senior partner in the Alliance, contributing many more soldiers than Britain to the Western Front. When Haig was appointed C-in-C of the British armies in France and Flanders at the end of 1915, his instructions from the British Government explicitly stated that:

> The special task laid upon you is to assist the French and Belgian Governments in driving the German Armies from French and Belgian territory ...[9]

*   *   *

General Sir Douglas Haig was the clear choice to succeed Field Marshal Sir John French as C-in-C because of the qualities of personal leadership and professional capacity demonstrated by his career so far, and which had won him the trust of military contemporaries and statesmen alike. In the judgement of Lord Haldane (educated at Edinburgh and Göttingen universities), who as Secretary of State for War in 1905-12 had worked with Haig when Director of Military Training, Haig 'had a first-rate General Staff mind'.

A son of the whisky-distilling family, Douglas Haig was, in his background, education, and world outlook, very much a product of the late Victorian and Edwardian upper-class, where 'new' money bought country estates (in the case of the Haigs, Bemersyde in the Scottish Borders), and was then accepted into the established landed gentry and aristocracy. He was educated at Clifton College (a leading English public school), Brasenose College, Oxford, and the Royal Military College, Sandhurst. Such an upbringing hardly helped to endear Haig to his later critics among the bourgeois intelligentsia. That he chose the cavalry as a career – commissioned into the 7th (Queen's Own) Hussars, later in command of the 17th Lancers, and later still becoming Inspector General of Cavalry in India – further doomed him in their eyes.

Yet to sneer at a man for being a cavalryman in the late nineteenth century and early twentieth century is like sneering at a soldier today for flying helicopters. For the cavalry were then the only available mobile means of reconnaissance, shock action in battle, and pursuit. This is why Haig, as Commander-in-Chief of the British Armies in France and Flanders during the Great War, believed that he must retain a cavalry corps in reserve in order to exploit a hoped-for breakthrough of the enemy's front. The primitive tanks of the time were too slow (at barely 2 mph; and only 8 mph for the lighter Whippets of 1918) and too mechanically unreliable for such a role.

The critics also forget that Haig's cavalry *did* successfully fulfil the role of exploitation during the Second Battle of the Somme in August 1918 (see below, pp.135–6), while in contrast the Germans were much handicapped during their great March offensive that year by want of cavalry to ride down British fugitives and seize rearward communication centres.

In any case, Haig had laid down before the war that cavalry must be adept at scouting, screening, and dismounted action with the rifle. In the mobile Marne campaign of 1914 and later on in Palestine, the British cavalry outmatched their opponents in all these roles.

It is therefore absurd to pillory Haig as a mindless military conservative for believing that cavalry had a present and future role. Not until the vastly improved tanks and motor-trucks of 1940 were cavalry finally rendered obsolete.

From his earliest days as a subaltern, Haig took his profession seriously indeed. He read widely in European military literature; he wrote his own treatise on *Cavalry Studies, Strategical and Tactical*; and, as a regimental commanding officer, was acknowledged to be a keen and able trainer of troopers and officers. When Chief Staff Officer to the Cavalry Division in the Boer War of 1899-1902 and then commander of a mobile column, he had shown energetic and decisive leadership. A colleague recorded:

> The thing that struck one most was his extraordinary ability to express in concise form, capable of being copied into a notebook on the field, important orders for the movement and disposition of troops. In this he was an absolute master.[10]

It was Haig's service under Haldane as Director of Military Training in 1906–09, when he drafted 'Field Service Regulations' (the British Army's first-ever tactical manual), that launched him towards the top: 1909-11, chief of staff to the Commander-in-Chief in India; 1912–14, General Officer Commanding Aldershot District; 1914, GOC I Corps in the retreat from Mons and the counter-stroke on the Marne.

During the First Battle of Ypres (October-November 1914) Haig's personal leadership under fire played a major part in repulsing a German offensive aimed at reaching the Channel coast. In 1915, he commanded the First Army in Sir John French's abortive offensives at Neuve Chapelle and Loos, where in Haig's judgement the opportunities for a breakthrough were lost because French was too late in committing his reserves to an exploitation of the initial break-in of the enemy defences.

This necessarily abbreviated *curriculum vitae* serves to demonstrate that Haig truly was well qualified by study and experience for the role of leading the largest expeditionary force ever fielded by Great Britain, in 1916 totalling fifty-six infantry divisions and five cavalry divisions organised in five separate armies, and with an average ration strength of nearly 1.4 million soldiers.[11]

*   *   *

In common with all the other commanders-in-chief of the belligerents, friend or foe, Haig was charged with the leadership of a mass technological organisation of a size and complexity unprecedented in human history. No civilian industrial cartel in the Britain of the day was anywhere near as huge as the army on the Western Front, with its workshops, supply depots, hospitals, road and rail network, and telecommunications net, all brought to completion under Haig's direction. How should a leader impose his will on such an organisation? How should he make it function as he wished? These are questions with which leaders still grapple today, in industry, government, and the public service.

Douglas Haig brought to his new role the values and the world outlook of his social class and the imperial Britain of his era. He did not, and simply could not, chat up the rank-and-file in Bonapartian style. He did not operate a deliberate public relations campaign like Field Marshal Montgomery or Lord Mountbatten in the Second World War. He was handicapped by his want of fluent speech. Nevertheless, there was no question about his personal authority. The record goes to show that he enjoyed the full confidence of those with whom he directly dealt, from his own staff and highly respected senior generals (like Sir Herbert Plumer and the Australian Sir John Monash) down to the level of divisional commands. It is harder to assess how he was regarded by his soldiers, whose horizon was necessarily limited to their own trenches and rest areas. Just the same, the British army on the Western Front was never to succumb to a crisis of morale or even actual disintegration such as eventually overtook the French and Russian armies in 1917, and the Austrian and German armies in the autumn of 1918. If the BEF had so succumbed, no doubt Haig would have got the blame. That it did not succumb must in fairness be attributed to Haig's leadership from the top, and to his understanding that soldiers' morale depended on regular rotation from the frontline to rest areas, on adequate leave, and even on plentiful rations.

The record also shows that Haig was the reverse of the obstructionist to new ideas alleged by his critics. His enthusiasm for military aviation dated from before the war. In 1915 he had pressed for the BEF to adopt gas warfare after its debut by the Germans. He was the first national C-in-C in the war to put his faith in the tank, committing it to battle on the Somme in September 1916, and thereafter asking for a thousand to be produced for the 1917 campaign – a target that in the event British industry was unable to meet.[12] It was Haig's idea to appoint a civilian businessman to re-organise and run his rail transport system.[13]

As Commander-in-Chief, Haig was confronted with four main challenges of leadership: cooperating with the French high command as a junior partner; struggling with the British prime minister and the cabinet over grand strategy; transforming his recently raised troops into an army professionally superior to the enemy; and, above all, defeating the German Army on his front.

Haig's record as a C-in-C of a national army within a coalition was exemplary. He enjoyed close and cordial relationships with the French generals fighting in battle alongside him (and sometimes under his command), as well as with successive French commanders-in-chief: Joffre in 1915–16, Nivelle and Pétain in 1917, and finally Foch as Allied Supreme Commander in 1918. Haig balanced personal courtesy towards his allied colleagues with firmness in regard to strategic decisions and the operational conduct of the war. It greatly helped that he had taught himself French; and, oddly enough, could express himself more fluently in that language than in English.

Far more difficult for him was dealing with Lloyd George as prime minister. No two leaders in war could have been more personally incompatible: Haig a reserved, tongue-tied Lowland Scot; Lloyd George a politically cunning, glibly eloquent Welshman – Haig the very model of an imperial officer, handsome, strong-jawed, splendidly moustached; Lloyd George a puckish-faced, twinkly-eyed charmer (especially of women). It rendered their relationship the more difficult that Haig suffered from the serious defect of becoming positively incoherent once he strayed off a written paper. An eyewitness recalled the scene when Haig at a pre-war conference in Cambridge in the presence of King George V and distinguished academics tried to extemporise his report on recent manoeuvres:

> In the effort he became totally unintelligible and unbearably dull. The University dignitaries soon fell asleep. Haig's friends became more and more uncomfortable; only he himself seemed totally unconscious of his failure. A listener, without other and deeper knowledge of the ability and personality of the Aldershot Commander-in-Chief, would have left the conference with the impression that Haig had neither ability nor military learning.[14]

This was why Lloyd George mistakenly put Haig down as bull-headedly dense. But Haig for his part saw the Prime Minister as a twister, and a strategically ignorant twister at that. This was not the best recipe for national leadership in a total war.

Haig was to become deeply reluctant to return to London from France for face-to-face meetings with the Prime Minister, where he knew he would be humiliatingly out-debated. Nor did it help smooth relations between Prime Minister and C-in-C that Haig's ally in Whitehall, the Chief of the Imperial General Staff, General Sir William (later Field Marshal Lord) Robertson, was a blunt-spoken soldier risen from the ranks who never failed to make it plain to cabinet members, and Lloyd George in particular, when he considered that they were talking out of their nether regions.

In consequence, there existed between the 'frock-coats' and the 'brass-hats' during the Great War neither the mutual personal respect nor the mutual trust that prevailed in the Second World War between Winston Churchill and his CIGS, General Sir Alan Brooke, despite their fierce arguments over strategy. Instead, strategic debate between Haig (and Robertson) and Lloyd George turned into a kind of positional warfare in which the combatants would give no intellectual ground to a despised foe.

How to defeat the Central Powers – the German, Austrian, and Ottoman Empires – that was the fundamental question which divided them. Haig's own strategic reasoning was straightforward enough. In the first place, Germany was by far the most powerful of those enemies; and, secondly, the German army constituted the mighty engine of German power. It followed that the Allies should concentrate their efforts on weakening, and ultimately wrecking, that engine. In Haig's judgement, this could only be achieved by engaging the main body of the German army in battle. And where was that main body deployed? On the Western Front: the front where the bulk of the French and British armies was also deployed. So Haig was certain that here must be the focus of the Anglo-French offensive effort.

Lloyd George, however, was unable to stomach so daunting a scenario. He had been deeply shaken by the total of killed and wounded in the Battle of the Somme in 1916: a total of a size without precedent in British military history although proportionately no greater than the losses suffered by the French and German armies at Verdun, or, for that matter, by the Union and Confederate armies at Antietam. But whereas Abraham Lincoln had had the sagacity and the moral courage to recognise that victory in a total war cannot come cheap in lives, Lloyd George flinched at the human cost. Whereas Lincoln had also understood that a total war cannot be won in peripheral theatres, Lloyd George's preferred grand strategy from 1916 onwards was to fight anywhere other than on the Western Front and against any foe other than the main body of the German army. This strategy of evasion he called 'knocking away the props' – as if Turkey or Bulgaria or even Austria-Hungary were propping up Germany rather than the other way about.

And whereas Lincoln gave Grant his unwavering support, even during the grim battles on the road to Richmond, Lloyd George would have liked to sack Haig.

Prevented from doing so by his own lack of moral courage and by the weakness of his political position as the Liberal leader of a coalition dependent on Conservative support, Lloyd George sought instead to undermine Haig's authority through intrigue. Early in 1917 he intrigued with the French government to have the British Expeditionary Force placed under direct French command; and in 1918 he was instrumental in setting up an allied Supreme War Council that he hoped would dictate strategy to Haig.

Neither expedient worked in the event. In 1917, Haig and Robertson successfully resisted the proposal to diminish the BEF into an army group under French control, while in 1918 Haig and Pétain (now French C-in-C) refused to give up control of their reserves to the Supreme War Council, and simply agreed their own arrangements for lending each other mutual support as necessary. So the Supreme War Council became a supreme talking shop, and Haig himself survived as the fully independent Commander-in-Chief of the British Empire's principal field army.

Nonetheless, the protracted struggle with his own head of government was the one challenge, the one source of strain, that Haig could have well done without. The struggle makes a dismal contrast with the harmonious and successful partnerships between Ulysses Grant and Abraham Lincoln, and Helmuth Graf von Moltke and Bismarck.

It must be borne in mind that Britain faced a unique problem in that, alone among the major belligerents, she had entered the war with just a small professional army instead of a mass army based on peacetime conscription. She therefore had to create, train, and equip a new mass army in utmost haste from 1914 onwards. When Haig took over as C-in-C in August 1915 this process was still far from complete. Peacetime regimental officers now found themselves in command of brigades or even divisions, while their staffs were similarly new to the job. The transformation of this inexperienced army into a force professionally capable of defeating the Germans on the Western Front therefore presented Haig with the third of his major challenges.

This, however, raised a further problem for Haig. Irresistible political and strategic pressures meant that he would have to commit his troops to battle even while this process of transformation was still going on: therefore two challenges in one.

And the battlefield was the harshest of classrooms, demanding from all ranks from Haig downwards a steep learning curve. This they did their diligent best to climb. Before a battle, the likely operational problems would be studied in detail: and after a battle there would be equally rigorous analysis of the lessons to be learned. Haig as Commander-in-Chief oversaw this learning process, personally convening conferences with his senior colleagues to discuss recent tactical and technical developments. The results of all the continual study were disseminated throughout the army by a copious flow of instructional pamphlets.

The core of the case made by his critics against Haig as a commander is that he launched frontal offensives against the German defences on the Western Front which had no realistic chance of success; and that, with callous disregard for the mounting casualties, he kept these offensives going month after month out of sheer obstinacy.

The critics first of all cite the Battle of the Somme in 1916 as evidence. But the critics ignore the fact that in 1916 Haig was not a free agent in making strategic choices. It was Joffre, the French C-in-C, who chose the Somme as the sector for the combined allied offensive of summer 1916, while Haig himself would have preferred Flanders. The German offensive at Verdun, bleeding the French army to death, impelled Joffre to demand that Haig launch his offensive on 1 July, not on 15 August as Haig had wished in order to give him more time to train and rehearse his citizen troops.

So it was in no way Haig's fault that he had to launch his half-trained rank-and-file led by ill-experienced commanders in a premature offensive against immensely strong defences manned by the best army in Europe. Nor was it his fault that he had to do so with inadequate artillery support: British industry had simply failed to produce enough guns and ammunition.

What *was* Haig's responsibility was the final plan of attack on the Somme. Although he himself wanted a short surprise bombardment at the moment of assault, he as a cavalryman yielded to the recommendation of the gunners that there must be a preliminary bombardment lasting five days. In the event, this bombardment cratered the ground without cutting adequate gaps in German barbed-wire entanglements or inflicting lethal damage on an enemy sheltering in deep dugouts. Then again, Haig wanted the infantry to attack by rushes in small groups, but gave way to the insistence of the commander of the Fourth Army charged with the offensive (General Sir Henry Rawlinson, an infantryman) that there must be a steady advance in successive lines because, in Rawlinson's view, the half-trained volunteers of 'Kitchener's Army' would be incapable of more subtle tactics. Here again Haig was tragically proved right, when on the catastrophic first day of the Somme offensive nearly 20,000 British infantry advancing in line as if on parade were slaughtered by artillery bombardment and then by machine-gun fire. Moreover, the subsequent weeks of fighting on the Somme equally proved that Haig had been right and Rawlinson wrong, because the infantry quickly learned to make tactical use of ground and to attack by short rushes under covering fire.

Was Haig, as a cavalryman, too willing to heed the advice of his artillery and infantry subordinates, including Rawlinson? Should Haig, as C-in-C, have overruled them? Those are questions still open for debate. There is another: given the calamitous failure of the First of July and then the creepingly slow advances month after month against a resolute German defence, should Haig have persisted with his offensive?

The answer must be that it was simply out of the question to call it off. In the first place, the French army was still fighting hard at Verdun: Day One on the Somme was Day 132 at Verdun. Secondly, from the summer into the autumn of 1916, the allies were carrying out a joint grand strategy for the first and only time in the war. They hoped to win the war that year by launching concentric offensives against Germany and Austria – by the Russians on the Eastern Front, the Italians on the River Isonzo, and the British and French on the Western Front.

Haig's final lunge on the Somme in September, spearheaded by the thirty-two available tanks, was intended as the British contribution to this joint effort. And the effort did indeed strain Germany and her armies close to breaking point, as Hindenburg and Ludendorff acknowledge in their memoirs. As for Haig's own offensive on the Somme, Ludendorff recorded that the battle had left the German army 'absolutely exhausted':

> [We] had to face the danger that 'Somme fighting' would soon break out at various points on our fronts, and that even our troops would not be able to withstand such attacks indefinitely ...[15]

And so in February–March 1917 he abandoned a swathe of occupied France and pulled back his front opposite the BEF up to forty-five kilometres to the 'Siegfried Stellung' (the 'Hindenburg Line' to the British), a formidable ten-kilometre-deep defensive system. This major retreat testifies to the severity of the beating inflicted on the German army by Haig's offensive.

*   *   *

Haig's 1917 offensive in Flanders, the Third Battle of Ypres (or Passchendaele in popular memory), presents a more complex problem, well analysed in John Terraine's book *The Road to Passchendaele*[16], a dossier of original documents relating to every aspect of the planning and execution of the offensive, from the political debates down to meteorological forecasts.

In the first half of 1917, the prospects for the allies were clouded with uncertainties. In March, Czarist Russia had undergone a revolution, but nobody could now be sure whether the new revolutionary régime would prosecute the war more effectively than the Tsar's government, or whether Russia was in fact militarily finished, as reports from allied observers with the Russian army suggested. On 6 April came the good news that the United States had declared war on Germany. Nonetheless, it would be the spring of 1918 before an American army of any size could be recruited, trained, equipped, shipped across the Atlantic, and deployed on the Western Front. In the meantime, what of France, hitherto the mainstay of the alliance?

After all the losses and disappointments of the past three years, France was suffering from profound war-weariness and corrosive social unrest, while the French army was undergoing its own crisis of morale and discipline. Although the French high command had informed Haig about this crisis, they had concealed from him the full truth that up to fifty-five divisions were affected by mutinies.

And last among the bad news, but certainly not least, the German U-boat campaign against allied merchant shipping rose to its peak in April, with Admiral Jellicoe, the First Sea Lord, warning that Britain faced national defeat if sinkings went on at the current rate.

Haig's proposed remedy for this across-the-board strategic plight was to launch the British and imperial divisions under his command – the last fighting-fit allied army – in a major offensive in Flanders, striking north-eastwards from the Ypres salient to clear the Belgian coast, capture its U-boat bases, and ultimately reach the Dutch frontier. Haig argued to the Cabinet that this offensive would encourage the Russians to fight on, take the heat off the shaken French army, and give French national morale 'something to feed on' until the Americans arrived.

A case could certainly be made that gripping the German army in battle in Flanders was the best way to hold the tottering alliance together until the Americans arrived – and that British inaction might have allowed the Germans to launch some decisive stroke of their own against the mutinous French army. But other aspects of Haig's hopes and arguments are far more dubious. In discussion with politicians he sometimes justified his planned offensive on the grounds that it would be a joint Anglo-French undertaking, not just the BEF alone, because Marshal Pétain, the French C-in-C, had promised him that the French Army would take part, as well as launch offensives of its own elsewhere on the Western Front. But sometimes he contended that his offensive was above all intended to take the heat off a French army which was for the moment *hors de combat*. So he was really placing an each-way bet.

Yet given what Haig did know about the state of the French army, it was either wishful thinking or deliberately misleading for him to rest his case for an offensive on a promise of full French co-operation. In the event, a single French army took over the coastal sector of the Flanders front, but played little part in the actual offensive.

The operational plan which Haig presented to the War Cabinet must seem extraordinarily optimistic in view of the failure of previous allied offensives to break through the deep German defence systems. No wonder Lloyd George was so sceptical when Haig spread his fingers over the map to illustrate his intended sweep up through Belgium to the Dutch frontier. It is a black mark against Haig's judgement that he should so readily be swallowing unjustified sanguine assessments by his intelligence chief (Brigadier General John Charteris) that the morale of the German troops opposite him was shaky, and that there was even a chance, in Charteris's words, that allied offensives 'will make final victory more assured and which may even bring it within reach this year'.[17] It is a further mark against his judgement that he retained his faith in Charteris despite a warning from the Chief of the Imperial General Staff in London that their own intelligence reports about Germany and the German army did not accord with Charteris's assessments.

The argument between Haig and the War Cabinet, or rather between Haig and Lloyd George, about the proposed offensive went on through May, June and July – even after the preliminary bombardment had begun; a criminal delay. Yet Lloyd George and his colleagues lacked the moral courage to forbid Haig's plan. Instead, and in Lloyd George's own words, 'It was decided that I should once more sum up the misgivings which most of us felt and leave the responsibility to Sir William Robertson and Sir Douglas Haig.'[18]

And so at long last, on 20 July (just eleven days before Z-Day) the War Cabinet authorized Haig 'To carry out the plans for which he has prepared'. It was therefore a Cabinet decision to launch the Ypres offensive: it was Lloyd George's responsibility as Prime minister; a responsibility he dodged in his memoirs.

Just the same, it was Haig's own military choice to locate his offensive at Ypres.

* * *

When the Third Battle of Ypres was closed down after three months of struggle, Haig's troops had only reached the village of Passchendaele, an objective for the first day. Therefore, in terms of the ambitious strategic aims which Haig himself had laid down, his offensive must be accounted a complete failure.

Nonetheless, in the course of the battle there were moments when a breakthrough seemed very near. In September, a month of dry weather in a wet summer, three set-piece onslaughts each time blasted on by some 1,300 guns and howitzers, brought Haig's army within sight of green fields and the German rear areas. It is worth remembering that in Normandy in 1944 it took the British and American armies nearly two months of hard slogging before they broke the German front and were able to begin a headlong pursuit. When does the willpower to keep an offensive going in order to break the enemy become sheer blind obstinacy? In the case of Third Ypres, that turning-point surely came when Haig insisted on attacking into November against the advice of his army commanders.

Yet Haig's onslaught, strategically abortive though it was, still inflicted serious damage on the German army, as Ludendorff himself well recognised:

> The army had come victoriously through 1917 [N.B., by knocking Russia out of the war]; but it had become apparent that the holding of the western front could no longer be counted on, in view of the enormous quantity of

material of all kinds which the Entente had at their disposal ... Against the weight of the enemy's material the troops no longer displayed their old stubbornness; they thought with horror of fresh defensive battles ...[19]

*   *   *

Haig's critics have argued that the campaigns of 1916 and 1917 demonstrate that he was a 'chateau general' out of touch with battlefield realities. The charge is ill-founded. Firstly, it made good sense to lodge a main headquarters in a chateau offering convenient office space and billets for a large staff. It was the equivalent of Hindenburg's and Ludendorff's headquarters in the hotels of the Belgian resort of Spa. In the Second World War the commanders of armies and army groups also often located themselves in chateaux, schlosses, or country mansions and for similar reasons (like Dwight Eisenhower before D-Day in Southwick House, near Southampton).

In any case, a commander-in-chief in a twentieth-century mass war cannot effectively exercise leadership from the frontline like Wellington. On the static Western Front, he could only command effectively from the centre of a telephone network of landlines, because this was where he could receive all available information with the least delay.

For the conduct of a major battle, however, Haig moved to an advanced headquarters located in a special train behind the particular fighting front: the equivalent of Montgomery's famous caravan, which at Second Alamein in October 1942 lay miles to the rear of the armour struggling in Rommel's maze of minefields. Nor did Haig remain desk-bound in his chateau HQ in between battles; he regularly visited armies, corps, and divisions in order to consult with their commanders and staffs.

Then again, and contrary to his critics' allegations, he was perfectly aware of the state of the ground over which his troops were fighting, as is proved by entries in his diary. Certainly the battlefield on the Somme degenerated into thick clinging mud, and certainly the terrain at Third Ypres became a swamp. Yet the critics forget that during the Second World War the Allied ground forces in Italy in the winter of 1943–44, and again on the Scheldt islands in 1944, were also fighting up to their necks in water and mud. On the Russian Front in 1942–45 the Wehrmacht floundered haplessly in deep mud during the autumn downpours and the spring thaws. It is unrealistic to expect a military leader campaigning like Haig in northern Europe to call off an offensive because of the weather.

Yet the critics' gravest charge against Haig as a leader has always been that a 'Lost Generation' of young men was needlessly and callously slaughtered in his offensives. Many people seem to think [ask your friends!] that the United Kingdom lost a million men or even more on the Western Front in 1914-18, whereas the true figure is 513,000.[20]

Were Britain's losses in fact much larger than those of her allies or the enemy? Great War casualty records offer a massive problem in themselves: a source of endless statistical dispute. Comparisons between opposing sides in the same battle are particularly difficult because of different systems of recording and classifying casualties. Haig's critics have always unhesitatingly opted for those guesstimates which show significantly higher British losses than German. Yet a battle on the Western Front did not consist of just one side attacking in the open against a defence ensconced in trenches, but of attack and counter-attack, bombardment and counter-bombardment. It is therefore probable that losses on both sides on the Somme and at Third Ypres would have been roughly equal, give or take a few thousand in totals numbering hundreds of thousands.

What is certain is that in terms of the percentage of the national male population between the ages of fifteen and forty-nine killed on all fronts during the Great War, Britain got off much more lightly than other belligerents: 6.7 per cent of the age group against Germany's and Austria's 10 per cent, and France's 12.5 per cent.[21] Britain's total loss was also smaller in proportion to national population than America suffered during the Civil War. On the quite exceptional day of 1 July 1916 the total of killed, wounded, and missing amounted to about 30 per cent of British troops engaged. That compares with Confederate losses of 28 per cent at Antietam and at Gettysburg, and Bonaparte's losses of 44 per cent at the Battle of Aspern in 1809.

The harsh truth is that a war against a powerful and determined opponent cannot be waged and won except at the cost of colossal casualties. There are no quick, cheap victories except in a 'cabinet' war for limited political aims, or between one efficient army and one incompetent army, as in the Franco-Prussian war of 1870 or the Franco-German war of 1940. A conflict between belligerents broadly equal in combat power inevitably means a protracted war of attrition. This was true of the American Civil War – true as well of the titanic contest between Nazi Germany and the Soviet Union in 1941–45, when the siege of Leningrad and the Battle of Stalingrad far surpassed the Somme and Third Ypres in loss of life and in the sheer horror and terror of the experience.

* * *

Third Ypres marked Haig's last attempt to solve the conundrum of the Western Front, when for the first time in history an abundance of manpower and firepower, together with the spade and the concrete mixer, enabled the opposing sides to create continuous and strongly-garrisoned systems of field fortifications 400 miles long: systems which could not be outflanked because at one end was the North Sea, and at the other, the frontier with neutral Switzerland.

Nevertheless, the trench stalemate would be broken, though in a fashion which

Haig at the end of 1917 could not have predicted, but which would afford him at last the chance of a war-winning victory.

References

1. As Prime Minister in the Second World War, Churchill was free to pursue his Mediterranean strategy, which led to the disasters in Greece and Crete in 1941, and to the prolonged and bloody march up Italy in 1943–45, where the commitment in troops and shipping-lift proved strategically cost-ineffective in the face of Kesselring's skilful defence. See Barnett, *Engage the Enemy More Closely*, chaps 8, 11, 12, 21, and 22.

2. Terraine, *The Smoke and the Fire*, p.102.

3. Longmans, Green, 1960.

4. Hutchinson, 1961.

5. Oxford University Press, 1975; paperback 1977.

6. Fussell, *The Great War and Modern Memory*, p.12. So Britanno-centric is this book (with little attention to the experiences of either Britain's ally France or her enemy Germany) in view of its reliance on the works of Robert Graves and Siegfried Sassoon, it should really be entitled 'The Royal Welch Fusiliers and Modern Memory'.

7. London, Hutchinson, 1963.

8. Cf., John Bourne and Gary Sheffield at the Centre for Great War Studies at Birmingham University.

9. *Haig as Military Commander*, p.170.

10. Ibid, p.43.

11. Cited in Butcher, *The BEF in the Great War Part 3 – 1916*, in Western Front Association *Stand To!* No.90, p.28.

12. One of Haig's critics, A.J.P. Taylor, revealed in a conversation with me that he had no idea that delays in the mass deployment of the tank was owing to the incompetence of British industry, and not to hidebound obstruction by Haig.

13. Eric (later Sir Eric) Geddes, former deputy general manager of the North Eastern Railway. He later became inspector-general, transportation, all theatres of war.

14. Cited in Marshall-Cornwell, op. cit., p.84.

15. Ludendorff, *My War Memoirs, 1914–1918*, Vol 1, p.307.

16. Terraine, *The Road to Passchendaele: The Flanders Offensive of 1917; A Study in Inevitability*.

17. Cited in Marshall-Cornwall, op. cit., p.233.

18. Lloyd George, *War Memoirs*, Vol II, p.1293.

19. Ludendorff, op. cit., pp.541-2.

20. *Statistics of the Military Effort of the British Empire*

22. Compiled from ibid.

CHAPTER 8

Brilliance and Betrayal

Lloyd George as War Premier

Unlike Lincoln, whose presidency virtually coincided in duration with the Civil War, David Lloyd George had a long and distinguished career in high office *before* and *after* his time as Britain's national leader in the Great War. From 1909 to 1915 he had served as Chancellor of the Exchequer in Asquith's Liberal Cabinet, and from 1918 to 1922 he was to serve as Prime Minister in the continued Liberal-Conservative coalition government. His wartime premiership from 1916 to 1918 was therefore just one episode in Lloyd George's political career: an episode to which he brought the same personal qualities and shortcomings as in his peacetime career.

In the judgement of Professor A. J. P. Taylor in his book *England 1914-1945*:

He was the most inspired and creative British statesman of the twentieth century. But he had fatal flaws. He was devious and unscrupulous in his methods. He aroused every feeling except trust. In all his greatest acts, there was an element of self-seeking. Above all, he lacked stability.' He tied himself to no men, to no party, to no single cause.[1]

According to Taylor, 'Manoeuvre was Lloyd George's last resource: some masterpiece of political tactics which would scatter his enemies.' And then again: 'Somewhere, somehow, he would find a dramatic rallying cry and sweep back [in a General Election] to renewed power.[2]

Here Taylor is referring to Lloyd George's doomed attempts in 1922 to cling on in Downing Street when the coalition government was at last falling apart; and falling apart not least because of deep Conservative mistrust of Lloyd George personally. Yet Taylor's harsh summing up of Lloyd George as a peacetime politician is just as true of Lloyd George as Britain's war premier. Here was the same opportunist fixer and political manoeuvrer, except that in wartime the objects of his deceits and stratagems were not political foes but the Chief of the Imperial General Staff and the Commander-in-Chief of the British Armies on the Western Front. All too soon, Sir William Robertson and Sir Douglas Haig found him (to use Taylor's words), 'devious and unscrupulous'; and it is certainly true that in these two soldiers he 'aroused every feeling except trust'.

Lloyd George devotes the floridly over-written 2,043 pages of his *War Memoirs* to telling his readers how superbly he performed as Minister of Munitions, Secretary of State for War, and finally Prime Minister; and how incompetent and wrongheaded were his predecessors in the field of munitions production and his military colleagues in the field of grand strategy. This monumental work of mendacious self-praise serves better as a revelation of Lloyd George's own character than as a historical reference work. In his determination to slander the generals, he sometimes blatantly contradicts himself. For example, he tells us that the War Office was hampered at the beginning of the war by a 'traditional reactionism. Its policy seemed ever to be that of preparing, not for the next war, but for the last or last but one...'[3] This, he says, accounts for the paucity of heavy artillery in 1914. But only two pages later he writes:

> It was not so much a question of unpreparedness at the outbreak of war. No one before the War contemplated our raising armies aggregating hundreds of thousands of men ... No blame can, therefore, be attached to the War Office ... for failing to have in store, at the outbreak of the war, a reserve of equipment and munitions for the hitherto undreamed-of-forces we were compelled to raise ...[4]

Although he records that on the outbreak of war the Cabinet raised the limit of voluntary enlistment to 500,000 men, he does not criticise himself and his fellow politicians in the Cabinet for settling for so small a number, and thereby failing to foresee the likely future scale of the war. Nor does he give corresponding credit to Haig (then a corps commander) and Lord Kitchener, the War Secretary, for warning at this time that the war must be expected to last several years.

Despite his penchant for deceit and manipulation, Lloyd George was an able and energetic administrator: a genuine fighter for the ordinary man against the power, national and local, of the then governing class. In an era when the mass meeting was still the main means of communication between politicians and the people, he spoke with beguiling eloquence. He was a master of the quick, witty retort to the heckler. As a Welshman of solid non-conformist middle-class origins – father a schoolmaster, uncle a small craftsman-employer, and himself (like Lincoln) a successful provincial solicitor before his political career – he was an outsider to the English public-school and Oxbridge ruling elite of the time. Unlike Lincoln, he was no worker with his hands, being notoriously maladroit. His deftness lay in speed of thought and quickness of utterance.

Lloyd George's career was motivated by a ruthless egotism, as he confessed to his future wife with admirable if uncharacteristic candour:

> My supreme idea is to get on. To this idea I shall sacrifice everything – except I trust honesty. I am prepared to thrust even love itself under the wheels of my Juggernaut if it obstructs the way ... [5]

Although Lloyd George opposed the Boer War as being an unjust attempt to coerce two small free republics, he was far from being a pacifist. The history of war fascinated him, and he was a great admirer of the Napoleon of romantic legend. Like all but a small minority of the Liberal Cabinet in August 1914, he believed that Britain must go to war because of the German invasion of Belgium, of whose neutrality Britain was a guarantor under treaty.

Lloyd George's wartime career falls into two main parts – the first in 1914-16 as the man who rallied the Home Front in the posts of Chancellor of the Exchequer, and then Minister of Munitions; and second in 1916-18, as the would be grand strategist in the posts of Secretary of State for War and then Prime Minister.

It was by masterminding and driving through a new industrial and technological revolution in 1914-16 as Minister of Munitions that he made his great contribution to the ultimate allied victory. The Britain that went to war in 1914 remained essentially true to the political and economic tenets of Victorian Liberalism: a belief in *laissez faire* competition in a free market, and a doctrinal horror of state intervention in commerce and industry. Armaments production for the small standing army of peacetime had been regarded as the specialised remit of the Ordnance Department of the War Office headed by the Master General of the Ordnance. Now in 1914-15 this same bureaucratic body was called upon to conjure up guns, ammunition, and equipment for an army of a million and a half engaged in trench warfare. The Ordnance Department sought the answer in its accustomed method of commercial contracting, with large orders placed with British armaments firms and abroad in the United States. Unfortunately, British and American manufacturers simply defaulted on the Ordnance Department's contracts, failing to deliver stated quantities of weapons and ammunition by stated dates. In the case of 18-pounder field-gun ammunition, for example, the contractors promised 420,000 rounds by August 1915, while the War office at least hoped for 215,000; but in the event only 118,000 were delivered.

By spring 1915 the British Expeditionary Force had virtually run out of shells. When this predicament was leaked to the press, banner headlines denounced the shortage as a 'Shell Scandal' caused by disgraceful Whitehall ineptitude. The scandal forced the demise of Asquith's Liberal government and its replacement by a coalition with the Conservatives. It also brought Lloyd George to the new post of Minister of Munitions, charged with blowing open the bottlenecks in production and, in future, providing the armed forces with all the weaponry and ammunition they wanted.

In his war memoirs, Lloyd George enjoys blaming the 'shell scandal' on the War Office and the Ordnance Department; and it is true that when still Chancellor of the Exchequer he had urged that orders should be placed not just with armaments manufacturers but also with the British engineering industry in general.

However, the Ordnance Department had resisted this on the grounds that only specialist firms could manufacture to the fine precision necessary.

In fact, Lloyd George and the Ordnance Department were both right; but in different time spans. Lloyd George was right in seeing that commercial contracting within an essentially peacetime market economy would not be sufficient; and that total war called for total industrial mobilisation under state direction. As he put it in June 1915, just after he had become Minister of Munitions:

We are fighting against the best-organised community in the world; the best-organised whether for war or peace; and we have been employing too much the haphazard, leisurely, go-as-you-please methods, which, believe me, would not have enabled us to maintain our place as nation, even in peace, much longer.[6]

But the Ordnance Department was also right in thinking that a broad-front, breakneck industrial expansion was beyond existing British resources in skills and suitable plant; and would result in muddles and bottlenecks in production, and, worse, sub-standard guns and ammunition. And in the short run, 1915-16, so it proved. Even the War Office programme, which Lloyd George condemned as small-minded, turned out in the event to be overambitious. According to the Official History of the Ministry of Munitions, 'Shortage of (skilled) labour and machinery and the failure of sub-contractors were in fact the principal causes of the breakdown of supply in the spring of 1915.'[7]

The inevitable lead-time in expanding war production meant that the bulk of the shells fired in the Somme preliminary bombardment in June 1916 (and for which Lloyd George stole the credit) resulted from *War Office* orders placed before he took over. And one factor in the failure of the Somme bombardment lay in the numerous dud shells that were later found littering the field. For the manufacture of shells and fuses demanded utmost precision – a precision which, just as the Ordnance Department had warned, was beyond the capability of contractors fresh to the business.

In his new post, Lloyd George soon discovered that such technological factors made it impossible swiftly to boost output. The years 1915-16 were marked by huge delays and shortfalls in output; serious discrepancies between the production of the different components in the same piece of kit. Just like the War Office in its more limited efforts, Lloyd George had to contend with Britain's underlying shortage of advanced engineering skills and factories. For while Britain was still strong in heavy industries such as shipbuilding (including warships and their guns), she had fallen behind America and Germany in advanced technologies like precision machine-tools, light engineering products, and drugs and dyes (the essential basis for producing high explosive). In peacetime she had depended on imports of such products.

In consequence, the task facing Lloyd George was nothing less than equipping Britain with the large-scale advanced technologies she had so far lacked: a new industrial revolution.

He brought to this daunting challenge the leverage of a senior cabinet minister, but, even more important, a personal dynamism and a fertile imagination untrammelled by bureaucratic procedure. He hired top businessmen to advise him and sit on his directing committees. Under the Ministry of Munitions Act of July 1915, he threw traditional Liberal *laissez faire* into the dustbin by taking state control of industrial plant and profits, raw materials, even labour. He initiated a major programme of constructing 'national', or state, factories for producing shells, fuses, and explosives. He sponsored new welfare measures in industry – canteens, proper wash-rooms, hostels. He tramped the country meeting the district munitions committees, and addressing public meetings and factory workers on the vital need for munitions. His skill as a negotiator and his instinct for the popular pulse was shown in 1915 when, as Chancellor of the Exchequer, he and the trade unions signed the so-called 'Treasury Agreement', by which the craft unions accepted the abolition of restrictive practices for the duration of the War, opening the way for mass production by new American machine-tools operated by semi-skilled or unskilled labour, often women. This was Lloyd George at his populist best.

And he succeeded in his new industrial revolution. As well as introducing assembly-line production in place of Britain's traditional craft-based batch manufacture, the Ministry of Munitions created new technologies that Britain had never had before, such as aircraft and aero-engines; drugs and dyes; and precision instruments and gauges. The output of electric power, essential to such new technologies, was doubled during the war. As a result of this industrial revolution, by 1918 Britain was not only supplying the armed forces of the Empire with all the kit and weaponry they wanted, but also supplying her allies.

Lloyd George's success as Minister of Munitions, together with his charismatic personality, made him the evident choice in December 1916 to replace the torpid Asquith as Prime Minister. His first care was to create a more effective machinery of central government. In place of the traditional Cabinet of around eighteen members, there would be a 'War Cabinet' of five members, supplemented by others when specifically required for a given topic. In a notable innovation, Cabinet meetings were to be minuted, and the minutes later circulated for action, information, or the record. To operate the new system with soldier-like exactitude, Lloyd George appointed as Cabinet Secretary a colonel of the Royal Marines, Maurice Hankey. Hankey was to remain in post for forty years. Lloyd George also transformed No. 10 into the civilian equivalent of a commander-in-Chief's headquarters staff, with a secretariat lodged in wooden huts in the Downing Street garden: hence, the nickname 'the Garden suburb'. It is from Lloyd George's innovations in the midst of a total war that derive Whitehall's central machinery today, headed by the Cabinet Secretary (and Head of the Civil Service), and serving a pre-eminently powerful Prime Minister.

Yet unlike Churchill in the Second World War, Lloyd George lacked a political firm base within the governing coalition. Whereas Churchill after 1940 would be leader of a party enjoying an overwhelming majority in the House of Commons, the Liberal Party in 1916 was now split between MPs who supported Lloyd George and those who remained loyal to Asquith. As a result, Lloyd George, a Liberal, now headed a coalition that owed its Parliamentary majority to his late political enemies, the Conservatives. In view also of personal Conservative links with the senior military figures, this signified that Lloyd George could not – or felt he could not – openly assert his authority over recalcitrant generals and admirals, as Churchill was to do in the Second World War. He would have to get his way, if he could, by deceit and manoeuvre.

Lloyd George took over as war leader at a time when the war had changed from a limited 'cabinet' conflict into a total war between peoples. At the end of 1916 public opinion in each belligerent state was still firmly resolved to fight on for 'victory'; and this despite the military failures of the year, despite the casualty lists constantly published in the newspapers, and despite rationing and a grey life of shortages. In Britain, many of those on the Left of politics who had opposed going to war in 1914 now saw the conflict as a crusade for liberal values and the destruction of German militarism. Only a small pacifist minority of the Liberal and Labour parties was in favour of peace at any price. As Lloyd George himself told an American journalist in September 1916, the British were 'determined to carry the fight to a finish':

> The whole world – including neutrals [i.e., America] of the highest purpose and humanitarians with the best of motives [i.e., President Woodrow Wilson] – must know that there can be no outside interference at this stage. Britain asked no interference when she was unprepared to fight. She will tolerate none now that she is prepared, until the Prussian military despotism is broken beyond repair.[8]

Yet at the end of 1916, it was *Germany* who militarily had had the best of the war so far, with her armies still occupying eleven French departments and almost all of Belgium. This advantage was reflected in the German peace terms as sketched in diplomatic feelers in the winter of 1916-17: Alsace-Lorraine to be wholly restored to German sovereignty; important French coalfield districts to be ceded to Germany; Belgium to become virtually a German protectorate; Germany to receive reparations from the allies. Such a peace was totally unacceptable to Britain or France. So a fight to the finish it had to be.

In the American Civil War Abraham Lincoln accepted that his political decision to fight the Confederacy to a finish would demand grinding the enemy's main army to pieces in remorseless battle, no matter the scale of casualties. Lloyd George, however, lacked both Lincoln's strategic insight and his moral courage. Right up to the spring of 1918 he was to look for some cheaper, easier way to bring Germany down than attacking the main body of her army entrenched on the Western Front. Thus at the core of Lloyd George's thinking as a war leader there lay a complete discordance between the end (victory) and the envisaged military means. As Haig's Chief of Staff, Major General Kiggell, bluntly told Lloyd George at the end of 1916: 'he had better make peace at once if England was trying to take up the line that heavy losses could not be allowed.'[9]

Yet the Battle of the Somme made Lloyd George all the more determined that there must be no more British offensives on the Western Front. He was a man of sensitive nature, even squeamish; somewhat of a hypochondriac. His mistress, Frances Stevenson, recorded in her diary the impact on Lloyd George of visiting in hospital in 1916 a friend's wounded soldier-son who had been shot through the head and partially paralysed. Lloyd George told Frances when he arrived home:

> You must take my mind off it all. I feel I shall break down if I do not get right away from it all. The horror of what I have seen has burnt into my soul, and has almost unnerved me for my work.[10]

As early as the beginning of 1915 Lloyd George, when Chancellor of the Exchequer, had urged on the Cabinet that the French should be left to defend the Western Front virtually on their own, while the British army should be shipped out to the Adriatic, there to open a Balkan front against Austria in conjunction with the Serbs and so, Lloyd George hoped, the Greeks and the Romanians. Like Winston Churchill dreaming of a similar Balkan coalition in 1941 during the Second World War, Lloyd George counted heads without taking note of the state of training, organisation, equipment, and ammunition stocks of the various armies that might take the field. Britain herself was then suffering from the desperate shortage of shells and guns, while the only fully operational reserve available to the British Empire in early 1915 was a single division, the 39th (Regular). But Lloyd George had his answer: 600,000 British soldiers for his Balkan front could be found from Territorials and the citizen volunteers of Kitchener's 'New Armies'. Yet to transport a force of 600,000 men from Britain to the Adriatic, put it ashore and then re-supply it for months on end was utterly beyond the available shipping lift. Lloyd George's own comment on the much smaller Anglo-French force landed at Salonika later in 1915 thus makes ironic reading:

> It is true that forces that numerically appeared to be very powerful were sent to Salonika; and there was every appearance of a formidable army of British, French, Serbians and Greeks, numbering in the aggregate hundreds of thousands... It was for offensive purposes reduced to stagnation and impotence by equipment so inadequate as to render this

conglomerate army quite incapable of making any effective attack on the enemy.[11]

Lloyd George's first idea of a grand-strategic plan for 1917, as argued to an allied conference in Rome in January that year which he himself had called, was to stand on the defensive on the Western Front, and transfer a mass of heavy artillery and other equipment to the Italian front, there to support an Italian offensive against the Austrians aimed at the Austrian port of Trieste. He hoped that this would ultimately lead to Austria's defection from Germany, and hence to Germany's own downfall. Surprisingly enough, General Cadorna, the Italian Commander-in-Chief, proved less than enthusiastic.

Lloyd George's second proposal was to send off to the Russian army not only surplus Anglo-French war production but even munitions designated for the British and French armies. This proposal fared no better with his allied colleagues.

So the Rome conference achieved nothing. Now the new French Commander-in-Chief on the Western Front, Robert Nivelle, proposed to launch a largely French grand offensive on the Aisne, which he claimed would break clean through the German defences in a single rush, and lead on to a quick victory and peace. Haig's allotted role in this venture was merely to carry out supporting attacks. Lloyd George jumped at Nivelle's proposal, for this was a Western Front offensive of which he could approve. In the first place, Nivelle was charming, glib, and even fluent in English (having an English mother): all that Haig and Robertson were not.

And secondly, in a remarkable exercise of deceitful manoeuvre designed to undermine Sir Douglas Haig, Lloyd George had secretly connived with Nivelle that the British commander-in-chief would become a mere army group commander under French orders.

At Lloyd George's prompting, Nivelle sprang this proposal on Haig and Robertson by surprise at a conference in Calais supposedly held to discuss rail transport problems. After much indignant objection by the two British generals, the scheme was limited to the duration of Nivelle's offensive only, and Haig was left with the right to appeal to his own government if he believed French orders were placing his army in danger.

But the consequence of this conspiracy between Lloyd George and the French C-in-C was finally to destroy all trust in the prime minister on the part of Haig and Robertson. Instead of open roundtable debates on British strategy such as would take place under Churchill, there were to be two mutually suspicious cliques, each with its own strategic agenda, each striving to outsmart the other, with ramifying harmful consequences to Britain's conduct of the war.

The third, and principal, attraction for Lloyd George of Nivelle's plan (as with Lloyd George's own suggested strategies for 1917) lay in that a nation other than the British would be carrying it out, and having its young men killed in the process. After all, if not the Italians or the Russians, then why not the French? As Lloyd George himself actually stated in Cabinet in June 1917 when still urging his Italian strategy in opposition to Haig's proposed offensive at Ypres,

> if the Germans came to the assistance of the Austrians, then you would be fighting them and wearing them out. But this would take place at the expense of the Italians and not our own men.

The implications of this strategic philosophy were extraordinary. Lloyd George wanted Britain's army in France and Belgium of some sixty first-class divisions to become largely an onlooker, while the increasingly worn-down French on the Western Front and Russians on the Eastern Front kept on fighting; and this at a time when an American deployment in France was clearly a long way off. It is hard to comprehend how Lloyd George could really believe that his preferred grand strategy could bring down the still-formidable German war machine.

Yet the failure of his conspiracy with Nivelle left him no less determined to unseat Haig and Robertson in the long run; in fact, the more so after his failure to prevent the Third Battle of Ypres. Largely thanks to his advocacy, it was agreed between allied political leaders in November 1917 that a Supreme Allied War Council should be set up, with the power to issue directives to national high commands. There was no question that some kind of unified grand-strategic direction of the war, as achieved between Britain and America in the Second World War, was desirable and overdue. But Lloyd George had as his primary aim the outflanking of Haig as a commander-in-chief in full control over theatre strategy and the deployment of his reserves; and the outflanking of Robertson as the government's chief military adviser. When the Supreme War Council began to function at Versailles in February 1918, the French, Italian, and American governments each appointed as their military representative on the Council either their Chief of the General Staff or a deputy Chief: Lloyd George did not. Instead he opted to appoint another general officer, co-equal in status with the CIGS: a functionally unworkable relationship. When Sir William Robertson refused to accept either of these compromised posts, General Sir Henry Wilson, a witty, glib, politician-like soldier, was appointed as Military Representative at Versailles. The prime minister would now be able to turn to Wilson for military advice instead of Robertson and Haig.

By stating his unwillingness to continue as CIGS under these circumstances, Robertson effectively dismissed himself, whereupon Wilson took his place as Chief of the Imperial General Staff, appointing a tame mouthpiece as the new British representative at Versailles. The shamefully disengenuous account in Lloyd George's war memoirs of this destruction of an able and honourable soldier only confirms him as a man who confused leadership with chicanery.

However, Lloyd George's concurrent attempt to use the Supreme War Council and its Executive War Board as a means of controlling Haig largely miscarried. Haig and his French opposite number, Pétain, adamantly refused to hand over their reserves to this Board, and made their own arrangements for mutual aid in a crisis. Nevertheless, Lloyd George still had one last strategem to pursue in his conflict with Haig. In order to prevent Haig from launching a renewed offensive in Flanders in spring 1918, the War Cabinet let him have only 174,000 reinforcements instead of the 600,000 he asked for: and this although the BEF was more than 100,000 men weaker in fighting troops in January 1918 than in January 1917.

This final devious attempt to emasculate Haig as commander in-chief very nearly led to outright military catastrophe when on 21 March 1918 the colossal German spring offensive crashed against Haig's inadequately manned and over-extended front (see below pp.000).

Just how needless, how culpable, was the Cabinet's withholding of reinforcements is shown by the fact that, in the two months *after* the moment of critical danger, almost 550,000 troops were sent from the United Kingdom to the Western Front.

Now all of Lloyd George's attempts to shackle or unseat the British commander-in-chief had miscarried. In consequence, it was under Haig's leadership that the British armies played a key role in the defeat of the great German spring offensive in March and April 1918; and then played the biggest part in the allied offensives in August-November that led to Imperial Germany's final defeat.

Yet even while Haig's troops were pounding the German army to the verge of disintegration and driving Erich Ludendorff, the German supreme commander, to demand that the German government sue for an armistice without delay, Lloyd George refused to believe that the war could be ended in 1918. In his enlightened strategic judgement, 1919 would be the year of allied victory, and it would be a victory won, so he believed, thanks to the American army and its unbloodied manpower.

*   *   *

The verdict returned by the historical record on Lloyd George as a national leader in a total war is plain enough: he was a pygmy compared with Abraham Lincoln – a pygmy in terms of staunchness of character and strategic understanding alike.

References

1. Lt Col Henri
1. Oxford, At the Clarendon Press, 1966, pp.192-3.
2. Ibid, p.189.
3. Ibid, Vol I, p.75.
4. Ibid, p.77.
5. John Grigg, *The Young Lloyd George*, p.67.
6. Ibid, p.155.
7. *History of the Ministry of Munitions*, Vol III, p.8.
8. Lloyd George, *War Memoirs*, Vol I, p.509.
9. Paul Guinn, *British Strategy and Politics, 1914-1918*, p. 206.
10. Frances Stevenson Diary, pp. 92-3.
11. Ibid, p.317.

CHAPTER 9

Saviour of an Army

Maréchal Pétain and the French Mutinies, 1917

Marshal Philippe Pétain has remained to the present day the focus of bitter controversy, especially in his native France. In 1916 he successfully defended Verdun against relentless German assaults. In 1917, as Commander-in-Chief, he saved the French army from widespread mutiny and restored it to fighting fitness. But then in 1940, after the allied armies had been routed by the German blitzkrieg, he successfully urged the French government to sue for an armistice, rather than fight on from French North Africa; and he thereafter became head of state in the collaborationist regime set up at Vichy in the zone left unoccupied under the armistice. Convicted after the Second World War as a traitor, the aged Pétain served out the rest of his life in a military prison. It was a remarkable rise and fall.

Yet Pétain the hero and Pétain the traitor were motivated by the same concern – to preserve the French soldier and the French people from avoidable suffering.

* * *

In the summer of 1917 Pétain's qualities as a leader were put to a test even sterner than the Battle of Verdun the year before. On 17 May, after spending just three weeks in Paris as Chief of the General Staff, he became Commander-in-Chief of the French army on the Western Front: an army in moral crisis after three years of fruitless offensives and colossal loss. Just three days later came a report of a mutiny in a divisional depot of the XXXII Corps. The firing charge for the mutiny was news that certain units in the depot were to be posted back into the line. A crowd of soldiers gathered in the cantonment to protest. Left-wing agitators harangued them, after which they sang the '*Internationale*' and went off to find the depot commanding officer.

Luckily for him, he was not at home, and so they had to content themselves with breaking into his quarters and smashing up his furniture. While the smashing was going on, the officers and NCOs of the depot kept out of the way, conduct which offers its own comment on the then quality of regimental leadership in the

109

French army. Next day the CO was visited by 'soldiers' delegates (on the new Russian revolutionary model), who presented a list of grievances. In the meantime, other troops in the depot refused to go on parade. Thus was set the pattern of events that would be repeated in all the later outbreaks.

From then on till the middle of June, Pétain was to receive news of up to eight fresh mutinies every day, until a total of fifty-four divisions, half the French army, had been affected.

A mutiny, signifying that the bonds of discipline and the psychological spell of respect for superiors have dissolved, must be one of the most unnerving experiences a leader at any level can face, let alone the head of a national army in wartime. It was some comfort to Pétain that troops actually on the fighting front seemed to be remaining staunch, even resisting heavy local German attacks. In almost every case the mutinies took place in units resting behind the line or in depots. A posting back to the trenches was the usual trigger for trouble, whereupon a mob of discontented soldiers would shout 'We want leave!' and 'We won't go up the line!' at their officers, while other soldiers simply staged sit-ins in their barrack huts. There would be protest marches to more singing of '*Internationale*'. In one camp a brigadier general got howled down and manhandled; in another the officers had stones chucked at them. One mutinying unit even took the road to Paris and had to be rounded up by cavalry. All these manifestations were fuelled by copious *pinard*, or rot-gut issue wine.

Although left-wing agitators were certainly doing their best to stir up trouble for their own political ends, there existed deep underlying causes of disaffection among the rank-and-file, as Pétain himself was to detail in his reports to his government: and all exacerbated by failures of leadership from the top of the army down to company commanders.

But it was General Robert Nivelle's disastrous grand offensive along the Aisne in April and May 1917 that actually triggered the mutinies. For the French poilu, this was one abortive attack too many. It must be remembered that already by the end of 1915 the French army had suffered nearly two million casualties in killed, wounded, and missing; and that in 1916 nearly 400,000 more casualties were suffered at Verdun alone. And victory still seemed as far off as ever.

At this grim moment in the war, General Nivelle (Joffre's successor as Commander-in-Chief) had kindled fresh hope by persuading the French government that a 'violent' and 'brutal' assault (his words) by a mass of forty French divisions would burst through the German defences in one bound, followed by a long-distance pursuit. Nivelle was really harking back to the nineteenth-century French military theorists who had fantasised about the decisive moral effect of an attack pushed to the extreme. He had promised his government and his soldiers that this time there would be no long attrition battle, but just a swift victory and an end to the war. Thus was the French army keyed up for one last effort. When instead his offensive degenerated into yet another murderous attrition battle, the crushing disappointment finally broke French morale. Yet by this time morale had already suffered because of muddled planning in the run-up to the offensive. Pétain cited a case of such mismanagement in a later report to the government:

> The troops put into the line on 19 April received successively information that they would attack on the 23rd, then the 25th, then the 29th, at last 3 and 5 May. Successive counter-orders of this kind are depressing in the extreme for those carrying them out. To prepare to attack is to face the probability of death. One can deliberately accept this idea once. But when they see the awful moment postponed again and again, the bravest and steadiest become demoralised. In the end, physical resistance and nervous tension alike have their limits. The troops who attacked on 5 May were at the end of their tether, having been in the frontline for seventeen days under intense and continuous fire.[1]

There was, however, a deeper cause of the mutinies. It lay in the pervasive defectiveness of French military administration; and especially where administration related to the soldier's wellbeing.

In the British and German armies there were efficient systems for feeding soldiers with regular hot food even in the trenches, and for providing them with good medical care and relatively comfortable rest camps. In the British army on the Western Front, there were plenty of canteens behind the line and private welfare centres like Toc H or the YMCA; there were sports and concert parties; regular leave; proper welfare facilities along the journey home. Moreover, British and German regimental officers were taught that it was a leader's prime duty to look after the welfare of his soldiers.

But none of this was the case with the French army. Instead it remained true to the muddle-through tradition set in the nineteenth century.

Leave was irregular and often unfairly allocated – a major grievance of the mutineers. The French soldier went on leave still in the filthy state in which he left the trenches; no showers and clean clothes as in the British army. When his train stopped en route, or even at the main Paris termini, there were no canteens, official or unofficial; nobody to guide him or look after him; no military policing of the drunk and disorderly; but instead plenty of agitators ready to subvert him.

According to a report rendered by Pétain, army rations in rest camps or in the line were inadequate, deficient in green vegetables, and badly cooked. Because field cooking equipment was so primitive and because of the distances that rations had to be carried, food in the trenches was, and to quote Pétain, 'congealed, dried up, dirty and often absolutely disgusting'. As for rest camps during periods out of the line, they were usually located in half-demolished villages, and, according to Pétain, 'totally without comfort'. No wonder the French soldier resorted more and more to filling his water-bottle with *pinard*, so adding widespread drunkenness to the other failings of the army.

Pétain therefore found himself picking up the bill for the bankruptcy of the French military tradition, alike in its Napoleonic belief in the decisive victory won by all forces united, and in its haphazard Napoleonic logistics.

But first of all he had to avert the imminent peril that the French soldiery might follow the contemporary Russian example and just go home.

It is hard to imagine a grimmer inheritance for an incoming commander-in-chief.

* * *

To the task of dealing with this inheritance, Pétain brought two advantages: his reputation as the victor at Verdun, and the authority conferred by his own imposing personality. A tall, fair-haired Pas de Calais man from a farming family, he reminded one CQG officer of 'a marble statue; a Roman senator in a museum. Big, vigorous, an impressive figure, face impassive, of a pallor of a really marble hue'.[2] His own *chef de cabinet*, Serrigny, later remembered his own first impression of Pétain: 'Cold, glacial even, this good-looking blond fellow, already going bald, attracted women and men alike by the intense gaze of his blue eyes.'[3] Another staff officer at GQG was similarly impressed:

> Pétain did not appeal to me only as a soldier; his greatness does not only derive from his skill at directing a battle, but emanates from his entire personality. No one evokes better than he what the Romans called 'great men'.[4]

To a degree unusual in generals of the time, Pétain felt a strong personal empathy with the rank-and-file and their hardships; perhaps *too* strong an empathy, given that command in war must involve sending men to their possible deaths. During the Verdun battle he would stand outside his headquarters and watch his soldiers marching past his headquarters on their way to and from the line:

> My heart lurched as I saw our young men of twenty going into the furnace of Verdun, and reflected that they would pass too quickly ... from enthusiasm in their first engagement to the weariness caused by suffering ... How saddening it was when they came back, either on their own as wounded or stragglers, or in the ranks of companies decimated by loss! Their stares seemed to be fixed in a vision of unbelievable terror ... they drooped beneath the weight of their horrifying memories. When I spoke to them, they could scarcely answer.[5]

Pétain came to the post of Commander-in-Chief, therefore, with the reputation of genuinely caring for the lives of his soldiers.

He also brought a new strategic and tactical realism. Long before the war he had opposed the French military theorists who believed that the attack could overcome the firepower of the defence by sheer aggressive élan conferring a decisive moral ascendancy. He had warned that the Nivelle offensive was a fantasy doomed to failure. He was to utter a similar warning in regard to Haig's 'Third Ypres' plan to clear the Belgian coast up to the Dutch frontier. For Pétain was a firepower man; an organisation man; a military technologist. His wartime exercise of command, from brigadier in 1914 to army group commander in 1916, had been notable for the weight of artillery employed and for painstaking tactical preparation. He had saved Verdun by massed batteries; by the unprecedented use of motor-transport supply along the single available road, the *voie sacrée*; and by a system of regular reliefs for battlefield units.

In dealing with the mutinies, Pétain judged that his first task must be to diagnose the causes. His initial reports to the Government detailed the effects of the Nivelle offensive on morale, and the long-term neglect of the soldier by military maladministration. Nonetheless, he also strongly blamed left-wing agitators in the ranks of the army, as well as the civilian agitators who swarmed in the railway stations trying to subvert soldiers travelling on leave. He condemned the freedom with which the French press spread defeatist and pacifist sentiments, and the feebleness of government in failing to curb this seditious propaganda. His complaint was justified. The unrestained criticism in the press of the current conduct of military operations could only corrode the morale of the soldier and likewise the home front's will to win. In particular, certain left-wing organs such as *Le Bonnet Rouge* and certain individual journalists were actually in German pay. Nonetheless, Minister of the Interior, Malvy, himself a Radical Socialist, refused to take action.

Pétain also identified another political cause of his army's disaffection: the unofficial so-called 'peace conference' due to be held in August 1917 in neutral Stockholm, and to be attended by delegates from the socialist parties of every belligerent country, should their governments let them go. As Pétain pointed out to French ministers:

> the idea of *Peace* and the word itself appear in terms of longing in the weekly journals. They give the widest and loudest publicity to the agitation worked up by the Socialist Party for the Stockholm conference ... The Papers, it is true, are almost unanimous in only contemplating peace with honour ... But the big word is let fall: *Peace*, approaching peace and, as many do not hesitate to describe it, *imminent*.

And the effects of all this on his troops?

> To dangle prematurely before the eyes of men who daily face death, men worn out by the misery of life in the trenches, the lovely mirage of peace is to wish deliberately to weaken all the moral resources and high ideals that have so far been the glory of the French army in this long war.[6]

It was owing to Pétain's protestations that the government refused passports to French would-be Stockholm delegates: a decision supported by 467 deputies (including many Socialists) in the French National Assembly, while fifty-two socialists voted against.

Yet, as Pétain rightly judged, the army's crisis of morale was only one aspect of a general crisis of morale affecting the French nation. The *union sacrée* of 1914 was now dissolving because of the effects of more than two years of vain sacrifice and suffering. Home-front discontent was inflamed by food shortages, coal shortages, unequal sacrifices across the social classes, resentment of war profiteers, and anger at the general incompetence of government. Moreover, the March revolution in Russia was providing both an inspiration and a blueprint for those political zealots on the Left who sought to exploit the national disgruntlement for their own purposes. It hardly helped when, on 4 June 1917, soldiers recruited from the French colony of Indochina fired on a demonstration of women war-workers in Paris, including wives of men at the Front. Wild rumours spread forward to the trenches that a bloody civil war had broken out in the capital: and the cry 'They're killing our wives there' spurred some mutinous units to take the road to Paris.

It was now even possible that France could succumb to revolution as had Czarist Russia only four months earlier, with all that such an eventuality would imply for the final outcome of the war. Whether or not this worst-case scenario came true depended, first and foremost, on Pétain's ability to restore the French army from mutiny to fighting fitness.

He began with a programme of identifying, and punishing, the ringleaders of the mutinies, while at the same time restoring the rule of military discipline and authority. He instructed his subordinate commanders:

> To excuse their not having done their duty, certain officers and NCOs hide behind the fact that since the incidents are collective in character, it is difficult to single out the leaders. Such a reason is not valid. It is always in fact possible to turn a collective act into an individual one. It is enough to give some man an order to carry out (beginning with the bad-hats). If they refuse, they are immediately arrested and sent for trial.[7]

But since 1914 military justice had had some of its powers emasculated for the sake of individual soldiers' rights. Indeed, courts martial with the power of summary sentencing had been abolished in favour of *conseils de guerre*, a more elaborately bureaucratic system where the appeal procedure could cause long delays. As recently as 20 April 1917 the C-in-C had also been deprived of his authority to confirm or commute a death sentence, which was instead vested in the President of the Republic himself, who in one case at least commuted the sentence merely because of political considerations. So Pétain demanded that the C-in-C be given back his powers over the death sentence; and on 9 June the Government conceded the demand. At the same time, and on his own responsibility, Pétain ordered that the *conseils de guerre* should operate in virtually the same way as the old *courts martial*, trying and sentencing prisoners without procedural delay.

Pétain's combination of firmness and humanity succeeded in swiftly overcoming the immediate crisis. From 10 June onwards the mutinies rapidly faded away; and on 20 June, five weeks after he became C-in-C, Pétain was able to report to the government:

> The relaxation has resulted from: (1) fear caused by the heavy punishments suffered by those most guilty; (2) action taken on the subject of leave; (3) the feeling experienced by the agitators that the general movement of revolt has failed because of a want of co-ordination...[8]

A letter from Pétain to his army commanders on 18 June gives an insight into his own thinking:

> I set about suppressing serious cases of indiscipline with the utmost urgency. I will maintain this repression firmly, but without forgetting that it applies to soldiers who have been in the trenches with us for three years and who are our soldiers.[9]

The figures confirm that in dealing with the mutinies Pétain did succeed in striking the right balance between severity and humanity. Of the 23,385 soldiers found guilty of mutiny or other military offences, only fifty-five men were actually executed: seven of them on the authority of the C-in-C and forty-eight after confirmation of sentence by the President of the Republic. The preferred form of retribution, visited on more than 23,000 men, was imprisonment in an overseas penal colony.

Meanwhile, Pétain was inaugurating long-term reforms of the French military system in all that related to the soldier's wellbeing. Home leave was the first reform on his agenda. As early as 2 June he instructed that the aim must be to give seven days' leave every four months; and that as much as half the muster roll of a formation being refitted in the rear could be sent on leave at the same time. He began the creation of all those welfare services behind the front and on lines of communication that the British soldier already took for granted: showers, change of clean uniform, motor transport from camp to station, canteens. He ordered 400,000 bunks for dugouts and rearward camps. He instructed that mobile cookers must be taken as far forward into the Line as physically possible. He reminded the French regimental officer:

> Supervision of food is as important for the soldier's health as for his morale. It is by concerning themselves with these details, apparently trivial, that company commanders will gain a deep and lasting influence over their men which will amply repay their trouble in time of battle.[10]

He also strove to curb drunkenness, ordering that 'wet' canteens be closed on the eve of departure for the front, and giving a word of advice to junior officers: 'In many units the example comes from the junior officers' mess ... where it is easy to get into the habit of drinking too much. The NCOs naturally follow in the same error...'[11]

In his diagnosis of the army's problems and his chosen cures, Pétain displayed shrewdness, psychological understanding, and sheer good sense. Yet, however wise may be the policy decisions made at a headquarters desk, effective leadership demands direct *personal* impact on the led. At times of crisis, wrote Clausewitz, 'the whole inertia of the mass rests its weight on the will of the Commander; by the light of his spirit, the spark of purpose, the light of hope, must be kindled afresh in others'.

Pétain completely understood this. As soon as he could safely get away from GQG, he toured his shaken army to enquire, to admonish, to encourage; to talk to all ranks. In turn, he encouraged others to talk freely to him about their problems. In the words of an instruction issued two days after he became C-in-C:

> A superior officer, in his relations with his subordinates, must at all times show himself approachable and friendly, willing to help them find solutions to the difficulties that hamper their work, ready to pass on any useful information and even to invite it.[12]

In all, Pétain visited ninety divisions in the months following the mutinies. Like a good regimental officer, he would carefully inspect kitchens and camp accommodation; he would personally look at the leave rosters. After inspecting a formal parade, he would gather round him an informal group of officers, NCOs and soldiers, inviting them to forget rank for a moment and speak frankly. He would start by giving his own views on the war situation; how France's allies were confident of victory; how America's enormous power was on its way. He would explain his own basic strategy in terms that soldiers could follow – reliance on firepower; avoidance of casualties. And then he would discuss such humble but vital matters as the quality of bread and other rations. According to one eye-witness, 'He spoke as man to man without trying to lower himself, dominating everyone with his spell ... He remained calm and impressive, truly the general-in-chief and with a regal presence.'[13]

He would end these talks by calling out men from the ranks who had earned decorations and personally pinning the medals on their chests.

Today such techniques of 'man-management' are commonplace enough in civilian life as well as in the armed services. But for a general in 1917, and a French general at that, such techniques were not obvious or commonplace; they were an innovation.

The suppression of the mutinies and the reforms of the military system were not, however, ends in themselves, but means to the end of restoring the French army as an instrument of war capable of defeating the German enemy in battle. However, Pétain had come to the post of C-in-C convinced that there must be no more grand offensives. The balance of forces on the Western Front, the power of the defence in depth, and the current state of military techology (strong in firepower but weak in mobility) ruled out a strategic breakthrough. Instead, he advocated what has become known to military historians as 'bite-and-hold' operations. In his own words:

> The method of wearing out the enemy while suffering the minimum casualties oneself consists in multiplying limited attacks, mounted with great artillery support, so as to strike the vault of the German edifice without pause until it collapses. When they can no longer rebuild the edifice, but only when, we will be able to go over to the pursuit.[14]

As for Pétain's theatre strategy, that was simple enough: wait for the Americans to arrive in 1918 with their millions of fresh, unblooded manpower.

The first of Pétain's 'bite-and-hold' limited offensives, at Verdun on 26 August 1917, displays the pattern: on the eleven-mile front of attack, no fewer than 60 per cent of the deployed force were gunners; only 40 per cent infantrymen. After an eight-day bombardment, the infantry went in, with objectives strictly limited to the furthest range of the guns. As soon as the infantry reached their objectives, capturing 10,000 German prisoners, Pétain closed the battle down. On 23 October he launched another limited operation at Malmaison on the Aisne, with 986 heavy guns and 624 field guns deployed on a seven-mile front. Because the ground won by Pétain's 'bite and hold' offensive outflanked the German position along the Chemin des Dames ridge, the enemy decided to evacuate it: a notable bonus.

Pétain's carefully stage-managed and low-cost victories served their purpose – they encouraged the nation, and they gave the army back its confidence.

He was no less innovative in regard to the defensive, abandoning the doctrine preached by such as General Ferdinand Foch that the frontline should be packed with troops, and that not a yard of ground should be yielded to the enemy. Instead he issued instructions for defence in depth, with the main battle position out of range of the enemy's opening bombardment. He wrote in his own hand on the original of his operational instruction:

Modern tactics are no longer Napoleonic tactics. They are dominated and conditioned by the progress of armaments, by the extraordinary growth in fire-power. 'Formation in line' is replaced by 'Formation in depth', whose organisation and cohesion rest primarily on the 'combination of all arms'.[15]

In order to re-indoctrinate the army with this concept, Pétain directed that divisions were to be pulled out of the line by rotation for thorough re-training and combined exercises, while army group commanders were to set up study centres for their officers. It was a remarkable programme to implement in the middle of a great war.

* * *

In 1918 the reformed French army was to play a major part in the defeat of the mammoth German spring offensives, and then in the victorious allied counter-offensives from June to November that brought imperial Germany to the point of abjectly requesting an armistice.

By rescuing the French army from despair and mutiny in 1917 and restoring it as a formidable military instrument, Phillippe Pétain therefore decisively affected the course of the Great War. This achievement lends a special weight to his views on the nature of leadership:

The true chief is one who knows how to ally firmness with wisdom, professional knowledge with resolution in action, the art of the organiser with that of the executor. It is thus that he wins confidence.

In this conquest of confidence, there is also the element of personal prestige: clear-sightedness justified by events, ability to avoid the false move, coolness in difficult circumstances, calm in adversity and modest in success.

In reality, confidence is not to be ordered, it is to be merited.[16]

References

1. Lt Col Henri Carré, *Les Grandes Heures du General Pétain*, p.82.
2. Jean de Pierrfeu, *C.O.G. – Secteur I*, Vol II, p.9.
3. General Serrigny, *Trente Ans avec Pétain*, Preface iii.
4. Pierrefeu, II, p.9.
5. Marshal Philippe Pétain, *La Bataille de Verdun*.
6. Quoted in Carré, pp.84–5.
7. Serrigny, p.147.
8. Carré, p.126.

9. Ibid, p.128.
10. Ibid, p.133.
11. Ibid, p.134.
12. Major General Sir Edward Spears, *Two Men Who Saved France*, p.105.
13. Pierrefeu II, p.35.
14. Serrigny, p.136.
15. General Laure, *Le Commandement en chef des Armées Francaises du 15 Mai 1917 á l'Armistice*, p.44.
16. Marshal Philippe Pétain, Le Devoir des Elites dans la Défense Nationale, p.29.

CHAPTER 10

Leader to Catastrophe

General Erich Ludendorff

In her hour of crisis in the Great War, Britain chose as her leader a politician of flair, imagination, and proven record – Lloyd George. He ran the war through a small War Cabinet of civilian ministers. Except for the armed forces themselves, the British war effort was master-minded by civilians – ministers, civil servants, businessmen. France in her hour of crisis chose Clémenceau, a ruthless civilian leader in the ferocious tradition of the First French Republic. And except for a brief period in 1914–15, the French war effort, like the British, was directed and administered by civilians.

It was very different in the German Empire. In Germany's hour of crisis in 1916 at the height of the Battle of the Somme and the French counter-stroke at Verdun, with Romania a fresh enemy, Germany called on two soldiers to lead the nation in the pursuit of victory: the veteran Field Marshal Paul von Hindenburg (born in 1848) as Chief of the Great General Staff and imposing figurehead; and General Erich Ludendorff as the executive brain. On 20 August, 1916, Ludendorff took up his post as *'First* Quartermaster General': a title which he insisted on because he would not accept the correct title of *Second* Chief of the General Staff (that is, 'second' to Hindenburg as Chief).

Ludendorff personified the restless energy and surging power of the German Empire; he also personified its ugliness, crudity and fatal political unwisdom. Under his *pickelhaube*, bright, keen protuberant eyes stared out of a suety, pudgy face ornamented by a straight nose, a bristling moustache, a pursed mouth, and sometimes an eyeglass. His head was round, hair cut short and bristly, his brow high and broad; a beefy neck bulged into the uniform collar. Ludendorff stood tall and straight, but his sword belt sagged slightly round and beneath a heavy stomach. His manner, his entire personality, expressed restless ambition and impatience, and enormous appetite for action.

A painter told Frau Ludendorff: 'Your husband gives me cold shivers down my back.' And Frau Ludendorff comments: 'Even in his family we knew that grim countenance. They used to say, "Be Careful! Look out! Today Father looks like a glacier."'

But he had not always been so grim. According to Frau Ludendorff,

There was a time when Ludendorff could be cheerful and free from anxiety. His features did not always wear that look of unbending obstinacy, the expression of a man whose feelings had been turned to ice.[1]

Ludendorff was the son of a small landowner turned businessman, born in 1865 in Kruszcevnia in the province of Posnan, which, as the Slavic name implies, lay in territory long disputed between Prussia and Poland. As a child he had shone at mathematics, and at the age of twelve achieved such high marks in the entrance examination to a Cadet school that he was admitted two grades above his age group. He likewise passed out top of his class at the Military Academy at Lichterfelde. While still a pupil at the *Kriegsakademie* at the beginning of the 1890s, he was recommended for the General Staff, the first rung in a steady climb up the ladder of promotion. In 1904 he was posted to the Second Section of the General Staff, responsible for planning Germany's mobilisation and deployment: a key function. Promoted in charge of this section in 1908, he fought a bitter battle to persuade the German government and Reichstag to sanction a huge increase in the size of the army in accordance with the requirements of the Schlieffen Plan. In 1913 the Reichstag finally authorised only two new corps instead of the three he wanted, with no further increases until after 1916. And Ludendorff found himself posted to regimental duty in Düsseldorf, with the result that he would not be the Younger Moltke's Chief of the Operations Section of the General Staff in the event of war. How might the Battle of the Marne have gone with the furiously energetic and aggressive Ludendorff at the nervy Moltke's side?

On the outbreak of war, Ludendorff was posted as Deputy Chief of Staff to the Second Army, charged with the surprise attack on Liège, and then as chief of staff to the general directly responsible for the attack. He seized this opportunity to prove his powers of leadership in the field by taking personal command of a brigade's attempt to rush the Belgian defences, thrusting forward between Liège's ring of modern forts, and accepting the surrender of the old Citadel. Militarily this surrender meant little, but symbolically it meant much, especially to the German media, which reported that Ludendorff had captured Liège single-handed. And so, even before Germany had completed her mobilisation and the *aufmarsch* of her massed armies, Ludendorff had made his reputation.

War was indeed his element. As he wrote to his wife even before the first shots were fired at Liège: 'I am thirsting for a man's work to do, and it will be given me in full measure.'

* * *

By the third week of August 1914, the commander of the German Eighth Army in

East Prussia, von Prittwitz, had decided to abandon the province in the face of offensives by two Russian armies outnumbering him by twenty-two divisions to nine. This defeatism cost Prittwitz his command, he being replaced by Paul Beneckendorff und von Hindenburg as the new army commander and Erich Ludendorff, the hero of Liège, as his Chief of Staff. It marked the beginning of a legendary partnership between two leaders with entirely opposite personal qualities. Ludendorff supplied the brainpower and the driving energy, while Hindenburg - massive in character, perhaps not very clever – provided the psychological flywheel in the partnership, levelling out Ludendorff's emotional oscillations.

Their problem was this: with just over 200,000 men and 600 guns, the Eighth Army was under attack by the Russian general Rennenkampf's First Army of nearly 250,000 men and 800 guns, and Samsonov's Second Army of nearly 300,000 men and 780 guns: formidable odds indeed. Nevertheless, the Russian advances were badly co-ordinated, with a wide gap opening up between the two armies. Ludendorff's simple and daring plan was to leave only a single cavalry division to face Rennenkampf's army in the east of the province, and concentrate the overwhelming bulk of German strength against Samsonov, down in the south. It much aided the German command in their planning that they could read the radio signals foolishly transmitted *en clair* between the two Russian headquarters.

The German onslaught on 26 August 1914 struck Samsonov's shambling army completely by surprise and destroyed it in the Battle of Tannenberg: a victory that would pass into German legend. Then, on 7 September, Ludendorff in turn attacked Rennenkampf in the Battle of the Masurian Lakes, and inflicted a lesser but still smashing defeat on him. These stunning successes made the reputation of the Hindenburg-Ludendorff team – the more so in view of the concurrent debacle of the Schlieffen Plan in the Battle of the Marne.

Nonetheless, historians have since disputed as to whether it was Ludendorff or the head of the Eighth Army operations section, Max Hoffman, who was really responsible for the strategy that led to these crushing German victories in the East. The answer seems to be that both men read the map alike; and that by the time Ludendorff arrived in East Prussia with *his* ideas, Hoffman had already ordered the major redeployments wanted by Ludendorff. Yet the crucial operational decisions were taken by Ludendorff alone.

On 1 November 1914 the Hindenburg-Ludendorff partnership was appointed to a new headquarters responsible for all German operations on the Eastern Front. The sheer length of this front meant that neither side could deploy enough troops and guns to create another Western Front-style trench stalemate. Instead, thinly-held gaps existed in between the major deployments, so offering the opportunity to exploit such weak enemy sectors by swift re-groupings of strength and bold breakthroughs – exactly Ludendorff's *forte*. During the campaigns of 1915 and

1916, this was to be the repeated pattern of German success, even if not without the occasional setback because of ponderous but determined Russian counter-strokes.

These victories won by Hindenburg and Ludendorff on the Eastern Front made them the obvious choice in August 1916 for supreme command of Germany's war machine in succession to von Falkenhayn, the now discredited architect of the disastrous offensive at Verdun.

* * *

Ludendorff 'is a first-class man to work with. He is the right man for this business - ruthless and hard.' So had noted Colonel Max Hoffman in his diary when Ludendorff took over in East Prussia in 1914.[2] His energy was so tireless as to suggest that for him toil was an addictive drug. Yet there was another side to this energy – a nervous tension barely under control. At moments of crisis, Ludendorff was prone to attacks of anxiety that came close to panic, and manifested by the countermanding and re-countermanding of orders, and by outbursts of uncontrolled anger. He had first revealed such loss of nerve during ticklish moments in the Tannenberg operation, and again at Masurian Lakes. In October 1914, during a complicated battle in Poland when the Austrians were retreating in the face of a Russian offensive, Hoffman recorded in his diary that 'Ludendorff has become frightfully nervous, and the chief burden lies on me ...'[3] In late 1915, when the Eastern Front had become static after deep German advances, Ludendorff could hardly bear having nothing to do. In Hoffman's words, 'Ludendorff is getting bored and keeps everyone on the run from morning to night. This restlessness – work for work's sake – is extremely uncomfortable for everyone around here.'[4]

For all the sharpness of Ludendorff's mind, it was very much that of a narrow professional; far more narrow than, for instance, either Haig or Robertson. His views on political, economic, and social matters were naive to the point of childishness, and yet it was now his responsibility to act as the nation's de facto leader in such matters. In regard to Germany's war aims, he was an extreme annexationist, telling the then Reichschancellor in 1915, 'if Germany makes peace without profit she has lost the war'.[5]

In December 1917, after the armistice with the new Bolshevik Government of Russia, Ludendorff outlined a scheme for a German colonial and economic empire in Poland and Western Russia: a scheme largely enforced on the hapless Bolsheviks by the Treaty of Brest-Litovsk in January 1918, by which Russia lost a third of her population, half her industry, and nine-tenths of her coal mines. Yet the military price of enforcing this ruthless peace was that in the winter of 1917–18, Germany could not transfer as many divisions from Russia to the West as might have been possible with less draconic terms, consequently weakening Germany's last throw for victory on the Western Front in spring 1918. Moreover, Brest-Litovsk, by showing in brutal fact just what a German peace meant, only served to stiffen the resolve of the allies to fight on for complete victory.

Thus Ludendorff lacked all understanding of wise state policy and the relation of grand strategy to it. He himself (in a book in 1935) turned Clausewitz's dictum that war is the instrument of policy on its back by stating that 'War is the highest expression of the national will to live, and therefore politics must serve war-making'.[6]

His naive economic and industrial policies contributed in large measure to Germany's ultimate defeat. It is true that the predominance of the army in Germany's life was rooted in her history. It is also true that Ludendorff as supreme war lord had to cope with the problems arising from the institutional confusions of the German Empire, a partly federal and partly centralised state: problems exacerbated by all kinds of rival and overlapping departmental responsibilities. Nonetheless, the grand policy blunders were all his own.

The grandest of these were the so-called 'Hindenburg Programme' of industrial mobilisation adopted at the end of August 1916, and the 'Auxiliary Service Law' of December 1916, which at least on paper made every German adult in and out of uniform liable for war service in industry or elsewhere. Up to the summer of 1916, German industrial mobilisation for war, like the British, had been related to basic civilian needs and the economic life of the nation as a whole, as well as to financial resources available through war loans. The Hindenburg Programme threw overboard all such constraints. According to a historian of the German war economy, the programme demanded 'not as much as is attainable, but rather definite increases of production by a definite time and at any price'.[7] The same historian devastatingly indicts the follies of the Hindenburg Programme as a whole:

> the Supreme Command decided to dismiss all financial considerations and to embark upon a programme whose practical feasibility ... had never been seriously investigated. The deadline for the fulfilment of the program, May 1917, was based on purely military calculations. The production quotas for weapons were set in a purely ad hoc fashion without any regard for the state of the powder supply ... Where the War Ministry had emphasized the utilization of existing plant facilities in an effort to save raw materials and manpower, the Hindenburg Program required an extraordinary amount of new plant construction. The effort to balance the manpower needs of the army and the homeland were, at least for the moment, abandoned ... the Hindenburg Program, in short, was a gamble in which the nation's finances and resources were recklessly exposed to exhaustion on the basis of unfounded expectations ... It had very little to do with either sound military planning or rational economics.[8]

The Hindenburg Programme really marked the consummation of a marriage between Ludendorff's ignorant pig-headedness, and shrewd lobbying by industrialists who wanted to make fortunes out of unlimited expansion of armaments production. Interestingly enough, however, the inspiration for the new programme had been provided by Haig's offensive on the Somme, and its alarming demonstration of the enormous output of munitions now being achieved by British industry.

The Hindenburg Programme led to catastrophic long-term consequences. In order to carry it out, labour had to be released from the army, which meant that when the new production quotas for weapons were achieved by July 1917, there were no longer enough soldiers to man all the weapons. When the ambitious target for explosives production was finally achieved in July 1918, steel output was not large enough to fabricate shells and guns in the quantities needed to make full use of the explosives. And the earlier War Ministry munitions programme which Ludendorff threw out would in fact have been large enough to supply all the requirements of Germany's great offensives in 1918.

But the Hindenburg Programme was not only economically illiterate in itself, it also had grave side effects on the German economy and German life as a whole, by worsening the deprivations and miseries caused by the allied blockade, and finally by late-1918 bringing the German home front to virtual collapse. In contrast, when during the Second World War Britain similarly devoted the major part of her national economy to war production, she could still keep civilian life going at a tolerable level thanks to abundant *American* supplies of food, raw materials, and dollar finance through Lend Lease.

Ludendorff the soldier therefore proved a war-losing blunderer as the leader of the home front. But what of him as the mastermind of Germany's national policy and grand strategy? What of him as leader of her armed forces in battle?

*   *   *

When he took over as 'Second Quartermaster General' in August 1916 Ludendorff's great fear was that what he called 'Somme battles' would break out elsewhere, and that the German army might not be able to resist the sheer weight of allied firepower. In the winter of 1916–17 he therefore had the Siegfried Line ['Hindenburg Line' to the British] constructed some twenty miles behind the existing Somme front; much shorter in length, and with a zone of defences in great depth. To this line the German army retreated in March 1917. Such a defensive measure hardly constituted an effective means of winning the war. In fact, Ludendorff saw no hope of defeating the allied coalition – Britain, France, Russia, and Italy – in land warfare. On the contrary, Germany's defeat at the hands of overwhelmingly superior allied strength seemed inevitable. Since Ludendorff ruled out all thought of a compromise peace, which would have meant giving up

Alsace-Lorraine and abandoning his ambition to turn Belgium into a kind of German protectorate, he had to look for some other way out.

That way was suggested by the German navy and by assorted economists. The economists, just as glib and certain with their calculations as economists are today, predicted that if a certain tonnage of British shipping could be sunk every month for six months, Britain would be economically strangled, her people starving, and her industries idle for want of raw materials. She would be compelled to sue for peace. The German navy for its part asserted that the U-boat could achieve this tonnage providing they were allowed to sink all ships on sight (even if neutral) within designated zones. The drawback lay in that such unrestricted submarine warfare would almost inevitably bring America into the war.

Nonetheless, Ludendorff remained all in favour. He was convinced that long before the United States could began to ship her forces in quantity across the Atlantic, the U-boat would have brought Britain down and ended the war. So on 1 February 1917 Germany launched her unrestricted U-boat campaign. At first the calculations of German admirals and economists were borne out: the tonnage of shipping sunk rose from 470,000 in February to 837,000 in April; and the First Sea Lord, Admiral Sir John Jellicoe, warned the War Cabinet that Britain would not be able to go on with the war if such a rate of sinkings continued. But in May 1917 the British adopted the convoy system, which served to empty the seas of merchant ships sailing alone, hitherto the U-boat's plentiful prey. Now, when a U-boat did manage to locate and attack a convoy, it found itself hunted down by escorting warships equipped with acoustic under-water detection apparatus ('ASDIC') and lethal depth-charges.

By July 1917 the rate of sinkings had dropped back to 558,000 tons, and by September to only 351,000 tons. Germany had lost this first Battle of the Atlantic. And by now American troops were on their way to France in numbers that increased month by month, for on 1 April 1917 the United States, provoked by losses of her own merchant ships and those of other neutrals, had declared war on Germany. This was the catastrophic outcome of a U-boat campaign which had anyway failed.

The German resort to unrestricted U-boat warfare had marked the triumph of purely military considerations over national policy, just like the invasion of neutral Belgium in August 1914. Yet again Germany's leadership had ignored Clausewitz's warning that

[It] is a senseless proceeding to consult the soldiers concerning plans of war in such a way as to pass purely military judgements on what ministers have to do; and even more senseless is the demand of theoreticians that the accumulated war material should simply be handed over to the field commander so that he can draw up a purely military plan for the war or for a campaign.

Just as the 'purely military judgement' to invade Belgium on 4 August 1914 had provoked Britain into declaring war, so the 'purely military judgement' to launch unrestricted submarine warfare had similarly provoked the United States.

With the failure of the U-boat, Ludendorff's 'magic bullet' for winning the war in 1917, he had to ponder over the strategic balance-sheet again. On the credit side, Russia was down and out, with an armistice eventually signed with the Bolsheviks on 16 December, while a German-Austrian offensive had driven the Italian army back from the Isonzo front to the River Piave with a loss of some 200,000 in prisoners alone. Yet the debit side made grim reading. The morale of the hungry German home front was now beginning to crumble, thanks in large part to the Hindenburg Programme's impact on the economy. Germany's allies – Austria, Bulgaria, and Turkey – were nearly at the end of their tether. Even the German Army, the mighty engine of the war, was showing signs of wear. Haig's offensive at Ypres, so decried by later British critics, had taken a fearful toll on the defenders, as Ludendorff well recognised:

> The army had come victoriously through 1917; but it had become apparent that the holding of the western front could no longer be counted on, in view of the enormous quantity of material of all kinds which the Entente had at their disposal ... Against the weight of the enemy's material the troops no longer displayed their old stubbornness; they thought with horror of fresh defensive battles and longed for a war of movement.[9]

In fact, he put it even more strongly:

> In the west the army pined for the offensive, and after Russia's collapse, expected it with the utmost relief ... It amounted to a definite conviction which obsessed them utterly that nothing but an offensive could win the war.[10]

Ludendorff's reading of his soldiers' state of mind reinforced his own convictions and aggressive temperament:

> The condition of our allies and of our army all called for an offensive that would bring about an early decision. This was only possible on the Western Front ... The offensive is the most effective means of making war; it alone is decisive. Military history proves it on every page. It is the symbol of superiority.[11]

Germany's grand-strategic conundrum in late 1917 lay in that, just as in 1914, she was faced with a two-front war. But instead of enemies (France and Russia) separated in *space* as in 1914, she now had to deal with enemies separated in *time*. At the moment the tired French and British armies stood alone on the Western Front but, from the summer of 1918 onwards, they would be joined by an

American army of over a million fresh, unblooded men. This would spell certain defeat because Germany's own reserves of manpower would by then be exhausted. Ludendorff's answer to the conumdrum was that Germany must smash the British and French armies before the Americans could arrive in force. So he opted for yet another enormous strategic gamble – to invest all that Germany had left by way of manpower and *materiel* into a grand offensive on the Western Front in the spring of 1918.

Characteristically, this was a military solution within a political vacuum. For Ludendorff had no clearly defined political objective, but merely a vague aspiration:

> Germany could only make the enemy inclined to peace by fighting. It was first of all necessary to shake the position of Lloyd George and Clemenceau by a military victory. Before that peace was not to be thought of.[12]

The Chief of the Operations Section of OHL(*Obersteheeresleitung*, or Supreme Headquarters) later wrote that the political aim was to make the allies acknowledge that, even with American help, they had no chance of winning the war, and had therefore better accept German terms. However, even this statement of the aim fell a long way short of what Bismarck would have reckoned to be a well-defined political purpose for a military campaign.

So from November 1917 onwards Ludendorff and his military colleagues settled down to plan an absurdity: military success as an end in itself. And the result of their planning was in purely military terms a *tour de force* of organisation, training, use of massed artillery, and sheer tactical enterprise on the battlefield.

The same cannot, however, be said of Ludendorff's final strategic design for his great offensive. In the course of long meetings in November and December 1917 he and members of OHL staff, together with army group chiefs of staff, thrashed out the alternative strategic options. One was for an offensive (codenamed GEORGE) across the River Lys in Flanders to take Douglas Haig's main body in flank and rear, and drive into that area between Ypres and the sea which contained his sprawling logistic base. Even a short advance would place Haig's armies in jeopardy – which is why Haig himself came to believe that this was where the principal German blow would fall. A second option was to attack on both sides of Verdun, bringing about a wide collapse in the French line. The third or 'centre' option (codenamed MICHAEL) was an offensive from the Saint Quentin sector, driving west-north-west in the direction of the Channel coast. But Ludendorff found it hard to choose:

> As is always the case, there was a great deal to be said for and against each proposal ... Strategically the northern attack had the advantage of a great, though limited, objective. It might enable us to shorten our front if we

succeeded in capturing Calais and Boulogne. The attack on Verdun might also lead to an improvement in our front ... The Centre attack [MICHAEL] seemed to lack any definite limit. This could be remedied by directing the main effort on the area between Arras and Peronne, towards the coast. If this blow succeeded, the strategic result might be indeed enormous, as we should separate the bulk of the English army from the French and crowd it up with its back against the sea. I favoured the centre attack ...[13]

But two of Ludendorff's most able subordinates considered this operation to be beyond Germany's available strength. Like the Elder Moltke, they reckoned that strategy should be tailored to the size of the available forces; and hence they favoured either the Verdun or the Flanders option. Nevertheless, Ludendorff finally chose MICHAEL, the offensive north of the Somme towards the Channel coast.

Thanks to troops railed across from Russia in the course of the winter of 1917–18, the MICHAEL forces consisted of forty-seven specially trained 'Attack' divisions and nearly 7,000 guns. Thirty-three of these divisions were deployed on the front of the British Fifth Army, which had only fourteen divisions to defend forty-two miles of line, some of it dilapidated trenches recently taken over from the French. Haig, having been refused the reinforcements for which he had asked, had opted to deploy his main strength in Flanders in defence of his vulnerable base area between Ypres and the sea.

By the third week in March, preparations for MICHAEL were complete. Ludendorff did not intend to allow his army commanders to use their own operational initiative in fulfilling the overall strategic plan, but instead that he himself would, in his own words, 'exercise a far-reaching influence on the battle'.

The offensive (or 'Emperor's Battle', as it had been dubbed in flattery of the Kaiser) opened in the misty morning of 21 March 1918 with a five-hour hurricane bombardment mixing mustard and phosgene gas with high explosive. This bombardment completely dislocated command and control throughout the British Fifth Army, and shattered its front-line defences. Then, using new deep infiltration tactics, the three MICHAEL armies drove forward. The over-stretched and poorly dug-in Fifth Army front was swamped, and part of the Third Army's front too; and by the end of the day Ludendorff had achieved the first-ever mass breakthrough on the Western Front. He therefore now had at least a sporting chance of achieving his ambitious objective: the Channel coast, and the splitting apart of the British and French armies – 1940 in 1918.

Whether that chance could be seized would critically depend on Ludendorff's operational judgement and steadiness of leadership, because from that very first day the MICHAEL offensive lost its strategic balance. The two armies tasked with the main thrust towards the west and north-west, the Seventeenth (General von der Marwitz) and the Second (von Below), made only slow and costly progress in the face of a stout defence by the British Third Army. It was the army supposed to act as a southern flank guard, the Eighteenth (von Hutier) that achieved the sensational success of the day, breaking clean through the overstretched front of the British Fifth Army. Two days later, with Hutier driving the Fifth Army back in disorderly retreat, it had become clearer still that MICHAEL was succeeding on the wrong sector.

If Ludendorff had now decided to exploit Hutier's breakthrough by concentrating all three MICHAEL armies in a thrust to the westward, he might well have driven the British and French apart, for by that day, 23 March, Pétain was already looking to cover Paris and Haig was looking to cover the Channel ports. Yet instead Ludendorff gave his three attacking armies diverging thrust-lines: to the north-west, to the west, and to the south. By these incoherent orders he threw away whatever chance of a decisive victory he had ever had.

By 25 March, the right-flank MICHAEL army, the Seventeenth, had fought itself to a standstill; the centre army, the Second, had also failed to achieve the objectives laid down in Ludendorff's orders two days earlier. Only the left-flank-guard army, the Eighteenth, had made some further slow progress.

On 26 March, when the worst of the battlefield crisis was passing, the alarm among the allied leaderships caused by the German breakthrough reached its own climax, in a hastily convened conference between the French and British prime ministers, their chiefs of staff, and commanders-in-chief in the town hall of Doullens. At this conference it was decided to appoint General Ferdinand Foch, that fiery fighter, as Allied Supreme Commander with authority to issue strategic directives to Haig and Pétain. Foch's appointment was of more symbolic than functional significance at that moment, because Haig and Pétain were already re-grouping their armies to form a new front blocking the German advance. Yet it demonstrated that Ludendorff's great offensive, far from 'shaking the position of Lloyd George and Clemenceau' as he had hoped, actually succeeded in forging an even closer military and political alliance between Britain and France.

Now Ludendorff changed his mind once again: a new offensive was to be launched round Arras with the aim of breaking the British front in that sector, and so enabling the Seventeenth and Second Armies at long last to fulfil their own objective of reaching the Channel coast. Meanwhile, the Eighteenth Army was to revert to a flank guard. Ludendorff's new orders failed to solve his problems: the attack at Arras was repulsed with heavy loss, while the Seventeenth and Second Armies had now completely run out of puff. Only the Eighteenth Army was still going slowly forward.

Ludendorff reacted to these setbacks by losing both his nerve and his capacity for coherent thought, shouting down the telephone at an army group commander in a violent fit of rage, and ordering fresh unrealistic objectives for his armies. But his troops were now exhausted after a week of marching and fighting, incapable of making progress against an enemy front becoming ever more solid as allied reserves came up. Then, on 28 March, Ludendorff at long last specified one single clear objective – Amiens. He was too late. Even Hutier's Eighteenth Army could do little more; its attacks petered out at Villers Bretonneux just short of Amiens in the face of stout resistance by Australian and British troops.

So the supreme German effort for 1918 – the heaviest blow with the maximum number of divisions – had failed.

Yet this was a reality that Ludendorff could not accept. He gave orders for a new offensive, codenamed GEORGETTE, to be launched on 9 April across the river Lys and in the Armentières sector, with an axis of advance towards Hazebrouck, a key British communications centre. GEORGETTE had a front of some twenty miles compared with MICHAEL's fifty, and only twelve 'attack' divisions compared with forty-seven in MICHAEL. Nevertheless, Ludendorff achieved a local breakthrough when three Portuguese divisions under Haig's command gave way. Otherwise the attackers found themselves in an exhausting struggle against a tough and well-conducted defence. By the end of April, GEORGETTE had petered out five miles short of Hazebrouck: another failure.

Moreover, in a worrying omen of decline, Ludendorff's soldiers had lacked the keen attacking zest shown on 21 March:

Our troops had fought well; but the fact that certain divisions had obviously failed to show any inclination to attack gave food for thought ... the way in which the troops stopped round captured food supplies, while individuals stayed behind to search houses and farms for food, was a serious matter. This impaired our chances of success ... But it was equally serious that our young company commanders and our senior officers did not feel strong enough to take disciplinary action, and exercise enough authority to enable them to lead their men forward ...[14]

Yet even now Ludendorff continued to believe that he could inflict a final defeat on the British and French armies. By launching limited offensives on the Chemin des Dames and then on both sides of Reims, he would draw French reserves away from the Flanders front, and so prepare the way for a culminating blow against the British alone.

Along the Chemin des Dames on 27 May German assault troops swarmed through troops and defences shredded by another hurricane bombardment, surging over the River Aisne and advancing ten miles in the day. Ludendorff had now to decide whether to halt the offensive since it had fulfilled its limited purpose, or to drive on in order to turn tactical success into strategic victory.

It was a choice presented to a man whose nerves and mind were already stretched taut by the strain of command and repeated disappointment: a man constantly on the telephone to his subordinate commanders, interfering over detail, nagging, chasing, raging. Ludendorff was not showing up well as a leader under pressure. Now he snatched at the opportunity presented by the breakthrough on the Aisne, ordering his troops to drive on. This they did, reaching the River Marne near Château-Thierry some forty miles from the offensive's start-line.

But Ludendorff found himself now out-generalled by his French opponent, Pétain, who refused to allow his reserves (including two American divisions) to be drawn piecemeal into a fast-flowing battle, and instead installed them with plentiful artillery support on a stop-line extending from the eastern fringes of the forest of Villers-Cotterets, along the river Marne, and thence to Reims. On this line, Ludendorff's offensive faltered, stalled, and died. A limited attack on 9 June on the French front between Noyon and Montdidier had to be halted by Ludendorff while it was struggling to penetrate the enemy's main position.

By now, in Ludendorff's words, 'not only had our March superiority in the number of divisions been cancelled, but even the difference in gross numbers was now to our disadvantage, for an American division consists of twelve strong battalions [n.b: compared with nine weak ones in a German division].'[15]

These factors compelled Ludendorff to ask himself whether he should now go over to the defensive, as his army commanders and senior staff officers were urging. 'But I finally decided against this policy, because, quite apart from the bad influence it would have on our allies, I was afraid that the army would find defensive battles an even greater strain than an offensive ...'[16]

On 15 July 1918 Ludendorff launched an offensive by fifty divisions (the very last scraping-up of his reserves) on both sides of Reims with the aim of encircling the city and its garrison, and opening a wide breach in the French front. West of the city, two Italian divisions gave way, enabling the attackers to gain a bridgehead over the Marne four miles deep, but still far short of the deep exploitation called for by Ludendorff's plan. East of the city the German assault troops suffered a crushing defeat at the hands of a French defence in depth. Ludendorff's response to this failure to make better progress was to rage away on the telephone to the chief of staff of the army in question.

Despite the defeat of this last offensive against the French, Ludendorff was still determined to launch his long meditated stroke against Haig in Flanders (codenamed HAGEN). However, while he was in conference about HAGEN with army commanders and chiefs of staff, news came in of a massive French counter-stroke from the cover of the forest of Villers-Cotterets against the western flank of the salient hanging down to the Marne. The German line had collapsed, and by midday eighteen French divisions headed by swarms of Renault light tanks had advanced four miles, endangering all the troops within the salient.

The response of the supreme leader of Germany's armies to this shocking news was to lose all self-control, even to the extent of turning his rage on Field Marshal von Hindenburg before the astonished eyes of headquarters staff. The scene was recorded by a staff officer in his diary. Over lunch, Hindenburg proposed that the solution to the crisis lay in summoning all troops, including those from Flanders, and launching them in a counter-stroke from north of Soissons against the flank of the French attacking group:

> Then all of a sudden, General Ludendorff joined in the conversation. He declared that anything of that sort was utterly unfeasible and must therefore be forgotten, as he thought he had already made abundantly clear to the field marshal. The field marshal left the table without a word of reply, and General Ludendorff departed, clearly annoyed and scarlet in the face.[17]

The scene was replayed even more dramatically after dinner that night, when Hindenburg, fingers spread over the map, quietly but clearly said: 'This is how we must direct the counter-attack, that would solve the crisis at once.'

> At this, General Ludendorff straightened up from the map and, with an expression of rage on his face, turned towards the door, letting out one or two words like "madness!" in profound irritation. The field marshal followed his First Quartermaster-General and said to him ... "I should like a word with you."[18]

Next morning the chief of staff of the Fourth Army found Ludendorff 'in a really agitated and nervous state'. Worse still was Ludendorff's continuing paralysis of strategic decision, unable to make up his mind whether to abandon his cherished HAGEN project for an offensive in Flanders. That would mean, after all, accepting that his entire gamble for 1918 had failed, with all the far-reaching effects on the morale of the home front and the confidence of Germany's allies.

It was not Ludendorff but Haig who put an end to this paralysis by launching an offensive on the Somme on 8 August by nearly half a million British, French, Australian, and Canadian troops, and led by 420 tanks, smashing through the German defence and advancing four miles. In Ludendorff's retrospective judgement, this was 'the black day of the German army in the history of this war...'[19]

Yet the real significance of this 'black day' lay in that it confirmed the lesson of the French counter-stroke of 19 July that the strategic initiative had ineluctably passed from Germany to the allies.

References

1. Cited in Barnett, op. cit., p.271.
2. Cited in Barnett, op.cit., p.272.
3. Goodspeed, *Ludendorff*, p.106.

4. Ibid.,p.138.
5. Ibid., p.117.
6. Ibid., p.247.
7. Feldman, *Army, Industry, and Labour in Germany 1914-1918*, p.153.
8. Ibid., p.154.
9. Ibid., p.278.
10. Ibid., p.279.
11. Cited in ibid., p.278.
12. Cited in ibid., p.281.
13. Cited in ibid., p. 285.
14. Ludendorff, p.611.
15. Ibid., p.637.
16. Ibid., pp.639-40.
17. Colonel Merz von Quirnheim, *Diary*, cited in Foerster, *Der Feldherr Ludendorff in Ungluck*, pp. 18-19.
18. Ibid.
19. Ludendorff, p.679.

Napoleon Bonaparte: the romantic ideal of a leader, but in reality a gambler with an unsound system of war and statecraft which condemned him to ultimate failure. (Taylor Library)

Abraham Lincoln, President of the United States of America, 1860–65. As supreme leader in the Civil War, he combined political vision and strategic grasp with a resolve to save the Union by destroying the secessionist confederacy of slave-owning states. (Library of Congress)

General George B. McClellan, C-in-C of the Union Army in 1861–62. Although an able organizer and trainer of troops, he shrank from conducting a remorseless war of attrition, costly in blood, against the southern Confederacy. (Library of Congress)

General Robert E. Lee, commander of the Confederate Army of Northern Virginia 1861–65, and C-in-C of all Confederate forces in 1865. Noble in appearance and personality, the very image of a great leader, he proved an ineffective battlefield commander. (Library of Congress)

General Ulysses S. Grant, C-in-C of all the Union armies 1864–65. 'A man of a good deal of rough dignity,' recorded a colleague, 'rather taciturn; quick and decided in speech'. He wore Lee down into defeat by an unrelenting campaign of attrition. (Mathew Brady: Library of Congress)

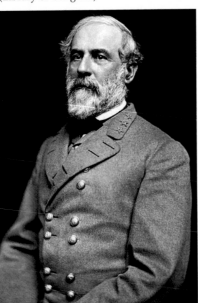

Field Marshal Helmuth Graf von Moltke, Chief of the Prussian (later German) General Staff 1857–88. His personal ascendancy sprang from a mastery both of strategic calculation and the logistical nuts-and-bolts of war in the field. (Public domain: UK)

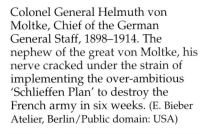

Napoleon III, Emperor of the French, Commander-in-Chief of the French armies in the war with Prussia in 1870, taken prisoner after the catastrophic defeat at Sedan. He was neither an able strategist nor a decisive leader: a Napoleon only in name. (Public domain: UK)

Colonel General Helmuth von Moltke, Chief of the German General Staff, 1898–1914. The nephew of the great von Moltke, his nerve cracked under the strain of implementing the over-ambitious 'Schlieffen Plan' to destroy the French army in six weeks. (E. Bieber Atelier, Berlin/Public domain: USA)

General (later Marshal) Joseph Joffre, French Chief of the General Staff and C-in-C, 1911–16. Unshaken by initial disasters in 1914, he finally wrecked the Schlieffen Plan by his well-timed counter-stroke on the Marne on 9–12 September 1914. (Public domain: UK)

David Lloyd George, Minister of Munitions 1915–16 and Prime Minister 1916–23. He looked for an easier way to defeat the German Empire than fighting her main army on the Western Front. His deviousness destroyed all trust between him and Haig. (Library of Congress)

General (later Marshal) Philippe Pétain. In 1916 he defended Verdun against ferocious German assault; and as C-in-C in 1917 restored army morale after widespread mutinies. He advocated 'bite-and-hold' offensives instead of attempts at breakthroughs. (Library of Congress)

Erich Ludendorff, First Quarter-Master General, and Germany's *de facto* supreme warlord from 1916 to 1918. Being a disastrous director of a war economy and a grand-strategic muddler, he was a major factor in his country's defeat in the Great War. (Library of Congress)

General (later Field Marshal) Sir Douglas Haig, C-in-C of the British armies in France, 1916–18. He believed that the war could only be won by defeating Germany's main army – on the Western Front. This he finally achieved in the campaign of 1918. (Library of Congress)

General (later Field Marshal) Erwin Rommel, commander of the German/Italian PanzerarmeeAfrika in the Western Desert, 1941–43. His renown as a leader in battle even captivated Winston Churchill, who paid public tribute to him as 'a great general'. (Bundesarchiv. Bild 101I-785-0287-08/Otto)

Admiral Isoruku Yamamoto, C-in-C of the Japanese fleet, 1939–43. He planned the air strike on Pearl Harbor on 7 December 1941, but recognized that this could only win time for Japan, and that America's superior national strength must eventually prevail. (US National Archives)

Air Chief Marshal (later Marshal of the Royal Air Force) Sir Arthur Harris, AOC-in-C Bomber Command, 1942–5. He relentlessly carried out political directives to cripple German industrial production by destroying the housing of the workforce. (HM Government/Public domain: UK)

General Sir William Slim (later Field Marshal Lord Slim). Known affectionately as 'Uncle Bill', he led the British Empire forces in Burma from defeat at the hands of the Japanese invaders in 1942 to the victorious re-conquest of the colony in 1945. (HM Government/Public domain: UK)

Admiral Sir Bertram Ramsay, Naval Commander Allied Expeditionary Force. He planned and commanded Operation NEPTUNE, the naval side of the Anglo-American landings in Normandy on D Day, 6 June 1944, the largest and most complex amphibious operation in history. (HM Government/Public domain: UK)

Marshal of the Soviet Union Georgi Zhukov. His ruthlessly tough leadership saved Moscow from the German invaders in 1941 and Stalingrad in 1942. His speciality lay in launching a well-timed offensive in massive strength against an overstretched enemy. (US National Archives)

General Dwight Eisenhower, Supreme Commander Allied Expeditionary Force. Though written off by Generals Brooke and Montgomery as a mere 'chairman of the board' he was superior to them in strategic judgement and in the conduct of large-scale operations. (US National Archives)

Adolf Hitler, *Der Führer* of the most formidable military and industrial power in continental Europe. He combined the personal magnetism of an evangelical preacher, the political ideas of an adolescent dreamer, and the managerial capabilities of a junior clerk. (US National Archives)

Winston Spencer Churchill, Prime Minister of the United Kingdom, 1940–45. A fighter by nature, and devoted to the cause of freedom and democracy, he found complete personal fulfilment in waging a victorious war against Hitler and the Nazi tyranny. (Yousuf Karsh/Library and Archives Canada/PA-165806)

CHAPTER 11

The Victor of 1918

Field Marshal Sir Douglas Haig

Despite the appointment of Foch as Allied Supreme Commander, the conduct of operations on the Western Front remained largely in the hands of the two national commanders-in-chief, Haig and Pétain. Being a good coalition general, Haig was careful to maintain a close professional relationship with Foch, who in the coming months was often persuaded to follow Haig's strategic advice. The British C-in-C carried the more weight because he commanded the most formidable allied army on the Western Front – much larger and far more experienced than the American Expeditionary Force under General John Pershing; and in better combat shape than a French army still convalescing after its moral crisis in 1917. It is a fact that, during the allied counter-offensives from July 1918 to the armistice of 11 November, Haig's British-Empire army was to take almost as many prisoners as the French, Belgian, and American armies put together.[1] For these reasons the final campaign on the Western Front can be fairly regarded as a contest of leadership between Haig, the imperturbable Lowland Scot, and Ludendorff, the highly-strung Prussian. In this contest, Haig quickly asserted a dominance of will which he was never to lose.

*   *   *

At 0420 hours on 8 August 1918 a hurricane bombardment by over 2,000 British guns and howitzers smashed down on the German front astride the River Somme just east of Amiens. But this 'Second Battle of the Somme' was very different from the disastrous opening day of the First Battle of the Somme on 1 July 1916. This time there was no ponderous fortnight-long preliminary bombardment, but instead a sudden destructive avalanche of fire that took the enemy by surprise. There was no slow and rigid advance by infantry as in 1916, but instead a battering ram of 342 heavy tanks and seventy-two of the new light Whippets rolling forward behind a creeping barrage, followed by an assault by fifteen Australian, Canadian, British, and American divisions, and three cavalry divisions – nearly 450,000 men in all. Overhead, the Royal Air Force (now the largest in the world) strafed all that moved on or behind the German front. As the tanks reared, loomed, and lumbered through the smoke and morning mist, enemy resistance collapsed. Cavalry (still the only means of rapid cross-country movement) rounded up demoralised German infantry, while Whippet tanks even surprised a corps staff at lunch. In that single day, Haig's troops inflicted losses of more than 27,000 in killed, wounded, and prisoners, and advanced four miles.

Ludendorff would record later that 8 August 1918 'was the black day of the German Army in the history of this war'. When divisional commanders reported to Ludendorff after the battle, he was told

> of behaviour which I had not thought possible in the German Army. Whole bodies of our men had surrendered to single troopers or isolated squadrons of cavalry. Retiring troops, meeting fresh divisions going bravely into action had shouted things like 'Blackleg' and 'You're prolonging the war'.[2]

This first devastating counter-stroke by Haig, coming so soon after the French offensive on 18 July, was enough further to buckle Ludendorff's nerve. In Ludendorff's own later words,

> The 8th of August put the decline of [our] fighting powers beyond all doubt, and in such a situation as regard reserves, I had no hope of finding a strategic expedient whereby to turn the situation to our advantage.[3]

On 10 August, he reported in this same tone of desperation to the Kaiser, whose response was equally bleak: 'I see we must balance the books, we are at the limit of our powers. The War must be brought to an end.'[4]

On 14 August, the Kaiser presided over a conference at OHL in Spa to examine what to do next. It ended in a decision to open up peace negotiations via Queen Wilhelmina of the Netherlands. Yet, typical of the incoherence of top German leadership, no peace formula was hammered out, and no timing agreed on. So no peace initiative followed – only drift. It would be the Allied armies, striking relentlessly home, who would decide Germany's policy for her.

* * *

The Second Battle of the Somme demonstrated how well the British armies in France and Flanders (from infantry section up to army command) had mastered their professional business since their debut in 1915-16. This mastery owed much to Haig's personal sponsorship of training programmes and of the systematic study of the lessons to be learned from current operations.

Yet the 8th of August and the subsequent advance to final victory demonstrated that Haig too had learned his lessons. In contrast to 1916 and 1917, he no longer thought in terms of a single grand breakthrough of the enemy front and a sweeping strategic exploitation. Nor did he mean to keep on attacking along one axis of advance as on the Somme and at Third Ypres. Instead, he would strike a succession of blows up and down the line. This strategy was adopted by Foch for all the allied armies. It greatly helped that Ludendorff's failed offensives had left the German front stretched out in bag-shaped salients vulnerable to such attacks.

In the aftermath of 8 August, Foch (now a Maréchal de France as well as Allied Supreme Commander) urged Haig to attack again on the Somme front on 16 August. But Haig, after consulting Rawlinson (Fourth Army commander) decided to postpone the operation because the enemy had now consolidated their defence again – whereupon Foch peremptorily called on Haig to carry out the attack. The British Commander-in-Chief refused to alter his decision, and on 14 August visited Foch in his HQ château to make clear to him, in Haig's words, that 'I was responsible to my Government and fellow citizens for the handling of the British forces'. In the event, Foch was genuinely persuaded by Haig's argument that it would better to strike later and on a fresh front further north.

On 21 August, therefore, the Third Army attacked between Arras and Albert, winning a limited success – limited because of the caution and rigidity of the battle plan. Disappointed, Haig signalled his army commanders:

> Risks which a month ago would have been criminal to incur ought now to be incurred as a duty. It is no longer necessary to advance in regular lines and step by step. On the contrary each division should be given a distant objective which must be reached independently of its neighbours.[5]

On 23 August the Third Army took Albert; the Fourth Army joined the offensive, widening the front of attack to thirty-five miles. In blazing summer heat, Haig's troops swept over the old Somme battlefield in the course of a single weekend. On 26 August, Haig launched the First Army to the attack on the River Scarpe. On 29 August, Bapaume fell to the New Zealand Division; on the 31st the Australian Corps took the powerful German bastion of Mont-Saint-Quentin near Peronne. The French army took Noyon.

According to the Bavarian official history, 'the German front ached and groaned in every joint under the unceasing blows delivered with ever fresh and greater force':

> The German divisions just melted away. Reinforcements, in spite of demands and entreaties, were not forthcoming. Only by breaking up divisions [10 in August alone] could the gap be more or less filled. The general and continuing crisis made it impossible to afford units the necessary rest and relief. In the circumstances, the troops deteriorated both spiritually and physically.[6]

On 2 September, Crown Prince Rupprecht of Bavaria, on returning to the front from sick leave, wrote in his diary that in Nuremberg,

> the inscription on a troop train was 'Slaughter cattle for Wilhelm & Sons'. Public feeling, for that matter, is not only very bad in Bavaria, but also in North Germany.[7]

Only next day a secret order by Ludendorff confirmed this grim judgement:

> An increase has recently taken place in the number of complaints received from home that men on leave from the front create a very unfavourable impression by making statements actually bordering on high treason and incitement to disobedience ... Instances such as these have a disastrous effect upon the morale of the people at home.[8]

Yet the defeats of August cruelly exposed Ludendorff's own fragility of morale. Even during his own MICHAEL offensive, he had displayed a lack of strategic realism coupled with twitchy prodding of subordinate commanders. The shock of the first allied counter-stroke on 18 July had reduced him to 'a really agitated and nervous state', according to a visiting army group chief of staff, while one of his own staff had cheerfully recorded in his diary: 'His excellency quite broken'. According to the same diarist, another visiting chief of staff had been

> very much disturbed by the appearance and nervousness of His Excellency. It really does give the impression that His Excellency has lost all confidence. The army chiefs are suffering terribly as a result of it. Hence telephone conversations lasting one and a half hours on the day's agenda.[9]

Now in August, Ludendorff reacted to the cumulative bad news from the front by explosions of rage instead of cool thinking; by the countermanding and re-countermanding of orders instead of consistent leadership; and by a stubborn refusal to sanction timely retreats. This was a man whose nerves were wound taut to snapping point.

And the month of September was to try Ludendorff even harder. On the 12th, the first all-American offensive of the war pinched out the salient of Saint Mihiel, east of Verdun, taking 15,000 German prisoners and 460 guns. Twelve days later, the German defence in depth in the tangled woodland of the Argonne was attacked by the United States First Army and the French Fourth Army. Although the German defenders inflicted heavy losses on the inexperienced Americans, they eventually lost a commanding height and 18,000 men taken prisoner.

On 28 September Haig attacked at Ypres, and in four days of fighting his troops drove the enemy back five miles and captured some 10,000 prisoners and 300 guns.

By this time Ludendorff had belatedly withdrawn his forces along the Somme-Aisne front into the Hindenburg (or Siegfried) Line, a ten-miles-deep maze of entrenchments, concrete bunkers, and barbed wire, divided into a forward (or delaying) position, a main battle position, and a rear position. On 27 September, Haig opened his attack on the Hindenburg Line with a hurricane bombardment and an advance by the Canadian Corps led by sixteen tanks. After two days of fighting the Canadians had won a lodgement six miles deep and twelve wide. On the 29th, the strongest sector of the Hindenburg Line (on the Canal du Nord) was breached by a British Territorial Division, the 46th Midland.

By now Ludendorff's nerve was completely shredded. According to some witnesses, the stress of cumulative bad news even caused him a temporary fit of hysterical paralysis. On 29 September (it was the day that Germany's ally Bulgaria signed an armistice), there took place a panic-stricken conference of top German leaders, at which an overwrought Ludendorff demanded an immediate armistice.

During the following days, disaster on the battlefield alternated with political crisis back at home. On 2 October Hindenburg and Ludendorff sent a staff officer to Berlin to tell a consternated Reichstag that 'each new day brings the enemy nearer his goal, and makes him less ready to conclude a reasonable peace with us. We must accordingly lose no time. Every 24 hours that pass may make our position worse.' Two days later, the new Imperial Chancellor, Prince Max of Baden, a prominent liberal, sent a message to President Woodrow Wilson asking for an armistice on the basis of Wilson's 'Fourteen Points', an idealistic programme for a peace settlement.

On 24 October, in a final act of folly, Ludendorff sent out a signal over Hindenburg's name, 'For the Information of All Troops', which stated that new and harsher terms from President Wilson 'is a demand for unconditional surrender. It is thus unacceptable to us soldiers'. This was too much for the Reichstag and the Court. On 26 October, Hindenburg and Ludendorff, the two architects of Germany's national defeat, were called for interview by the Kaiser in the Berliner Schloss. Both men offered their resignations, but only Ludendorff's was accepted. The interview marked, wrote Ludendorff in his memoirs, 'some of the bitterest moments of my life'.[10]

Meanwhile Douglas Haig was riding success as if it were a charger. Every passing week had made him the more certain that 1918 would see the final defeat of the German army, and an end to the war.[11]

On 5 October his Australian, New Zealand, Canadian, and British divisions swept through the remainder of the Hindenburg Line. By now the average strength of a German battalion was down to 545 men – perhaps 250 rifles. On 17 October, Haig's troops occupied Lille and Douai, abandoned by the enemy. That same day, the British Fourth Army attacked German positions along the River Selle, and in three days' fighting took 5,000 prisoners and sixty guns. On 19 October Courtrai and Bruges fell to advancing British troops and the enemy evacuated the entire Belgian coastline.

Only the Armistice of 11 November saved the German army on the Western Front from final rout and disintegration. Crown Prince Rupprecht of Bavaria had reported to the Imperial Chancellor in late October that a division could only be reckoned as the equivalent of one or two battalions; that there was a severe shortage of artillery; and that in some armies 50 per cent of the guns were without horses. Rupprecht continued:

> The morale of the troops has suffered severely and their power of resistance diminishes daily. They surrender in hordes whenever the enemy attacks, and thousands of plunderers infest our base areas. We have no more prepared positions, and no more can be dug ... We cannot sustain a serious attack, owing to a lack of all reserves.

'Whatever happens,' he went on, 'we must obtain peace before the enemy breaks into Germany; if he does, woe on us!'[12]

In terms of sheer scale, the German army on the Western Front suffered in 1918 the worst military defeat in history so far.

And in bringing about that defeat, the soldiers of the British Empire under the leadership of Field Marshal Sir Douglas Haig had played a far larger part than any other allied army. Between August and November they had taken 188,700 prisoners as against 196,070 by the French, American, and Belgian armies put together. They had captured 2,840 guns as against 3,775 by all the rest of the allied armies.

It is an achievement which Haig's critics seem not to have noticed.

*   *   *

The defeat of the German field army on the Western Front acted as the demolition charge that brought down the whole structure of the German Empire. On 29 September, Ludendorff had demanded that his government sue for an immediate armistice. On 4 October, the new Reichschancellor, Prince Max of Baden, duly approached President Wilson. On 3 November, the High Sea Fleet at Kiel mutinied rather than make a sortie against the British Grand Fleet. On 5 November, Ludendorff's successor, General Wilhelm Groener, reported that 'We can hold out long enough for negotiations. If we are lucky, the time might be longer; if we are unlucky, shorter ...'

By now the German home front, dismayed by grim news from the Front and demoralised by hunger, was crumbling too. In Berlin, where the Kaiser's grenadiers had once goose-stepped brilliantly by, shabby mobs ranged about. On 9 November, while armistice negotiations were in progress at Compiègne,

Spartacists (German Communists) seized the imperial palace in Berlin and proclaimed a soviet republic. Their rivals, the Social Democrats, retorted by proclaiming a socialist republic from the steps of the Reichstag. Next morning the Kaiser abdicated and fled to Holland. At 0500 on the 11th the hapless German delegates signed the armistice terms; and at 1100 the guns ceased fire.

References

1. The British took 188,700 prisoners, as against 196,070 by the French, Belgians and Americans together.
2. Ludendorff, p.683.
3. Ibid, p.684.
4. Niemann, *Kaiser und Revolution*, cited in Barnett, p.253.
5. Cited in Marshall-Cornwall, p.282.
6. Cited in John Terraine, *To Win a War: 1918 The Year of Victory*, p.130.
7. Diary, cited in *Military Operations France and Belgium 1918 Vol IV*, p.414.
8. Cited in Terraine, op.cit., pp.148–9.
9. von Quirnheim, Diary, cited in Barnett, op.cit., p.338.
10. Cited in Barnett, op. cit., p.357.
11. It says much for the strategic sagacity of Lloyd George and Henry Wilson (the CIGS) that they were planning for a 1919 campaign.
12. Diary, cited in Terraine, op.cit., pp.206–7.

PART III:

The Second World War 1939–1945

CHAPTER 12

Leader from the Front

Generalfeldmarschall Erwin Rommel

On 12 February 1941, Lieutenant General Rommel arrived in Tripoli, the capital of the Italian colony of Libya, to take command of the newly arriving *Deutsches Afrika Korps* and then, if it were possible, save Tripolitania from the British Western Desert Force, which five days earlier had cut off and destroyed the Italian Tenth Army (Marshal Graziani) in the battle of Beda Fomm, south of Benghazi. Rommel had to put fresh heart into the beaten Italians; he had to organise his German troops as they arrived piecemeal; and do so in desperate haste. And he himself, like his troops, was a novice at desert campaigning.

His operational assessment was grim enough:

> On 8th February, leading troops of the British army occupied El Agheila [on the border between Cyrenaica and Tripolitania]... Graziani's army had virtually ceased to exist. All that remained of it were a few lorry columns and hordes of unarmed soldiers in full flight to the west. If Wavell [C-in-C Middle East] had now continued his advance into Tripolitania no resistance worthy of the name could be mounted against him.[1]

This was exactly the judgement made by Wavell himself and Major General Richard O'Connor, commander of Western Desert Force.

Had Western Desert Force now advanced to Tripoli, there would have been no desert tournament between opposing armoured armies lasting two years, and Erwin Rommel would not have become the legendary champion of that tournament. Fortunately for him, however, Winston Churchill ordered Wavell and O'Connor to halt their advance, and despatch their battle-hardened formations to Greece in a foredoomed attempt to save that country from a German invasion in overwhelming strength. In the desert, Wavell could only stand on the defensive.

Nonetheless, it was his judgement that Rommel could not be ready to attack until mid-April 1941 at the earliest. He was therefore content to entrust the defence of Cyrenaica to an untried general (Philip Neame) commanding a hastily assembled force consisting of a brigade group of Australian infantry and a single poorly-equipped armoured brigade new to the desert. But Wavell had utterly misjudged his opponent. On 31 March, Rommel in person led his *Afrika Korps* forward in his first desert offensive.

This development came as much a surprise to the German high command as it did to Wavell, because they had simply expected Rommel to organise a defence against a British advance on Tripoli. As Rommel put it in a letter to his wife in Germany:

> Dearest Lu; we've been attacking with dazzling success. There'll be consternation among our masters in Tripoli and Rome, perhaps in Berlin too. I took the risk against all orders and instructions because the opportunity seemed favourable.[2]

Like a boxer fast on his feet and quick to exploit his opponent's mistakes by swift and devastating punches, Rommel hounded the ill-coordinated, slow-reacting British defenders of Cyrenaica back in disorder. Such was his headlong speed of advance that his troops even captured the opposing commander, General Neame, and with him General O'Connor, who had been sent up from sick leave in Egypt to 'advise' Neame. With O'Connor's capture, the British Middle East Command lost the one general who would have been capable of matching Rommel in boldness and unorthodox manoeuvre: a major calamity with far-reaching effects on the course of the campaign.

By mid-April Rommel had isolated the fortress of Tobruk and put it and its Australian garrison under close siege, meanwhile advancing to the Egyptian frontier. In this debut as a desert general he had not only saved Tripoli from imminent danger, but also inflicted a sensational defeat on the forces of the British Empire, wiping out all the gains of O'Connor's victories during the winter of 1940–41. And he had made a personal reputation as a leader constantly on the move with his forward troops. In newsreels and press photographs he presented the very image of a panzer general: rugged features beneath a be-goggled uniform cap, a checked cotton scarf tucked into an open-necked shirt, and the Iron Cross and the *Pour le Mérite* medal pinned to his breast. On the soldiers of the British Army as well as on his own soldiers, Erwin Rommel was already casting a leader's spell.

* * *

Rommel was born in 1891 in Heidenheim, Wurttemberg, far from the bleak north German plain that was the home of Prussian militarism. Nor was there any military tradition in his family, for his father and grandfather were both schoolmasters. He grew up as one of five children, and as a young pupil at the local grammar school was a dreamy and indolent boy without much interest in either games or books. Yet adolescence triggered a complete change of temperament. He began to display his future characteristics as a soldier: practical ingenuity, intense enthusiasm; delight in physical prowess. He became a keen skier and cyclist, later graduating to motorcycles, which he immediately took to pieces to find out how they worked. This being the era of the Wright Brothers and Blériot, Rommel and friends built their own full-size glider, although in the event they never got it off the ground. His fascination with flight inspired him to think of a career as an engineer with the Zeppelin airship company but, in July 1910, faced with his father's opposition to this idea, Rommel instead enlisted in the Wurttemberg army. Yet all through his military life he was to display the characteristics of an engineer: a fascination with solving practical problems; an urge to supervise operations on site rather than from a desk, especially when a job seemed to be going wrong.

In the German Empire created by Bismarck, each federal state like Wurttemberg retained its own distinct army within the imperial whole. Nevertheless, it was the army of Prussia, the largest state within the Empire, and led by the *junker* gentry, which dominated the rest. Rommel, middle-class and in the Wurttemberg service, was thus doubly an outsider. Like his future adversary, Bernard Montgomery, he devoted himself as a young officer to mastering his profession. Since he scorned the evening delights of garrison towns in favour of study, and neither smoked nor drank, it is not surprising that his fellow subalterns found him altogether too serious.

While he was a student at the war academy in Danzig in 1911, he met his future wife, Lucie Maria Mollin. Theirs was to be the closest and most affectionate of relationships: throughout his campaigns Rommel would write to her almost every night, his letters revealing a man his subordinates and soldiers never knew. Being a born warrior, resourceful, aggressive, indifferent to danger and hardship, he relished his frontline service in the Great War of 1914–18, first in France and later in Romania and Italy. During the German and Austrian breakthrough of the Italian front at Caporetto in 1917, Rommel, in temporary command of six companies of infantry, penetrated twelve miles deep into the Italian defence system, captured a tactically important hill, and took 9,000 prisoners. For this exploit he was awarded the *Pour Le Mérite*, Germany's highest military decoration.

After the war he faced professional stagnation in an army limited by the Versailles Treaty to 100,000 officers and men, and in any case dominated by the Prussian élite. Yet, thanks to his distinguished record as a front-line soldier as well as his sheer professional merit and zeal, he gradually climbed the ranks. His standing within the officer corps was enhanced by his lectures as an instructor at the Infantry School at Dresden in 1929–33, emphasising boldness, bluff, and manoeuvre, as well as by the publication of his manual on tactics, *Infanterie Greift An* (*Infantry Strikes Home*), based on his Italian experiences.

Rommel met Hitler for the first time in 1935, when the Führer came to inspect his battalion of mountain troops. Like all German officers at the time, Rommel regarded Hitler as a well-meaning patriot who had thrown off the restrictions of the Versailles Treaty on the size of the army, and restored Germany's standing in the world. As a career soldier concerned with immediate professional matters, Rommel was not pondering deeply on wider political or moral issues. Yet the day of Hitler's inspection of his battalion provides a foretaste of the ambiguous relationship that would exist in wartime between the soldier and the tyrant. When Hitler's black-uniformed SS life-guard tried to line up in front of Rommel's own soldiers, Rommel refused to present his battalion for inspection until the SS were moved – which they duly were.

In this same year of 1935, Germany created her first three panzer divisions, embodying the new concept of fast-moving tank warfare advocated by German thinkers like von Manstein and British theorists like J. F. C. Fuller and Basil Liddell Hart. But when the Second World War broke out in September 1939, Rommel was not serving with a panzer division, but as commander of the Führer's personal escort battalion. He owed this appointment to Hitler's own request the year before, the Führer having been deeply impressed with *Infanterie Greift An*. It may also have helped that Rommel was not the kind of Prussian military aristocrat who made the jumped-up Hitler feel uneasy.

By now Rommel had matured his own philosophy of personal leadership, telling cadets at a military academy in 1938:

> Be an example to your men, both in your duty and your private life. Never spare yourself in your endurance of fatigue and privation, and let your troops see that you don't.

When, on 10 May 1940, Hitler launched 137 divisions in a blitzkrieg against France, Belgium, and the Netherlands, Rommel was commanding the 7th Panzer Division in the northernmost of two panzer corps charged with the crucial task of smashing the French front on the River Meuse, and then scything a way through to the English Channel in order to cut off the Allied Northern Army Group. This marked Rommel's debut as a commander of a major formation in war, and he embraced the opportunity with positively boyish enthusiasm. When the attempt of his assault troops on 13 May to cross the Meuse in inflatable rubber boats was repulsed by the enemy, Rommel himself went forward to take command, organising a pontoon ferry for his tanks and crossing the river in the first wave of assault craft, and then personally directing the breakout from the initial bridgehead. By nightfall on the 14th he had smashed his way into open country. He was utterly absorbed by battle, completely happy, writing to his wife:

> Dearest Lu: Everything wonderful so far. Am way ahead of my neighbours. I'm completely hoarse from orders and shouting. Have had three hours' sleep ...[3]

After only five days of battle, Rommel and his fellow panzer commanders had smashed a sixty-mile-wide gap in the allied front and were riding for the sea. He took a simple pleasure in his burgeoning fame as commander of the 7th Panzer Division (dubbed 'the Ghost' by German media because of the speed of its advances), and he asked his wife to 'cut out all the newspaper articles about me, please. I've no time to read at the moment, but it will be fun to look at them later'.[4]

On 20 May the neighbouring panzer corps reached the English Channel at Abbeville, so isolating the Allied Northern Army Group (including the British Expeditionary Force). Yet on this same day a small British force of tanks and infantry launched a short-lived local counterstroke southwards into Rommel's flank near Arras. Though Rommel easily blocked this attack, it shook the nerve of the German command all the way up to Hitler himself, who already feared that the panzer spearheads might be cut off and crushed by a massive allied counterstroke. The panzers were therefore halted for three days in order to give time for the supporting infantry divisions to come up. This delay made possible the allied retreat to Dunkirk and the evacuation to England of over 338,000 troops, including the bulk of the BEF.

On 5 June 1940 the Germans launched the second phase of the blitzkrieg: a general offensive across the Somme and the Aisne by 104 divisions against forty-nine French divisions and just a single British. In a fresh display of personal leadership and tactical opportunism, Rommel conducted his tanks across an unguarded railway bridge over the Somme, catching the enemy unawares. In two days Rommel was through the feeble allied defence and thrusting towards Rouen at up to forty-five miles a day. On 10 June his 7th Panzer Division reached the English Channel at St Valéry-en-Caux, trapping a French army corps and the British 51st (Highland) Division. Exultantly he wrote to his wife:

> The battle is over here. Today one corps commander and four divisional commanders presented themselves before me in the market square of St Valery, having been forced by me to surrender. Wonderful moment![5]

Barely six days later, Rommel ended his campaign by capturing the major port of Cherbourg, having advanced 150 miles in a single day. On 22 June the French Government led by Marshal Pétain signed an armistice. Germany's great enemy of 1914–18 was down after just six weeks of fighting.

Rommel's record as a panzer leader during this astonishing campaign had made him a clear choice for command of the new *Deutsches Afrika Korps*: a choice soon vindicated by his rout of the troops of Cyrenaica Command in March and April 1941. Just the same, this success only concluded the first act of a two-year-long campaign.

* * *

The Western Desert is a vast wasteland of gravel and thorny scrub stretching from the Nile delta in Egypt (Britain's main base in the Middle East) right across Cyrenaica (then a province of the Italian colony of Libya). The only metalled road hugged the coast, linking a string of ports like Mersa Matruh, Tobruk, and Benghazi. Only in the Jebel Achdar ('the green mountains') south of Benghazi was there a fertile countryside. The Desert therefore provided a perfect arena in which mechanised armies could manoeuvre against each other without encumbrance. It was war in its purest form, with the pendulum of fortune swinging between the *Afrika Korps* and the Eighth Army (created in September 1941). In November and December, the Eighth Army launched its first major offensive: the aim to lift the siege of Tobruk, bring Rommel's armour to battle, and destroy it. In the event, the British advance became bogged down in a sprawling tank battle in the desert between the Egyptian frontier and Tobruk. At a critical moment, Rommel took his panzers off on a foray deep into the British rear in the hope of panicking General Sir Claude Auchinleck, the C-in-C Middle East, into retreat. The foray achieved nothing, for Auchinleck, far from being panicked, was resolutely driving the Eighth Army on towards Tobruk. Although Rommel won a tactical success against the British armour after his return to the main battlefield, his *Panzergruppe* had now fought itself out, with its tank strength down from 250 to thirty. On 8 December he ordered a retirement to El Agheila on the border between Cyrenaica and Tripolitania, which he reached on 5/6 January 1942.

Rommel's conduct of the 'Sidi Rezegh battles' (as they became known in British annals) had displayed him at his best as a leader at the head of his panzer troops and at his worst as the overall director of large and complex operations. He had indeed suffered a major defeat, placing Tripolitania yet again in danger of a renewed British westwards advance.

However, just as Churchill had saved Rommel in March 1941 by stripping Wavell of his best troops and sending them to Greece, so now he saved Rommel again by diverting troopships with two divisions intended for Auchinleck on to Singapore, now under threat from a Japanese advance through Malaya. Auchinleck's loss of strength went on: 6th and 7th Australian Divisions were despatched to the Far East along with an armoured brigade group. The forward defence of Cyrenaica was now entrusted to 1st Armoured Division, as yet untried in battle, with four infantry divisions and the 7th Armoured Division lying back in reserve.

In the evening of 21 January 1942 Rommel, leading one of his battlegroups in person, began one of his most brilliant displays of military agility and opportunism, repeatedly switching the axis of his advance to the bemusement of a slow-thinking British command and thus defeating the Eighth Army in detail. After routing and scattering the 1st Armoured Division, he captured Benghazi on 29 January, along with a huge treasure-trove of stores and fuel. Six days later the campaign came to rest in a fresh equilibrium when a re-grouped and reinforced Eighth Army stood fast in a prepared defensive position at Gazala (east of the Jebel Achdar), and Rommel's supply line by motor transport had been stretched to its limit.

It was time for both sides to ponder their future strategy.

* * *

Since his arrival in North Africa in February 1941, Rommel had been compelled to work within the frustrating constraints of a joint Italo-German chain of command. He was nominally a subordinate of Marshal Bastico (nicknamed 'BOM-Bastico by German officers) and through him to the Italian high command (meaning Mussolini) and the German high command (meaning ultimately Hitler). It had proved a wearying business trying to agree a common operational strategy. Moreover, Rommel was wholly dependent for supplies and reinforcements on Italian merchant shipping and oil-tankers sailing from Italian ports, and escorted by the Italian navy. Hence his campaign lay at the mercy of the competence and zeal of Italian authorities. It is no wonder, then, that his signals traffic with Rome was often thick with pleas for urgently needed stores, kit, and fuel – and especially when the Royal Navy's surface ships and submarines were disrupting trans-Mediterranean traffic from Italy to Libya.

It did not help Rommel in contending with these problems that he was a poor coalition general, unable to conceal his impatience with, even contempt for, the professional shortcomings of the Italian army and its officers.

In regard to grand strategy, Rommel fundamentally differed from his own supreme command – above all, Hitler. As he wrote later:

> They failed to see the importance of the African theatre. They did not realise that with relatively small means we could have won victories in the Near East which in their strategic and economic value, would have far surpassed the conquest of the Don Basin. Ahead of us lay territories containing an enormous wealth of raw materials, which could have freed us from all our anxieties about oil.[6]

Such a strategy would also destroy British dominance of the Middle East, and permanently sever the imperial lifeline between the United Kingdom and India. However, Rommel failed to comprehend that Hitler's obsession with the war with the Soviet Union was less inspired by strategic or economic considerations than by sheer ideology: hatred of 'Jewish' bolshevism; the vision of *Lebensraum* for the German *volk*, meaning an empire of subject peoples extending to the Urals. For Hitler, and indeed the German high command (schooled as they were in Continental warfare), the Mediterranean theatre, and Rommel's campaign, were never more than a sideshow.

Yet for Churchill and General Sir Alan Brooke (Chief of the Imperial General

Staff) the contrary was true. The Mediterranean and Middle East had been the focus of Britain's war against the Axis powers ever since the French alliance had fallen apart in June 1940. In particular, the extinction of the Western Front meant that the North African Desert offered the only place where the land forces of the British Empire could engage Axis armies in battle.

In consequence, the ration strength of Middle East Command had increased to half a million men by the summer of 1942, with a vast military/industrial base (mostly located in Egypt) developed in support. After the deployment of a German air corps in Sicily in January 1941, the direct route to Egypt through the Mediterranean became impassable except for the occasional heavily-escorted convoy of desperately needed supplies and weaponry. As a result, Middle East Command came to depend for reinforcements and re-supply on the 12,000-mile ocean route from Britain round the Cape of Good Hope, up the east coast of Africa, and finally through the Red Sea to Suez.

In view of this colossal strategic investment by land and sea, Churchill had again and again nagged his Cs-in-C Middle East (first Wavell, and then Auchinleck) to go over to the offensive in the Desert without delay. It was Churchill's intellectual weakness to add up totals of military manpower without taking into account their true state of combat-worthiness; and to add up totals of British tanks without taking into consideration such tiresome facts as that their armour and guns – and their mechanical reliability – were for the most part inferior to their German equivalents. Now, in the spring of 1942, Churchill was at it again, urging Auchinleck to launch the Eighth Army into an attack that would pre-empt a coming German offensive as revealed by Bletchley Park's Ultra decrypts of Enigma signals. He even gave Auchinleck an ultimatum on 10 May that he must attack by the end of June, or resign. Auchinleck, however, refused to hazard the Eighth Army against such opponents as Erwin Rommel and *PanzergruppeAfrika* before he reckoned that it was truly fit for battle.

The British intention to launch an offensive was well-known to the Axis command thanks to the decrypting by B-Dienst (the equivalent of Ultra) of signals to Washington by the American military attaché in Cairo. At a conference in Obersalzburg between Hitler, Mussolini, Rommel, General Kesselring (C-in-C South), and Cavallero, chief of *Commando Supremo*, sanction was given to Rommel to pre-empt this offensive with one of his own – aimed at destroying the British armour and capturing the port of Tobruk. But once Tobruk was taken, the offensive was to halt, and the principal Axis effort in the Mediterranean switch to an assault on the British island fortress of Malta.

On 26 May 1942 Rommel led 15th and 21st Panzer Divisions, plus the 90th Light Division, into their greatest offensive, and, as usual, against superior numbers. Thanks to B-Dienst's decrypts, he knew the broad layout of the Eighth Army's Gazala Line: a 'mine-marsh' extending from Tobruk to Bir Hacheim, with three defended localities ('boxes' in the jargon of the time) along its rear garrisoned by a total of two infantry divisions and an infantry brigade. Rommel's plan of attack was simple, bold, but unjustifiably optimistic. Posting his Italian infantry divisions opposite the British Gazala Line, he would sweep round the Line's southern flank at Bir Hacheim, drive north and cut the coast road behind the Eighth Army.

His direct opponent, Lieutenant General Neil Ritchie, the Eighth Army commander, was a slow-thinking stodge of a conventional soldier, whom Auchinleck had been advised long beforehand was not up to the job. Nonetheless, Auchinleck, having already sacked one Eighth Army commander (Cunningham during CRUSADER), decided that he could not sack another. Instead, he would act as Ritchie's long-distance mentor. This was a decision that would prove disastrous for the Eighth Army and for both men personally.

In the first place, Ritchie ignored Auchinleck's advice to concentrate all his armour behind the centre of his line astride the Trigh Capuzzo track, where it would be equally well placed to meet a direct attack on the Gazala Line from the west or a flanking movement from the south. Instead, Ritchie deployed his armoured and motorised divisions well forward south of the Trigh Capuzzo, and, what's more, with their units separated. Rommel was thus enabled to trample through the surprised British formations one by one, even overrunning the headquarters of 7 Armoured Brigade. Only when Rommel had driven far into the Eighth Army's rear, did British superiority of numbers begin to tell.

In particular, the panzer divisions received an unpleasant surprise on encountering American-supplied Grant tanks, well-armoured and with a 75mm gun in a sponson and a 37mm gun in the turret. These could outmatch all but a handful of Rommel's own tanks.

After two days of fighting, Rommel found his offensive stalled, and his panzer divisions immobilised by want of fuel. It was a supreme test for his leadership as a battlefield commander. In the middle of a sandstorm, he himself brought up the vital supply trucks loaded with jerry-cans, and guided them through a gap in the British armour. Then followed one of his most unorthodox strokes of generalship. He breached the enemy 'mine-marsh' from the rear, so opening up a short and direct line of communication with his own base. He then withdrew into a bridgehead on the British side of the minefields in order to re-group and re-supply his army.

Too late Ritchie launched a counter-stroke against this bridgehead, by now protected by a well-sited anti-tank defence. Partly because of poor coordination between the British armour and infantry, the counter-stroke broke down in failure. Now Rommel was free to resume his offensive. His first objective lay in Bir Hacheim, the southern anchor of the Gazala Line, and garrisoned by Free French troops; and he was there in person to direct the assault. The fall of Bir Hacheim on 11 June after a stout defence marked the finish of the Gazala Line. Once again Rommel swept north towards Tobruk and the sea, and on the way colliding with the Eighth Army's two armoured divisions. There ensued a sprawling battle in an area of desert south of Tobruk aptly dubbed by the British 'the Cauldron'. In this crucial fight, Rommel was mightily aided by the utter confusion and indecision within all levels of the British command, as well as by his knowledge of current British deployments thanks to B-Dienst's ability to read British radio traffic.

In just two days he virtually destroyed Eighth Army's remaining strength in tanks, exultantly writing to his wife:

> Dearest Lu: The battle has been won and the enemy is breaking up. We're now mopping up the encircled remnants of their army. I needn't tell you how delighted I am. I've been living in my car for days and have not had time to leave the battlefield ...[7]

He had now been fighting for three weeks, and yet his energy, his will to victory, seemed quenchless. On 18 June he closed the ring round Tobruk, which Churchill had insisted must be held as an isolated 'fortress' even though its perimeter defences had fallen into decay since the siege of 1941. Now it was held by a hastily installed garrison mostly drawn from the 1st South African Division. On 20 June Rommel launched his assault, and by the evening Tobruk and 30,000 prisoners were in his hands. This was the moment of Rommel's greatest triumph, marked by the Führer by promotion to field marshal, at fifty the youngest in the German Army. Rommel had not only inflicted a crushing defeat on the Eighth Army, but had also dealt a humiliating hammer-blow on Winston Churchill himself who, while staying as a guest in the White House, was told the news of Tobruk's fall by President Roosevelt.

To his troops Rommel issued an order of the day:

> Your spirit of attack has cost the enemy the core of his field army, which was standing poised for an offensive. Soldiers of the *PanzerarmeeAfrika*! Now for the complete destruction of the enemy. I shall call on you for one more great effort ...[8]

But to his wife he wrote: 'Hitler has made me a field marshal; I wish he had given me one more division.'

As the wreckage of the Eighth Army retreated pell-mell before him in what British soldiers dubbed 'the Gazala Gallop', the very completeness of Rommel's triumph exposed him to a dangerous temptation – the temptation to motor on deep into Egypt, to Alexandria and the Nile. According to the strategy agreed with the German and Italian high commands before his offensive, now was the time to call a halt so that Axis resources by land, sea, and air could be switched to taking Malta. For without the elimination of Malta as a British air and naval base, it would be impossible to ship enough supplies across the Mediterranean to nourish a large-scale offensive deep into Egypt, Palestine, and Iraq.

Yet the sheer momentum of victory pulled Rommel onwards, in turn pulling the Axis's entire Mediterranean strategy in behind him, for he won Hitler's and Mussolini's sanction to continue his advance. On 23 June 1942 his troops crossed the Egyptian frontier and began a headlong pursuit towards Alexandria.

But now he faced a new opponent: General Sir Claude Auchinleck, the C-in-C Middle East, who had sacked Ritchie and taken over direct command of the Eighth Army. Auchinleck decided to fight a battle on what the British media misleadingly dubbed 'the Alamein Line'. A 'Line' it was not, for the defence consisted of three separate defended localities ('boxes') at fifteen-mile intervals across the forty-mile gap between the Mediterranean and the impassable Qattara Depression. The right flank was anchored by the 'box' at El Alamein on the coast, blocking the railway and the road to Alexandria.

On 1 July 1942 Rommel led the Panzerarmee forward in an attempt to break through this new British defence. His strength was now down to 2,500 Germans and sixty tanks, while his soldiers were so exhausted by five weeks of fighting without relief that only Rommel's power of leadership kept them moving. Auchinleck was being only too accurate when he told the Eighth Army in an order of the day: 'The enemy is stretching to his limit, and thinks we are a beaten army. He hopes to take Egypt by bluff. Show him where he gets off.'

Rommel planned to pass the Panzerarmee round the south of the Alamein 'box' in an attempt to reach the sea and cut off the British garrison – a repetition of his successful outflanking manoeuvres in May which had led to the fall of Tobruk. But this time he ran into an ambush by massed British artillery. In his own words, 'British shells came streaking in from three directions ... Under this tremendous weight of fire, our attack came to a standstill. For two hours I had to lie out in the open.'[9]

It was the beginning of a three-week duel between Rommel and Auchinleck – swaying, desperate fighting; thrust and counter-thrust. Gradually Rommel found himself outfought and outmanoeuvred. Gradually he felt Auchinleck wrest from his grasp the initiative that he had enjoyed so long. In his anguish at being baulked of final victory just when it had seemed so near, he sought mental relief in writing every night to his wife. On 17 July he reported:

Things are going downright badly for me at the moment. The enemy is using his superiority, especially in infantry, to destroy the Italian formations one by one, and the German formations are much too weak to stand alone.[10]

Rommel could not know that, thanks to Ultra decrypts of his Enigma signals traffic, the enemy knew at only twenty-four hours' delay exactly where his German and Italian formations were deployed. By inflicting reverses on the Italians, Auchinleck compelled Rommel to divert his German divisions from attacking to shoring up his own front. On 17/18 July the 1st Australian Division trampled through the Trieste and Trento divisions and began to roll up Rommel's front from north to south. Only by hurrying every last German reserve to the threatened sector could Rommel manage to avert a general rout:

> Dearest Lu: Yesterday was a particularly hard and critical day. We pulled through again. But it can't go on like this for long, otherwise the front will crack. Militarily this is the most difficult period I've ever been through. You know what an incurable optimist I am. But there are situations where everything is dark.[11]

From now on his mind no longer turned on how to consummate victory but on how to avoid retreat. His great summer offensive was over, and it had failed. His defeat by Auchinleck in this First Battle of Alamein marked not only the turning-point in the Desert war but also in Rommel's own life. Ahead lay the nagging ill-health that is born of disappointment and frustration – desert sores, an infected liver, a duodenal ulcer.

On 31 August he attempted one last shot at forcing his way through into the Nile Delta, his opponent now being Lieutenant General Bernard Montgomery, the new commander of the Eighth Army (Auchinleck had been sacked by Churchill as C-in-C, Middle East on 8 August). Rommel's plan of attack was a repetition of his favourite manoeuvre of a swing round the enemy's southern flank towards the coast, and this time it went hopelessly wrong. The panzer divisions first had to struggle forward in soft sand under heavy British air attack, but then, when they swung north, they ran up against a well-prepared defence along the west-to-east Alam Halfa ridge – minefields, weapon-pits, a powerful gun-line. Here Rommel's offensive stalled and died. The Battle of Alam Halfa was Montgomery's first victory: it was the springboard of his fame. Yet all the credit for the defensive plan belonged to Auchinleck and his engineers, who had laid out and installed the Alam Halfa defences before Montgomery even arrived in Egypt.[12]

In the wake of his defeat at Alam Halfa, Rommel could only await a British offensive launched with forces that would far outweigh his own, thanks to the new weaponry and fresh divisions flowing in abundance to the Eighth Army. In the meantime, his own health was growing worse, with fainting fits, nasal congestion, and chronic stomach troubles. It could not have helped his state of mind that despite prolonged efforts he had failed to persuade the Italian and German high commands to send him adequate supplies and reinforcements.

Late in September he returned to Germany to receive his field marshal's baton from the Führer's own hand, and then went into hospital in the Austrian Alps. While he was recuperating, his staff and troops worked hard to complete the defences that he had planned for the Alamein position: really an updated 'Hindenburg Line' in the desert between the sea and the Qattara Depression, consisting of a five-mile-deep maze of minefields, barbed wire, weapon-pits, anti-tank guns and field artillery.

In the Second Battle of Alamein, launched by Montgomery on 23 October 1942, the *PanzerarmeeAfrika* was heavily outweighed in numbers and firepower. It could muster only 200 gun-armed German tanks and 300 Italian 'self-propelled coffins' against 1,100 British tanks, including some 270 American-supplied Shermans, more formidable than all Rommel's armour except for his thirty German Panzer Mark IVs. Moreover, the enemy enjoyed complete command of the air, able to bomb anything that moved. Yet Rommel's defence in depth wrecked Montgomery's master plan to drive straight through into open desert in the first twenty-four hours of battle, with the British armoured divisions brought to a standstill in the midst of German minefields. Montgomery now had to think again; and opted for a Great War-style battle of attrition where his superiority in tanks, artillery, and sheer manpower must eventually prevail.

On 25 October Rommel flew in straight from hospital to take command of the *Panzerarmee* in its desperate fight, but there was little he could do to prevent it being remorselessly ground down day after day. On 2 November Montgomery at last broke through into open desert. Yet Rommel with only ninety tanks against 700 now fought one of his most brilliant panzer actions in order to win time for the bulk of his army to make good its retreat:

> Dearest Lu: the battle is going heavily against us. We're simply being crushed by the enemy's weight. I've made an attempt to salvage a part of the army. I wonder if it will succeed. At night I lie open-eyed, racking my brains for a way out of this plight for my poor troops. We are facing difficult days, perhaps the most difficult that a man can undergo.[13]

Next day, however, Hitler sent him an order that the army must stand fast at Alamein and fight to the end, whereupon Rommel obediently cancelled his instruction to retreat. Then on 4 November Hitler gave him permission to retreat after all – a delay that handed Montgomery a thirty-six-hour advantage in mounting a pursuit.

The stupidity of Hitler's 'stand fast' order, coupled with his callous willingness to expose the *Panzerarmee* to annihilation at Montgomery's hands, served seriously to undermine Rommel's respect for the Führer's military judgement.

Now began a new feat of leadership on Rommel's part – the conduct of a retreat of 1,400 miles back to his base at Tripoli while vastly outnumbered and often immobilised for want of fuel. His very personal legend now served as his army's shield, for Montgomery would only follow him up with the utmost caution, fearing to be another victim of a sudden thunderbolt counter-stroke. Although Ultra decrypts of Enigma signals told him that Rommel was at times down to some thirty-fifty tanks and fuel for only four-five days, Montgomery still insisted on preparing major set-piece assaults whenever Rommel paused in his retreat. By the time these assaults were launched (at El Agheila and Buerat), Rommel had already slipped away.

In January 1943 Rommel linked up with the Italo-German Fifth Panzerarmee under General von Arnim which had been landed in Tunisia after the Anglo-American invasion of French North Africa back on 8 November 1942 (Operation TORCH). On 20 February 1943 Rommel won his last but short-lived offensive success, when by dint of personal leadership in his old style he bustled the inexperienced Americans out of the Kasserine Pass. But when on 6 March he attacked the Eighth Army at Medenine farther to the east, he was easily repulsed by Montgomery's well-sited defence, strong in anti-tank guns and field artillery.

It was now clear to Rommel that for the Axis army to remain any longer in Africa was now, in his words, 'plain suicide'. On 9 March he flew off to Hitler's headquarters in the hope – vain of course – of persuading Hitler to withdraw from Tunisia in good time.[14]

As for Rommel himself, he had left Africa for ever.

* * *

His achievement in command of *Deutsches Afrikakorps/Panzergruppe/PanzerarmeeAfrika* elevates Rommel to the first rank of leadership in war. He conducted three victorious offensives against the Eighth Army, and in the third of these, the Gazala battles of May-June 1942, he inflicted the biggest single defeat suffered by British and Imperial forces in either of the two wars against Germany. As a leader he not only dominated the minds of his own soldiers but also those of the enemy as well – and of their commanding generals.

More than that, he came to dominate the mind of the British prime minister himself. 'Rommel, Rommel, Rommel, Rommel,' exclaimed Churchill in Cairo in August 1942, 'what else matters but beating him?'[15]

Between 1941 and 1943 Rommel had kept in play the principal land-war effort of the British Empire against the Axis powers, with a total Middle East ration strength of half a million soldiers drawn from Australia, India, New Zealand, South Africa, and the United Kingdom, plus a huge logistical base, and a 12,000 mile-long maritime line of communication from Britain to Suez. Moreover, he had attracted a British strategic commitment utterly out of proportion to its meagre military results. In the biggest battle fought by the Eighth Army against Rommel (Second Alamein), it engaged only the equivalent of four and a half German divisions (two panzer and one motorised, plus the 164th Infantry Division and a parachute brigade serving as infantry), as compared with the 190 then being engaged by the Red Army on the Eastern Front.

Rommel's two-year campaign in the desert must therefore be accounted one of the most remarkable examples in history of a successful strategic diversion on the grand scale.

*   *   *

On 31 December 1943 Rommel was appointed C-in-C of Army Group B in France, charged with defending the Netherlands, Belgium, and France against the Anglo-American invasion expected sometime in 1944. It was Rommel's first active operational command since he left Tunisia, being employed instead by Hitler on such tasks as reporting on the situation in occupied Greece and organising an army group for the defence of northern Italy. It had not been a happy year. He had begun to question whether Germany could possibly win the war in the face of America's colossal output of munitions. He had exchanged angry words with Hitler when the Führer accused his soldiers of throwing away their weapons at Alamein. As his trust in Hitler's judgement began to crumble and his country's fate became more and more overshadowed, Rommel was beginning to find that a patriot's duty was not as simple and straightforward as he had once assumed.

Now he was commanding an army group beset with grievous problems and weaknesses. After three years of mass slaughter on the Russian front, the German army was no longer the superb instrument of 1940. Rommel found that the coastal defences (anyway incomplete) were garrisoned by elderly Germans, or by renegade Poles, Russians, and Yugoslavs, while his panzer divisions were understrength and also too few in number for the extent of territory to be defended.

Nevertheless, in the winter and spring of 1944 he set to work with all his old dynamic energy and resourcefulness, always on the move, always on site like a good engineer. His naval opposite number, Admiral Ruge, recalled later:

> He got up early, travelled fast, saw things very quickly, and seemed to have an instinct where something was wrong ... He had a knack of handling men and talking to them. Wherever we went at this time in France, he spoke freely to all ranks. He explained his ideas to them clearly and patiently, and told them exactly what he wanted them to do.[16]

He displayed the practical ingenuity of the young man who had loved taking motor-cycles to pieces in order to discover how they worked. On fields suitable for the landing of glider-borne troops he installed an array of wooden stakes, nicknamed 'Rommel's Asparagus' by his soldiers. In his own hand he drew designs for obstacles to landing-craft approaching likely invasion beaches: underwater metal 'tank-traps', as well as masses of stakes capped with explosive charges. And his soldiers came to believe that their general was obsessed with land-mines, for they laid between five and six million for him along the coast in the first five months of 1944. Even so, Rommel was thinking of fifty million, if he were granted the time.

Unlike von Rundstedt, his immediate superior, Rommel was adaptable and clear-sighted enough to recognise that classic counter-strokes in depth, demanding large-scale movement by road or rail, were now ruled out by allied command of the air. He believed that the only hope of defensive success lay in halting the invasion forces on the beaches, and then destroying them by prompt local counter-attacks.

Montgomery himself paid tribute to Rommel's achievements and military judgement when in May 1944 he told a high-level conference of allied leaders:

> Rommel is an energetic commander; he has made a world of difference since he took over. He is best at the spoiling attack; his *forte* is disruption; he is too impulsive for the set-piece battle. He will do his best to 'Dunkirk' us.[17]

Rommel's proposed strategy of forward defence caused acrimonious argument within the German command structure, with von Rundstedt urging that the six available panzer divisions should be held well back from the coast in order to deliver a classic counter-stroke. Hitler for his part ensured his own commanding authority by dividing operational responsibilities between Rundstedt (C-in-C West) and Rommel (C-in-C Army Group B). The result was an ultimately disastrous compromise, whereby Rommel was allotted three panzer divisions out of six, while Hitler, far-off in his HQ at Rastenburg in East Prussia, retained direct control of the other three.

On D-Day (6 June) and thereafter, all Rommel's fears came true. Hitler only belatedly released the panzer divisions in reserve, and these, being stationed well back from the coast, could only crawl haltingly towards the invasion front under the lash of allied bombing. A single counter-attack on D-day by a battlegroup of 21st Panzer, cutting through a British beachhead almost to the sea, showed what might have happened if Rommel had had his way.

On 12th June, Rommel signalled OKW:

> The strength of the enemy on land is increasing more quickly than our reserves can reach the front. Our operations in Normandy will be rendered partially impossible by the overwhelming superiority of the Allied Air Force ... the enemy has complete control over the battle area and up to sixty miles behind the front ... Our position is becoming extraordinarily critical. I request that the Führer be informed of this.[18]

On 17 June Rundstedt and Rommel met Hitler in an unused headquarters bunker at Margival, near Soissons. The ensuing angry confrontation marked the climax of their attempts to convince the Führer that the battle of Normandy was already lost and that the army must be withdrawn before it was destroyed. But all they got was one of Hitler's renowned shouting fits. Back at Rommel's headquarters at la Roche Guyon, Rommel and his Chief of Staff, General Hans Speidel, came to the conclusion that peace negotiations ought to be opened with the Western Allies as soon as possible.

On 15 July Rommel tried for the last time to shine the grey light of strategic reality into the closed-up bunker of Hitler's mind, signalling him:

> The troops are everywhere fighting heroically, but the unequal struggle is nearing its end. It is urgently necessary for the proper conclusion to be drawn from this situation. As C-in-C of the Army Group, I feel myself in duty bound to speak plainly on this point.[19]

Five days later Rommel's staff-car was hit by cannon-fire from a Royal Air Force fighter-bomber on a road near the appropriately named village of St Foi de Montgomery. His seriously-wounded driver lost control of the car, which veered off the road, struck a tree stump, and turned over. Rommel was thrown from the vehicle on to the road, causing him a triple fracture of the skull.

Two days later, while he was lying in a hospital bed at Vesinet near Paris recovering from an operation on his head, anti-Hitler plotters launched an attempt to assassinate the Führer in his East Prussian headquarters and simultaneously mount a coup d'état in Berlin. It all went wrong: Hitler himself was not killed but merely wounded by a bomb inside a despatch-case left in his conference room by Colonel Klaus von Stauffenberg, while the attempt to seize power in Berlin failed because of bungled execution by the plotters and the prompt and ruthless response of the commander of the Berlin *Wachtregiment*.

Although Rommel himself had taken no part in the plot, he was unwittingly incriminated by a leading plotter, General von Stülpnagel (the Military Governor of Paris). After the failure of the coup d'état, Stülpnagel tried to commit suicide, but the shot only blinded him. As he came round in hospital after an operation, the Gestapo heard him cry out: 'Rommel! Rommel!' This was enough to provoke the Gestapo into hunting Rommel down.

On 8 August Rommel was moved at his own insistence from France to his home at Herrlingen, near Ulm, in order to avoid capture by the fast advancing allies. While he continued his convalescence, a so-called 'People's Court' tried the leaders of the bomb plot after they had been savagely tortured. Most of the accused were then cruelly hanged by piano wire. On 7 September Rommel learned that his chief of staff in France, Hans Speidel, had been arrested by the Gestapo. Despite his own growing danger, Rommel wrote to Hitler in Speidel's defence:

> Speidel showed himself to be an outstandingly efficient and diligent chief of staff. I cannot imagine what can have led to his removal and arrest.[20]

When a month later he was ordered to go to Berlin, ostensibly for an interview with General Jodl (Wehrmacht chief of staff), he refused to go, on the grounds that he was not yet fit enough to travel. As he himself observed, 'I'm not that much of a fool. I know these people now. I'd never get to Berlin alive.'[21] Instead, they came for him. On 13 October he was told by telephone that two generals would visit him next morning, whereupon he told his son Manfred that they were either going to offer him a new post or take him before a People's Court.

He received his visitors in full uniform, including his old 'Afrika' tunic. They told him that he could either die by the poison they had brought with them (his death to be announced as a 'brain seizure') and receive a state funeral, or be arraigned before the People's Court for treason, which would also entail punitive measures against his family and staff. He took the poison.

It was von Rundstedt, as Germany's senior field marshal, who gave the funeral oration as Rommel's coffin draped in a swastika flag lay in state in the town hall of Ulm. The oration had been written for him by Goebbels' propaganda ministry, and referred to Rommel as 'this tireless fighter in the cause of the Führer and the Reich, imbued with the National-Socialist spirit. His heart belonged to Adolf Hitler.'[22]

No other single incident in the history of the Third Reich better illustrates the moral rottenness that was the soul of Nazism.

References

1. Liddell Hart (Ed), *The Rommel Papers*, p.94.
2. Lewin, *Rommel as Military Commander*, p.36.
3. *Rommel Papers*, p.7.
4. Ibid, p.43.
5. Ibid, p.66.
6. Cited in Lewin, op. cit. p.107.
7. Liddell-Hart, op. cit., p.224.
8. Ibid, p.232.
9. Ibid, p.246.
10. Ibid, p.257.
11. Ibid, pp.257–8.
12. When in my 1960 book *The Desert Generals* I pointed out that that Montgomery's victory at Alam Halfa owed itself to Auchinleck's plan and preparations, it caused sharp controversy. However, this has now been confirmed by official records not open to research in 1960, but used by Niall Barr, op. cit.
13. Liddell-Hart, op. cit., p.320.
14. Hitler's refusal to order a timely withdrawal from Tunisia resulted in the surrender of 100,000 men to the Allies in May 1943.
15. Cited in Lewin, op. cit., p.143.
16. Young, op. cit., pp.192 & 196.
17. Cited in Lewin, op. cit., p.221.
18. Young, op. cit, pp.205–6.
19. Liddell-Hart, op. cit., p.487.
20. Ibid, p.500.
21. Ibid, pp.501–2.
22. Young, p.242.

CHAPTER 13

The Reluctant Gambler

Admiral Isoruku Yamamoto

It was owing to the leadership of Admiral Isoruku Yamamoto, Commander-in-Chief of the Japanese Combined Fleet, that a reluctant United States of America was finally propelled into the Second World War. On the peacetime[1] Sunday morning of 7 December 1941, Japanese carrier-borne aircraft executed Yamamoto's operational plan to cripple the US Pacific Fleet at anchor in Pearl Harbor, Hawaii, and succeeded in sinking five battleships and seriously damaging seven others. Yet only when the raid was already in progress did the Japanese ambassador in Washington deliver Japan's formal declaration of war. Four days later, Nazi Germany also declared war on the United States. And so the mighty consequence of Yamamoto's carrier-strike was to turn a European conflict – Great Britain and the Soviet Union versus Nazi Germany and Fascist Italy – into a world war. By design and by default, therefore, Yamamoto had altered the course of twentieth-century history. This renders him of peculiar interest as a man and as a leader.

*   *   *

The youngest son of an old Samurai family, he was given the name 'Isoruku' (meaning 'fifty-six') because his father was fifty-six years old when Yamamoto was born in 1884. The family's circumstances were modest enough despite the social rank of 'samurai', his father being a hard-up schoolmaster, and Yamamoto's childhood home a simple wooden house in the small town of Nagoaka, in the north of the main Japanese island of Honshu, an area where harsh climate and rugged terrain bred a tough and sturdy race. His father was in fact so hard-up that he could not afford Yamamoto's school textbooks, and the boy had to make his own handwritten copies. As a youth, Isoruku showed a talent for painting, and even thought of becoming an artist.

This austere childhood became all the harsher because of his father's coldness towards him. When a favourite son died, Yamamoto's father actually said that he wished that it had instead been Isoruku.

THE LORDS OF WAR: FROM LINCOLN TO CHURCHILL

The future admiral grew up in a society that remained as feudal in its values and social structure as Europe back in the middle ages – with each man having his proper place in the hierarchy, from the poorest peasant up to the divine Emperor at the pinnacle; and each man owing total loyalty – fealty – to his superior in rank. Like all Japanese boys, Yamamoto was brought up to believe that the highest morality lay in dutiful obedience to the Emperor. The state religion, Shintoism, struck the same note, laying down that the Emperor was truly a God, descended from the Goddess of the Sun.

Yet in the late-nineteenth century and early-twentieth centuries, this profoundly traditional society was embarking on a headlong Western-style modernisation: new heavy industries; a new navy copied from Britain's Royal Navy; an army and an education system – a constitution too – copied from Bismarck's Germany. Such was the environment of cultural paradox in which Yamamoto was to make his career. In 1904 he graduated from the navy academy at Etajima, where a modern Western naval officer's training was combined with ancient Japanese warrior games like Kendo, more like medieval European jousting than cricket. In the following year he was serving as a junior officer in the flagship at the Battle of Tshushima, when the new Japanese navy shatteringly defeated the Russian fleet – the first-ever victory of an Asiatic state over a European power. Yamamoto's mother sent him off to war with a specially-made handkerchief on which his father had inscribed a valedictory message:

> Please fall for the Emperor and your country. Even when the flower of the warrior falls, it will still have a beautiful fragrance.

In the event, Yamamoto's flower did not fall at Tshushima. He was nonetheless badly wounded, in peril of losing an arm, although in the event he only lost two fingers from his left hand. However, this mutilation had a lasting effect on him, as his son remembered:

> The left hand was a scar and a matter of pride and inferiority at the same time. He made an extraordinary effort not to lag behind because of it. Even when he went up the gangways of ships, he would go up very quickly, and when he was well into middle age, all his movements were of a young person.[2]

Yamamoto even feared that the mutilation might prove hereditary, and when his son was born, his first question was to ask whether the baby had his full complement of digits.

In 1915 he was adopted by a childless noble family called Yamamoto, so bestowing the surname by which history remembers him. Three years later he married, choosing his bride on the practical grounds that she seemed sturdy and healthy, and should be able to stand up to hardship.

162

THE RELUCTANT GAMBLER

While Yamamoto served with the Imperial Navy during the Great War, Japan was continuing to pursue an expansionist policy overseas, with the particular objective of turning a weak and disunited China into a protected market for Japanese industry. She had in fact embraced imperialism just when it was being renounced by European states on the score that it was the immoral exploitation of subject peoples. While Japan had been very keen to adopt Western technology, she had no matching interest in adopting Western liberal values, but remained a society intensely traditional and inward-looking. In the 1920s and 1930s this was particularly true of the Japanese armed forces.

Yet Yamamoto himself was a remarkable exception. In 1919–21 he studied English in the United States, taking the opportunity to travel widely: Boston, Harvard University, Detroit (home of the vast automotive industry), the Texas oilfields, and across the border into Mexico. Shortage of cash compelled him to live as cheaply as possible; and while in Mexico he lodged in an attic bedroom in a third-class hotel, existing on bread, water and bananas. This mode of existence prompted the Mexican authorities to ask the Japanese embassy to confirm the identity of a certain Isoruku Yamamoto, supposedly a naval officer.

His three years in America left Yamamoto with a profound impression of American industrial power:

> Because I have seen the motor industry in Detroit and the oilfields of Texas [he wrote to a friend], I know Japan has no chance if she goes to war with America, or if she starts to compete in building warships.

When he returned in 1927 as the naval attaché in Washington, his admiration for America extended beyond her industries to her values. To a friend learning English he recommended that he should read a biography of Lincoln:

> Have you seen a picture of Lincoln's birthplace? You cannot find such a poor house even in Japan. Until his death he worked for the freedom of man.
>
> A man of will completely believes in himself. Sometimes they do not believe in God and may make a mistake. Of course, Lincoln did make mistakes, but that does not diminish him. A man is not God. Because he makes mistakes, it renders him human, and that's only why we love him. He is full of human elements. If he had lacked these, he could not have led other men. It is because he had some weaknesses that he could forgive others, and sympathise with them and help them.[3]

This letter reveals much about his concept of leadership, and indeed much about the man himself.

Unlike a British naval officer of the time, Yamamoto was socially uninhibited to the point of eccentricity. During a party evening in the passenger liner taking him to Washington in 1927, he turned handstands in the first-class lounge; and later, as an admiral, repeated the trick on the deck of his flagship. His family and friends thought that when he walked along the street throwing roasted peanuts in the air and catching them in his mouth, he had the air of a mischievous small boy.

Indeed, he hated pomposity and formality: for example, when Commander-in-Chief of the Fleet, he came up with a novel way to help a staff officer who was finding it difficult to plan a complicated exercise. Yamamoto invited him to his cabin and told him to sit down, whereupon the officer immediately leaped up again - for Yamamoto had booby-trapped his seat with upturned drawing-pins. Said the Admiral, 'Surprise and fantasy in a situation are useful points to bear in mind.'

Yamamoto was one of the first officers in any navy to be convinced that the key to victory at sea in the next war would lie in carrier-borne aviation. In 1923 he became executive officer at the Kasimagaura Naval Air Training Centre, and had himself trained as a pilot. He set out to convince his airmen that naval flying was a serious and highly technical profession, not a kind of sport. He thus helped to lay the foundations of the undoubted superiority of Japanese maritime aviators at the beginning of the war in the Pacific and South-East Asia in 1941.

As station commander at Kasimagaura, he was not popular at first, perhaps because of his taciturn manner, but gradually won the respect of his cadets. 'He was usually very quiet and hardly said anything [a pilot remembered], but he had a strange charm which made his men love him.' He liked to play Japanese chess with the young officers and listen to their talk. When they needed baseball equipment, he went off to Tokyo one weekend and won the money gambling. Yet he was also a man of deeply felt emotions. At his instigation, a small shrine was set up at Kasimagaura to all the pilots killed in accidents, and he would pray there every morning, while he also kept a black book listing their names, and these he would read as a kind of meditation.

In 1934, now a Vice Admiral, he went to London as the chief naval member of the Japanese delegation taking part in the preparatory meetings for the forthcoming international conference on naval disarmament. This was a time when Japan was at a turning point in her relations with the rest of the world. In 1930 a period of relatively liberal and moderate foreign policy came to an end, and henceforth the Japanese government was to be dominated by hardliners at the head of the army and navy. This signified opposition to any disarmament treaty that would limit the size of the Imperial Japanese Navy, as well as an ambition to carve out an empire in China and elsewhere in the Far East and Pacific. In 1931 the Japanese army had occupied the Chinese province of Manchuria, an act of annexation that provoked condemnatory sermons in the League of Nations at Geneva, but no further action. A half-hearted attempt by Japan in 1933–34 to reach a settlement with Britain and America (on the basis that these powers accepted that China fell within Japan's sphere of economic and strategic interest) had come to nothing; and thereafter the nationalistic pressure groups which wanted to expand the army, the navy, and the Japanese empire came to dominate Japanese policy. So Japan did not send a delegation to the London naval conference in order to negotiate a compromise, but to demand an end of the 1922 Washington Treaty, which had limited the Japanese navy to nine battleships as against fifteen each for the United States and Great Britain, and call instead for a common upper limit for all three powers.

In deliberate snub to the British conveners of the conference, Yamamoto was chosen to lead the Japanese delegation because he was a mere vice admiral when other powers would be sending their chiefs of naval staff (and full admirals). A report on him by the British naval attaché in Tokyo before the conference is fascinating because of the light it casts on Yamamoto's personality as seen by a snobbish western sailor:

> I had not met him before and I was astonished to find that the Ministry of Marine had selected an officer of his type to carry out what must be a mission of some importance to his country. He is far from being the best type of naval officer, being, as far as I could gather on short acquaintance, a man of little charm and extremely abrupt manner. He is ... apparently well known as an inveterate gambler; in fact, he stated that his greatest interest is gambling in any form and poker in particular. It may be that his skill at this game has earned him his present appointment.

Once in London, Yamamoto had to follow a very specific instruction from Tokyo that he must settle for nothing less than parity of tonnage with Britain and America. Given his own world outlook, this was for him personally an awkward and ambiguous role. Nonetheless, in a personal conversation with the British First Sea Lord (Admiral of the Fleet Lord Chatfield) he expressed the hope that a compromise might be reached whereby Japan would gradually reach naval parity with America while remaining inferior to Britain. Yamamoto took pains, however, to remind Chatfield that 'this conversation was purely private, that it was his own personal idea, and not that of his government'.

After a hard day in conference, Yamamoto, the inveterate gambler, would invite his three colleagues in the delegation into the sitting-room of his hotel suite for games of either poker or bridge that could last until three in the morning. He justified this addiction on the score that it was his duty as a gunnery officer to study the law of probability, which applied equally to the fall of shot and the fall of cards.

After abortive negotiations lasting from autumn 1934 into 1935, Yamamoto and the Japanese delegation obeyed orders from Tokyo to walk out of the conference. It seems that Yamamoto was genuinely sorry about the breakdown of the London talks, writing to his geisha mistress, Chuyiko, that he had done all he could to make it succeed, but that he had begun to feel he was being used as a tool.

He even thought of retiring, and jokingly told a friend, 'When I resign from the Navy, I'm going to Monte Carlo to become a gambler.'

With the breakdown of the London conference, Japan would now embark on greatly increased building programmes for all kinds of warships but especially battleships and aircraft carriers. Yamamoto had already done much to promote the carrier arm. In 1932 he had been put in charge of naval aviation's technical department, which entailed close collaboration with Mitsubishi, the aircraft manufacturer. The eventual result of this collaboration was the Zero, the best carrier-borne fighter aircraft on either side at the start of the war with the United States. In 1933 Yamamato had taken command of the First Aircraft Carrier Squadron, flying his flag in the *Akagi*, an attack carrier of almost 30,000 tons. Under his leadership the air squadrons trained hard at navigation, dive-bombing, and landing and take-off operations. By now he had become within the Imperial Navy the standard-bearer of airpower in its rivalry with the still very influential battleship faction, which in 1938 laid down the 18-inch gun, 65,000-ton super-battleship *Yamato* (to be swiftly sunk in 1944 by American carrier-borne aircraft).

In 1936 Yamamoto became Vice Minister of the Navy and celebrated the appointment by giving a party for journalists at which he did his renowned handstands and rolled an egg from one end of the room to the other by blowing on it. However, his new post meant that he was now navigating in the turbulent waters at the centre of the Japanese governmental system, where the army and the navy fought each other for dominance over civilian ministers, all in the name of the Emperor. Japanese political life now extended to assassinations by extreme militarists; and in February 1936 young officers from one such group murdered the Inspector General of Education, the Lord Keeper of the Privy Seal, the Finance Minister, the Grand Chamberlain, and the Prime Minister's brother, in mistake for him.

This then was the atmosphere of menace, violence, and instability in which Yamamoto, as a junior minister, tried as best he could to slow the march of fanatical militarists and navalists towards territorial conquest and a possible collision with the United States and Great Britain. When, in 1937, the Japanese army invaded the heartland of China, he expressed his fury to friends at what he believed to be a dangerous error of policy. In vain he sought to warn the expansion-mongers about America's immense reserves of strength. But the right-wing extremists simply regarded him as a coward for wishing to avoid war; and he became so convinced that he himself stood in danger of assassination that in May 1939 he wrote his will. When in August that year he was appointed Commander-in-Chief of the Combined Fleet, it was partly in order to send him to sea for his own safety.

On coming aboard the flagship *Nagato*, he told his staff: 'Well, it's nice being commander-in-chief, isn't it? Being Vice Minister of the Navy is just like being a high-class servant or caretaker.'[4] But in a letter to a friend on 15 September 1939, just a fortnight after the Second World War had begun in Europe, his tone was more serious:

> I am pleased to be in command of such a fleet. At the same time, I realise the greatness of my responsibility. I feel I am completely cut off from the world and can devote myself to my work for the Navy.[5]

By 'my work' he meant bringing the fleet to the highest pitch of operational efficiency. Except in size, the Japanese Navy was already superior to the United States Navy in fighting power, being equipped with faster and more heavily gunned ships in most classes, more destructive torpedoes, and – most important of all – more efficient carrier-borne aviation.

As a leader, Yamamoto won the unconditional trust, and indeed affection, of his subordinates:

> he was very kind and he always kept his promises [recalled his private secretary during the 1930s]. That was his outstanding characteristic. He was a very methodical person, scrupulous person. He was unusual - not like ordinary people. You felt you were being overpowered by him, although he was quite a small person. In a way, he was stubborn because once he made up his mind he wouldn't change it. His determination was always so strong to finish whatever he had decided to do.

Another member of his staff remembered his selflessness: 'He was so good to his subordinates. For instance, if something he undertook went off well his subordinates got the credit for it. If it didn't go well, it was his responsibility.'

While Yamamoto was busy training his fleet, Japan began to steer a course of policy that must inevitably lead to a collision with the United States and the United Kingdom. The expansionists were greatly encouraged by the German victory over France and by Britain's precarious global situation; and in September 1940 the Japanese government signed a Tripartite Treaty of alliance with Nazi Germany and Fascist Italy. Yamamoto judged this action to be 'quite irrational': Japan was being 'very foolish as she will be shocked to find what America can do to threaten her economically.' This proved a shrewdly accurate prediction. From summer 1940 onwards, the US began to impose embargoes on supplies of raw materials to Japan, limited at first but gradually becoming more and more severe. Undeterred, Japan coerced the hapless Vichy-French government in September 1940 into conceding air and naval bases in French Indo-China, whereupon the US responded by embargoing exports of scrap-iron and steel. In a continuation of her southward expansion, Japan occupied southern Indo-China in June 1941. There followed in August a total ban by America, Britain, and the Netherlands on all trade with Japan.[6] Most important of all, the embargo included oil, so confronting Japan with the early prospect of industrial paralysis and an army and navy immobilised for want of fuel. Either she accepted a compromise with the West, meaning withdrawal from China and Indo-China, which to the hard-liners in Tokyo was out of the question, or she went to war to conquer the British and Dutch colonies whence came the supplies of oil and essential raw materials (including rice, the Japanese staple diet).

War it was to be. In the past, Yamamoto had tried and failed to convince the fanatical Japanese nationalists of the dangers of risking a conflict with America. Unlike them, he had never exaggerated Japan's strength, let alone sneered like them at America for the peaceable demeanour of her foreign policy. He well knew that America possessed enormous industrial resources: and he also knew, as he told a friend, that the Americans had an American spirit that was just as strong as 'the Japanese spirit' about which the nationalists were always raving. But he was a patriot and steadfastly loyal to his Emperor. Having failed to persuade his colleagues and government that a war with America would be a disaster for Japan, he now put all his energies and talents into fighting it as effectively as possible. For him there was no question of resignation: the warrior code demanded his obedience.

Nevertheless, he made clear to his superiors his pessimistic assessment of Japan's long-term prospects in a war:

> If you force me to fight, I will show some real action for the first six months or a year. But if the fighting continues for two or three years, I do not have any confidence whatsoever.[7]

Strategic planning for such a conflict had begun in the 1930s, and was intensified from 1940 onwards. The naval staff reckoned that Japan must attack in 1941, when her current shipbuilding and repair programme would be complete, and before America had time to develop an overwhelming superiority at sea.

The question for the Japanese Navy now was how best to fight this war. It had been the broad strategic concept throughout the 1930s that while amphibious forces conquered the British and Dutch empires in South-East Asia (Malaya, Borneo, Java, and Sumatra), the main Japanese fleet would stand on the defensive in the central Pacific in order to parry an expected advance by the US Fleet from Hawaii westwards to relieve the Philippines (an American protectorate) and its US garrison.

In January 1941 Yamamoto threw this defensive strategy against the Americans overboard. Instead, he would destroy the American Pacific Fleet altogether by a surprise carrier-strike launched within thirty minutes of a Japanese ultimatum expiring. Here we see Yamamoto, the admiral who believed in the superiority of airpower over the gunpower of battleships. Here too was Yamamoto the lifelong gambler and student of chance – the man who had counselled a staff officer about the importance of an element of surprise and fantasy in war planning.

THE RELUCTANT GAMBLER

From January to September 1941 Yamamoto's basic idea of a strike on Pearl Harbor was worked out in detail, debated in conferences, and played out in war games over a large-scale model of the Pearl Harbor anchorage and the capital ships alongside. Yamamoto left the planning of the operation to those who were going to have to carry it out. As Admiral Genda, who took a leading part in the planning, recalled:

> He wasn't going to permit argument as to whether or not they were going to do it, but he was going to let those in charge do it the way they pleased. If someone asked for six aircraft carriers, they got six; if they needed so many aircraft, then they got so many. If some wanted to approach from the north, he said O.K., you approach from the north. In these matters lay the secret of his greatness as a leader ...[8]

From September onwards the carrier group and its air crews again and again rehearsed their tightly timed attacks. On 5 November Yamamoto signalled 'Combined Fleet Operation Order Number One', incorporating all the previous staff studies. Two days later the Navy ministry fixed the provisional date for the attack for 8 December (7 December American time). On 1 December the Japanese government made its final decision, leaving its delegation in Washington to go through the motions of negotiating a settlement. A letter to a friend gives a glimpse of Yamamoto's own state of mind at this time:

> I believe the situation has come to the worst. It's terrible to think this is God's will, but we cannot say whether this is good or bad. I think Japan's future is going to be very difficult now. I have determined to do my duty, which is completely opposite to my personal convictions. It is a heavy fate. Do you think that this is God's will too?[9]

On 26 November 1941 the carrier strike force left the Kurile Islands on its secret and circuitous 3,000 mile route towards Pearl Harbor – six carriers, two battleships, three cruisers, nine destroyers and tankers. Ahead sailed an advanced force of twenty submarines, some carrying midget submarines to penetrate inside Pearl Harbor. On 4 December Yamamoto bid farewell to his family before joining his flagship with the main fleet in Japan's home waters.

The strike achieved complete surprise, despite all sorts of clues to the coming onslaught available to the American command, from deciphered Japanese diplomatic signals to radar detection of the attacking aircraft, misinterpreted as an expected fly-in of American bombers to Hawaii. When the last wave of Japanese aircraft returned to their carriers, the US Pacific Fleet had been knocked out as a fighting force of big-gun battleships. The whole Pacific and all the waters of south-east Asia lay wide open to Japanese conquest.

Yet there was one shadow on this astounding success: the American aircraft-carriers had not been at anchor in harbour as expected, but somewhere out at sea on exercise. Their lucky survival was later to prove the decisive factor in swinging the fortunes of the war.

On the American nation the Pearl Harbor strike served as a shrillest possible call to arms. Owing to delays in deciphering signals within the Japanese embassy in Washington, Yamamoto's aircraft were already attacking Pearl Harbor by the time the Japanese ambassador presented his country's declaration of war to the State Department. America therefore took the attack to be an act of outright treachery. 'Remember Pearl Harbor' became the national rallying cry. It may be questioned whether there would have been a comparable wave of outrage and anger if Japan instead had merely launched a conventional invasion of the Philippines. It may even be doubted whether the United States would have found itself at war at all if Japan had restricted her aggression to just the British and Dutch colonies in the Far East.

In Japan the astounding success at Pearl Harbor generated a mood of positively hysterical glee. Yamamoto did not share this national euphoria, writing to his sister:

> It seems that everyone is getting very excited, but at such a critical moment for the country it is much better if everyone kept more quiet and be faithful in carrying out their own tasks seriously and with patience. It's no use making much over the sinking of three or five battleships. Japan may win or Japan may be beaten from now on. I believe the fight for the Navy is just beginning. I will do my best but it is hard to tell what might happen.[10]

In fact, Yamamoto hoped that the government would use his victory to open peace negotiations, and even to offer to evacuate occupied territories. However, as he wrote, 'because the government is on top of the world now, it's difficult for them to see things seriously and do it.'

Yet in any case there was no chance at all that America would negotiate in the aftermath of Pearl Harbor. Instead, and just as Yamamoto had forewarned, she set about mobilising at breakneck speed her vast industrial and military potential. The temporary advantage won by Japan at Pearl Harbor must inevitably yield in a year or so to an overwhelming American naval superiority.

Two days after Pearl Harbor the British battle-cruiser *Repulse* and battleship *Prince of Wales* were sunk off Malaya by Japanese torpedo-bombers and, in February 1942, a hastily assembled squadron of British, Dutch, and American cruisers was overwhelmed in the Battle of the Java Sea, so consummating the destruction of European seapower in the Far East. By the end of April Japan had completed her conquest of an empire that rendered her economically self-sufficient.

Yamamoto nevertheless recognised how vulnerable this vast new imperial periphery must be to counter-offensives by resurgent American sea power. So in

June 1942 he decided to launch a major operation with the purpose of destroying the enemy's remaining maritime strength in the Pacific before new American fleets could reach the seas from the shipyards.

His operational plan reveals once again Yamamoto the gambler: Yamamoto the poker-player seeking to bluff an opponent into a mistaken call. He intended first to despatch an amphibious task-force to attack the American island base of Midway, a stepping-stone to Hawaii and Pearl Harbor itself. This move would, he hoped, entice what was left of the US Pacific Fleet, including its two available aircraft-carriers, to steam to Midway's defence, whereupon the American task-force would be ambushed by the entire Japanese Combined Fleet – eight aircraft-carriers (four of them large 'attack' carriers), eleven battleships, twenty-two cruisers, and sixty-five destroyers, plus a screen of twenty-one submarines. On 21 May 1942 the fleet steamed out of Hashira naval anchorage to the cheering of onlookers and the blessings of Shinto priests; and on 4 June 1942 the battle was joined.

It did not go at all according to Yamamoto's plan. In the first place, the Americans had broken the Japanese electro-mechanical ciphers (equivalent of the German Enigma), and therefore knew that a Japanese raid on the Aleutian Islands off Alaska was a mere diversion, and that Midway was Yamamoto's true destination. Secondly, while Japanese intelligence had reckoned on only two American aircraft-carriers being available, a third, the *Yorktown* (damaged in the Battle of the Coral Sea in May), had been made fit for sea thanks to a prodigious feat of work in the dockyard. And finally, there were critical flaws in Yamamoto's own over-elaborate plan for deploying his fleet. He had divided it into separate task-forces too distant one from another to lend each other immediate mutual support. In particular, the four big 'attack' carriers were steaming some 300 miles ahead of the battleship force under Yamamoto's direct command, and out of communication with the flagship because of the radio silence imposed by Yamamoto for the sake of 'surprise'. Furthermore, the Japanese ships were tactically handicapped by lack of radar.

In the ensuing battle, Yamamoto lost all four of his big carriers, unluckily caught without air cover because their aircraft were all on deck being re-fuelled and re-armed between sorties. The Americans only lost the *Yorktown*. Even with eleven battleships to none, Yamamoto would not risk another lethal American air strike, and he turned the Combined Fleet for home. This was the first naval battle in history to be decided by aircraft alone – the first where the surface ships never sighted each other.

Defeat and disaster subject a leader to the severest possible test of character. Yamamoto passed this test, telling his tearful and near-hysterical staff: 'I will apologise to the Emperor myself. It's all my fault. Do not speak badly of the carrier force.'

But how deeply he was hit personally by this defeat was shown when he retired to his cabin for several days with severe stomach cramps.

Japan had lost a battle that ranked with Trafalgar in historical importance. Now there must ensue a war of attrition which she was bound to lose, just as Yamamoto had always feared, and which he likened to a sumo wrestling match. In December 1942 he wrote to a friend:

> Even though America has lost one warship after another it does not seem to bother her at all. I think America's national power is immense and also that her national courage is remarkable.

By 1943 he saw more clearly than ever that Japan was heading for defeat, while he himself was now desperately tired and war-weary; even, in the Japanese fashion, eager for his own death. And this release came to him on 18 April 1943 when his aircraft was intercepted and shot down near Guadalcanal in the south-west Pacific by American fighters which knew his exact course and schedule, thanks to the breaking of the Japanese ciphers.

In his will, drafted in May 1939 when he feared assassination, Yamamoto had written:

> For a warrior, dying for one's country is the most honourable thing. It makes no difference whether the death is on the battlefield or at home. It is easy to die like a warrior on the battlefield but it is difficult to die for a principle. The grace of the Emperor is great, and Japanese history is as long as eternity. I cannot help but think about Japan's future. My personal honour, life or death is of no concern.

References

1. The Japanese ambassador in Washington did not present Japan's declaration of war until after the Pearl Harbor strike was launched.
2. Unless otherwise sourced, all quotes from Yamamoto's family or former colleagues are taken from interviews conducted by the BBC for the 1973 television series 'The Commanders'.
3. Agawa ...
4. Agawa, p.000.
5. Loc.cit.
6. The Netherlands Government in exile, sovereign power in the Dutch East Indies.
7. Agawa.
8. Interview with BBC television, 1973.
9. Agawa, loc. cit.
10. Ibid.

CHAPTER 14

From Defeat into Victory

General Sir William Slim

On 13 March 1942 Major General William Slim, who barely a week earlier had been serving in Iraq as GOC of 10th Indian Division, took up command of I Burma Corps or 'Burcorps', in an improvised headquarters in the Law Courts at Prome, some 120 miles north of Rangoon, the capital of the British colony of Burma and already in the hands of the Japanese invaders. Although he was charged with the task of defeating any further enemy advance, especially towards the Burmese oilfields, he quickly found that he had been plunged into the worst of all plights for a military leader, that of taking over an already desperately compromised campaign. His predecessor in command had prematurely blown the bridge over the Sittang river east of Rangoon while 17th Indian Division lay still on the far side. Since then the Japanese had pursued their favourite outflanking manoeuvre of moving on foot or on bicycle across country, and then blocking the roads behind British forces dependent on motor transport.

To oppose this formidable and fast-moving enemy, Slim could only field the 4,000 exhausted men who still remained of the 17th Indian Division after the Sittang disaster, plus the Burma Division, a scratch formation in no way fit to take on the Japanese. In any case, 17th Indian Division had only just finished recruit training, and, moreover, in preparation for the North African desert, not the Burmese jungle and rubber plantations. Morale among rear echelon troops verged on the panicky, while Burcorps was devoid of organised structure of any kind, even a headquarters staff. For allies, Slim could only look to Chinese troops of unknown quality under their American commander, General 'Vinegar Joe' Stilwell, a notorious hater of 'Limeys'. Wrote Slim in his memoirs:

> This was not the first, nor was it to be the last, time that I had taken over a situation that was not going too well. I knew the feeling of unease that comes first at such times, a sinking of the heart as the gloomy facts crowd in; then the glow of exhilaration as the brain grapples with problem after problem; lastly the tingling of the nerves and the lightening of the spirit, as the urge to get out and tackle the job takes hold.[2]

In 'tackling the job' Slim possessed two assets. The first was that both his divisional commanders were personal friends from his own regiment, the 6th Gurkhas: Major Generals 'Punch' Cowan of 17th Indian Division and Bruce Scott of Burma Division. And the second lay in the impact of his own leadership.

*   *   *

Slim's origins were highly unorthodox for a British general. He was born in 1891 in Bristol into the genteel lower-middle-class world of an H. G. Wells novel, and, after the family moved to Birmingham, educated at King Edward's School. He began his working life as a student teacher and then as a clerk on a high stool at Stewart and Lloyds, the Birmingham steel firm. Although in that era a grammar-school boy had precious little chance of becoming an officer in the British army, Slim was already fascinated by things military. Having been in the school cadet corps, he managed to wangle himself into the University Officer Training corps as a lance corporal. The outbreak of the Great War in 1914 freed him forever from his clerk's high stool. For Kitchener's 'New Army' of volunteers needed officers, and Slim, as a non-commissioned officer in his school's Officer Training Corps, was just the type; and so off he went to Tidworth Camp in Hampshire as a second lieutenant commanding a platoon of the Royal Warwickshire Regiment. It is therefore not true, as legend sometimes has it, that he rose from the ranks while serving in the Army.

Right from the start, Slim had found his vocation. He was to write years later of this period of his life:

> I have commanded everything from a section of half a dozen men to an
> Army Group of a million and a half, and I still look back to the time when
> I commanded a platoon as the best command I ever had.

Slim was badly wounded in the shoulder at Gallipoli fighting alongside the 6th Gurkhas, who so impressed him that he asked to join them when he received a commission in the Indian Army after the war. His choice of regiment was important in terms of his future style of leadership because Gurkha soldiers were volunteers coming from yeoman-farmer stock. To command such men required not just the giving of orders but true leadership - humanity and humour as well as firmness.

As adjutant of his regiment in the 1920s Slim proved meticulous and exacting. In his own words:

> it is not enough to be efficient; the organisation must look efficient. If you
> enter the lines of a regiment where the Quarter Guard is smart and alert
> and the men you meet are well turned out and salute briskly, you cannot
> fail to get the impression of efficiency. You are right: ten to one the unit is
> efficient.

By the time the Second World War broke out in 1939 Slim had distinguished himself as a student at the Imperial Defence College (today the Royal College of Defence Studies); as Commandant of the senior officers' school in India; and as a successful short-story writer for Blackwood's Magazine. In 1940-41 he served in the Middle East, fighting the Italians in Ethiopia, the Vichy-French in Syria, and then, as GOC 10th Indian Division, surviving Russian toasts in vodka after British and Soviet troops had jointly occupied Iran in order to eliminate German influence and secure a direct route from the Persian Gulf for Western aid to the Soviet Union.

Now, in March 1942, he was for the first time shouldering responsibility for an entire campaign.

* * *

Slim appreciated that his only hope of stopping the Japanese was to concentrate his two divisions (which were now separated by the jungle-covered mountain ranges of the Pegu Yomas), join with Stilwell's Chinese, and regain the initiative by launching a well-directed counter-stroke. By 3 April 1942 he had at least succeeded in re-uniting Burcorps north of Prome. But to regain the initiative with tired and ill-trained troops unavoidably stretched over too wide a front proved impossible. Time and again his plans crumbled to dust as the Japanese infiltrated behind him and forced him to scramble back in retreat. Time and again his powers of judgement and decision, his sheer fortitude, were put to the test. By 14 April the Japanese were close to the Yenangyaung oilfields, and Slim on his own responsibility ordered that the installations be destroyed and the oil tanks fired. On the 17th the bulk of Burma Division under Major General Bruce Scott was cut off amid the flames. An attempt by Stilwell's Chinese troops to break through the encircling enemy failed. The only hope now lay in a combined British-Chinese counter-attack due to be launched on the following day. Yet Scott asked Slim's permission to try to break out that very night, on the score that his soldiers were exhausted and without food or water.

> Scott was the last man to paint an unduly dark picture [wrote Slim in his memoirs]. I knew his men were almost at the end of their strength ... I could not help wishing that he had not been so close a friend. I thought of his wife and boys ... .

For Slim personally this was the grimmest moment of the campaign. Yet eyewitnesses remembered how gently, courteously, and yet with iron authority Slim told Scott that he must stay put until the planned counter-attack next day. When Slim stepped out of the radio van he faced a half-circle of his own staff and of Chinese liaison officers:

> They stood there silent and looked at me. All commanders know that look.
> They see it in the eyes of their staffs and their men when things are really
> bad, when the toughest soldiers want holding up, and they turn where they
> *should* turn for support – to their commander. And sometimes he does not
> know what to say. He feels very much alone. 'Well, gentlemen,' I said,
> putting on what I hoped was a confident, cheerful expression, 'it might be
> worse.' One of the group, in a sepulchral voice, replied with the single word:
> 'How?' I could cheerfully have murdered him, but instead I had to keep my
> temper. 'Oh,' I said, 'it might be raining.' Two hours later, it was ...

The counter-stroke failed: Scott had to abandon his guns and transport and scramble
out as best he could. On 28 April Slim's superior, Lieutenant General Sir Harold
Alexander, ordered him to withdraw Burcorps to India. The final retreat across the
Irrawaddy and the Chindwin and then up the Kabaw valley was marked not only
by relentless Japanese attempts finally to trap Burcorps, but also by extremities of
exhaustion and thirst in the appalling heat, and by the ravages of malaria and
dysentery. Every man from corps commander down to private soldier was haunted
by the fear that at any time the monsoon rains could dissolve the mountain track
that led to India, and so deliver them to the enemy. In Slim's own words:

> Men's nerves were wearing thin. I do not altogether wonder that I said to
> myself at this time, 'If somebody brings me a bit of good news, I shall
> burst into tears'. I was never put to the test.

In the event, it was the monsoon that saved Burcorps by bringing its Japanese
pursuers to a halt, up to their necks in mud.

It says much about the impact of Slim's leadership that at the end of so dreadful
a campaign his troops retreated into India as formed bodies under their officers,
marching past their corps commander as he stood by the roadside, and cheering
him. Slim remarked of this moment:

> To be cheered by troops who you have led to victory is grand and
> exhilarating. To be cheered by the gaunt remnants of those you have led
> only in defeat, withdrawal and disaster, is infinitely moving - and
> humbling.

Nevertheless, he had succeeded in the most exacting test of military leadership –
that of successfully conducting a perilous retreat. But Slim himself, pondering the
course of the campaign with characteristic modesty and self-awareness, saw it
differently:

> The most distressing aspect of the whole disastrous campaign had been the
> contrast between my generalship and the enemy's ... For myself, I had little
> to be proud of; I could not rate my generalship high ...

Nevertheless, the experience, confronted in this unflinching way, served to mature and toughen Slim as a leader where it might have destroyed a lesser man. When in October 1943 he was appointed to command the new Fourteenth Army in Assam, he brought to the task an armour-steel resolve to smash the Japanese in battle and re-conquer Burma. The defeat of 1942 proved the essential moral foundation for the victory to come.

*   *   *

Yet the new army commander faced a challenge of leadership more daunting than faced any other British general in the Second World War. The jungle where his British, Indian, Gurkha, Burmese (and, later, East and West African) soldiers lived and fought was itself a potent enemy of morale. It was close and claustrophobic, full of strange noises; heaven-made for Japanese ambushes. It was suffocatingly hot and humid, or, during the monsoon, a liquid world of rain and mud. Its wild-life comprised poisonous snakes, poisonous insects, leeches, ticks, malarial mosquitoes. The border of Assam and Burma was a very long way from home, and Fourteenth Army and South-East Asia Command occupied a place in British newspapers a very long way below the glamorous and well-publicised exploits of the Eighth Army in the Mediterranean theatre. Likewise, South-East Asia was still bottom of the list for equipment and supplies.

Above all, the Fourteenth Army – like the Americans and Australians in the Pacific theatre – faced a peculiarly formidable, and indeed terrifying, enemy in the Japanese. Conditioned by their culture and their religion to embrace death in battle for the Emperor as a supreme happiness, and to regard surrender as dishonour beyond bearing, they had the unpleasant habit of literally fighting to the last man. They also appallingly mistreated their prisoners, even where they did not actually tie them to poles and use them for bayonet practice. Slim's new task of leadership was made even more difficult because in the early months of 1943, British and Indian troops in Burma had once again been humiliatingly outfought by the Japanese. Prodded by an ever-impatient Winston Churchill in London, General Sir Archibald Wavell, the Commander-in-Chief in India, had launched a premature offensive down the Arakan peninsula on the west coast of Burma. The operation stalled before powerful Japanese defences, whereupon an enemy counter-offensive struck the attackers in the flank and tumbled them back to their start-line.

The only bright spot in terms of morale lay in what Slim called 'the somewhat phoney propaganda' that followed Orde Wingate's first Chindit operation behind the Japanese lines in February-April 1943.

Wrote Slim later:

Against us was that record of defeat, that lack of basic amenities, the discomfort of life in the jungle, and, worst of all, the feeling of long separation from home. The British soldier, especially, suffered from what he felt was the lack of appreciation by his own people and at times of their forgetfulness of his very existence. The men were calling themselves a 'forgotten army' long before some newspaper correspondent seized on the phrase. This feeling of neglect had sunk deep. There was a good deal of bitterness in the army.

He fully recognised how dangerous a threat to the spirit of his army was posed by the terrain itself:

> It could fairly be described as some of the world's worst country, breeding the world's worst diseases, and having for half the year at least the world's worst climate. To move even small pack-caravans from Burma to India was so difficult that no proper trading route existed.

In fact, supply was the limiting factor on operations along the India-Burma frontier – something Churchill could never grasp. Slim's army in Assam depended on a rickety 600-mile line of communication: broad-gauge railway from Calcutta, then metre-gauge railway; a ferry over the Brahmaputra river; and then more metre-gauge railway up into the hills to the main operational base at Dimapur. This railway had been built to carry tea from the plantations, with a carrying capacity of 600 tons a day. Now Slim's engineers strove to improve the line – and keep it open in the face of floods, bombing, landslides, and even an earthquake. By 1944 its capacity had been raised to 4,400 tons a day. Beyond the railhead at Dimapur, the roads to the forward areas had to be carved out of the hillsides by human muscle because of lack of machines.

But to Slim, morale remained the key problem he must solve:

> I felt there was only one way to do it, by direct approach to the individual men themselves, by informal talks and contacts ... Whenever I could get away from my HQ I was in those early months more like a Parliamentary candidate than a general ... except that I never made a promise.

He would joke in Gurkhali with Gurkha soldiers, talk in Urdu to the Indians; and with the British squaddie find the homely, human comment which exactly hit the mark. When addressing a gathering of soldiers he gave his standard spiel:

> Well, I'm not here so that you can just look at my face – I'm no oil painting – but I'm here so you can see the man who's going to bugger you about.

A hospital matron remembered how when Slim visited the sick and wounded, 'he sat on the beds and chatted to the boys, leaning his chin on his stick"[3] Slim did indeed make immense efforts to improve the state of health and hygiene in his army. When he took command, the malaria rate was 84 per cent of its total strength. By 1945 it was down to one case per thousand soldiers per day. Since the whole theatre was short of supplies, he encouraged self-help and ingenuity in all the measures to make the army healthier and also more comfortable out of the fighting line, such as better rest camps.

However, Slim's skills as an organiser who cared for his soldiers, as a 'parliamentary candidate' (in his words) talking with his 'constituents', or even his impressive outward appearance, cannot by themselves account for the trust, or faith even, that he came to evoke from his army. Every great leader of fighting forces must be able to evoke this faith in himself as a talisman; to inspire the feeling in the ranks that if he is at the helm, all will be well, however ghastly things may look. With Slim the secret lay in a combination of *military* ability – professional competence and knowledge, strategic inventiveness – and sheer integrity and strength of character. Those who served closest to him during his command of Fourteenth Army testify to these qualities. Here was a man big of physique, deep voiced, with a jutting jaw which – however unscientifically – men took as a proof of stubborn resolution. Slim's whole personality exuded strength and calm.[4] These qualities were coupled with a powerfully commonsensical mind. In the judgement of Brigadier 'Taffy' Davies, Slim's Chief of Staff during the first Burma campaign,

> He could think terribly simply, get through any problem and find the right answer. And having found the answer he was equally capable of handing it on to his subordinates with the greatest of clarity and simplicity.

According to Air Vice Marshal Stanley Vincent, commander of the tactical air force in Burma, 'His effect was immediate; honesty, sterling worth – you trusted in what he said as genuine.' Lieutenant General Sir Geoffrey Scoones, commander of IV Corps in the hard-fought Battle of Imphal-Kohima in 1944, was to recall Slim as

> a chap who gave you confidence. The reason is that he knew his job, which is the basis of the confidence of troops in any commander. He was straightforward and no frigging about. He was a very strong character – very strong convictions.

General Sir Ouvry Roberts, who as a major general commanded the 23rd Division in the same battle, reckoned in retrospect that Slim 'had the best brain of any of the generals who rose to the top'. His Chief Engineer, Major General 'Bill' Hasted, later had this to say: 'The key word in his case is 'trust' - his ability to trust people and in so doing to get the best out of them in endeavour and initiative. Trust begets trust and therefore everyone in turn trusted him.' And according to Colonel Nigel Bruce who, as his ADC, saw him at close quarters throughout the campaign,

> Slim was a simple but profound man. His relaxations were walking and reading. *Deep* reading – mysticism and philosophy and religion. He wasn't

just a soldier, but a man of very deep spiritual understanding. This was his inner strength.

But of course the whole purpose of Slim's campaign of projecting his leadership was to forge an instrument that could defeat the dreaded Japanese in battle. The turning-point came with a second battle in the Arakan Peninsula in February 1944 – and the first battle fought by the new Fourteenth Army under Slim's command. General Mutaguchi, commanding the Japanese Fifteenth Army in Burma, planned for 1944 a major offensive into India in order to capture Slim's main base area in the plain of Imphal, and so pre-empt a combined British and Chinese concentric invasion of Burma. As a preliminary diversion the Japanese 55th Division was to attack in the Arakan, surrounding and destroying in turn the 7th Indian and 5th Indian Divisions of Lieutenant General Sir Philip Christison's XV Corps. On 4 February 1944 Mutaguchi began the well-tried, and so far successful, ploy of infiltrating behind the British frontline troops and cutting them off.

In the past this ploy had always induced the British to turn back to clear their communications. But this time it failed to work. On Slim's orders, the British forces stayed put even though surrounded – and were air-supplied by American transport aircraft. Meanwhile, ferocious Japanese attacks on the 7th Indian Division's defensive perimeter – the so-called 'admin box' – were fought to a standstill. When Slim launched two reserve divisions into the battle, the Japanese gave up and retreated, with XV Corps following up in pursuit.

Slim had prepared for this success with commendable thoroughness. He had deployed half the total strength of his army to the Arakan in order to ensure victory in the land battle. In conjunction with the American General Old, commanding the US Combat Cargo Force, he and his staff had pre-planned the air-drop operation in detail, including packing programmes for the supply of a force larger than a division for several days. In Slim's words, 'Everything that it would require, from pills to projectiles, from bully beef to boots, was laid out, packed for dropping, at the airstrips.'

Yet the outcome had still depended on the skills and staunchness of the British and Indian troops on the ground. By outfighting the Japanese, they had demonstrated the high morale and professionalism in Fourteenth Army brought about by Slim's leadership.

In Slim's own judgement, this second battle in the Arakan marked the turning point in the Burma Campaign: 'It was the first time we had won a battle on a spot where we had previously lost one.' For the first time too, 'a British force had met, held, and decisively defeated a major Japanese attack ... The legend of Japanese invincibility in the jungle ... was smashed.'

But the battle in the Arakan marked only the opening phase of the 1944 campaign. Slim himself had been preparing a major offensive to be launched from

Assam's Imphal plain into Burma. This had entailed the stocking of large supply depots around Imphal, as well as the forward deployment of attack divisions. As it happened, Mutaguchi had been accelerating preparations for his own offensive aimed at occupying this same Imphal-Kohima area, and in particular capturing the main British base and railhead at Dimapur.

Once Slim became aware of these enemy preparations, he abandoned his own offensive plans in favour of enticing the Japanese on to ground of his own choice in the Imphal plain, and there smashing the enemy by superior numbers and firepower. He would then launch a counter-offensive against the enfeebled enemy that would carry Fourteenth Army forward into Burma.

Unfortunately, Mutaguchi launched his offensive a week earlier than Slim had expected, thanks to the drastic expedient of providing no logistic support for his attack divisions, in the belief that they would be able to supply themselves from captured British dumps. As bad luck would have it, Mutaguchi's early advance caught Slim at a moment when he had committed the most serious strategic misjudgements of his career. Firstly, Slim had unbalanced Fourteenth Army by committing six divisions to the Arakan offensive and leaving only three deployed on the Kohima-Imphal front, even though he later justified this decision on the score that he needed overwhelming strength in the Arakan to make sure of success. Secondly, he wrongly appreciated that he would have time to switch divisions back from the Arakan to Imphal before the Japanese could attack. And, thirdly, he made a capital error of calculation in regard to his planned defensive battle in the Imphal plain, for instead of ordering his forward divisions back in good time to concentrate for the battle, he left it to the corps commander, Scoones, to decide when they should begin to retire. But Scoones was late in issuing his own order, despite warnings from his divisional commanders that Japanese were massing for attack.

The result was that instead of withdrawing in good order to the 'killing ground' where Slim had hoped to smash the Japanese, 17th and 20th Divisions had to fight their way back in great danger of encirclement and defeat in detail. Slim's defensive battle was therefore out of balance from the very beginning. He himself acknowledged later with characteristic honesty that he had blundered:

> It was an error that was likely to cost us dear ... Kohima with its rather scratch garrison and, what was worse, Dimapur with no garrison at all, were in deadly peril. As I contemplated the chain of disasters I had invited, my heart sank.

So instead of the comfortable smashing-up of the Japanese from prepared positions, there took place a confused, desperate, and prolonged close-range struggle, a kind of Verdun on jungle-clad hills. Soon the garrisons of Kohima and Imphal were completely cut off and dependent on air supply, while Kohima especially lay in terrible peril. Now what counted was cool-headedness in judging where and when to feed in reinforcements – and, more than that, the raw quality of leadership needed to maintain the confidence and cohesion of troops and commanders.

And this quality of leadership Slim provided in full measure. General Scoones recalled:

> When he flew into Imphal during the battle, he was unflappable. We would exchange what we thought were funny jokes. Bill was always cheerful – not like one visitor who said: 'I don't see how you can survive ...'

Ouvry Roberts (GOC 20th Division) was to say:

> I never saw him despondent at any time. He showed no sign at all that things were going wrong at Imphal ... He would get out of his jeep and say, 'Hello, Ouvry, how's things?' Very casual. Then he'd ask me to introduce him to some officers, ask them questions, try and see and hear as much as he could for himself, assess morale for himself. Then of course he loved to talk to his Gurkhas. He had a quiet authority ...

Gradually the grip of the now disease-ridden and starving Japanese round Imphal and Kohima was prised open by relieving forces ordered up by Slim; and on 10 July 1944 General Mutaguchi finally ordered his beaten troops to retreat. He had lost 53,000 men killed in battle or died of disease out of his initial strength of 85,000.

Thus by sheer personal leadership in the battle itself – and the staunchness of his troops, Indian and British – Slim had redeemed his earlier errors, and won a crushing victory. Now the way was open for the re-conquest of Burma.

The campaign would be the first in history to be supplied for the most part from the air: an innovation that owed itself by the close teamwork between Slim and the commanders of the American and British air forces in the theatre.

Slim's offensive began with an advance through the monsoon rains from the Indian frontier to the River Chindwin, which Fourteenth Army crossed in December 1944 by means of the longest Bailey prefabricated bridge in the world. With a firm bridgehead over the Chindwin, Slim could prepare to smash the still powerful Japanese army defending central Burma. His plan was to fight a decisive battle in the Shwebo plain north of the River Irrawaddy, where his superiority in airpower and armoured forces could best be brought to bear. Slim was quite sure that this was where the enemy would elect to fight him:

> I relied on my knowledge of the Japanese and on the mentality of their high command as I had known it ... I thought he would never dare to lose face by giving up territory without a struggle.

Yet in the event Slim proved utterly mistaken. The Japanese, now under a new commander, Kimura, instead withdrew behind the mile-wide barrier of the Irrawaddy. Slim therefore had to think again. The resulting new plan, EXTENDED CAPITAL, can justly be called a strategic masterpiece. He would cross the Irrawaddy *north* of Mandalay with XXXIII Corps and lock the Japanese in a frontal battle, so convincing them that this was to be his main thrust. Meanwhile, his IV Corps (now commanded by Lieutenant General Frank Messervy) would secretly make a southward flank march, cross the Irrawaddy where least expected by the Japanese, and then strike east towards Meiktila, deep in the enemy's rear, and the nodal point of his communications.

In terms of arrows drawn on the map, EXTENDED CAPITAL appears splendidly simple, but the logistical problems and the operational risks were alike enormous. The southward flank-march of IV Corps to the crossing point over the Irrawaddy would take it along 400 miles of abominable track. The corps would then have to cross the mile-wide Irrawaddy without any of the specialised craft and equipment available in the European or Pacific theatres. Moreover, absolute secrecy was vital to success. It is therefore little wonder that the 400-mile flank march of IV Corps in February 1945 constituted the period of greatest tension during Slim's time in command of Fourteenth Army. His air force colleague, Air Vice Marshal Vincent (who shared a joint HQ with Slim) remembered that 'it was the only time he got a little on edge'. His ADC, Nigel Bruce, recalled that when Slim one day caught two officers having their lunch rations before their soldiers had been fed, 'Slim lost his temper; he was cold and terrifying.'

He himself later confessed to the anxieties which he had sought to conceal at the time:

> sometimes doubt and fear slunk in upon me. I was asking so much of them [his troops] - was it too much? Success depended on what? Luck? A Japanese pilot streaking the tree-tops, an enemy agent with a wireless set crouched above the track counting tanks – and Kimura's divisions would move, the muzzles of his guns swing towards our crossing places. Imagination is a necessity for a general, providing it is a *controlled* imagination. At times I regained control of mine only by an effort of will, of concentration on the job in hand. And then I walked once more among my soldiers, and I, who should have inspired them, not for the first or the last time, drew courage from them.[5]

But when on 14 February 1945 IV Corps won a bridgehead across the Irrawaddy at Pagan against only light opposition, Slim had achieved the complete strategic surprise for which he had hoped. A battlegroup of armour, infantry and guns under 'Punch' Cowan swept eighty miles across open country to Meiktila, and captured it four days later. Now came frenzied Japanese counter-strokes in their attempt to re-take the town, the key to their entire position in central Burma. Slim flew up to the front in order to lend personal support to Cowan, who was conducting this crucial battle. He was impressed with Cowan's performance:

> To watch a highly skilled, experienced, and resolute commander controlling a hard-fought battle is to see, not only a man triumphing over the highest mental and physical stresses, but an artist producing his effects in the most complicated and difficult of all the arts.

At one point, Slim left Cowan's side to go forward with a party of officers to watch bunkers being cleared of Japanese only a few yards away – only to discover that their party was in the direct line of fire from a Sherman tank attacking the bunkers from the opposite side. In his own words, 'one army commander, one corps commander, one American general, and several less distinguished individuals adopted the prone position with remarkable unanimity.'

Despite the desperate ferocity of the Japanese as they strove to clear their communications, they were beaten off, with the result that the entire Japanese defence in the Mandalay-Meiktila area now collapsed. Slim's stunning victory marked the end of any serious Japanese attempt to defend Burma. On 18 March 1945 Slim issued an operation order for 'the capture of Rangoon at all costs and as soon as possible before the monsoon'. His purpose was to cut off the remaining Japanese forces in Burma before they could escape into Thailand. Yet this final chase brought its own trials and anxieties. Slim's tanks and motor transport were worn-out and liable to break-downs, while air supply was interrupted by the low clouds of the impending monsoon. In its southward advance from Mandalay to Rangoon the Fourteenth Army swapped the dusty dryness of the Meiktila battlefield for rainstorms and steamy, stifling heat, debilitating to already desperately tired troops. In the face of any hold-ups to the advance, Slim's customary mask of calm for the first time slipped. When one truck driver took the opportunity to have a much-needed 'kip' because the truck in front had got stuck in the mud, he was awakened by the loud noise of his door being wrenched open:

> I found myself confronted by no less a person that the Army Commander who was demanding in a very irate voice what the bloody hell I was doing sitting on my backside when there was a truck stuck in front of me and I should be doing something about it.

In remarkably short order, everyone present was 'heaving like mad and I was rather intrigued to find that beside me was the Army Commander, with his shoulder behind the truck pushing hard as well.'

On 2 May 1945, Rangoon, capital of Burma, was captured – not, however, by Slim and his soldiers despite their supreme effort, but to a force landed from the sea by Admiral Lord Louis Mountbatten, Supreme Allied Commander, South-East Asia.

It was at this moment of victory that Slim's superior, General Sir Oliver Leese (Commander Allied Land Forces South-East Asia), a Montgomery man from Italy, decided that Slim was 'tired' and not the man to command the planned forthcoming seaborne invasion of Malaya, and so effectively sacked him. Leese contended later it was all a misunderstanding, but Slim was quite certain from what Leese had said to him that he had indeed been sacked. His reaction to this dismissal at the very moment of his final triumph provides a further insight into his greatness of character:

> It was a bit of a jar [he wrote to a padre friend] as I thought the Fourteenth Army had done rather well. However, he [Leese] is the man to decide. I have had to sack a number of chaps in my time, and those I liked best were the ones who did not squeal. I have applied for my bowler hat and am awaiting result.

There followed much frantic signalling between various headquarters in South-East Asia Command, and between that Command and the Chief of the Imperial General Staff in London, who was outraged at Leese's action. The result was that Leese got 'the bowler hat' instead of Slim, and 'Uncle Bill' (as Slim's soldiers affectionately called him), became Commander Allied Land Forces South-East Asia in Leese's place.

On 12 September 1945, a month after Japan's unconditional surrender, Slim was present when there took place in Singapore the formal surrender of all Japanese forces in South East-Asia.

> I looked at the dull impassive masks of the Japanese generals and admirals seated opposite. Their plight moved me not at all. For them, I had none of the sympathy of soldier for soldier ... I knew too well what these men and those under their orders had done to *their* prisoners. They sat there apart from the rest of humanity.

General Douglas MacArthur, who had taken the Japanese national surrender on behalf of the allies, had instructed that the ceremony of yielding up swords to the victors should not be enforced. Mountbatten and Slim simply ignored this edict:

> In South-East Asia [wrote Slim] all Japanese officers surrendered their swords to British officers of similar or higher rank. Field Marshal Terauchi's sword is in Admiral Mountbatten's hands; General Kimura's is on my mantelpiece, where I always intended that one day it should be.

References

1. *Defeat into Victory* was the title given by Lord Slim to his own acccount of the Burma campaign, and cannot be bettered as a terse summing-up of Fourteenth Army's achievement in 1942–45.

2. Slim, *Defeat into Victory*, p.27. All further quotations from Slim himself are from this book, unless otherwise cited, and are reproduced by permission of the Second Viscount Slim. All eyewitness quotations from Slim's colleagues and subordinates are from personal interviews conducted in 1973 for the BBC television series 'The Commanders'.

3. Interview for the BBC Television series 'The Commanders'.

4. Slim is the only one of the leaders in this book that I have met personally. This was in the 1960s, at the end of his life, when he was Governor of Windsor Castle. I had written to him to ask him for information about the South-east Asia theatre of war, and he responded by asking me to lunch at the Castle. The outward characteristics were just as one expected: the bigness of physique, the deep voice, the general impression of massive strength and calm. But other things, even in that brief time together, showed me what it was about him that made him a great leader of men. Firstly, his look of appraisal when we shook hands: not unfriendly but with the quality of making me feel that if I were going to measure up to his standards, I would have to try bloody hard. The second thing about him was his modesty and courtesy, given who he was and who I was – the way he encouraged me to talk, rather than talking about himself as Montgomery did when I visited him. And the third thing was that when I had aired various facile opinions, he would quickly offer a comment so well-informed on the topic, so devastatingly sensible, as to make one feel a pretentious ass.

5. Slim, p.534.

CHAPTER 15

Fire Raiser in Chief

Marshal of the Royal Air Force
Sir Arthur Harris

Arthur Harris ('Bert' to his friends; 'Bomber' Harris to the media) conducted the only British offensive in the Second World War to rival the attrition battles on the Western Front in the Great War for sheer duration and the percentage of the attacking force killed in action. Bomber Command's total losses in aircrew (all volunters, all by army standards officer-quality even if NCOs) came to 57,000 – twice the 'Lost Generation' of subalterns on the Western Front so lamented in national memory. And while the Second Battle of Alamein in 1942 lasted a mere fortnight and the Battle of Normandy in 1944 some six weeks, Bomber Command's main offensive against German cities lasted for some three years, with operations carried out night after night, month after month, and against an ever more formidable enemy air defence system. To conduct such an offensive demanded supreme powers of leadership.

I wonder if the frightful strain of commanding a large air force in war can ever be realised except by the very few who have experienced it. The commander of a bomber force has to commit it every twenty-four hours. Every operation is a major battle, and [since] much depends on the outcome, success is as vital and disaster as grave, as on any other occasion when the whole of a force engages the enemy.

So Harris wrote in his war memoirs. And he went on:

In addition, there is the continuous and fearful apprehension of what the weather may do, especially in the climate of north-west Europe. I should have been able to justify myself completely if I had left the whole force on the ground, if I had done nothing whatever, on 9 occasions out of 10 ... It is best to leave to the imagination what such daily strain amounts to when continued over a period of years.[1]

* * *

The grand-strategic decision to seek Germany's defeat by means of bombing her industrial machine to a standstill was taken by Winston Churchill and the War Cabinet twenty months before Harris became Air Officer Commanding-in-Chief of Bomber Command on 23 February 1942. With the collapse of France in June 1940, Britain was left fighting Nazi Germany on her own except for relatively small contingents by land, sea, and air from the Dominions (Australia, Canada, New Zealand, and South Africa) and India. The United States of America remained resolutely neutral, while the Soviet Union and Nazi Germany had concluded a pact of friendship. And even if Britain herself survived the current threat of a German invasion, she could never raise an army large enough to defeat the Wehrmacht in battle and liberate Western Europe. How then in the summer of 1940 could she hope to win the war?

> there is one thing that will bring the enemy down, and that is an absolutely devastating, exterminating attack by very heavy bombers from this country upon the Nazi homeland. We must be able to overwhelm him by this means, without which I do not see a way through.[2]

So wrote Winston Churchill to Lord Beaverbrook (Minister of Aircraft Production) on 8 July 1940. The War Cabinet could only agree. All possible resources should be devoted to the manufacture of bombers on the largest feasible scale, along with a parallel programme for training the aircrews.

At long last, therefore, was to be fulfilled the vision of the airpower prophets who in the 1920s and 1930s had proclaimed that future wars would be decided not by mass armies slogging it out on the ground, but by the bomber striking at the enemy's heartland.

* * *

The airpower prophets had been inspired by the bomber's modest debut during the Great War. In 1917 the Germans had attacked London and other targets in South-east England with huge Gotha four-engined biplanes, technological wonders though few in number. By Second World War standards the Gothas caused little damage and inflicted few casualties. However, the psychological impact on the British people was out of all proportion. For the first time in history their capital city and other inland conurbations had been bombarded by a foreign power, so destroying their traditional sense of immunity to the violence of war. Of immediate concern to the War Cabinet, local absenteeism in the aftermath of an air raid caused alarming falls in industrial output.

The War Cabinet's first response to the Gotha raids was to re-organise Britain's home-based fighters and anti-aircraft batteries into a new command, the Air Defence of Great Britain. But in the second place they decided that Britain must have its own four-engined heavy-bomber force, which would fly from bases in northern France to attack industrial targets in the Rhineland. It was entitled the 'Independent Air Force' in order to distinguish it operationally from the tactical air squadrons along the Western Front. Nevertheless, production problems in Britain's new aero-engine factories meant that the war had ended before the Independent Air Force had grown large enough to launch a mass offensive.

From the modest results actually achieved by the bomber in the Great War the prophets of airpower in the 1920s fantasised visions of vast air-fleets in perfect formation reducing whole cities to rubble. In 1921 an Italian General, Giulio Douhet, published a widely influential book, *The Command of the Air*, which envisaged the bomber smashing 'the material and moral resources of a people'. Similar science fiction disguised as rational analysis was published in Britain in the 1920s by such prominent strategic thinkers as J. F. C. Fuller and Basil Liddell Hart, whose books imagined the simultaneous obliteration of a dozen great cities and the collapse of civilised life.[3]

Yet by far the most important British evangelist in the 1920s of airpower as a winner of wars was Air Chief Marshal Sir Hugh Trenchard (later Marshal of the Royal Air Force the Viscount Trenchard), nicknamed 'Boom': a man of imposing presence and formidable power of will. Trenchard had commanded the Independent Air Force in the final year of the Great War, and during the 1920s was Chief of Air Staff in the newly-created Royal Air Force. He and his successors never ceased to hammer home to politicians (and to rival service chiefs) that hostile bombers could inflict mortal damage on Britain; never ceased to preach that the only answer to this threat lay in creating a bomber fleet even bigger than the enemy's and able to inflict even worse damage on his cities. The politicians duly took fright. In 1932 the Prime Minister, Stanley Baldwin, famously pronounced that 'the bomber would always get through'.

By this time the Air Staff had convinced Whitehall that by 1939 the German air force would be able to drop 2,000 tons of bombs on the first day of an air offensive. In 1934, Winston Churchill told the House of Commons that around 30,000 to 40,000 people would be killed or maimed in London within a week, and that some 3 million would flee the capital. In 1936 the film 'Things to Come' sensationally depicted these horrors for the benefit of a mass audience.

Nevertheless, the Air Staff later had to admit that its pre-war estimates of the impact of German bombing were largely 'crystal-gazing'. Moreover, the development after 1936 of radar (enabling enemy bombers to be readily intercepted by defending fighters) served to nullify the assertion that the only answer to the bomber was retaliation by even more bombers. Priority in aerial rearmament was therefore switched to fighters, a decision eventually vindicated by Fighter Command's defeat of the Luftwaffe in the Battle of Britain.

It was only therefore because of Britain's desperate national plight in 1940 that the bomber evangelists once again found themselves preaching to receptive listeners. But once again their extravagant claims were soon mocked by operational reality. Far from navigating accurately at night to selected German industrial targets, Bomber Command in 1941 could barely find and hit a large town. Moreover, the technical problems involved in the design, development, and large-scale manufacture of bombers meant that at the beginning of 1942 Bomber Command's available operational strength normally amounted to only about 500 aircraft.

Puffed-up promises contrasted with dismal performance – such, then, was Arthur Harris's inheritance on taking up his post as AOC-in-C Bomber Command on 23 February 1942.

*   *   *

'Bert' Harris was not yet fifty: ruthless, belligerent, and tough: a man flamboyantly outspoken, with a short-fused temper rendered even shorter by a stomach ulcer. His opposite number at RAF Coastal Command at the time, Air Chief Marshal Sir John Slessor (later Lord Slessor), said of him in a 1970s interview:

> He is a man who is singleminded. A desperately cynical character quite unhelpful to interservice relationships. I am not blaming him: he thought he had the secret of winning the war; he simply would not admit to himself that there was anything we needed to do anywhere else ... Nothing mattered to Bert but Bomber Command. He had great guts ...[4]

Field Marshal Sir Gerald Templer remembered Harris as a fellow student at the Camberley Staff College in the late 1920s:

> Many of the people had more brains but no one with a stronger character. It was also apparent that he had the most awful chip on his shoulder: we didn't know why ... I think it was that, for some reason which escaped all of us, he thought we would look down on him because he was a South African ...

Harris soon became notorious for his blunt, even crude, manner of speech and his loathing of bureaucratic circumlocution. As a student at the Staff College he opined that the British Army would never accept the tank until it could eat hay, and shit. When during the Second World War his Chief of Staff sent him a long and wordy paper describing ten different ways of attacking a target, Harris scrawled across the title page in capital letters: 'TRY FERRETS!'

Harris's background was nevertheless typical of the British imperial governing class: his father a member of the Indian Civil Service, and he himself educated at an English public school. As a young man he went off to mine gold in Rhodesia in an era when this newly settled colony somewhat resembled the old American 'Wild West' in its frontier style of life. Here Harris tried his hand at farming, as well as driving mule-teams and four-horse coaches. During the Great War he joined the Rhodesia Regiment as a bugler, but, after some hard marching in hot weather, decided (in his own words) 'to find some way of going to war in a sitting posture'. He found the way as a wartime commissioned officer in the Royal Flying Corps, rising to lead a night-fighter squadron. In the 1920s he commanded a night-bomber squadron in England and a troop-carrying squadron in Iraq. Bored with this humdrum transport role, he fitted his aircraft with bomber racks, though without permission. In 1934 he was appointed Deputy Director of Plans in the Air Ministry, where he played a key role in getting the technical specifications approved for the new heavy bombers which he would later command in war. In 1938 and again in 1941 he visited the United States as a member of British delegations arranging production of equipment for the Royal Air Force. Although all this was valuable experience, his time in the Air Ministry confirmed his contempt for deskbound bureaucrats and pedantic bureaucratic procedures – a loathing which only served to fire up his anger when as AOC-in-C Bomber Command he came into dispute with the men of Whitehall.

Since Harris's acerbic views and uncomfortable character were well known, why was he appointed to lead Britain's strategic air offensive? Certainly, no one could gainsay the range of his professional experience, nor his executive ability. The key to his appointment lay, however, in Bomber Command's operational record so far: dismal in itself, but also damaging to the Royal Air Force's standing with the political leadership in comparison with the Army and Royal Navy. In these present circumstances, what had once seemed Harris's professional vices now appeared as virtues. Here was surely the pilot whose drastic action could save the strategic air offensive from fatally stalling.

* * *

Harris began by laying on a colossal public-relations exercise, codenamed Operation MILLENNIUM. On 20 May 1942 he put into the air every single aircraft he possessed, 1,258 in all (including training aircraft and crews in training), and launched them against the city of Cologne on the Rhine. In his own later words:

> The dangers were many and obvious. If anything went wrong – and this was to be in many ways a wholly new type of operation – then I would be committing not only the whole of my first-line strength but absolutely all my reserves in a single battle.[5]

The raid turned out to be a stunning success. The city lay sprawled beneath a clear sky and a virtually full moon. In three hours Bomber Command dropped 1,500 tons of bombs on this gift of a target, wrecking 600 acres of buildings and raising a pall of smoke 15,000 feet high. British losses were only twenty-nine aircraft, a mere 3.5 per cent of the attacking force.

This astonishing demonstration, dubbed the 'Thousand Bomber Raid' by the BBC and British newspapers, achieved two major things: it revived the spirit of Bomber Command, giving the crews an enduring faith in their new C-in-C; and it convinced Churchill that the bomber was still worth backing. Soon after the raid, Harris wrote off to the Prime Minister a very characteristic missive:

> The success of the 1,000 plan has proved beyond doubt in the minds of all but wilful men that we can even today dispose of a weight of air attack which no country on which it can be brought to bear can survive. We can bring it to bear on the vital part of Germany. It only requires the decision to concentrate it.[6]

And he went on to state again the long-cherished fundamental tenet of the airpower faith:

> It is imperative if we hope to win the war to abandon the disastrous policy of military intervention in the land campaigns of Europe, and concentrate our air power against the enemy's weakest spots.

Yet although Harris certainly convinced Churchill that the bomber offensive was still worth backing, the Prime Minister no longer believed as he had in 1940 that this was the *only* way to win the war. He now regarded it as one among several means of bringing Germany down. For by 1942 both the United States and the Soviet Union had become belligerents, and on the Russian Front the Wehrmacht was locked in colossal battles with the Red Army. Even as early as October 1941 (a month before Pearl Harbor) the Prime Minister had written a masterly letter to the Chief of Air Staff refuting the whole concept of a single decisive weapon:

> One has to do the best one can, but he is an unwise man who thinks there is any *certain* method of winning this war, or indeed any other war between equals in strength. The only plan is to persevere ...[7]

Nor did the thousand-bomber raid mark the opening of a sustained offensive against German cities. It took a further year to solve all the technical and industrial problems involved in producing enough heavy bombers, effective bombs, pyrotechnic target markers, and, above all, electronic navigational and target-locating kit.

Of the three four-engined bombers under development, the Short Stirling proved just too heavy, and unable to attain its specified performances in height or speed, although experienced pilots could get it up to its designed operating altitude.

The Avro Manchester, with two Rolls Royce Vulture engines, had to be abandoned as a failure but, redesigned with four Rolls Royce Merlin engines, became the Lancaster, the outstanding night bomber of the war.

Although the overall number of aircraft in Bomber Command was little larger at the beginning of 1943 compared with the beginning of 1942, the proportion of four-engined bombers carrying much heavier bomb-loads had risen from a quarter to four-fifths. Moreover, now becoming operational were two crucially important British target-finding devices, codenamed Gee and Oboe. Both worked from ground systems in Britain which monitored the bombers' course towards the target. Gee's range was 300-400 miles and gave a position accurate at best to less than half a mile. It worked by enabling an aircraft navigator to fix his position by radio pulses from three triangulated ground transmitters. Oboe proved the most exact blind-bombing device of the Second World War for operations at night, in bad weather, or in industrial haze. The system was based on two ground transmitters located in Britain. A bomber force would fly along a semi-circular radio-beam at the range of the target and centred on one ground transmitter. When this beam was intersected by a second beam aimed straight at the target, it signalled the moment to drop the bomb-load.

Since it proved impossible to manufacture enough Oboe sets to equip every bomber, the Air Ministry's Directorate of Bomber Operations decided to create a special Pathfinder force of aircraft equipped with Oboe and manned by selected crews. Having pinpointed the target by Oboe, the Pathfinders would mark it brilliantly by coloured flares on the ground and in the air, whereupon the stream of heavy bombers would simply unload their bombs on to the markers.

Yet Harris bitterly fought against the formation of the Pathfinder force, writing in his memoirs:

> I was entirely opposed to the creaming off the best crews in all groups in order to create a corps d'élite in a special group. This could be calculated to have a bad effect on morale in the Command as a whole ...

He wanted each of the six Groups in Bomber Command to form their own pathfinders, but, after a rancorous dispute, the Air Ministry overruled him. Harris's stubborn opposition to a separate and distinct pathfinder force was an early example of his absolute refusal to listen to arguments that clashed with his own rock-solid convictions. He was also motivated, however, by a fierce disdain for the Directorate of Bomber Operations in the Air Ministry, and especially for the Director himself, on the score that this officer was a mere Group Captain. Harris' own account of the quarrel gives in full pungency the true flavour of the man:

> Junior officers were to my mind quite needlessly named director of this and that, and they imagined themselves as commanders in the field of the command they were supposed to direct - a very nice job, too, because they

thought – mistakenly – that they were running the show without having to take responsibility for the results.

I looked upon C-in-Cs in the field as responsible people who were not to be bothered by the trumpery opinions of young Jacks-in-office ...[8]

In January 1943 Harris and General Ira Eaker, commanding the US 8th Air force in Britain, received a new directive from the Combined Chiefs of Staff as a result of the summit conference between Churchill and Roosevelt at Casablanca:

Your primary object will be the progressive destruction and dislocation of the German military, industrial, and economic system, and the undermining of the morale of the German people to a point where their capacity for armed resistance is fatally weakened.[9]

*　*　*

The mass offensive so long dreamed of by the prophets of airpower really began on the night of 5 March 1943, when nearly 400 of Harris's bombers struck at Essen in the Ruhr, home of the Krupp works, the largest single industrial site in Europe. This was just the first operation in the five-month-long Battle of the Ruhr: five more attacks on Essen; five on Duisburg; four on Cologne; two on Dusseldorf; two on Dortmund; three on Bochum. In Harris's own triumphant words later, 'Nothing like the whole succession of catastrophes which overcame the cities of the Ruhr and North-west Germany in the first half of 1943 had ever occurred before ...'

Aerial photographs justified this claim. Every building within entire urban areas was left as a roofless shell – not only industrial plant but also houses and tenement blocks. According to optimistic but fallacious calculations by Churchill's trusted scientific mentor, Professor Frederick Lindemann (ennobled as Lord Cherwell in 1941), it was within the capability of Bomber Command to render the German workforce homeless, and thereby cripple war production.

However, like all battles of attrition, the bomber offensive cost the attackers dear as well. Between the beginning of April 1943 and the end of July 1943 no fewer than 858 aircraft and their precious trained crews were lost, mostly shot down by night-fighters guided by ground radars.

But Harris was no more deterred by setback and loss than had been Grant during the battles in the Wilderness of Virginia in 1864 or Haig on the Western Front in 1916 and 1917. On 24 July 1943 he launched the Battle of Hamburg: four colossal smashes, each by nearly 800 bombers, on successive nights. This time the German radars were blinded by cascades of metal foil, codenamed 'Window'. On this now virtually defenceless city fell nearly 9,000 tons of bombs, more than half the weight being incendiaries. The effects were truly cataclysmic. In the later account by the chief of the Hamburg fire service:

Clouds of sparks sucked along the streets at about 50 feet a second firing more and more buildings. Little whirlwinds rushed in the streets. Flames with 10, 15, 20 metres length leaped from one side of the street to the other. The centre of Hamburg was going up like a chimney.

The whirlwinds reached speeds of up to 170 miles per hour, and the temperature in the heart of the fires rose to 800 degrees C.[10] Even large trees were sucked out of the ground. In that one week in Hamburg 45,000 people died, two-thirds as many as were killed in air raids in the whole of Britain over the entire course of the war.

It was the judgement of Albert Speer, Reichsminister for armaments production, that a rapid succession of raids on the Hamburg scale would bring Germany to defeat. But Bomber Command was operationally constrained by the often adverse weather conditions over northern Europe, coupled with the strength of air defences round key targets. Despite these constraints, Harris unwaveringly pursued his strategy of area bombing. To Churchill he reported on 3 November 1943 that nineteen German towns had been 'virtually destroyed', plus a further nineteen 'damaged'.[11] He proclaimed to Churchill that 'We can wreck Berlin from end to end, if the USAAF will come in on it. It will cost between 400–500 aircraft. It will cost Germany the war.'[12] He argued that 'the Lancaster force alone should be sufficient but only just sufficient to produce in Germany by April 1, 1944 a state of devastation in which surrender is inevitable.' This of course would render unnecessary the planned Normandy invasion.

Harris's onslaught against Berlin lasted from 18 November 1943 into March 1944. Each of sixteen grand attacks entailed a round trip of some 1,600 miles from airfields in eastern England, often in the foulest of winter weather. Furthermore, greater Berlin was a sprawling conurbation rather than a city like Hamburg – too large and too diffuse an objective to be destroyed by Harris's available strike-force, especially since many other targets were also to be attacked. Harris had quite simply got his calculations wrong.

Moreover, he had taken on the German night-fighter defence at the peak of its effectiveness. The enemy had found the answer to 'Window' in an entirely new operational system. Information about the course and height of incoming bomber streams was fed from observer posts to regional operations centres, whence fighter controllers would direct their airborne pilots towards their targets by radio-telephone. The precise location of individual British bombers could then be pinpointed by radars mounted in night-fighters like the Junker Ju88. Once located in this way, the slow, lumbering Lancasters with their puny .303 machine guns were easy prey to attackers equipped with cannon specially adapted to blasting them from below on their blind-sides.

The battle of attrition over Berlin (and other cities) lasted for five months. The cumulative strain tested the moral strength of Harris's aircrews to the limit, and in a few cases beyond. Repeatedly they had to leave the comfort of the base, perhaps even of a married quarter or a lodging with wife and family in a nearby village, and take off into a long night full of mortal hazard. If they returned, they would find that many familiar faces were no longer to be seen in the mess. How, then, did Harris inspire them to keep going?

Curiously enough, he practised none of the conventional arts of leadership, such as giving inspirational addresses or issuing rhetorical orders of the day in the style of a Bernard Montgomery. Harris never toured the bomber stations and talked to the crews, but instead remained personally remote in his headquarters in High Wycombe. He much occupied himself with his public relations campaign to 'sell' the bomber offensive to allied political leaders and other personages. At his official residence, Springfield House, he would show his guests large albums (bound in blue leather) full of dramatic 'before-and-after' aerial photographs of bombed German cities. Indeed, he himself reckoned that he was so busy directing operations and trying to convince the allied leadership that Bomber Command could win the war that he had no time to visit his bases.

Unsurprisingly therefore, aircrew veterans agree that for them Harris was an unknown figure. Yet they nevertheless acknowledge that in some mysterious fashion they were indeed conscious of his ruthless will to win, and his devotion to their cause. According to Dr Noble Frankland, the official historian of the strategic air offensive, and himself a former bomber pilot, Harris's presence 'was very strongly felt and I can only describe it as a kind of electricity'.[13] His crews relished the stories, true or not, about their leader's outrageous rudeness to anyone in or out of uniform, however senior, who dared to challenge his opinions.

On Harris himself the responsibility of conducting this prolonged campaign of attrition imposed an appalling strain. Yet his nerve was never shaken. His resolve never wavered. For here was a man driven by a primitive urge to smash the enemy to pulp. A senior colleague remarked that, of all the top British service leaders of the war, Harris was the only one who really did hate the Germans. Back in 1940, Harris had watched from the roof of the Air Ministry as the fires raged round St Paul's Cathedral, and had then remarked to a friend standing beside him, 'Well, they are sowing the wind.' Now in 1943, he, Arthur Harris, found rich professional fulfilment in supplying the whirlwind.

Nonetheless, if his aircrews were to have an odds-on chance of completing their allotted tour of thirty operations, he had to keep total losses of aircraft down to below 4 per cent of an attacking force. Yet by January 1944 Bomber Command was losing over 6 per cent in raids on Berlin, 7 per cent in raids even farther afield. In one attack on Leipzig the loss of aircraft mounted to nearly 10 per cent. On the night of 30 March 1944 Bomber Command suffered its worst single disaster of the war during an attack on Nuremberg – ninety-four aircraft down out of 795 despatched: a loss of 11.8 per cent. Even Harris himself now came close to admitting that he faced defeat, writing to the Air Ministry on 7 April 1944 that 'the strength of the German defences would in time reach a point at which night-bombing attacks by existing methods and types of heavy bomber would involve percentage casualty rates which could not in the long run be sustained.'[14]

By the beginning of 1944, the American 8th Air Force, attacking key industrial targets such as ball-bearing works by day, had also been defeated by the German defence. The American fighter aircraft – Mustangs and Thunderbolts – lacked the range to escort the bombers all the way to the target. After they turned back for home, even the heavily-gunned B-17 and B-24 bombers flying in close formation were no match for the latest German fighters, especially the superb Focke-Wulf 190 and its destructive cannon. In two raids on the ball-bearing centre of Schweinfurt in August and October 1943, 16 per cent and 20 per cent of the attacking forces were shot down[15] – a rate of loss impossible to sustain for long.

Nor had the allied air offensive inflicted fatal damage on German war production, which, reaching its peak in 1944, continued to supply all the aircraft, tanks, guns, and ammunition required by the Wehrmacht – in certain cases, more than could be utilised in the field. For Albert Speer, as Reichminister for Armaments, had masterminded the dispersal of key technologies across the country, even installing plant operated by slave labour in disused mines. Even in urban areas now reduced to heaps of rubble, industrial output was still maintained thanks to the resilience and adaptability of managements and workforces. Bomber Command's Battle of the Ruhr is estimated to have cost the region only about one-and-a-half months' output, while the American attacks on aircraft factories failed to prevent production from steeply climbing. In one instance, aircraft workers operated temporary assembly lines set up outside their bombed factory, and this despite freezing winter weather.[16] Far from breaking the morale of the industrial population, therefore, allied bombing actually served to stiffen it by arousing patriotic anger.[17]

Thus the belief of the pre-war prophets and the wartime bomber barons like Harris that airpower could win a war all on its own was comprehensively betrayed by events.[18] Armies on the ground would be needed after all – and that meant armies on the ground of western Europe.

Yet it would be wrong to write off the bomber offensive of 1943 as a sheer misuse of resources. No one can state with certainty how much larger German war production might have been if there had been no such offensive. But what *is* certain, as Albert Speer has pointed out, is that the defence of Germany against the bomber amounted to a virtual 'Second Front' diverting resources from the Eastern Front in Russia, where in 1943-44 the Wehrmacht was struggling (and failing) to hold its ground against the Red Army. Air defence of the Reich demanded thousands of anti-aircraft guns; it engrossed the production of radar sets and other specialised kit; and it entailed the widespread construction of massive reinforced concrete air-raid shelters. Moreover, the concentration on producing fighter aircraft, a purely defensive weapon, meant that Germany was now increasingly short of aerial striking power.

So while the bomber had not proved a war-winner in its own right, it still remained (as Churchill had judged in 1942) a potent weapon along with others in the allied armoury.

* * *

During the six-month period before the launch of the Normandy invasion on 6 June 1944 the longstanding and bitter dispute between Harris and the Air Ministry about the most cost-effective way to employ Bomber Command reached a crisis. Whereas the Air Ministry urged Harris to attack key sites in the German war economy, such as petrol-from-coal plants, ball-bearing factories, and essential but vulnerable transport links like canals and railways, Harris belligerently argued that attacks on such targets were merely what he called 'panaceas'; and that only area bombing could cripple the German war economy. He chose to disregard the operational evidence that Bomber Command was now capable of hitting a specific industrial target rather than just a city. This whole episode showed him personally at his most abrasive, and in debate at his most extravagant.

In the spring of 1944, however, this dispute became subsumed in a much larger one, when the Anglo-American Combined Chiefs of Staff directed that henceforward the prime task of both British and American heavy-bomber forces must be to cut the French transport system to pieces, so isolating the forthcoming invasion area. This directive was anathema to Harris, partly because it would take his bombers away from enemy urban centres, partly because he still believed that he could win the war without the need for an invasion. He was affronted that Bomber Command was to be reduced to the role of aiding the army and navy.

Only after the most vehement protests and what can only be termed 'go-slows' in implementing the directive, did Harris finally give way over precision bombing and over paving the way for the invasion. On 16 March 1944 Bomber Command displayed its new capability to hit specific targets by flattening the vast Trappe railway marshalling yard outside Paris. This was the opening move in the plan to isolate the forthcoming Normandy battlefield and its hinterland by destroying rail links, by cratering roads, and by demolishing key bridges over rivers like the Seine. And the plan proved a decisive success. It is fair to say that, without this devastation by British and American heavy bombers before and after the Normandy landings, the invasion could not have succeeded.

In turn, the advances of the allied armies after the victory in Normandy made possible the final triumph of the strategic air offensive against the German war economy. For now the German early-warning radars were no longer on the Channel coast, but back on German soil, while Bomber Command's Gee and Oboe ground stations had been brought forward from England to the German frontier. On 1 November 1944 the Air Ministry directed Harris to destroy petrol-from-coal plants because it was known that the German armed forces were desperately short of fuel; and to attack nodal points in the enemy transport network. But Harris, still true to his faith in area bombing, pigheadedly resisted the directive. From November 1944 into January 1945 an angry correspondence[19] flamed away between him and Air Chief Marshal Sir Charles Portal, Chief of the Air Staff. Harris claimed that his bombers had 'virtually destroyed' forty-five out of sixty major German cities. 'Are we,' he wrote, 'now to abandon this vast task which the Germans themselves have long admitted to be their worst headache just as it nears completion?' All that was required, he went on, was the destruction of Magdeburg, Halle, Leipzig, Dresden, Chemnitz, Breslau, Nuremberg, Munich, Coblenz, and Karlsruhe; and the further destruction of Berlin and Hanover.[20] Portal's reply was coldly dismissive:

> I have, I confess, at times wondered whether the magnetism of the remaining German cities has not in the past tended as much to deflect our bombers from their primary objective as the tactical and weather difficulties which you describe so fully ... I would like you to reassure me that this is not so. If I knew you to be as wholehearted in the attack of oil as in the past you have been in the matter of attacking cities I should have little to worry about.[21]

Yet Harris continued to denounce the oil plan as 'another attempt to seek a quick, clever, easy and cheap way out'; and in January 1945 he put forward a revised shopping list of German cities which he wanted to destroy.[22] He told Portal that he had 'no faith' in selective bombing policies and 'none whatever in this present oil policy', and proceeded to ask the Chief of Air Staff to 'consider whether it is best for the prosecution of the war and the success of our arms, which alone matters, that I should remain in this situation'.[23]

The resignation of the celebrated Commander-in-Chief of Bomber Command at this stage of the war would have constituted a highly unwelcome news story (except in Berlin), as well as being greatly damaging to the morale of the aircrews. So Portal wisely chose to ignore Harris's veiled threat, and wrote back with teeth-gritting diplomacy:

> I willingly accept your assurance that you will continue to do your utmost to ensure the successful execution of the policy laid down. I am very sorry that you do not believe in it but it is no use my craving for what is evidently unattainable. We must wait until after the end of the war before we can know for certain who was right ...[24]

This dispute between Portal and Harris, at once personal and strategic, shines the harshest light on the flaws in Harris's character as a leader. The blunt-spoken forcefulness had coarsened to such an extent that his superior, the Chief of the Air Staff, found him impossible to deal with. The steel-willed perseverance with a chosen offensive strategy had degenerated into sheer myopic obduracy.

Portal's measured reprimands had their effect, however. The proportion of Bomber Command attacks devoted to petrol-from-coal plants rose from 14 per cent in the last quarter of 1944 to 26 per cent in January-May 1945, while the proportion devoted to area bombing dropped from 58 per cent to 37 per cent (the remaining 16 per cent accounted for by attacks on purely military targets or transport).[25]

In the event, the combined offensive by Bomber Command and the US 8th Air Force in the last months of the war completed the destruction of Germany's petroleum industry that had already been largely accomplished by American daylight bombers at huge cost by the end of 1944. The Luftwaffe and the panzer divisions alike were now immobilised by want of fuel. After the war, Harris himself acknowledged that the oil plan was one 'panacea' that had worked.

The 37 per cent of Bomber Command's effort still devoted to area bombing signified a systematic working through the shopping list of those German cities so far little damaged. Dresden certainly figured in this list. The War Cabinet and the Air Ministry discussed the possibility of a smashing attack on a great city in order to inflict a final blow on the morale of the German people, and at the same time assist the Red Army's invasion of eastern Germany by wrecking a key road and rail centre behind the German front. Churchill himself wrote to the Air Minister, Sir Archibald Sinclair, on 26 January that he was more interested in further attacks on German cities than harrying the retreat of the Wehrmacht on the Eastern Front. Next day the Combined Targets Committee directed that Dresden was to come second only to Berlin as a target. Bomber Command and the US 8th Air Force were therefore ordered to attack it at the first opportunity.

Nonetheless, Harris and his Deputy AOC-in-C (Air Chief Marshal Sir Robert Saundby) entertained serious misgivings about the Committee's choice. Less was known about Dresden than about previous city targets; it lay at extreme range; and it was perilously close to Czechoslovakian cities and to the Red Army's advancing front. So, on 13 February, Harris specifically asked SHAEF (Supreme Headquarters Allied Expeditionary Force) for formal clearance for the operation.

It is therefore entirely wrong that Harris should have been later scapegoated for the destruction of Dresden when the responsibility plainly lay with his superiors all the way up to Churchill himself.

On the night of 24 February 1945, Bomber Command fulfilled the directive of the allied top leadership by torching Dresden; next day the US 8th Air Force followed suit with an avalanche of high explosive. German deaths, civilian and military, are estimated to have amounted to between 35,000 and 40,000.

For the first time, however, reports in the British media about the destruction of a German city ignited a widespread blaze of moral indignation, leaving a smouldering aftermath in journalism and history books that was to last into the twenty-first century.

But what made 'Dresden' any different from Berlin, Hamburg, or Essen, the destruction of which had only upset the odd bishop?

Harris had his own very characteristic answer, conveyed in a letter to the Deputy Chief of the Air Staff:

> I would not regard the whole of the remaining cities of Germany as worth the bones of one British grenadier. The feeling over Dresden could easily be explained by a psychiatrist. It is connected with German bands and Dresden shepherdesses.[26]

*　*　*

On 1 April 1945, Churchill minuted the Chiefs of Staff Committee and the Chief of Air Staff:

> It seems to me that the moment has come when the question of so called 'area bombing' of German cities should be reviewed from the point of view of our own interests. If we come into control of an entirely ruined land, there will be a great shortage of accommodation for ourselves and our Allies ...[27]

Five days later, the Air Staff ordered Harris to halt the area offensive.

Since January, when the allied leadership had directed Harris to continue Bomber Command's attacks on German cities, the grand strategic context of the war had drastically changed. Back then the Wehrmacht had still been fighting doggedly against the Red Army on a front extending from the Baltic down into Hungary, and against the Anglo-American armies in the Rhineland. But by the beginning of April, the Wehrmacht's resistance on the Western Front and on the Eastern Front was crumbling fast into final collapse. The strategic air offensive had quite simply become redundant.

Yet this swift change in the fortunes of war cannot justify the cold callousness with which the British hierarchy from Churchill downwards treated Harris and Bomber Command after Germany's surrender on 8 May. It was as if that hierarchy was now ashamed of the onslaught on German cities, partly perhaps because of the public relations backlash from the Dresden raid. Churchill in his victory broadcast to the nation vaunted the achievements of just about every facet of the

British war effort, military and civilian, but with the one exception of bomber operations.

This slight on Bomber Command and its valiant aircrews was deeply hurtful to Harris.

Even more to the point, no campaign medal was ever issued for the strategic air offensive: no equivalent to the Africa Star or Burma Star, or the Battle of the Atlantic medal. Harris made it clear that he would only accept a peerage if the aircrews and groundcrews who had served under his command were themselves honoured by a medal. To this day, they never have been.

References

1. *Bomber Offensive*, p.000.
2. Cited in Hastings, *Bomber Command*, 1979), p.116.
3. Douhet, *The Command of the Air*, Fuller, *Tanks in the Great War*, p.314. Liddell Hart, *Paris*, p.47. In America in 1923, General 'Billy' Mitchell scored a progaganda success by sinking a surrendered German battle-cruiser, unarmed and at anchor. Mitchell's passionate advocacy of the bomber was eventually to bear fruit in the unavailing attempts by the United States Army Air Forces to win the Second World War by daylight bombing.
4. Unless otherwise sourced, all quotations from contemporary witnesses are from interviews conducted for the 1974 BBC Television series 'The Commanders'.
5. Harris, op. cit., pp.108–9.
6. Webster and Frankland, *The Strategic Air Offensive Against Germany 1939–1945*, pp.340–1.
7. Hastings, op. cit., p.121.
8. Harris, op. cit., p.49.
9. Cited in Hastings, op. cit., p.185.
10. Lowe, *Inferno: The Devastation of Hamburg, 1943*, p.200. See this book for an excellent detailed account of the Battle of Hamburg.
11. Webster and Frankland, op. cit., Vol II, p.47.
12. Ibid, p.48.
13. Interview for the BBC television series, 'The Commanders'.
14. Webster and Frankland, Vol II, op. cit., p. 193.
15. Ibid, p.228.
16. Ibid, pp. 222-223.
17. Harris himself had never believed that bombing would break the morale of a nation like the Germans, any more than the Luftwaffe's raids in 1940–41 had broken British morale.
18. The seductive fallacy that airpower alone could decide international conflicts was to delude governments during the remainder of the twentieth century and into the twenty-first. Notable examples are NATO's interventions in Kosovo in 1999 and Libya in 2011.
19. See Webster and Frankland, Vol III, pp.82–90, and Probert, *Bomber Harris: His Life and Times*, pp.307–12.
20. Webster and Frankland, op.cit., Vol III, p.82.
21. Ibid, p.84.

22. Ibid, pp. 92–3.
23. Ibid.
24. Ibid, p.93
25. Hastings, op. cit., p.334.
26. Cited in Hastings, p.344.
27. Noble and Frankland, op. cit., Vol III, p.117.

CHAPTER 16

NEPTUNE'S Admiral

Admiral Sir Bertram Ramsay

'Nothing could be more wrong. It was excellent planning and execution ...'

In these simple words, written with pencil in his pocket diary six weeks after D-Day, did Admiral Sir Bertram Ramsay, Naval Commander Allied Expeditionary Force (ANCXF), sum up Operation NEPTUNE, the remarkable feat of transporting the allied armies and all their weapons and equipment from England to the Normandy shore on D-Day.

Too often historians of D-Day and the Normandy campaign neglect NEPTUNE and concentrate on the conduct of the land battle once the invasion forces reached the beaches – almost as if the English Channel were just a conventional 'no man's land'.[1] Yet in fact to get those armies safely to the beaches entailed (in Ramsay's own words in the Introduction to Neptune Naval Orders)

> probably the largest and most complicated operation ever undertaken and involves the movement of over 4,000 ships and craft of all types in the first three days.

Operationally, too, NEPTUNE presented far greater hazards than the allied landings in North Africa in 1942 or Sicily and Italy in 1943. Instead of the tideless Mediterranean with its often fine weather, there would be the English Channel with its steep tides and all its unpredictability of wind and sea even in summer. There would be dense minefields to bar the passage of the invasion armada, U-boat and E-boat ambushes, and finally a maze of underwater obstacles and the guns of the Atlantic Wall.

Operation NEPTUNE and the ensuing assault across the beaches by landing forces would be the greatest of gambles. For D-Day was the one and unrepeatable opportunity to re-establish the Western Front, defeat the German Army in battle, and open the way for an eventual invasion of the Third Reich. On this one card America and Britain were staking the outcome of the war.

So even Nelson had not carried such a weight of responsibility as the Naval Commander Allied Expeditionary Force, Admiral Sir Bertram Ramsay.

* * *

A Scot whose family had moved from the Highlands to the Lowlands, Ramsay combined stubborn advocacy of what he believed to be professionally right with an outgoing personality that did much to soothe ruffled relationships within the allied supreme command in 1944. Professionally, he was a very modern type of admiral, formerly on the directing staffs of the Naval Staff College and the Imperial Defence College, and a keen believer in a staff system. In 1935 he had resigned from the Royal Navy because as Chief of Staff, Home Fleet, he had clashed with the then C-in-C, Admiral Sir Roger Backhouse, an old-fashioned officer who believed that the C-in-C should do everything himself down to the smallest detail. While on the retired list, Ramsay was asked to report on the condition of Dover as an operational defended port. This paved the way for his appointment on the outbreak of war as Flag Officer Dover Command in the rank of vice admiral, and reporting direct to the Admiralty.

In May 1940 it fell to him as Flag Officer to organise at a week's notice the evacuation of as many as possible of the 400,000 soldiers of the British Expeditionary Force and the First French Army now trapped round Dunkirk against the sea by elements of two German army groups. Since his headquarters were located in an old Great War electric-dynamo room inside the white cliffs of Dover, the forthcoming operation was named DYNAMO: it perfectly summed up the hectic pace and driving energy of the evacuation now directed by Ramsay. He and his tri-service staff had to organise, schedule, and route (and re-route) the traffic between British ports and Dunkirk of a motley armada of vessels ranging from destroyers and cross-channel passenger ferries to river motor-boats and cutter-rigged cockle-boats. This traffic was exposed to constant attack by Stuka dive-bombers and machine-gunning and cannon-fire from Messerschmitt Bf109 fighters, as were the wide Dunkirk beaches and the two lattice-work wooden moles that alone enabled the loading of passenger ferries. Reichsmarschall Göring had promised Hitler that his aircraft could finish off the BEF, and his aircrews would do their ruthless best to redeem the promise.

Ramsay gave an inkling of his own state of mind in a letter to his wife as the evacuation got under way:

> I have on at the moment (it's 1 a.m.) one of the most difficult and hazardous operations ever conceived and unless le bon Dieu is very kind there will be certain to be many tragedies attached to it. I hardly dare to think about it & what the day is going to bring with it ... how I would love to cast off the mantle of responsibility which is mine & become just peaceful and retired once again ... All my staff are completely worn out & yet I see no prospect at all of any let-up ... As for my ships they have not a moment's rest unless they are damaged badly.[2]

It did not help that the First Sea Lord, Admiral Sir Dudley Pound, back in London did not seem to comprehend how desperate was Dover Command's struggle to save the BEF, even withdrawing Ramsay's big modern destroyers for convoy work, and refusing to relieve his exhausted ships' companies. In a letter to his wife on 7 June, when DYNAMO was over, Ramsay gave as a principal cause of strain 'the continuous struggle with the Admiralty to make theory see the necessity of giving [way] to what is practical.' The telephone line between DYNAMO's operation room and the Admiralty was busy with Ramsay's blunt protests. As he diplomatically phrased it in his despatch on DYNAMO: 'Verbal representations being made to the CNS [Chief of Naval Staff], authority was received for the return to Dover Command of the modern destroyers released the night before.'[3]

It had originally been hoped that at best some 45,000 soldiers could be rescued, but when DYNAMO came to an end on 4 June, the total brought safely home had reached 338,226.

In Ramsay's words in a letter to his wife, 'The relief is stupendous. The results beyond belief.' And he had no doubt as to why the operation had proved so successful, telling her without false modesty that 'We can always count on the glorious deeds but less often on good direction and management ... my staff were so well chosen & so efficient that they worked like a perfect machine.'

DYNAMO proved Ramsay's cool nerve in a crisis, his steadiness of judgement, and his ability to mastermind a complex amphibious operation even in the worst of circumstances. In August 1942 he was appointed Deputy to Admiral Sir Andrew Cunningham, ANCXF (Allied Naval Commander Expeditionary Force), in organising Operation TORCH, the forthcoming invasion of Vichy-French North Africa. Cunningham, a great fighting admiral, was very content to leave it to Ramsay as deputy ANCXF, working within the London headquarters of General Dwight Eisenhower (the Supreme Allied Commander), to plan the complex interlocking naval movements. Ramsay was thus occupying a key position in this, the inaugural integrated Anglo-American command structure.

Between 3 and 20 October 1942 there were issued over Ramsay's signature the eight bulky parts of 'Ton' [TORCH Operation Naval Orders], laying down the broad strategic plan, the routeings of convoys and task forces out from the United Kingdom to their launch points off Algiers and Oran, and giving detailed tactical instructions for the assault landings themselves. For the first time in history a naval expedition had been organised and planned with the kind of elaboration and exactitude that had long characterised the mounting of grand offensives on land.

And despite temporary local setbacks in the face of Vichy-French resistance, the landings were everywhere successful. Hitler's response was to rush troops by sea and by air into Tunisia. This proved to be a major strategic blunder, because the resulting land campaign was to end on 12 May 1943 with the surrender of 230,000 Axis troops trapped against the sea round the city of Tunis.

By now, however, planning for the invasion of Sicily (Operation HUSKY) had caused major ructions in the allied high command, with Ramsay, Naval Commander Eastern Task Force, in the middle of them. He was confronted with a plan 'which had been concocted and approved right up to the highest plane; in fact a 'fait accompli'. The 'highest plane' consisted of Eisenhower, General Sir Harold Alexander (British C-in-C Middle East), Air Chief Marshal Tedder, and Ramsay's own boss, Admiral Cunningham. Nonetheless, Ramsay was so horrified at the operational implications of the proposed strategy that he protested to Cunningham, who simply suggested that Ramsay might try to persuade Montgomery (Eastern Task Force ground force commander) to change it. Montgomery was in fact only too willing to do so, and with Ramsay's full concurrence produced an entirely novel plan which concentrated the British landings into a single lodgement on the eastern coast of Sicily south of Syracuse. However, Montgomery, incensed by all the bumbling in high places, added to his brief statement of his plan a crisp ultimatum that 'so far as the army is concerned all planning and work is now to go ahead along the lines indicated'.

> Monty has thrown a spanner of considerable size into the works [reported Ramsay to his wife in April] & in doing so has caused almost complete disruption of work besides increasing, if possible, his unpopularity ... I have all the time to try & modify his remarks to suit his audience & it is curious how quite unable he is to see the effect he causes or in fact to care in the least what that effect is ...[4]

Ramsay was also encountering problems with Admiral Sir Andrew Cunningham, the British C-in-C Mediterranean, who wanted to 'keep everything very tight in his own hands':

> It seems that he regards anything to do with combined operations as anathema & that the RN must keep well clear & all to themselves. I on the other hand have had diametrically opposite views and consider the army & Navy as one for thinking, planning and action. He is of the 'true blue' school and I am not.[5]

These fraught preliminaries to Operation HUSKY called for all Ramsay's talent for oiling the machinery of allied teamwork while standing fast on key operational questions.

At noon on 9 July 1943, eve of D-Day for HUSKY, he assumed command of the Eastern Task Force, as its component squadrons from Britain, Tunisia, Tripolitania, and Egypt rendezvoused south of Malta. 'After the months of tiresome planning,' he wrote to his wife two days later, 'it is a treat to *do* things instead of write or talk about them.' The past irritation of signals from Cunningham 'worded most rudely' gave way to the exhilaration of being at sea 'with my flag flying' and in command of a great enterprise.

Just as in TORCH, meticulously detailed planning of a complicated operation led to complete success on the British landing beaches, with Montgomery's army solidly ashore. On 19 July, Ramsay, his task completed, struck his flag.

*   *   *

In view of Ramsay's record as a successful planner of large-scale amphibious operations and his proven talent at teamwork with soldiers and airmen, and with American colleagues as well as British, it passes belief that the then First Sea Lord, Admiral of the Fleet Sir Dudley Pound, could recommend that another officer[6] be appointed Allied Naval Commander Expeditionary Force for Operation OVERLORD, the invasion of Normandy scheduled for summer 1944. But Churchill would have none of it, arguing that he was 'sure that Admiral Ramsay would be a far better appointment for this purpose on account not only of his natural abilities but his unique experience in conducting a great overseas descent ...'[7]

On duly taking up the command in October 1943, Ramsay was clear in his mind that success must depend on close cooperation between himself and General Sir Bernard Montgomery, ground force commander Allied Expeditionary Force. Yet as Ramsay well knew, Montgomery's egotism and his inability to realise the impact of his personality made him a difficult colleague. For this reason, Ramsay even moved into the same block of flats as Montgomery in the spring of 1944. 'He's not the ideal messmate, Monty,' confided Ramsay to his wife, 'as he apparently must always lead the stage, which gets a bit boring. But he is almost always interesting. He and I get on well together and he listens to my advice and generally acts on it.'

In fact, Ramsay was to have a larger problem in his relations with his naval subordinate commanders, British and American. He found Rear Admiral Kirk (the American commander-designate of the Western Task Force) a pompous and whingeing fusspot; and at the beginning of May characterised two letters from Kirk about the threat from German E-boats as 'hysterical':

> he has quite lost his sense of proportion besides being rather offensively rude. My opinion of him decreases steadily. He is not a big enough man to hold the position he does.

Rear Admiral Vian (British commander-designate of the Eastern Task Force), a man of dark and difficult nature, added to Ramsay's stresses. At a meeting in March, Vian struck him 'as being a little helpless & requires to be given so much guidance on matters which I feel he could work out for himself'.

*   *   *

Right from the start of taking up his command, Ramsay had been absolutely clear as to the fundamental principle that must inspire planning for NEPTUNE: 'it is the responsibility of the Navy to land the army as they require.' It followed from this that 'a sound military plan subsequent to the [amphibious] assaults must be the basis of the whole operational plan ...'

The existing plan inherited by Ramsay, Montgomery and Dwight Eisenhower (as the Supreme Commander) was for an initial assault by three divisions on a thirty-mile front along the Bay of the Seine in Normandy, a sandy shore with good access inland over flat country, and with the port of Cherbourg within relatively easy reach. However, Montgomery (with Eisenhower's endorsement) decided that, in order to win a secure lodgement on D-Day, the width of the invasion front must be increased from thirty miles to fifty. This entailed increasing the assault forces from three divisions to five, with two in reserve for the immediate follow-up. And this in turn demanded the enlargement of the shipping lift and the escorting naval forces by no fewer than 216 landing craft, fifty-four assault ships, three cruisers, twenty-seven destroyers and many smaller vessels.

Here was Ramsay's first great headache – and a major test of his principle that it was the navy's job to land the army as it required. For the allies simply did not possess in the European theatre enough landing craft to put five divisions ashore in Normandy *and* also carry out a simultaneous landing in the South of France (ANVIL) on which the Americans had set their minds. This dilemma now provoked what Ramsay called 'a cross-Atlantic game of ball' between Washington and London which lasted from late January until 24 March 1944, when the American Chiefs of Staff finally gave way and accepted that ANVIL must be postponed in order to release craft for NEPTUNE/OVERLORD.

Thus it was only now, little more than two months before D-Day as then scheduled, that Ramsay knew for certain that he would have enough vessels to carry out the complex plans on which he and his staff had been working hard since January.

On 10 April 1944, 'Operation NEPTUNE – Naval Orders' [ON] at last went to print, thanks to a final burst of work by a production line of typewriters driven by a team of Wrens [the Women's Royal Naval Service]. The consummation of three months of meticulously thorough staff work under Ramsay's direction, it ran to 579 pages, plus numerous detailed appendices, and divided into twenty-two sections. 'Operation NEPTUNE – Naval Orders' defined the task of the allied navies on D-Day as

the safe and timely arrival of the assault forces at their beaches, the cover of their landings, and subsequently the support and maintenance and the rapid build-up of our forces ashore ...

'ON' laid down in detail the organisation, scheduling and routeing of the D-Day armada - a blueprint that would be exactly implemented on D-Day. Firstly, the supporting warships were divided into a Western Task Force (three battleships, one monitor, nine cruisers, and twenty-five destroyers under Rear Admiral Kirk USN), charged with supporting the American First Army; and an Eastern Task Force (two battleships plus one in reserve, one monitor, eleven cruisers and forty destroyers under Rear Admiral Vian RN), charged with landing the British Second Army. Both task forces were sub-divided into naval 'forces' each corresponding to one of the five assaulting army divisions and their beaches [cf, naval 'Force G' - 'Gold' beach, 50th British Infantry Division].

These naval 'forces' boasted a wealth of specialised vessels developed since early experiments back in the 1920s, and proven in action during the North African and Italian landings. According to ONNO, such vessels would total six headquarters ships and fifty-five Landing Ships (Infantry) converted from peacetime liners or cross-channel ferries; six Landing Ships (Dock) and (Repair); 236 Landing Ships (Tank), oceangoing 4,000 tonners with bow-ramps, carrying up to sixty tanks and 300 soldiers; 248 Landing Craft (Infantry) and 837 Landing Craft (Tank), plus others adapted for special purposes like twenty-nine Landing Craft (Flak) and thirty-six Landing Craft (Rocket).

Nor was this all, for 'ON' went on to list the smaller landing craft that would be carried in the landing ships and lowered by davits into the water for the final run-in – 502 Landing Craft (Assault), each carrying thirty soldiers and their kit; 464 Landing Craft (Mechanised) to ferry armoured vehicles and transport from ship to shore; Landing Craft (Support) equipped with smoke-projectors and machine guns; and last but not least the invaluable American DUKWs, the 2.5 ton amphibious trucks each carrying twenty-five soldiers, and capable of over 6mph on water and up to 50mph on land].[8]

'ON' next laid down that the assault forces (together with their warship escorts and minesweepers) were to assemble (and load) in south-coast ports from Plymouth round to Newhaven; and the two follow-up forces in Felixstowe on the east coast, in the Thames estuary, and in ports west of Plymouth. The first of the build-up groups needed to swell the D-day assault forces into a great army – and Ramsay reckoned the build-up plan to be of 'unique and major importance' – were to be brought together and pre-loaded in the Bristol Channel (American) and the Thames (British). The naval covering forces charged with protecting the flanks of Neptune against U-boats and E-boats were ordered to assemble in the Bristol Channel and the Thames; and most of the heavy bombardment units (battleships, monitors and cruisers) in the Clyde and in Belfast Lough.

Also slotted by Ramsay and his staff into the jigsaw were the exact timings and routeings of the cross-Channel follow-up convoys on and after D-day that would be so vital for feeding military reinforcements and supplies into the lodgement areas -and not forgetting the unwieldy concrete components of the two

Mulberry artificial harbours due to be towed across the Channel by 158 tugs and installed off the Normandy shore by D+18, plus the unit that would lay the Pluto petroleum pipelines to Normandy across the bed of the Channel.

Ramsay's orders laid down in the minutest detail (complete with diagrams and timetables) the interlocking movements of this mass of vessels of every shape, size, and speed so that they would arrive off the Normandy shore in correct sequence on D-Day – beginning with two midget submarines (X-Craft), which were to station themselves off the enemy shore on D minus 1 as markers to guide assault waves to the right beaches.

From an assembly area south of the Isle of Wight (Position Z) the five assault forces were to sail southwards down 'The Spout' and on through the German minefield barrier via ten channels to be swept ahead by minesweepers. This barrier worried Ramsay far more than the threat from U-boats or E-boats:

> There is no doubt [he wrote in his diary in March] that the mine is our greatest obstacle to success, and if we manage to reach the enemy coast without becoming disorganised & suffering serious loss we shall be fortunate.
>
> It is a most complicated operation & however we [he and Vian] looked at it we could find no satisfactory solution of how best to sweep the channels of the faster groups & bombarding ships. In the end I decided that the only way out was to find 2 more flotillas made up from existing flotillas & employ them to sweep the cruisers through to their bombarding positions.

'ON' gave detailed instructions for this, the largest minesweeping operation of the war. In the first of four main phases, two channels two-miles wide for each of the five assaulting amphibious forces would be simultaneously swept. The channels would then be marked along their sides by buoys bearing flags or lights. Ramsay's orders emphasised that 'good navigation on the part of the Fleet minesweepers is of utmost importance', and laid it down that the minesweepers must keep to their sweeping courses even if (in his words) 'heavily engaged', because the assault forces following astern 'relied solely on them for safety'.

The disembarkation of the assault troops from the landing ships and the run-in to the beaches were no less meticulously planned. The process was divided into sixteen timed stages, ranging from H-Hour minus 120 minutes (arrival at the lowering points of the first Landing Ship [Tank] group with amphibious tanks) to H minus 60 (bombarding ships open fire), H minus 10 minutes (first group of rocket-equipped landing craft open fire), H minus 7.5 minutes (amphibious tanks touch down on the beach) to H-Hour itself, the infantry assault. At H plus 30 minutes, assault landing craft would bring in the first infantry reserves and the obstacle clearance units to deal with 'Rommel's asparagus' (explosive-tipped metal stakes); between H plus 75 and H plus 105, it would be the turn of Landing Craft (Tank) to touch down with self-propelled artillery and priority motor transport.

On 9 May Ramsay notified Eisenhower that the naval plan would be frozen as from the 12th. On 25 May, all holders of 'Operation NEPTUNE - Naval Orders' were instructed to open them. Three days later, they were notified that D-Day would be 5 June.

Taken all in all, 'Operation NEPTUNE - Naval Orders' constitute a masterpiece of planning and staff-work never surpassed in their scope and thoroughness, and in the scale and complexity of the problems solved. Just the same, wrote Ramsay in his diary,

> I am under no delusions as to the risk involved in this most difficult of operations and the critical period at around H-Hour when if initial flights are held up success will be in the balance ...

At 0415 on 4 June Eisenhower and his senior commanders met in Southwick House, near Portsmouth, to consider the latest weather report, which was, so Ramsay recorded in his diary, 'BAD':

> The low cloud predicted would prohibit use of Airborne Troops, prohibit majority of air action. The sea conditions were unpromising but not prohibitive. I pointed out that we had only accepted a daylight assault on the understanding that our overwhelming air & naval bombardment would be available to overcome the enemy coast & beach defences. SAC [Supreme Allied Commander] decided therefore to postpone assault for 24 hours. Force U (Utah beach] and O [Omaha) would have started and must be recalled. The weather got progressively worse after midday ... as the day went on the forecast became more fully justified.

At 2100 that day, there began an even more fraught commanders' conference chaired by Eisenhower, as a gale of wind rattled the windows of Southwick House (his HQ) and rain squalls battered the glass. No record was taken of this meeting, and recollections differ as to its outcome. But Ramsay was certain that the decision to go was taken at this evening conference -and taken because the meteorologists were predicting a gap in the bad weather in the forenoon of the 6th.

Ramsay forthwith issued the necessary naval orders, including the final fixing of H-hours for each landing area – 0725 for Sword and Gold beaches, 0735 for Juno's right wing; 0745 for Juno's left wing; Omaha and Utah 0630, because of the American wish to hit the beaches an hour earlier than the British and Canadians. When at 0415 on the 5th, Eisenhower and his commanders conferred yet again, the weather prophets 'came in smiling', so recorded Ramsay in his diary: 'It was therefore decided to let things be & proceed. The wind was still fresh & it is clear that forces will have an uncomfortable initial journey, improving as the day proceeds.'

Throughout that day the log-jams of shipping in the estuaries and harbours of southern England broke up, as the NEPTUNE armada sailed in due sequence towards Position Z (or 'Piccadilly Circus') south of the Isle of Wight, and then down 'The Spout' towards the Normandy coast. Some 2,700 vessels (not counting the 1,900 smaller landing craft carried in the landing ships) were on the move - vessels ranging from 30,000 ton battleships to Thames barges on tow. No fewer than 195,000 sailors (navy and merchant marine, more than half of them British, manned this fleet, with its cargo of some 130,000 soldiers, 12,000 vehicles, 2,000 tanks, and nearly 10,000 tons of stores.

The hazardous approach march – to use the military term – through the German minefields went perfectly, with the minesweepers starting to clear channels in the early evening of the 5th, and then sweeping ahead of the advancing assault forces right through the night hours. Once through the mine barrier, the assault forces spread out to the lowering or bombarding positions specified in the diagrams in 'ON'. By now a night-time blast by Bomber Command on German beach defences and gun positions had finally woken up an enemy who had believed that the weather was too rough for an invasion.

The tactical planning of the naval bombardments, disembarkations of the assault forces from the landing ships, and the actual assaults on the beaches had been delegated to the national naval and military task-force commands, though in the case of the Eastern (British and Canadian) Task Force sector, under Ramsay's supervision. In this sector, D-Day was to go broadly according to plan, but on the Western (American) Task Force sector, serious operational misjudgements imperilled the whole allied enterprise.

Whereas in the British and Canadian sectors, landing craft were disembarked from the landing ships about eight miles off shore, giving them about two hours on choppy seas to reach the beaches, the American command chose to unload eleven miles off shore (out of range of German shore batteries) which meant a three hours' run-in - three hours of seasickness for cold and fearful soldiers. Whereas at 0530 British battleships and cruisers opened a two-hour bombardment of enemy coastal defences, the American bombardment did not start until 0550, even though H-hour for the American assault forces was fixed at one hour earlier than for the British and Canadians. In the vain hope of surprising the enemy, Admiral Kirk had opted for a preliminary bombardment lasting only thirty to forty minutes, and which failed to neutralise the German batteries. Meanwhile the US Army Air Forces harmlessly dropped 1,300 tons of bombs in the fields beyond the enemy gun positions.

Once ashore, four out of five allied assault forces succeeded in fighting their way off the beaches despite incidental muddles and mishaps, such as getting entangled in 'Rommel's asparagus' while under fierce enemy fire. But in the case of Omaha beach, the day went dangerously wrong.

The troubles began with the eleven-mile run-in on puke-inducing choppy sea. All but five out of thirty-two amphibious tanks foundered, and thirty-two out of fifty howitzers went down in swamped DUKWs. Many other landing craft in the Omaha task force also foundered, including those equipped for clearing Rommel's asparagus when exposed at low water. As a result, only a few paths could be cleared before the tide rose and covered the obstacles again.

With the first assault waves thus unable to get ashore, an enormous marine traffic-jam built behind them. Orderly formation and sequence of movement disintegrated into a formless mass. Those troops who did manage to reach the beaches found themselves pinned down before high bluffs and a concrete seawall under sustained German fire. Only by late afternoon was the muddle at sea and on shore sorted out and the enemy driven back inland. Although Omaha was to become a heroic American legend, celebrated in a Hollywoood movie, it was in truth a near catastrophe caused by poor leadership.

How poor was that leadership is made clear by pencil-written comments by Ramsay in his pocket diary after he visited Omaha (along with all other invasion beaches) next day:

> The blockships [for the Mulberry harbour] had just arrived & were hanging about awaiting someone to tell them what to do. LSTs & ships & craft of all sizes anchored anywhere. No LSTs unloading, the beaches littered with stranded craft and no traffic going on between beach & ships. *Augusta* [Admiral Kirk's flagship] was anchored one and a half miles from shore. But complete absence of activity prevailed ...[9]

* * *

While the soldiers fought on D-Day for secure lodgements ashore, the allied navies were ferrying across the Channel the reinforcements and vital supplies needed to build up the allied armies faster than the enemy could build up his army by road and rail under the flail of allied air attack. On that first day alone, ships flying the White Ensign and the Red Duster put ashore over 75,000 British and Canadian soldiers, over 6,000 vehicles (including 1,000 tanks) and over 4,000 tons of stores. By the end of a week, 54,186 vehicles and 104,428 tons of stores had been unloaded in the American, British, and Canadian sectors. After ten days this seaborne traffic had swelled the Allied Expeditionary Force to thirteen infantry divisions, three airborne divisions, and three armoured. In Ramsay's own words, 'What they achieved was remarkable'.[10]

Then, on 19 June, the traffic was brought virtually to a standstill by a full gale, an immeasurably more disruptive force than U-boats or E-boats, and a fresh anxiety for the ANCXF. An eyewitness wrote of the gale:

> It came from the north, with a touch of east in it, and that was the worst direction, for it piled up the seas on our north-facing beaches and created the very condition which is the mariner's ancient peril and ancient dread: a lee shore, on which even great ships can meet their doom, and small ones are smashed to matchwood. Most of ours were small ones, and they stood offshore, head to wind, riding it out. There must have been hundreds in peril there ... The full flood of our supplies had dried up to a trickle ...[11]

Worst of all, the storm did serious damage to the British Mulberry artificial harbour and virtually destroyed the American one. It fell to Ramsay as ANCXF to improvise alternative methods of supply as well as organise the repair work on the Mulberries. Until the captured port of Cherbourg was cleared of obstructions at the beginning of August, all supplies to the American army had to be unloaded straight on to pontoon piers off the beaches. Though the main stores pier of the British Mulberry was re-opened on 29 June, it was only on 19 July, when the pier for Landing Ships (Tank) pier came back into operation, that the harbour was fully repaired. By the end of the month it was handling 11,000 tons of stores, nearly 4,000 men and over 400 vehicles a day: a remarkable recovery.

When Ramsay formally wound up NEPTUNE as an operation distinct from OVERLORD on 24 June, the allied navies and merchant marines had landed 714,000 men, over 110,000 vehicles and 260,000 tons of stores. Thanks to this supreme effort, the Allied Expeditionary Force was now solidly deployed on the new Western Front, and the German defenders of Normandy were on their way to a crushing defeat. When the Battle of Normandy finally ended in the third week of August with the enemy's total defeat and rout, the victory belonged as much to the sailors under Ramsay's leadership as to the soldiers under General Omar Bradley and General Sir Bernard Montgomery, for by this time the allied navies and merchant marines had shipped to France over two million men, some 440,000 vehicles and over three million tons of stores.[12]

Ramsay had achieved the objective set out in the Introduction to Operation NEPTUNE Naval Orders:

> to carry out an operation from the United Kingdom to secure a lodgement on the Continent from which further operations can be developed.

*　*　*

Because the Anglo-American land campaign entirely depended on supplies brought in by sea, Ramsay in his continuing role as ANCXF played a critical part in a heated debate between Eisenhower and Montgomery over future allied strategy in north-west Europe (see Chapter Seventeen). At the beginning of September, with Montgomery's 21 Army Group advancing into Belgium, it seemed for a heady moment that the enemy was in such disarray that the allied pursuit could roll straight on into Germany. Montgomery argued for concentrating the bulk of allied forces on a 'narrow-front' thrust north of the Ardennes aimed at the Ruhr, while Eisenhower contended that available logistic resources were simply not large enough to sustain such a thrust. In particular, the allies lacked sufficient port capacity. Of the major French Atlantic ports held by the Germans as fortresses, Cherbourg, finally captured on 1 July, had been so comprehensively sabotaged and booby-trapped that only now was it beginning to be of some use, while le Havre did not even fall until 12 September. Of the Channel ferry ports, Boulogne did not fall until 22 September, Calais until 1 October, and Dunkirk not until the end of the war. Only Ostend fell without delay, although wrecked cranes and demolished quays meant that it took until the end of September for daily unloadings to reach 1,000 tons, and until November for a wide enough channel to be cleared into the harbour. The one piece of good news was that Antwerp fell to the British 11th Armoured Division on 4 September. This deep-water port lay conveniently close in rear of the 21 Army Group.

There was however a snag. It lay eighty miles up the Scheldt from the North Sea, and the German army held ground to the south and the river and Dutch islands to the north. As Ramsay confided to his diary, 'Antwerp is useless until the Scheldt Estuary is cleared of the enemy.' On the day before the port fell, he signalled SHAEF 'For Action', with copies to Montgomery, to state that it was 'essential' to open the ports of Antwerp and Rotterdam (the latter in fact not to fall till the end of the war). Eisenhower himself immediately hauled in this warning. When he signalled Montgomery next day to reject his 'narrow-front' strategy, he remarked that the ports of Havre and Antwerp 'are essential to sustain a powerful thrust into Germany'.[13] Yet Montgomery gave priority to capturing Boulogne and Calais, and, worse still, left the Scheldt still uncleared in his rear while he launched his abortive offensive towards Arnhem on 16 September.

With the prospect of a long winter campaign ahead, the allied supply position now became hideously precarious. All once again turned on ships and ports. On 5 October Ramsay attended a conference of army group and air Cs-in-C (plus Sir Alan Brooke, Chief of the Imperial General Staff) at SHAEF to discuss future strategy. According to Ramsay's diary for that day

> Monty made the startling announcement that we could take the Ruhr without Antwerp. This afforded me the cue I needed to lambast him for not having made the capture of Antwerp the immediate objective at highest priority, & I let fly with all my guns at the faulty strategy we had allowed. Our large forces were now practically grounded for lack of supply, & had

we now got Antwerp and not the [Arnhem] corridor, we should be in a far better position for launching the knock-out blow ... I got approving looks from Tedder & Bedell Smith [Eisenhower's chief of staff], and both of them, together with CIGS, told me after the meeting that I had spoken their thoughts & that it was high time someone expressed them.

Yet Montgomery's narrow vision was so focused on his wished-for narrow-front offensive that it was not 16 October that he at last ordered that the opening of the port of Antwerp was to be given 'complete priority over all other offensive operations ...'.[14]

Admiral Ramsay and Lieutenant General G. C. Simonds (II Canadian Corps) jointly planned the capture of the Dutch islands of South Beveland and Walcheren (commanding the Scheldt from the north) as a combination of frontal attacks overland along the dykes that linked the islands and seaborne landings by the Royal Navy. The bitterly fought campaign in waterlogged ground lasted from 24 October until 8 November. Meanwhile, Ramsay deployed more than ten squadrons of minesweepers to clear eighty miles of estuary and river, and on 26 October three coasters reached Antwerp. Yet it was not until 28 November that the first convoy of nineteen Liberty ships came alongside the quays. Antwerp was at last open for business, no fewer than sixty days after the city had been first captured.

The Allied Expeditionary Force's supply crisis now passed. From November onwards through the winter and then the spring of 1945, sea communications would feed the armies on the Western Front with all they needed, first to defeat the German counter-stroke in the Ardennes in December, then to chew their way forward to the Rhine in a series of attrition battles, and finally to burst over the Rhine in April 1945 in the climactic offensive of the war against Nazi Germany.

When on 7 May 1945, General Alfred Jodl, Chief of Staff of the German Armed Forces High Command, signed the unconditional surrender of all land, air, and sea forces, the admiral who had contributed so much to this ultimate triumph of Operations NEPTUNE and OVERLORD was not there to witness the fulfilment of his endeavours. For Sir Bertram Ramsay, ANCXF, had been tragically killed on 2 January 1945 when his aircraft crashed on take-off from a snow-covered airfield in France.

References

1. Cf., Hastings, *Overlord: D-Day and the Battle for Normandy 1944*; D'Este, *Decision in Normandy: the Unwritten Story of Montgomery and the Allied Campaign*; Beevor, *D-Day: the Battle for Normandy*.
2. Churchill Archives Centre, letter of 27 May 1940. Ramsay Papers, RMSY 8/10. All letters to his wife in this chapter are cited by permission of his son, Major General Charles Ramsay.

3. Despatch.

4. Ibid.

5. Letter to his wife of 7 April 1943, in RMSY 8/23.

6. Admiral Sir Charles Little, C-in-C, Portsmouth Command. Did Pound pedantically rule out Ramsay because he was technically on the retired list?

7. Cited in Roskill, *Churchill and the Admirals*, p.233.

8. DUKW stood for production serial letters: D for year of origin, 1942, fourth year of the war; U for 'Utility'; K for front-wheel drive; W for six-wheeled.

9. Loc. cit.,

10. ADM 234/366, p.119, citing ANCXF Report, Vol I, p.95.

11. RMSY 8/26, diary for 7 June 1944.

12. ADM 234/363, BS No. 49, 'The Campaign in North-west Europe, June 1944–May 1945' (1952), p.3, cited in Barnett, *Engage the Enemy More Closely*, p.837.

13. Barnett, op. cit., p.847.

14. Ibid, p.849.

CHAPTER 17

Coalition Supreme Commander

General of the Army Dwight Eisenhower

On 15 May 1944, three weeks before the scheduled launch of the Anglo-American landings in Normandy, Field Marshal Sir Alan Brooke (Chief of the Imperial General Staff) confided to his diary his professional opinion of the man who would lead this, the greatest amphibious operation in history:

> Went straight from home to St Paul's School to attend Eisenhower's final run-over plans for cross-Channel operations. The King, PM, Smuts and all Chiefs of Staff were present. The main impression I gathered was that Eisenhower was no real director of thought, plans, energy or direction. Just a co-ordinator, a good mixer, a champion of inter-allied cooperation, and in those respects few can hold the candle to him. But is that enough? Or can we not find all qualities of a commander in one man?[1]

This is just one among many references in the Alanbrooke diaries to Eisenhower, varying from the merely patronising to the highly critical. And Field Marshal the Viscount Montgomery of Alamein follows Alanbrooke in admiring Eisenhower as 'a military statesman' while questioning his capacity as a commander in chief in the field. First comes the praise:

> I know of no other person who could have welded the Allied forces into such a fine fighting machine in the way he did, and kept the balance among the many conflicting and disturbing elements which threatened at times to wreck the ship ...[2]

And then the disparagement:

> I would not class Ike as a great soldier in the true sense of the word. He might have become one if he had ever had the experience of exercising direct command of a division, corps, and army - which unfortunately did not come his way ...[3]

Yet Alanbrooke and Montgomery both got Eisenhower wrong. For he was not only the most brilliantly successful leader of coalition armies since the Duke of

Marlborough, but also – repeat also – extremely able as a strategist and a director of large-scale operations in the field. Indeed, Eisenhower is unique among top commanders of all belligerent nations in the Second World War for sheer *range* of talents and understanding.

* * *

As the examples of Haig and Joffre, Haig and Nivelle, in the Great War go to show, military alliances between nations are the trickiest of machines to make run smoothly, and to steer in the right direction. However, in 1942 the top leadership of the recently formed grand alliance between the United States and Great Britain decided on a daring experiment – to create a single *integrated* allied headquarters and command structure for the planning and execution of the forthcoming invasion of Vichy-French North Africa (Operation TORCH). It was an experiment without precedent in history. If it were to succeed, it would demand outstanding qualities in the man put in charge: psychological insight; sound practical judgement; and, above all, the ability to weld together in a joint team the soldiers, sailors and airmen of two nations with very different military traditions.

To this challenging post was appointed Major General Dwight D. Eisenhower, Assistant Chief of Staff in charge of War Plans in the Department of Defense in Washington: a little-known soldier without famous victories or great battles behind him.

* * *

Eisenhower came from just the same sort of background as Grant and Lincoln – a country boy, reared to practical skills; a hard life in a poor but loving family. He was brought up in Abilene, Kansas, some twenty miles west of the geographical centre of the United States, and a community which exemplified the traditional American virtues of neighbourliness, self-reliance, and a pioneer simplicity. Eisenhower's grandparents had reached Abilene from Pennsylvania by covered wagon in 1878, in the final stage in a wandering that had carried the Eisenhowers from Bavaria via Switzerland and Holland to America in 1741. The Eisenhowers had always been Mennonites, a German Protestant sect with a hatred of war; and so young Dwight received a simple and strict moral upbringing, complete with Bible reading on Sundays. Dwight's father worked as a mechanic in a creamery and the family lived on 'the wrong side' of Abilene's rail tracks. Dwight himself, as the third of six brothers, had to take his share in lighting up stoves, digging the vegetable patch, and looking after animals and poultry. At school he was renowned for his hard punching, especially when aimed at boys from the 'right side' of the rail track. In summer the Eisenhower boys would hawk vegetables round this enclave of wealth and privilege, where disdainful treatment by the householders left him with a lifelong detestation of snobbery and pretentiousness, coupled with an ability to treat every kind of person, from monarch to private soldier, as his personal equal.

He did not excel at school either academically or for diligence and, after leaving school, drifted through a series of temporary jobs – firing boilers, loading wagons and finally acting as night foreman at the creamery. Here again Eisenhower's early life has much in common with the early lives of Ulysses Grant and Abraham Lincoln.

When a friend suggested that he ought to apply for a place at the US Naval Academy at Annapolis, Eisenhower reckoned that he would be equally happy to go either to Annapolis or to the Military Academy at West Point. Since a vacancy occurred at West Point, that is where he went, thereby perhaps depriving America of a great admiral. Cadet Eisenhower did not shine as a cadet at West Point, standing ninety-fifth in his class for all-round conduct, whereas Cadet (later General) Omar Bradley stood sixth. A member of the directing staff wrote later of him:

> We saw in Eisenhower a not uncommon type, a man who would thoroughly enjoy his army life, giving both to duty and recreation their fair values, but we did not see in him a man who would throw himself into his job so comprehensively that nothing else would matter.[4]

But he scored in other ways. He was popular without courting popularity, for his fellow cadets responded to his genuineness and balanced personality.

Only when commissioned as a young officer did he display the professional zeal lacking in his years at West Point. During the Great War he proved an able trainer of new recruits, finishing up in command of the training centre for tank crews at Camp Colt, Maryland: a record which earned him a Distinguished Service Medal. With the return of peacetime, however, the army shrank back to a tiny core of regular soldiers, and with that shrinkage came career stagnation for the officer corps. A major in 1920, Eisenhower was still a major fourteen years later. Nevertheless he could at least read books on strategy and military history, and thanks to this study he passed out of Fort Leavenworth Command College in 1925 first out of 275 students. In 1927 he was assigned to the American Battle Monuments Commission, with the job of gathering material for a guide book on the French battlefields of the Great War fought over by the American Expeditionary Force. General John Pershing, the wartime C-in-C of the AEF, reported that Eisenhower 'has shown superior ability not only in visualising his work as a whole, but in executing its many details in an efficient and timely manner'.[5]

The slow march of a peacetime career took Eisenhower through the Army War College in 1928 and next year to the War Department in Washington as a major on the staff of the Assistant Secretary of War. This post involved him in the preparation of plans for large-scale industrial mobilisation in the event of war, so locking his mind on to such broad questions as technological resources, transportation plans, sources of strategic raw material, and modes of co-operation between government agencies and industry. For a future allied supreme commander, this was valuable experience. It happened that at this time Eisenhower's brother Milton was also in Washington, serving as Director of Information in the Department of Agriculture; and Dwight learned much through Milton about the political environment in which America's military leaders had to operate.

In 1935 Eisenhower was posted to Manila, capital of the Philippines, the islands ruled by the United States since their conquest from Spain in 1898 but soon to become an independent Commonwealth under American protection. His task was to serve as Assistant Military Adviser to President Quezon, working under the Chief Military Adviser (and effectively commander-in-chief of the Philippine forces), General Douglas Macarthur. Eisenhower was later to describe this episode in his life as 'learning dramatics under Douglas MacArthur'.

Now for the first time in his career, Eisenhower had to work with foreign troops and a foreign government. He succeeded by the simple means of getting himself liked and trusted. President Quezon himself recorded that

> of all Ike's qualities the one I regard most highly is this: whenever I asked Ike for an opinion I got an answer. It may not have been what I wanted to hear, it may have displeased me, but it was always an honest and straightforward answer.

By the time of the Japanese attack at Pearl Harbor on 7 December 1941, Eisenhower had progressed from 'military adviser' to chief of staff of a Philippine division and then of an army. A week after Pearl Harbor he returned to Washington to take up a new post as Assistant Chief of Plans, in which capacity he participated that December in the Anglo-American summit conference which decided the future grand-strategic priorities of a global war: first, to defeat Nazi Germany, and, second, to defeat the Japanese Empire.

In February 1942 General George Marshall, the US Chief of Staff, appointed Eisenhower to be his Assistant Chief of Staff in charge of 'War Plans' – and specifically the projected allied invasion of French North Africa, Operation TORCH. In June, Marshall asked Eisenhower to prepare a draft directive for an allied supreme commander, or, in other words, draw the blueprint for integrated inter-allied command. When Eisenhower submitted his draft directive, Marshall asked him whether its terms suited him, since he was the man who was going to have to carry it out. Marshall's personal backing then proved decisive in the process by which the Combined (Anglo-American) Chiefs of Staff came to select Eisenhower to be Allied Supreme Commander in TORCH. Throughout the rest of the war, Marshall continued to give Eisenhower his loyal support – a key asset in times of dissension within the alliance. Theirs was a relationship founded on complete mutual trust and shared qualities of balance and good sense.

It is difficult to comprehend why Alanbrooke and Montgomery should think that Eisenhower lacked the experience to be an allied supreme commander. After all, Alanbrooke's only previous operational experience in the present war had been to command a corps in the disastrous Dunkirk campaign of 1940; Montgomery's to command a division in that same campaign. In contrast to the two British generals' narrowly military formation (and indeed narrowly military vision), there is the *variety*, the *breadth*, of Eisenhower's earlier career.

That he was to prove so cumulatively successful as a supreme allied commander lends a special interest to his own wartime view on how that role should be performed: a view expressed in the form of advice in September 1943 to Admiral Lord Louis Mountbatten, who was about to become Supreme Allied Commander in South-East Asia:

> The written basis for allied unity of command is found in directives issued by the CCOS. The *true* basis in the earnest co-operation of senior officers assigned to an allied command ... *Never permit any problem to be approached in your staff on the basis of national interest.*[Eisenhower's emphasis]
>
> An allied Commander-in-Chief must be self-effacing, quick to give credit, ready to meet the other fellow more than half-way, must seek and absorb advice and must learn to decentralise. On the other hand when the time comes that he himself feels he must make a decision he must make it in a clean-cut fashion and on his own responsibility and take the blame for anything that goes wrong whether or not it results from his mistake or from an error on the part of a subordinate.

Eisenhower continued:

> You may say that an Allied Commander-in-Chief is not really a commander and if you are thinking of the picture you have of commanding a battlefleet or a destroyer flotilla, you are correct. But on the other hand, in no sense of the word is he a figurehead or a nonentity. He is in a very definite sense the Chairman of the Board, a Chairman that has very definite executive responsibilities. He must execute those duties firmly, wisely and without any questions as to his own authority and responsibility.
>
> The point I make is that while the set-up may be somewhat artificial, and not always so clean-cut as you might desire, your personality and good sense *must* make it work. Otherwise *Allied* action in any theater will be impossible.[6]

This letter has been here quoted *in extenso* because it embodies the quintessential

'Ike' as a man as well as a leader. Here is the kind of common sense to be found in Abraham Lincoln and the Duke of Wellington: a quality which is in fact far from common in human affairs.

At the very outset of creating the first integrated Anglo-American command structure in 1942, Eisenhower made it clear that he would not tolerate any diminution of his own authority and responsibility as supreme commander. The British War Office had issued its own directive to General Sir Kenneth Anderson, the British land force commander, which simply repeated the terms of that given to Haig in the Great War, authorising Anderson to appeal to his own government if and when he believed that an order from Eisenhower endangered his army. Such a directive stood in blatant contradiction to the new integrated command structure, whereby Eisenhower was serving as an *allied* commander responsible to an *allied* authority, the Combined Chiefs of Staff, and thence to the Prime Minister and President jointly.

Eisenhower immediately wrote to General Sir Hastings Ismay (chief of Churchill's personal staff) to register his strong objection:

> I think the wording of the directive is such as to weaken rather than to support the spirit that should be developed and sustained among all ranks in this great enterprise.[7]

His letter resulted in a fresh directive from the War Office to Anderson: 'You will carry out any orders issued by him [Eisenhower].'

As well as setting up this novel integrated allied command structure and planning Operation TORCH, Eisenhower also faced major problems in his capacity as commanding general of the American expeditionary forces in Britain, all of them being green troops fresh from training camps. In a letter in September 1942 to a general in charge of training back in the United States, he deplored the poor professional standards among American troops stationed in the United Kingdom, and stated how the problem should be rectified:

> The first is the highest order of discipline and smartness in the individual. This applies to Junior Officers, who are the only ones who can produce the necessary standards among the enlisted mass. The second point is perfection in platoon training. I am constantly astounded by the mediocre type of troop-leading we find in the small units.
>
> The third point is the handling of motor transport. Through all our manoeuvres in the United States, this was our weakest point and it still is.[8]

Eisenhower thought that his officers were far too slack in tackling this question of discipline, reporting to Marshall in October 1942:

> I find that all my senior commanders are still inclined to regard *inexcusable* failures and errors with too tolerant an eye; I am hammering

away at them, and shall not hesitate to relieve anyone who does not grasp the point and insist upon attainment of proper standards.[9]

On into 1943 he kept blasting away on the topic of slackness in bearing or conduct:

I must insist that every officer, regardless of rank, sets a constant example to enlisted men. If he fails to do so, more drastic action is indicated. Soldierly conduct on the part of all will not only improve our chances in any tactical operation but convince the British that we are here not as muddling amateurs but as earnest, competent soldiers who know what we are about.[10]

He did not hesitate to sack even a general once he had lost confidence in him, as in the case of Major General Fredendall, commanding II US corps, who had proved dismayingly hesitant during Rommel's temporarily successful counter-stroke in Tunisia in February 1943. Eisenhower instructed Fredendall's replacement, George Patton:

You must not retain for one instant any man in a responsible position where you have become doubtful of his ability go do the job. We cannot afford to throw away soldiers and equipment, and, what is even more important, effectiveness in defeating our enemies, because we are reluctant to damage the feelings of old friends. This matter frequently calls for more courage than any other thing you will have to do, but I expect you to be perfectly cold-blooded about it.[11]

Yet Eisenhower's ability to carry out his own precepts was severely tested when in a well-reported incident in Sicily in 1943, Patton slapped the faces of two soldiers in hospital who were suffering from what in the Great War would have been called 'shell-shock', but who in Patton's reckoning were just malingerers. Eisenhower now had to weigh Patton's appalling conduct against the fact that he was an outstanding American field commander at a time when these were in short supply. In Eisenhower's own words in a report to Marshall later:

The problem before me was whether the incidents were sufficiently damaging to Patton and his standing in his army as to compel me to relieve him, thus losing to the United Nations his unquestioned value as a commander, or whether a less drastic measure would be appropriate.[12]

Eisenhower's answer was to fire off a ferocious personal 'rocket' to Patton:

If there is a very considerable element of truth in the allegations, I must so seriously question your good judgement and your self-discipline as to raise serious doubts in my mind as to your future usefulness. I assure you that such conduct will *not* be tolerated in this theatre no matter who the offender may be.[13]

And he instructed Patton to apologise to the individual soldiers concerned and, if necessary, do so before his whole army. He also sent two generals to Sicily to examine the facts of the case, and report back on what Patton's army now thought of him. In the event, Patton did publically offer his apologies. As Eisenhower later wrote to Marshall:

> I decided that the corrective action as described above was adequate and suitable in the circumstances. I still believe this decision was sound. As a final word it has been reported many times to me that in every public appearance of Patton before any crowd composed of his own soldiers, he is greeted by thunderous applause.[14]

Back in 1942 Eisenhower had had to cope with a similar dilemma, but one rendered all the trickier because of political complications. The prominent individual in the case was Admiral François Darlan, long the right-hand man of Marshal Pétain, President of the Vichy-French regime, in collaborating with the German occupiers of France. This made him an arch-villain in the eyes of British and American politicians and publics.

Darlan had arrived in French North Africa as Pétain's personal representative just before the Torch landings took place. In that capacity he ordered the French forces in North Africa to cease their hitherto tenacious resistance and allow the allies to complete their occupation. Soon afterwards Eisenhower officially recognised Darlan as High Commissioner in France's North African colonies. However, Eisenhower's action excited a furore of moral indignation in Britain and, to a lesser extent, in America, on the score that here was the Allied Supreme Commander putting into power a Vichy traitor. Moreover, had not Eisenhower exceeded his authority? Winston Churchill for one thought so. Eisenhower justified his appointment of Darlan on the grounds of sheer practical common sense. He reported to the Combined Chiefs of Staff: 'Without a strong French government of some kind here we would be forced to undertake complete military occupation. The cost in time and reserves would be tremendous ...'

And two days later, after Churchill had made his protest, Eisenhower wrote to Marshall:

> I am not repeat not committing ourselves to anything that is not repeat not essential to immediate operations, and God knows I'm not repeat not trying to be a kingmaker. I am simply trying to get a complete and firm military grip on North Africa, which I was sent down here to do.
>
> I do not repeat not understand why anyone should think that I am trying to set up a political regime, or why it should be thought I fail to realise the crookedness or unpopularity of Darlan ... But I do feel that the Allies should not repeat not hesitate to take advantage of any favourable situation in that line that this fellow can bring about.[14]

As it happened, an assassin's bullet conveniently put an end to the Darlan problem a month later.

In April 1943 Eisenhower's debut as a supreme allied commander ended in triumph, when all the Axis forces holding out round Tunis surrendered.

There is no space here to narrate Eisenhower's further Mediterranean campaigning in Sicily and Italy in 1943, except to say that the British official history, *The Mediterranean and Middle East* and Eisenhower's own papers make it clear that he was as closely and actively involved as in TORCH. It is impossible to read his correspondence without being impressed with the good sense, energy, and all-round capability with which he applied to problems ranging widely from high allied policy to inter-allied relations; to military discipline, training, and tactics; and to logistics, especially the available lift by road and air.

In January 1944 he took up his post in London as Supreme Commander Allied Expeditionary Force, responsible for planning and carrying out Operation OVERLORD, the landings along the Normandy coast, and by far the largest and most complex combined operation in history. No other military leader before or since has taken up a comparable challenge.

First and foremost, Eisenhower, as Supreme Commander, took on his own shoulders all the weight of the major decisions. Others may have carried out detailed studies of different aspects of the operation and submitted draft plans, but the final responsibility was always his. In the second place, it fell to him alone to make certain crucial operational decisions. For instance, the preliminary air plan called for the destruction of key French communications points round the Normandy battlefield – railway junctions and marshalling yards, bridges, road nodal points (often in towns or villages). Churchill grew so uneasy about the likely French civilian casualties (which he feared might amount to as many as 15,000) that he strongly pressed Eisenhower to scale down the whole air offensive. Eisenhower responded by making tactful cosmetic reductions – such as delaying attacks on major centres of population until just before D-Day – but he was not to be budged even by the Prime Minister on the need to execute the plan as a whole. In his own words in a letter to Churchill,

> The 'Overlord' concept was based on the assumption that our overwhelming Air Power would be able to prepare the way for the assault. If its hands are to be tied, the perils of an already hazardous operation will be greatly enhanced.[16]

So the air offensive went ahead.

Eisenhower's powers of decision were again sternly tested (along with his military judgement) when a month before D-Day his air C-in-C (Air Chief Marshal Sir Trafford Leigh-Mallory) warned him that the projected landings of the American 82nd Airborne Division would result in failure and heavy casualties.

Intelligence indicated that the glider-borne and parachute troops of 82nd Airborne would run into extremely tough German opposition, and that in any case the chosen landing areas were not suitable for gliders. Yet the deployment of 82nd Airborne behind the enemy front at the base of the Cotentin Peninsula was seen as one of the essential keys to success on D-Day.

Eisenhower signalled back to Leigh-Mallory:

> You are quite right in communicating to me your convictions as to the hazards involved and I must say that I agree with you as to the character of these risks. However, a strong airborne attack in the region indicated is essential to the success of the whole operation and it must go on. Consequently there is nothing for it but for you, the Army Commander and the Troop Carrier Commander, to work out to the last detail every single thing that may diminish these hazards ...[17]

Eisenhower's decision was to be vindicated when on D-Day ferocious small-unit fighting by the soldiers of 82nd Airborne[18] created confusion and unease behind the German defence of the Cotentin.

In hindsight, the success of the D-Day landings and the eventual victory in Normandy may seem almost inevitable, but that was far from the case before the event. For OVERLORD was going to be by far the largest, most complicated, tri-service operation ever mounted; and even when put ashore the invasion forces would be fighting a redoubtable and well-prepared opponent. So it was no wonder that, in Eisenhower's own contemporary words, 'as the big day approaches, tension grows and everybody gets more and more on edge':

> This time, because of the stakes involved, the atmosphere is probably more electric than ever before. In this particular venture we are not merely risking a tactical defeat, we are putting the whole works on one number. A sense of humour and a great faith, or else a complete lack of imagination, are essential to sanity.[19]

D-Day had been provisionally fixed for 5 June. But June came in with a Channel gale. On the 4th, Eisenhower postponed OVERLORD for twenty-four hours. Next morning the weather was just as bad, making a crossing impossible for landing craft loaded with troops. But a further postponement would mean waiting for weeks until the tides and their timings came right again. Such a postponement must damage the morale of invasion forces keyed up to fight, while also giving the Germans under Field Marshal Rommel more time to strengthen their coast defences. Then on 5 June a senior British meteorologist predicted that the weather would improve for twenty-four hours over 6 June, then get worse again.

To go or to postpone? No military leader has ever had to take a decision more fraught with risks or more loaded with potentially catastrophic consequences. Now

Eisenhower rose to true greatness as a leader, telling his assembled senior commanders and staff:

> This is a decision I alone can take. After all, that is what I am here for. We will sail tomorrow.

*   *   *

Eisenhower was also fully prepared to take personal responsibility for the failure of Overlord if that should happen. To meet such a contingency he wrote a draft communiqué in his own hand on the eve of D-Day:

> Our landings in the Cherbourg-Havre area have failed to gain a satisfactory foothold and I have withdrawn the troops. My decision to attack at this time and place was based on the best information available. The troops, the air and the navy did all that bravery and devotion to duty could do. If blame attaches to the attempt it is mine alone.[20]

*   *   *

The course of the Normandy campaign brought Eisenhower a new problem of leadership in the shape of his relationship with General Sir Bernard Montgomery, his ground force commander (and C-in-C, 21 Army Group). The tension between them arose partly from differing views over operational *strategy*; partly from Montgomery's childlike self-obsession and obliviousness to his effect on others, making him an extraordinarily awkward colleague. For Eisenhower he presented the novel puzzle of how to deal with a difficult subordinate, this time of another nationality and, what was more, a British hero.

The original plan for OVERLORD had called for Caen and the airfields to the south of the city to be captured on D-Day. In the event, Montgomery was stopped short of Caen by 21st Panzer Division; and, despite repeated British frontal offensives, the objectives for D-Day were not finally reached until some six weeks later. On 18 July Montgomery launched Operation GOODWOOD, a climactic blow to the south-east of Caen with three armoured divisions in column, and preceded by carpet-bombing by Bomber Command. His orders gave 'the direction of Falaise' as the thrust-line, while in a press conference beforehand he clearly implied that the operation was intended to lead to a breakthrough. In the event, however, his advance was stopped short by German anti-tank guns deployed in depth. Did he really hope for a breakthrough and then a deep advance along the shortest route to the Seine, so cutting the communications of all the German armies south of that river? In his *Memoirs* he was to argue that the purpose of all his attacks in the Caen sector was simply to attract the bulk of the German armour away from the Americans, and so make it possible for them to break through a weakened enemy front (which they successfully did at St Lô on 25 July).

But in the meantime Eisenhower had become increasingly anxious that the enemy might impose a stalemate on the allied armies, cramped as they then were into a narrow lodgement along the coast. He urgently needed forward airfields because his tactical air forces were still largely operating from the United Kingdom, so limiting their time over the battle-zone. He also needed the space to deploy much larger ground forces and their logistic resources. His anxieties had been shared by Eisenhower's Royal Air Force colleagues, including his Deputy Supreme Commander, Air Chief Marshal Sir Arthur Tedder.

But Montgomery scorned their fears, believing (along with his American opposite number, Omar Bradley) that Eisenhower failed to understand the strategy with which he himself had agreed. Alan Brooke for his part sourly confided to his diary that it was 'clear that Ike knows nothing about strategy'.

Who was right? Although Montgomery, an outstanding organiser and director of an attrition battle, was correct in predicting that there would be no prolonged stalemate in Normandy, it remains open to question whether he truly intended to break clean through in the GOODWOOD battle south-east of Caen, and failed. Was Eisenhower's concern (as Supreme Commander) in June and much of July about the failure to win space for forward airfields and for the expansion of ground forces really so misjudged?

This controversy proved only the prelude to a second and much more serious dispute between Eisenhower and Montgomery that lasted from the immediate aftermath of the victory in Normandy in late August right on through September. Should the allied armies advance all together on a broad front towards Germany, as the Supreme Commander wished? Or should all available logistic resources and a portion of Bradley's 12 Army Group be allotted to Montgomery's 21 Army Group (as Montgomery was urging), in order that the resulting mass of forty divisions on a relatively narrow front would be able to drive north of the Ardennes all the way to the Ruhr? This strategy, Montgomery was convinced, could end the war in 1944.

It must be remembered that this debate was taking place when the allied armies still lay south of the three great Dutch rivers, the lower Rhine, the Maas, and the Waal: potentially formidable barriers when defended by German troops. That was one consideration. A second consideration was that, in order to free logistic resources in support of Montgomery's 'narrow-front' advance, the rest of the allied armies would have to be halted.

Of course, Montgomery's advocacy of the 'narrow-front' strategy dovetailed very neatly into the case he was also making for his re-appointment as ground force commander of all the allied armies (the post which had lapsed at the end of the Normandy campaign). Eisenhower as Allied Supreme Commander was clear that such a re-appointment would be utterly unacceptable to Bradley (12 Army

Group) and other American formation commanders, as well as politically out of the question back at home. As for the 'narrow front' strategy itself, Eisenhower judged that this would be logistically impossible to sustain, and operationally very hazardous. In September 1944 the allies still only held two major ports on the Continent: badly-damaged Cherbourg, and Antwerp in Belgium. All French ports other than Cherbourg remained fortresses in German hands. Antwerp was unusable because the River Scheldt, linking it to the sea, was commanded by German forces along its north bank – forces which Montgomery, despite repeated urging from Eisenhower, had neglected to eliminate. The allied armies were therefore largely still dependent on supplies unloaded over the Normandy beaches or through the remaining Mulberry artificial harbour, and then brought forward by a perpetual long-distance rotation of trucks.

Eisenhower therefore pointed out to Montgomery that the ports of Antwerp and le Havre were essential to sustain a powerful offensive north of the Ardennes and into Germany; and he flatly stated that 'No allocation of our present resources would be adequate to sustain a thrust to Berlin'.[21]

In a letter to Marshall on 14 September, Eisenhower gave his considered judgement on Montgomery's 'narrow-front' strategy:

> Examination of this scheme exposes it as a fantastic idea. First of all, it would have to be done with the ports we now have. The attack would be on such a narrow front that flanking threats would be particularly effective and no other troops in the whole region would be capable of going to its support. Actually I doubt that the idea was proposed in any conviction that it could be carried through to completion; it was based on wishful thinking, and in an effort to induce me to give to 21st Army Group and to Bradley's left [wing] every ounce of maintenance there is in the theatre.[22]

If Eisenhower's critics require proof of his shrewdness as a strategic thinker, this masterly letter affords it.

Less admirable, however, was his decision to sanction Montgomery's proposed operation to cross the three big Dutch rivers (including the lower Rhine) by a series of airborne landings to seize the bridges, followed up by ground forces. MARKET GARDEN was launched on 17 September and ended in failure on the 25th with the destruction of the British 1st Airborne Division at Arnhem.[23] This operation has been analysed again and again in detail to establish just what went wrong. The essential point is, however, that MARKET GARDEN suffered exactly the fate which Eisenhower had foreseen for Montgomery's vastly more ambitious scheme to drive deep into Germany, with Berlin as the ultimate objective. Had that thrust run into stiff German opposition and flanking counter-strokes when far forward somewhere north of the Ruhr, the result could have been a catastrophe dooming the whole allied campaign in the West.

As it was, even mounting MARKET GARDEN had strained logistic resources to the limit. Eisenhower warned Montgomery that 'we are squarely up against the situation which has been anticipated for months, and our intake into the Continent will not repeat not support our battle'. On 13 October he urged on Montgomery yet again how vital it was to open up the port of Antwerp:

> I do not know the exact state of your supply, but I do know what a woeful state it is throughout the American and French forces. By comparison you are rich![23]

By now Montgomery's earlier disagreements with Eisenhower had turned into a general critique of his leadership as Supreme Allied Commander. In letters more and more blatantly insubordinate, Montgomery signalled his contempt for Eisenhower's concepts of grand strategy and his rejection of the present allied command structure.

For Eisenhower this insubordination presented him with his worst problem of leadership as a coalition supreme commander. After all, Montgomery was not a fellow American like Patton, but a British general, and, moreover, a British general hero-worshipped by the British public and media, and backed by Alan Brooke, the Chief of the Imperial General Staff. Patient diplomacy having failed, Eisenhower signalled Montgomery in mid-October to warn him:

> if you, as the senior commander in this theatre of one of the great allies, feel that my conceptions and directives are such as to endanger the success of operations, it is our duty to refer the matter to higher authority for any action they may choose to take, however drastic.[25]

Although Montgomery replied that 'you will hear NO more on the subject of command from me', this proved to be far from the case.

All through November he kept grinding on about the need for a single ground force commander for all the allied armies in the West (and who else but himself?); and at the end of December, after the defeat of Hitler's Ardennes offensive, he was at it again. In an extraordinary letter couched in the tone of a schoolmaster to a pupil, he told Eisenhower that in the coming 1945 campaign all offensive power should be assigned to a single thrust north of the Ruhr, with 'one man directing and controlling the whole tactical battle'.[26]

By this time Eisenhower's stock of patience had been wholly depleted. With the support of British members of his own staff, he wrote to Montgomery that their differences must now be referred to the British and American governments, who would have to decide whether to retain either himself in command or Montgomery.

Montgomery was only saved from inevitable dismissal by the personal diplomacy of his chief of staff, Major General 'Freddie' de Guingand, who persuaded him to write Eisenhower a grovelling letter of apology.[27]

Of *all* Eisenhower's worries and anxieties in 1944, the most needless was having to deal with Montgomery.

* * *

At the beginning of 1945 the Anglo-American high command was very much better placed than Foch, Pétain, and Haig at the beginning of 1918. Whereas in 1918 Czarist Russia had collapsed, releasing some forty German divisions for a massive German blow on the Western Front, in 1945 the Red Army of the Soviet Union was about to renew the colossal offensives on the Eastern Front which in 1944 had taken it to the borders of East Prussia, to the Vistula, and deep into Hungary; and which had inflicted irreplaceable losses on the Wehrmacht of over 900,000 soldiers. When to this total is added the 553,000 soldiers lost by the Wehrmacht in the West since D-Day,[28] it is clear that the allies on both fronts now faced a very much weakened enemy.

On 9 January Churchill reported to Eisenhower the signal received from Stalin the previous day that the Soviet Supreme Command had decided 'regardless of the weather, to commence large-scale operations against the Germans along the whole Central Front not later than the second half of January'.[29] In fact, the Red Army struck on 12 January in an offensive which by the beginning of February had taken it from the Vistula to the Oder, within forty miles of Berlin.

This emergency compelled Hitler to switch panzer divisions from the Western Front to the Eastern: a fact revealed to the Anglo-American high command by Ultra decrypts in the course of February. Throughout the coming battles inside Germany Ultra was also to provide continual and highly valuable insights into enemy readings of allied intentions as well as of forthcoming German movements.[30]

Not until 20 January did Eisenhower submit his plans for the 1945 campaign to the Combined Chiefs of Staff. The British, in the form of the abrasive personalities of Field Marshal Montgomery (21st Army Group) and Field Marshal Sir Alan Brooke (Chief of the Imperial General Staff), had continued to urge that there should be a single grand offensive north of the Ruhr by 21st Army Group plus the American 12th Army Group, the remainder of the Western Front being reduced to a defensive. This single thrust should be directed by Montgomery, the loser of Arnhem, who would be restored to the post of allied 'ground force commander'. But this hope was now finally squashed by Eisenhower, on the score that such an extra intermediate command level would be redundant and lead to 'great duplication in personnel and communications'.[31] As for operational strategy, Eisenhower himself agreed (as he wrote to Marshall on 10 January) that the main weight of the offensive should lie on the allied left flank, and that on the right flank south of the Moselle 'the whole task is defensive'.[32] Nevertheless he judged that simply to stand on the defensive in the centre would not adequately secure the southern flank of the principal thrust. He therefore decided that in the first phase of the campaign (an advance to the Rhine) not only 21st Army Group but also the American 12th Army Group (Bradley) would take the offensive, in the latter's case along the axis Prum-Bonn.

Eisenhower could not agree with Montgomery that once across the Rhine the allies should confine themselves to a single thrust-line to the north of the Ruhr. As he wrote to Marshall on 15 January, the fact that this constituted 'an invasion route of the first importance' was 'equally obvious to the German, and if he concentrates in its immediate defense, I may not have the necessary overwhelming superiority to force a satisfactory breakthrough'. He therefore wished to enjoy 'the ability to maneuver', meaning, for example, 'the ability to advance also on Frankfurt and Kassel, rather than to rely on a single thrust in the north'.[33]

On 20 January the Supreme Commander fleshed out his preliminary thinking into 'an appreciation and plan of operations for the winter and spring of 1945' submitted to the Combined Chiefs of Staff:[34]

These operations fall into three phases:

• Phase 1 - The destruction of the enemy forces west of the Rhine and the closing of the Rhine.
• Phase 2 - The seizing of bridgeheads over the Rhine from which to develop operations into Germany.
• Phase 3 - The destruction of enemy forces east of the Rhine and advance into Germany.

In Eisenhower's judgement, if the bulk of the enemy could be destroyed west of the Rhine, 'the remaining phases will be immeasurably simplified'. In regard to Phase 2,

operations across the Rhine north of the Ruhr offer the greatest strategic rewards within a short distance, but this area will be most strongly held by the enemy. An advance in the Frankfurt area offers less favourable terrain and a longer route to vital strategic objectives. Depending on the degree of enemy resistance it may be necessary to use either or both of these two avenues.[35]

This broad scenario was to be fulfilled in the event. Yet the sequence of the phases offers a striking contrast with the pattern of Red Army offensives first established in the counter-stroke at Stalingrad in November 1942, whereby a sudden smashing blow with massed divisions and stunning firepower burst the enemy front asunder, followed by a phase of exploitation and pursuit. Instead, Eisenhower had opted for opening phase of attrition to write down the enemy's reserves – what Haig had called 'the wearing-out battle' – which only then would be followed by a breakthrough to 'the green fields beyond'.

And the nature of the battle itself during Phase 1 would have been familiar enough to veterans of the Great War. Operation VERITABLE, the offensive by Crerar's First Canadian Army (II Canadian Corps and XXX British Corps), its objective the Rhine between Xanten and the Dutch frontier, opened on 8 February with a bombardment by more than 1,000 guns, followed by a barrage lifting ahead of the infantry and tanks. Thereafter, the attackers, 450,000 strong, fought their way south-eastwards between the Maas and the Rhine week by week against General Schlemm's First Parachute Army: a struggle (often in drenching rain) from one natural feature to another, one village or farm to another, through mud sometimes so waterlogged that all vehicles were bogged down except for the wide-tracked Churchill tank. The German defences too would have been familiar enough to veterans of Third Ypres, consisting of three defensive belts each of two or three lines of trenches and fortified villages or farms, the whole protected by minefields and barbed wire. Given the German talent in both wars for launching vicious local counter-attacks, it was no wonder that Operation VERITABLE became, in Eisenhower's words, 'a bitter slugging match'.[36] The historian of the British 11th Armoured Division described its experience in Operation BLOCKBUSTER (a later phase of VERITABLE) on 26 February as 'a slow, miserable and costly operation ... confronted by impenetrable forests, impassable bogs, numerous craters, roadblocks, mines and every form of demolition ...'[37] Only on 8 March was the objective of the Rhine between Xanten and the Dutch frontier finally reached, when General Schlemm completed an orderly withdrawal across the river. This had indeed been an updated Great War battle of attrition conducted ably enough by a Great War general out of his time, Field Marshal Montgomery.

Back on 23 February the American Ninth Army (General Simpson, under command of Montgomery's 21st Army Group) on the right flank of the First Canadian Army had launched Operation GRENADE, a parallel offensive directed at the Rhine between Xanten and Dusseldorf. Here the principal obstacle lay in the flooded River Roer. Nonetheless, the Ninth Army quickly won bridgeheads up to four miles deep against a weaker defence than opposite the Canadians and British, and thereafter began an advance which brought it to the Rhine opposite Dusseldorf on 1 March and to all its objectives along the river by the 5th.

The attrition battles of VERITABLE and GRENADE had cost the allies dear enough – 15,500 Canadian and British casualties, and just under 7,300 American.[38] But it had cost the enemy much more: 51,000 prisoners and an estimated 38,000 killed or seriously wounded.[39]

For Hitler had played exactly into Eisenhower's hands by refusing the request of Field Marshal Model (Army Group B) to organise a main defence behind the Rhine, and instead instructing him and General Blaskowitz (Army Group H, opposite the British and Canadians) to fight for the Rhineland west of the river. He thus condemned to a murderous battle of attrition his weary, discouraged, and heavily outnumbered troops, short of armour and without air cover. Hitler had indeed no strategy for the campaign in the West in 1945 other than to order his commanders to fight for every inch of ground.

Meanwhile, the US First and Third Armies (in General Omar Bradley's 12th Army Group) between the US Ninth Army's right flank and the Moselle had been carrying out Operation LUMBERJACK, with the objective of closing up to the Rhine between Dusseldorf and Mainz. Once the First Army had crossed the flooded River Roer the enemy's resistance took on the character of a fighting retreat except for a brief stand by panzers on the Erft Canal. American advanced guards entered Cologne on 5 March and by the 7th the entire city was in American hands. On the same day the right-flank corps of First Army, having swung south-eastwards, reached the Rhine at Remagen, and seized the Ludendorff bridge, the one Rhine bridge that the Germans had failed to blow in time.

Without hesitation, Eisenhower decided to exploit this opportunity by ordering Bradley to secure a bridgehead across the river with at least five divisions. In the meantime the Third Army (Patton) had reached the Rhine between Remagen and Coblenz.

On 8 March Eisenhower issued a fresh directive which definitively altered the balance of his strategy even further away from a single thrust by 21st Army Group to the north of the Ruhr, and towards a greater effort along the front south of the Moselle. Although he confirmed the date for 21st Army Group's assault crossing of the Rhine at Wesel as 24 March, he also ordered the US 6th Army Group (General Jacob Devers), to 'initiate offensive operations in the Saar' with the object of keeping

> all possible German forces away from the main effort in the north, by defeating the enemy west of the Rhine, closing on the Rhine from the Moselle southward and establishing bridgeheads over the Rhine in the Mainz-Mannheim sector.[40]

The hardest task in these operations fell to the 6th Army Group's Seventh Army (Patch), which had to break through the Siegfried Line between Saarbrucken and Lauterburg and then fight its way through the thickly-wooded hills of the Palatinate to reach the Rhine between Mainz and Mannheim. In a pincer movement, Patton's Third Army (on the right flank of the 12th Army Group) was at the same time to attack south-east across the Moselle towards the Rhine between Coblenz and Bingen. Despite tough enemy resistance at first, the two armies had within a fortnight cleared the entire Palatinate up the line of the Rhine, surrounding the bulk of the German Seventh Army, taking 107,000 prisoners, and seizing a second bridge over the Rhine, at Oppenheim.[41] By 25 March German resistance everywhere west of the Rhine had ceased.

A historian of the Western Front in the Great War cannot fail to be struck by the similarity of Eisenhower's strategy of successive blows along a broad front against an overstretched enemy and that of Haig and Foch between August and November 1918. In Eisenhower's case he brilliantly fulfilled his aim of gutting the German army west of the Rhine in order decisively to weaken its defence of the river and the German heartland beyond. The number of prisoners alone amounted to 280,000.[42] Moreover, this success on the grand scale serves completely to vindicate Eisenhower's broad-front strategy so persistently opposed by Montgomery and Brooke.

To the success of these attrition battles the allied tactical air forces greatly contributed by attacking enemy road and rail communications, defensive positions, and troops and transport on the move. In a single week during operations in the Saar sector, the American 1st Tactical Air Force flew over 8,000 sorties.[43] On 22 February over 9,000 aircraft (strategic bombers as well tactical air) from bases in England, France, Holland, Belgium and Italy took part in Operation CLARION, involving targets across an area of 250,000 square miles, from Emden to Berlin, Dresden, Vienna, and Mulhouse, and aimed at key communications links.[44] By now the strategic bomber forces had finally smashed the German war economy as a whole to a standstill,[45] with steel plants, oil-from-coal plants, gas-works and power stations reduced to wrecks. By March petroleum production had altogether ceased. Moreover, bombing had left the German transport infrastructure in ruins, with major canals breached and emptied, rail and canal viaducts dropped, marshalling yards cratered. Coal still being mined could not be moved from the pitheads, nor munitions from underground factories still in production. This was total economic paralysis.

On 11 March, Hitler replaced Rundstedt as Oberbefehlshaber West with Field Marshal Albert Kesselring, who had conducted such a skilful and dogged defence of the Italian peninsula against the odds since 1943. However, in the face of some eighty-five allied divisions he could only field fifty-one, most of them down to a strength of about 5,500 soldiers, and these increasingly dispirited and prone to desert. He was also desperately short of armour.[46] Here was a situation beyond the recuperative powers even of the 'Smiling Albert' of his nickname.

On 13 March Eisenhower confirmed in a directive that Montgomery's 21st Army Group would carry out the planned crossing of the Rhine at Wesel (Operation PLUNDER) on 24 March, while Bradley's 12th Army Group would break out from its bridgeheads south of Mainz and thrust towards Frankfurt.[47]

In preparing Operation PLUNDER, Montgomery knew from Ultra decrypts and Army 'Y' radio intercepts that the enemy's defence consisted of a thin crust of understrength and overextended formations, with 2nd Parachute Division, for example, holding a front of thirty-three kilometres.[48]

Montgomery organised his assault crossing with his usual meticulous thoroughness, building up a maximum preponderance of manpower and firepower.

For three days beforehand the British Second Tactical Air Force attacked German army and Luftwaffe installations in the neighbourhood of Wesel. The assault crossing on the night of 23 March was covered by the fire of some 3,500 guns. After the first waves of troops had gained a lodgement, Bomber Command dropped 1,100 tons of high explosive on the town of Wesel. When divisions of the British Second Army and the American Ninth were firmly ashore, parachute and gliderborne troops of the British 6th Airborne and the American 17th Airborne Divisions were landed behind the enemy front north of Wesel (Operation VARSITY). The hopelessly outnumbered and outgunned German 1st Parachute Army were unable to prevent 21st Army Group from winning by 27 March a bridgehead some thirty-five miles wide and twenty miles deep .

Montgomery now issued orders for a breakout and a pursuit to the Elbe: on the left, Second Army (with its left wing thrusting for Hamburg); on the right, Ninth Army (its right wing directed on Magdeburg, with a swing south round the Ruhr).

Meanwhile, on 24 March, Eisenhower had signalled the Combined Chiefs of Staff that the victories west of the Rhine 'has resulted as planned in the destruction of a large proportion of available enemy forces on the Western Front':

> While not desiring to appear overoptimistic, it is my conviction that the situation today presents opportunities for which we have struggled and which we must seize boldly. The dash and daring in First and Third Army sectors have gotten us two bridgeheads very cheaply which can be consolidated and expanded rapidly to support a major thrust which will assist the northern operation and make our exploitation effective.[49]

In fact:

> While we are continuing to plan for and to be ready to meet stern resistance, it is my personal belief that the enemy strength on the Western Front is becoming so stretched that penetrations and advances will soon be limited only by our own maintenance.

In a directive to army group and army commanders next day Eisenhower confirmed that the final offensive into the German heartland was to consist of two main thrusts – Montgomery's north of the Ruhr, and a second one south of it by Bradley, the two army groups encircling the whole Ruhr industrial region by linking up in the area Paderborn-Kassel.[50]

On 1 April the US Ninth Army (in Montgomery's 21st Army Group) and the US First Army completed that encirclement, so trapping the whole of Army Group B and two corps of Army Group H. For over a fortnight General Model fought on, attempting two breakouts in conjunction with efforts at relief by other German forces, but on 18 April the Ruhr pocket was finally eliminated along with twenty-one enemy divisions. No fewer than 325,000 prisoners fell into allied hands, while

Model himself committed suicide. Meanwhile, by the end of March, the US First and Third Armies (in Bradley's 12th Army Group), the Seventh Army (Devers' 6th Army Group), and the First French Army were all well over the Rhine and advancing eastwards. Thanks to Sigint the allied command knew the dire straits to which the enemy field forces were now reduced: it was clear that coherent German resistance was nearing its end.[51]

Yet Eisenhower as Supreme Commander was already looking ahead to the operational problems involved in effecting a tidy junction with the Red Army advancing from the east. He signalled Stalin personally on 28 March to suggest that 'the best axis on which to effect this junction would be Erfurt-Leipzig-Dresden' – signifying that the principal thrust-line for his own forces after the encircling of the Ruhr would lie in the centre (on the axis Kassel-Leipzig), not in the north in the 21st Army Group sector, as Montgomery and Churchill were still urging. In fact, despite their indignant protests, he proposed to remove Simpson's US Ninth Army from Montgomery's command in good time to strengthen his proposed central thrust.

There now blew up the last great Anglo-American row of the war over strategy. While Montgomery's motivation in arguing that his thrust for the Elbe should take strategic priority is obvious enough Churchill's intervention on the other hand was prompted by considerations of politics and national prestige. In the first place, he signalled Eisenhower that he wished Simpson to remain under Montgomery in order to 'avoid the relegation of His Majesty's Forces to an unexpectedly restricted sphere'.[52] But more importantly,

> If the enemy's resistance should weaken, as you evidently expect ... why should we not cross the Elbe and advance as far eastward as possible? This has important political bearing, as the Russian Army of the south seems certain to enter Vienna and overrun Austria. If we deliberately leave Berlin to them, even if it should be within our grasp, the double event may strengthen their conviction, already apparent, that they have done everything.[53]

Churchill put this view even more strongly to Roosevelt on 1 April:

> If they also take Berlin, will not their impression that they have been the overwhelming contributor to our common victory be unduly imprinted in their minds. And may this not lead them into a mood which will raise grave and formidable difficulties in the future?[54]

Roosevelt, however, refused for such political reasons to overrule the military judgement of the Supreme Allied Commander.[55] And Eisenhower himself remained convinced that Berlin was no longer a prime military objective, and that the priority lay in arranging a tidy junction with the Red Army. In any case, he was very conscious (as Churchill did not seem to be) that the Red Army already lay within forty-fifty miles of Berlin, while his own armies were still some 250 miles from the city. This did not offer good odds on the Western allies winning the race. After a flurry of signals running on into the middle of April, Eisenhower's strategy stood unchanged.

But was Churchill's proposal well-judged even on the political plane? The boundaries of the three occupation zones into which Germany was to be partitioned after her defeat had been formally agreed in a Protocol signed at the Yalta summit conference in February 1945, with Berlin designated as a tripartite enclave deep inside the Soviet zone. As it was, the end of the war found Anglo-American forces occupying almost half that part of the Soviet zone which lay west of the agreed inter-zonal boundary along the rivers Oder and Neisse; and from which they then did withdraw.[56] A race to Berlin – or Prague – must surely have brought about an open confrontation with Stalin. Was this the time do so, with the Allied Expeditionary Forces and the Red Army face to face in the field? And when one catastrophic European conflict was only just ending? Nor should be left out of account the tremendous Western public admiration for the war effort of the Soviet Union and the victories of the Red Army. It is thus hard not to conclude that the idea of a race to Berlin displays Churchill at his most impulsive.

The campaign of 1945 was now well into its final phase, with the German Army suffering the kind of rout and collapse which it had inflicted on the Polish Army in 1939, the French Army in 1940, and the Yugoslav and Greek armies in 1941. The racing allied advances were only briefly slowed by uncoordinated local German counter-attacks on a river or canal, in a village or a wood. By 18 April, when the Ruhr pocket surrendered, 21st Army Group had reached the Elbe at Lauenburg, had freed the north and east of the Netherlands, and lay some forty-fifty miles from the German North-Sea and Baltic coasts; the 12th Army Group was on the Elbe and had taken Bayreuth; and the Sixth Army Group, wheeling south-eastwards, was nearing Nuremberg and Stuttgart. Two days earlier the Red Army launched its final offensive of the war, smashing through German defences on the Oder and on 25 April surrounding Berlin – the same day that Soviet and American advanced guards met at Torgau on the Elbe, splitting the Reich and its armed forces into two. Yet even now some German formations rallied and offered a hard fight, such as the last stand of First Parachute Army in defence of the Bremen-Oldenburg area against Montgomery in the second half of April. But the final days of April and the first days of May saw the Anglo-American armies run the final furlong of their race. On 2 May the British 11th Armoured Division reached Lubeck on the Baltic; next day the garrison of Hamburg surrendered; and on 4 May General-Admiral von Friedeburg unconditionally surrendered to Montgomery all German forces in the Netherlands, northwest Germany (including the Friesian Island and Heligoland), and Denmark. For Montgomery personally, this marked the crowning moment of his long march from Alamein. In the south, the US Seventh Army took Augsburg and Munich on 30 April, and pressed on to the Brenner Pass (making contact with the US Fifth Army in Italy) and Salzburg. Meanwhile the US Third Army captured Linz in Austria and Pilsen in Czechoslovakia, and was nearing Prague.

On 7 May, at Eisenhower's headquarters in Reims, General Alfred Jodl, Chief of Operations, *Oberkommando der Wehrmacht*, signed the unconditional surrender of all the German armed forces on every front.

General Eisenhower, Supreme Commander Allied Expeditionary Force, then made a signal to the Combined Chiefs of Staff:

> The mission of this Allied force was fulfilled at 0241, local time, May 7th, 1945.[57]

References

1. Quoted in Danchev and Todman (Editors), *War Diaries 1939–1945; Field Marshal Lord Alanbrooke*, p.546.
2. Montgomery of Alamein, *Memoirs*, p.540.
3. Ibid.
4. Davis, p.146.
5. Ibid, p.220.
6. Chandler, *The Papers of Dwight David Eisenhower; The War Years*: IV, p.2231, Note 1.
7. Ibid, .604.
8. Ibid, p.585.
9. Ibid, p.591.
10. Ibid, p392.
11. Ibid, p.1011.
12. Ibid, pp.1571–2.
13. Ibid, p.
14. Ibid, pp.1572–3.
15. Ibid, p.379.
16. Ehrman, *Grand Strategy*, Vol. V, p.302.
17. Chandler, op. cit., pp.1894–5.
18. Celebrated in the 2010 television drama series, *Band of Brothers*.
19. Chandler, op. cit., pp.1806–7.
20. Ibid, p.1908.
21. Ibid, p.2120.
22. Ibid, p.2144.
23. A veteran of Arnhem once told me, 'They called it "Market Garden", and we certainly bought it.'
24. Chandler, op. cit., pp.2221–2.
25. Ibid, p.2125.

26. Montgomery of Alamein, op. cit., p.318.

27. Ibid, p.319.

28. Ziemke, *Stalingrad to Berlin. The German Defeat in the East*, p.412.

29. Chandler, op. cit., p.2231, Note 1.

30. Hinsley et al, *British Intelligence in the Second World War: Its Influence on Strategy and Operations*, Vol. III, Part II, pp.670–84.

31. Ibid.

32. Eisenhower to Marshall, cited in Chandler, op. cit., p.2419.

33. Chandler, op. cit., p.2431.

34. Ibid, p.2450.

35. Ibid, p.2451.

36. Ellis, *Victory in the West*, Vol. II, p.264.

37. *Taurus Pursuant*, p.85, quoted in Ellis, op. cit., p.273, Note 2.

38. Ellis, op. cit., p.277.

39. Ibid.

40. Quoted in ibid, p.284.

41. Ibid, p.283.

42. Ibid, p.284.

43. *Report by the Supreme Commander to the Combined Chiefs of Staff on the Operations in Europe of the Allied Expeditionary Force, 6 June 1944 to 8 May 1945*, p.144. No account is given of the operations of the British tactical air forces in Terraine, *The Right of the Line: The Royal Air Force in the European War, 1939–1945*.

44. *Supreme Commander's Report*, op. cit., p.116.

45. Webster and Frankland, *The Strategic Air Offensive Against Germany 1939–1945*, Vol. III: *Victory*, Part 5, pp.183–205.

46. Bidwell, 'Kesselring', in Barnett (Ed), *Hitler's Generals*, p.286.

47. Chandler, op. cit., pp.2536–7.

48. Hinsley, op. cit., pp.686–7.

49. Chandler, op. cit., p.2539.

50. Ibid, p.2542.

51. Hinsley, op. cit., pp.688–90.

52. Signal of 31 March 1945, cited in Chandler, op. cit., p.2563, Note 2.

53. Ibid.

54. Ibid.

55. See Woodward, *British Foreign Policy in the Second World War*, pp.516–18, and Note on p.518.

56. See Sharp, *The Wartime Alliance and the Zonal Division of Germany*, Chapter V for an analysis of this whole question in its political and military aspects.

57. Chandler, op. cit., p.2696.

CHAPTER 18

Stalin's Marshal

Georgi Zhukov

On 22 June 1941 Adolf Hitler launched Operation BARBAROSSA, a totally unprovoked attack on the Soviet Union, a country with which only two years earlier he had concluded a treaty of friendship. The attack began with the destruction by the Luftwaffe of much of the Soviet air force on its airfields, followed by an avalanche of nineteen panzer divisions (with 3,550 tanks) and 116 infantry divisions which took the Soviet defence between the Baltic and the Black Sea completely by surprise. For Stalin had refused to heed British warnings from Ultra decrypts of German Enigma signals that his country was about to be attacked; and, worse still, had ordered that the Red Army be deployed forward along the frontier, instead of well to the rear and out of range of the initial shock of an enemy offensive.

The combination of Stalin's mistakes and the war-hardened fighting skills of the enemy led to an unfolding military catastrophe. In a series of gigantic battles of encirclement during June, July, August, and September, the Wehrmacht destroyed the main part of the Red Army then stationed in European Russia: 300,000 prisoners taken round Byalystok and Minsk; 600,000 round Kiev; and another 600,000 round Viazma. By October the Germans had advanced some 400 miles into the Soviet Union, and, after defeating a Soviet counter-stroke at Smolensk, were now fairly launched on the last 200 miles to Moscow.

To the Soviet leadership the situation seemed ever more desperate, for the defence of Moscow depended either on the exhausted survivors of earlier battles, or on green troops rushed to the front. And Stalin himself seems to have suffered a temporary nervous crisis after the initial disasters for which he bore so much responsibility. The very survival of the Soviet Union now seemed in doubt.

On 5 October 1941 Stalin recalled to Moscow General Georgi Zhukov (at that time commanding the defence of Leningrad) and briefed him on 'a very grave situation' that had developed on the front west of Moscow. No one knew the true state of the fighting. Stalin instructed Zhukov: 'You are to go at once to the Western Front Headquarters to investigate the situation thoroughly. Phone me from there at any hour, day or night.'[1] Zhukov set off immediately by car: 'On the way I studied the situation on the map with the aid of a torch. I was very sleepy, so every now and then I made the driver stop, and took short runs to stave off sleep.'[2]

His tour of inspection took him through the countryside of his childhood, even to within ten kilometres of the village where his mother and other kinsfolk were still living. He wanted to call on them, but had no time. 'I asked myself what would happen to them if the fascists came to their village; what would happen to General Zhukov's relatives. Shoot them, surely.'[3] So he later arranged for them to be evacuated.

Back in Moscow on 8 October 1941 he submitted a grim situation report to Stalin: a large group of the Red Army had been surrounded at Viazma; Tula, a major armaments centre south of Moscow, was in danger; and German armour might at any time burst through the weak Soviet defence at Mozaisk on the direct route to Moscow.

Two days later Stalin appointed Zhukov C-in-C of the West Front. On his leadership now depended the fate of Moscow, and even of the Soviet Union itself.

*   *   *

Zhukov was forty-five years of age, short in stature, barrel-chested, with the thick, square hands of a peasant. A hard-riding horseman and a keen hunter, he was the epitome of crude physical strength. In an army little given to polish or refinement, he already enjoyed a reputation as an outstandingly tough and ruthless commander. Although he could be jovial, he was better known for the savagery of his temper in the face of neglect of duty or professional incompetence. Yet this toughness was united with a first-class mind, wide military experience, and profound strategic study. Zhukov was also a devoted member of the Communist Party because, being a peasant by birth, he could never have reached his present rank but for the Revolution.

He was brought up in a one-roomed wooden cabin in Byelorussia. His mother, strong enough to lift and carry a 180-pound sack of grain, worked in the fields, while his father, a cobbler, had to eke out the family income by going to Moscow for casual work. As a small boy, Zhukov would help with the village haymaking and harvest. At the age of ten he was apprenticed to a furrier (an uncle) in Moscow, where life consisted of long hours of work and frequent beatings. But in his teens he took to reading at night, starting with Sherlock Holmes stories, but moving on to serious study of mathematics, geography and science.

In August 1915, a year after the outbreak of the Great War, he was called up for service in the army of Czar Nicholas II, and joined the Novgorod Dragoons. The training was tough and the discipline hard, even brutal. Nevertheless, Zhukov qualified for an NCO course. This was training which he never forgot and which marked the real start of his military career. In 1916, having won two St George's

Crosses for his part in capturing a group of German officers, he was blown off his horse by a mine, and hospitalised with concussion and damaged hearing.

When the revolution broke out in March 1917, Zhukov's unit was among the first to form a 'soldiers council' (or 'soviet') under Bolshevik leadership. For Zhukov himself, Communism seemed to promise a society free from the degrading poverty of his own upbringing; to promise an end to privilege and exploitation. Next year he joined the newly-created Red Army. As a cavalryman he took part in the Red Army's victories in 1919–20 over the 'White' counter-revolutionary armies supported by western powers, but was again wounded. In 1923, at the age of only twenty-seven, he was promoted to the command of a cavalry regiment. 'I was very excited,' he wrote in his memoirs. 'My new position was quite an honour and very responsible. To command a regiment has always been considered a most important stage in mastering the military profession.'[4] Three years later his divisional commander reported that he was

an energetic and decisive commander. Thanks to the work of Comrade Zhukov in education and combat training, the regiment rose to the required standard in all respects. He should be promoted to brigade commander and one-man chief.[5]

The term 'one-man chief' signified that he was deemed so politically trustworthy that he need not share authority with a Communist Party commissar, but would in future be himself responsible for his soldiers' political guidance.

It was as a regimental commander that Zhukov first made his name as a ruthless martinet, as he himself recalled in his memoirs:

Looking back, I admit that at times I was too exacting, not always sufficiently tolerant of my subordinates. I was exasperated by any slackness in work or demeanour. Some men could not accept this. But my firm belief is that no one has the right to lead an easy life at the expense of another's honest work. This is particularly important in the army, whose men will one day defend their country in life-and-death fighting.[6]

In 1930, after seven years in regimental command, he became brigade commander in the 7th Samara Division, one of the first to be experimentally converted from horses to tanks. This proved a key episode in his career, calling out all his energy and professional dedication. Konstantin Rokossovsky, his then superior officer and later a brother marshal, reported that Zhukov was a leader

of strong will and decisiveness. He possesses a wealth of initiative and skilfully applies it to his work. He is disciplined, he is exacting and persistent in his demands [on his brigade]. He loves military matters and constantly improves himself.[7]

In the 1930s Zhukov (now Assistant Inspector of Cavalry) was in charge of battle training and helped to draft the Red Army's new tactical manuals, with their emphasis on deep offensive thrusts. Later, as commander of the 4th Cavalry Division and then III Cavalry Corps, he became a strong advocate of mechanisation and armoured warfare.

In 1937 the Red Army was seriously shaken as an institution when, owing to Stalin's pathologically suspicious mind, its leaders (from the Chief of the General Staff, Mikhail Tukhachevsky, downwards) were put on trial for treason. More than two-thirds of the officer corps (including Tukhachevsky himself) were shot: thirteen out of eighteen army commanders; fifty-seven out of eighty-five corps commanders; and 110 out of 195 divisional commanders. It is not clear how or why Zhukov escaped these purges. Perhaps it was because he was well-known to be a committed Communist who compelled his subordinates to study the classic heavyweight treatises on Marxism-Leninism, so putting his loyalty beyond question. Or perhaps it was because he belonged to Stalin's military favourites, the old Civil War cavalry clique. In any case, the purges opened the way to promotion for younger officers like himself.

In June 1939 Zhukov arrived on the hot, dusty plateau of Mongolia to take up the command of the army tasked with defeating powerful Japanese forces which had encroached from occupied China on to Soviet territory. The coming battle would take place in a barren wilderness 400 miles from the nearest railhead, and Zhukov would be fighting Japanese troops toughened by their long war with the Chinese. He was well aware that he had been given this appointment in order to test his competence for high command: a test he simply had to pass.

The battle of Khalkin-Gol (so called from the river that ran through the battle area) served as the prototype of all Zhukov's later military operations. Firstly, he sharpened up his army by ferocious tours of inspection, instantly dismissing any subordinate who showed the slightest slackness or hesitancy. He built up an overwhelming strength in tanks, guns, and aircraft. He concentrated his assault forces so secretly that the Japanese never even knew that they existed. When Zhukov struck home on 20 August 1939 he achieved complete surprise, smashing through the Japanese flanks to encircle large formations, and finally driving the enemy back in rout. He had indeed proved himself.

On his return to Moscow he met Stalin for the first time:

> Stalin's appearance, his soft voice, the depth and solidness of his judgement, his knowledge of military affairs, the attention with which he listened to my report – all this impressed me indelibly.[8]

Zhukov for his part certainly impressed Stalin, who appointed him to head the Kiev Military District, the largest in the country; and then in December 1940 to be Chief of the General Staff. When Zhukov protested that he had never worked on a staff, but always in the field, Stalin answered that it was the Politburo's decision. So that was that. Upon Zhukov now fell the main weight of preparing the defence of the Soviet Union. The work entailed close collaboration with Stalin himself, and fundamental differences of strategic judgement soon became apparent. When in the early months of 1941 evidence (such as German troop movements from the West of Europe to the East) accumulated that Nazi Germany was preparing to attack the Soviet Union, Zhukov urged that the Red Army be brought to a state of readiness. But Stalin refused, partly because he just would not accept that Hitler was intending to attack, partly because he believed that Hitler might use Soviet precautionary deployments as an excuse for aggression. Zhukov acknowledged in his memoirs that he should have expressed his views more forcefully:

> I do not disdain responsibility for the fact that perhaps I did not prove to Stalin in a sufficiently convincing manner the necessity of bringing our Army to combat-readiness. Possibly I did not enjoy enough influence with him to do this.[9]

Just the same, even Zhukov himself was taken by surprise by the power, weight, and speed of the German onslaught in Operation BARBAROSSA after it was launched on 22 June 1941:

> Neither the People's Commissar for Defence, nor myself, nor my predecessors, expected the enemy to concentrate such huge numbers of armoured and motorised troops, and, on the first day, to commit them to action in powerful, compact groups.[10]

As the Soviet armies reeled back in disaster, and nerves began to stretch taut in the Kremlin, Zhukov found himself in sharp disagreement with Stalin. In July he warned that the next German manoeuvre would be to cut off the Soviet army group round Kiev in the Ukraine, and that therefore it should be evacuated in good time. But Stalin utterly refused to sanction the abandonment of Kiev, the ancient capital of Russia, and lost his temper, a terrifying phenomenon. According to Zhukov, Stalin in a rage 'virtually changed before one's eyes ... he grew pale; his gaze became lowering and spiteful. I knew of few daredevils who could hold out against Stalin's anger and parry the blow.'[11]

Zhukov now proved to be one of those daredevils. On the grounds that his advice was being ignored, he offered his resignation as Chief of the General Staff, and was posted instead to command the Reserve Front. However, his act of moral courage served only to enhance Stalin's long-term respect. On 10 September 1941 Stalin sent him to take over the demoralised defence of Leningrad, now threatened by fast-advancing German spearheads. He arrived there in a bloody, brutal rage, hardly able to bring himself to talk to his predecessor, the veteran but now broken Marshal Voroshilov. Like the NCO he had once been, Zhukov set about kicking the defenders of Leningrad into line. He ordered officers and rankers alike not to retreat another step, on pain of instant execution by firing squad. He drove his troops into repeated counter-attacks regardless of loss.

Yet he was not without a caustic sense of humour. To an engineer officer constructing dummy wooden tanks to deceive the Luftwaffe, he remarked that soon the Germans would tumble to the deception and start dropping wooden bombs.

Zhukov's ruthless leadership succeeded in preserving Leningrad from an immediate fall, and instead there began one of the longest and grimmest sieges in history.

Now he had become commander-in-chief of the West Front defending Moscow. He was without doubt the right man for so desperate a situation. His native ruggedness of character had inter-reacted with a harsh upbringing and an exacting career to make of him a veritable heavy tank of a leader – powerfully engined in willpower and energy; thickly armoured against the shocks of adversity; a stable gun-platform in judgement; and yet manoeuvrable mentally over the most difficult terrain, whether strategic or political.

*   *   *

Zhukov knew that he must work a miracle of re-organisation and recovery, and in the utmost haste – a new defence in depth to be created; fresh reserves to be formed. First of all, however, he must impose his leadership on his tired and discouraged soldiers. He must infuse them with his own pugnacious will to win, and give them back their faith in victory. So he began with his generals. When Rokossovsky (now commanding Sixteenth Army) successfully appealed to the Chief of the General Staff against an instruction by Zhukov not to retreat, Zhukov signalled Rokossovsky:

> I am the commander of troops on this front: I revoke the order for the withdrawal of troops, and order you to defend the existing line and not retreat one step further.[12]

Stalin himself, in his mounting anxieties, presented another problem, for Zhukov found that his own strategic recommendations often ran counter to the dictator's ideas. In November, when Stalin wanted to forestall the next German blow by launching counter-attacks, he and Zhukov had (in Zhukov's words) 'a none too pleasant conversation'. Zhukov told Stalin that 'we cannot commit the Front's last reserves to counter-blows of doubtful success'. But Stalin 'snapped out in displeasure', telling him, 'Consider the question of counter-blows settled. Report your plan of operations tonight.'[13] The counter-attacks duly took place – and duly failed.

On 15 November the German High Command launched Operation TYPHOON, the final lunge for Moscow and victory. Though slowed up by mud and rain, and then by the first frosts and snows, the German panzer spearheads began to swing round to the north and south of the capital, and the Soviet defence showed signs of cracking and buckling. An anxious Stalin telephoned Zhukov to ask: 'Are you sure we'll be able to hold Moscow? It hurts me to ask that. Answer me truthfully, as a communist.' And back from Zhukov went the assurance, 'By all means, we'll hold Moscow. But we'll need at least two more armies.'[14]

Nevertheless, by the end of November the front, in his words, 'curved dangerously, forming weak spots here and there. The irreparable seemed likely to happen at any moment. But the soldiers had not lost heart.'[15] On Zhukov himself the strain of leadership in such desperate circumstances was appalling:

In the period of particularly bitter fighting from 16th November to 8th December, I never had the chance to sleep for more than two hours a day, and then only in cat-naps. To keep up my strength and ability to work I had to resort to brief but frequent physical exercises outside in the frost, to strong coffee and sometimes to a twenty-minute ski run.[16]

It can hardly be wondered that, in Rokossovsky's delicate words, 'our front commander sometimes was guilty of unnecessary abruptness ...'[17]

Behind the struggling army, the citizens of Moscow (including many women) were digging fresh defences in the city outskirts. For the conflict had now become 'the Great Patriotic War,' with the Communist Party serving as the instrument of the Russian people's hatred of the invader who had bombed and burned his way town by town, village by village, across their Motherland.

Meanwhile, fresh divisions were being railed 3,000 miles across from Siberia and Mongolia. Yet Zhukov insisted on grouping these formations to the east of Moscow in readiness for an eventual grand counter-offensive. He was determined that the enemy must first be stopped by the divisions already in the line.

By 4 December the Wehrmacht had stumbled to a halt some twenty miles short of Moscow, its offensive energy completely drained after five months of continual attacking. Worse, it was now beginning to suffer the impact of a Russian winter, with soldiers in summer uniforms crippled by frostbite and with the very lubricants in motor vehicles and weaponry frozen solid. Already, by 29 November, Zhukov had divined the enemy's weakness, advising Stalin that 'the Germans had been bled white' and that the time had come for the long-prepared counter-offensive.

On 5 December the Red Army struck across the snow, breaking the overstretched German front and snapping overstretched German nerves. Just as at Khalkin-Gol, Zhukov had brought off a complete and perfectly-timed strategic surprise, for the German command never suspected that the Red Army possessed such fresh, unused forces and in such strength. The enemy fell back in a headlong retreat that came near to panic-stricken rout, while Zhukov mercilessly hounded his troops on in pursuit. The least sign of hesitation on the part of subordinate commanders evoked furious signals threatening summary arrest. Nonetheless, Zhukov himself had reached the limits of even his powers of endurance. According to an eyewitness, 'Zhukov gave the impression of being completely tired out. His eyes lay deep in their sockets and were very red. The need for sleep seemed to have overcome him and his voice sounded hoarse. He was still keeping going by superhuman efforts.'[18]

Zhukov's winter offensive drove the enemy back some ninety miles on the Moscow sector and up to 200 miles elsewhere along the West Front. By killing stone dead Hitler's hopes of utterly destroying the Red Army and demolishing the Soviet state in a single campaign, Zhukov had swung the course of history.

*   *   *

But for the moment Zhukov had no more to give. As he was to recount to Eisenhower in 1945:

> When finally the crisis was over, I fell into such a deep sleep, no one could wake me up for a long time. Stalin called me on the telephone twice. He was told 'Zhukov is asleep and we cannot wake him'. Stalin replied: 'Don't try to wake him, until he wakes up by himself.' During my deep sleep the troops had moved forward at least eight to ten miles – so it was certainly a pleasant awakening.[20]

There was soon to be a far less pleasant awakening, because, with the panic over, Stalin began to interfere again in the conduct of the war, telling a staff conference that now was 'just the time for a general offensive'.[21] But Zhukov warned Stalin that the Wehrmacht still retained great combat strength, while the Red Army's own offensive powers were limited after its colossal losses in the summer battles. He urged that the Soviet effort be concentrated on the front west of Moscow. If there were offensives elsewhere as well, the troops involved 'will only unjustifiably sustain great casualties and wear themselves out'.[22]

Nevertheless, Stalin insisted on having his way. During the winter of 1941–42 the Red Army launched attacks all along the front from Leningrad to the Ukraine but only achieved local gains at high cost against an ever more effective German defence. The chance was forfeited of scoring a major strategic success west of Moscow with all possible forces united. So, yet again, events had proved Stalin's judgement wrong, and Zhukov's right.

Just the same, the desperate battle for Moscow and the winter counter-offensive had given both men a deep respect for each other. It marked the beginning of a relationship – sometimes amicable, sometimes acrimonious – which was to shape Soviet strategy for the rest of the war.

There now ensued a four-year struggle of offensive and counter-offensive, advance and retreat, all amounting to a war of attrition more costly in human life and more dreadful for the frontline soldier to endure than the trench stalemate in the Great War. And yet, just like the Western Front in 1914–18, the Eastern Front in 1941–45 was where the outcome of the war between the Allies and Germany was decided – and decided in battles that eventually gutted the German Army and brought Germany down in defeat.

The struggle on the Eastern Front was, moreover, the most colossal ever waged: colossal in geographical extent, with a front extending to over 3,000 miles at the maximum; and colossal in loss of life, amounting in the case of the Soviet Union to some twenty million military and civilian dead.[19] It was also the most ferocious of struggles, being fuelled by bitterly opposed ideologies, National-Socialism and Marxist-Leninism, and conducted by two ruthless tyrants, Adolf Hitler and Josef Stalin. Soldiers with shaky morale in either army faced a stark choice: take a chance at going over the top, or accept the certainty of a bullet from your own side in the back of your head.

In August 1942, at the height of the second German summer offensive, Stalin appointed Zhukov Deputy Supreme Commander of the Soviet armed forces, or, in effect, deputy to himself. On 27 August Stalin despatched his new deputy to Stalingrad, his namesake city on the west bank of the Volga, now encircled by the German Sixth Army and under siege. Once again Zhukov was called upon to defeat a German offensive in full career, and roll it back:

> I knew that the Battle of Stalingrad was of outstanding military and political importance. With the fall of Stalingrad the enemy command would be able to cut off the south of the country from the centre. We would lose the Volga, which was a vital waterway.[23]

Yet Zhukov was fortunate in that his opponent this time was Adolf Hitler, who, knowing himself to be a much cleverer strategist than his generals, had taken over supreme direction in person of all German military operations everywhere. By the time Zhukov took command at Stalingrad it had become clear that Hitler had divided his forces between two axes of advance: the one towards Stalingrad and the Volga, and the other southwards across the River Don and down towards the Caucasus oil-fields. However, after the German Sixth Army placed Stalingrad under siege and began to fight its way into the city block by block, 'Stalingrad' became for both sides a symbol, a talisman, like Verdun in 1916. In consequence, the battle festered into the most ferocious encounter fought anywhere in the Second World War, with desperate men slaughtering each other in the rubble for possession of some corner of a ruined factory.[24]

At the beginning of September, Stalin, far off in Moscow, began to fear that the city was about to fall, and ordered Zhukov to launch a relieving attack on the besiegers with troops from outside the city. When Zhukov objected that such an attack would be premature and would not succeed, Stalin nonetheless ordered it to take place, resulting in a costly failure. It was Zhukov's own judgement that forces strong enough for a decisive counter-stroke could not be assembled before mid-November. In the meantime the defenders of Stalingrad (the Sixty-second Army under Lieutenant General Chuikov) had simply got to hang on with a minimum trickle of reinforcements. And, for two frightful months, hang on they did. But all this time Zhukov was patiently and secretly assembling powerful forces for his counter-stroke.

And just as during the battle of Moscow the previous year, Zhukov shrewdly divined the moment when the German effort was utterly spent. When he put his plan of attack to Stalin,

> Stalin listened attentively. By the way he smoked his pipe, smoothed his moustaches, and never intervened even once, we could see that he was pleased. The Stalingrad operation implied that Soviet forces would henceforth enjoy the initiative. We had confidence that the coming counter-offensive would be successful ... .[25]

On 19 November 1942 Zhukov launched Operation URANUS, a smashing blow from the north deep into the rear of the German Sixth Army in Stalingrad, coupled with a second blow from the south. The Romanian divisions holding the fronts on both flanks of the Sixth Army quickly gave way. Four days later Zhukov's two assault forces met at Kalach on the River Don, completing the encirclement of General Paulus's Sixth Army. Just as at Khalkin-Gol in 1939 and on the Moscow front in 1941, Zhukov had achieved maximum surprise and impact by a counter-stroke with forces the enemy never suspected could exist, and timed for the moment of the enemy's moral and physical exhaustion.

Yet Zhukov was not present to witness this consummation of his victory. Even before the launch of his counter-offensive on 19 November, he had left the Stalingrad sector to oversee the preparation of other offensives along the Eastern Front, leaving it to Chuikov to conduct operations.

The Stalingrad campaign marked the turning-point of the war waged against Nazi Germany by the grand alliance of the Soviet Union, Great Britain and the United States of America. Nazi Germany had suffered a catastrophe from which neither her military strength nor her confidence in victory would ever recover. For Zhukov personally the battle also proved a turning-point. His strategic judgement had been triumphantly vindicated, and his talent for directing great operations in the field had been brilliantly confirmed. In his relationship with Stalin he became henceforward far more of a mentor, far less of a mere subordinate. And Stalin, unlike Hitler, was big enough to accept as a true colleague a strong-minded and blunt-spoken soldier. In Zhukov's words, 'I know from my own war experience that one could safely bring up matters unlikely to please Stalin, argue them out and finally carry the point.'[26] At the same time, Zhukov's own respect for his formidable supreme commander grew deeper:

Stalin's visitors were invariably struck by his candour and his uninhibited manner of speaking, and impressed by his ability to express his thoughts decisively, his inborn analytical turn of mind, his erudition and retentive memory, all of which made even old hands and important personages brace themselves and be on the alert.[27]

Nonetheless, working with Stalin demanded all Zhukov's own tank-like strength of character: 'Many-sided and gifted as Stalin was, his disposition could not be called even. He was a man of strong will, reserved, fervent and impetuous.'[28] In July 1943 there came another clash of opinions between the two of them, after Zhukov had stopped a German panzer offensive at Kursk by a model defence in depth. When the enemy began to withdraw, Stalin wanted to launch an immediate counter-stroke, but Zhukov and General Vassilevsky (Chief of the General Staff) disagreed:

It cost Vassilevsky and myself great pains to convince Stalin that there should be no haste and that the operation should be started only when everything was absolutely ready. The Supreme Commander-in-Chief had to agree with our arguments ...[29]

On 3 August 1943, 'when everything was absolutely ready', the Soviet counter-stroke was launched south of Kursk, and brought down a great section of the enemy front like a bulldozed wall.

This was the first in a continual succession of mighty blows up and down the Eastern Front which within a year were to sweep the Wehrmacht off Russian soil and back towards the Reich itself. It fell to Zhukov to orchestrate these offensives, and, if need be, take personal command: Autumn 1943, liberation of the Ukraine; January 1944, the relief of Leningrad; March and April, 1944, the advance to the Carpathian borders of Hungary and Romania; June, the liberation of Byelorussia; July, the destruction of the enemy's Army Group Centre and the advance to the Vistula; January, 1945, the advance to the River Oder, only sixty miles from Berlin.

The key to these successes lay in sheer mass – mass of firepower (whether conventional artillery or batteries of 'katyusha' rockets); mass of armoured vehicles; and, above all, mass of manpower, which enabled Soviet commanders to disregard casualty rates that would have appalled their western counterparts. As Zhukov told Eisenhower in 1945,

If we come to a minefield, our infantry attack exactly as if it were not there. The loss we get from personnel mines we consider only equal to those we would have got from machine guns and artillery if the Germans had chosen to defend the area with strong bodies of troops instead of minefields.[30]

Mass manpower demanded mass supplies of rugged and easily operated weaponry. The outstanding example of this formula lay in the T-34 tank, fast, well-armoured, well-gunned, and mechanically reliable. Yet it should not be forgotten how great was the contribution of United States factories to the mobility of the Soviet armies, for as many as 409,526 American jeeps and trucks, and 325,784 armoured vehicles were shipped to the Soviet Union either by the Arctic convoys to Murmansk or overland from the Persian Gulf through Iran.[31]

By 1944 Zhukov had matured into a master of this mobile warfare on a gigantic scale. A colleague remembered:

> Operations were prepared by him with scrupulous care. He grasped all their aspects, worked them out in detail, calculated, checked with the army commanders, played them on maps and sand-tables. He strictly controlled, and rigidly demanded, the fulfilment of the plan and orders, making those responsible answerable for shortcomings. And it is true that not all military chiefs were pleased ...[32]

For Zhukov's style of leadership remained as rough and ruthless as ever. One of his harshest critics wrote later that the 'rudeness which many commanders of my generation connected with the name of Marshal Zhukov was not his only self-indulgence. His belief in the right to insult, to humiliate, his subordinates, was transmitted like an infection.'[33]

And yet the personal strain on Zhukov of planning and conducting one great battle after another was intense. In his own words, 'All this taken together, plus continuous lack of sleep and physical and mental tension, had a most telling effect ...'[34] He was kept going – like his fellow commanders, like his soldiers, like the Russian nation – by an implacable hatred of the German invader. His own avenging spirit dated from the autumn of 1941, when he had seen the distant fires that marked the progress of the enemy advance on Moscow:

> I asked myself how and with what should the Soviet people repay the enemy for the suffering he was leaving behind in his bloody wake. With the sword, and with the sword alone, by ruthlessly destroying the enemy brute.[35]

On 1 April 1945 Stalin signed the order for the Soviet offensive to take Berlin: it was to begin no later than the 16th, and, in order to forestall any Anglo-American attempt to move on the city, it was to be completed in no more than twelve to fifteen days. He charged Zhukov and his First Byelorussian Front with this crucial task. As Zhukov explained in his memoirs,

We had never before had to capture such a big and well-fortified city as Berlin. The forthcoming battle was a very special operation which defied comparison with any other. My forces would have to pierce a continuous zone of formidable lines of defence, well organised in depth, starting from the Oder, and all the way back to Berlin.[36]

For this offensive to fail would be for the Soviet Union an immeasurable catastrophe, political as well as military. As he mulled over the coming operation, Zhukov searched his memories of the battle for Moscow in 1941, analysing (in his words) the errors of the adversaries in order that he might profit from the experience.

At 0500 hours on 16 April he launched his sixty-eight infantry divisions and over 3,000 tanks, supported by the fire of some 42,000 guns and mortars, along a direct thrust-line from the Oder to Berlin. But this time he failed to achieve his customary surprise. The enemy, in a classic German tactic dating from the Great War, had already withdrawn the bulk of his forces to well-prepared defences in the rear. As Zhukov admitted in his memoirs:

We had somewhat underestimated the complexity of the terrain in the area of the Seelow Heights. Emplaced ten to twelve kilometres away from our start-line and deeply dug-in behind the reverse slopes, the enemy managed to afford his troops protection against our artillery fire. Above all, it is I who must shoulder the blame for this shortcoming.[37]

The failure provoked Stalin into a fury that sprang partly from his anxiety lest the Western allies should reach Berlin first. Giving Zhukov a ferocious reprimand, he ordered Zhukov's neighbouring front commander and bitter rival, Marshal Koniev, to take Berlin. This in turn enraged Zhukov. According to a correspondent of the Red Army newspaper *Red Star* who was an eyewitness, 'Zhukov, a man with all the marks of an iron will about his face, and a man who did not like to share his glory with anyone, was extremely worked up.'[38]

In his anger and frustration Zhukov was utterly determined to smash his way into Berlin ahead of Koniev by sheer weight of attack. To the commander of the First Guards Tank Army, he snapped, 'Well, get moving!'[39] By 21 April, Zhukov's troops had mangled their way through the defenders of the Seelow Heights and on into the northern suburbs of the German capital. On 25 April Zhukov's and Koniev's forces met west of Berlin, completely cutting off the city, along with Hitler and his close entourage in the *Führer Bunker* under the *Reichschancellery*. Now Soviet troops began to fight their way towards the city centre through streets shattered by Soviet bombardment and British air raids. 'In Berlin,' wrote Zhukov in his memoirs, 'the wounded did not leave the battlefield. They all pressed forward.'[40]

At 1500 hours on 30 April (almost the same time that Hitler shot himself)

General Kunetzov reported to Zhukov, 'Our Red Banner is on the Reichstag! Hurrah, Comrade Marshal!'

On 2 May the remnants of the German garrison of Berlin surrendered. To Zhukov had fallen, after all, the supreme prize of Berlin. On the 8th he represented the Soviet Union when, at Eisenhower's headquarters in Reims, General Jodl signed the unconditional surrender of all German forces everywhere. To Zhukov too fell the honour of taking the salute at the Allied victory parade in Berlin, and later at the Soviet victory parade in Moscow. These honours were well merited. For Marshal Georgi Zhukov, Hero of the Soviet Union, had done more than any other Allied military leader to destroy the main engine of German national power, the German Army.

References

1. Zhukov, *Memoirs*, p.321. Further references to this work in the present chapter are simply cited as *Memoirs*.
2. Ibid.
3. Ibid, p.324.
4. Ibid, p.78.
5. Chaney, *Zhukov*, p.17.
6. Ibid, p.97.
7. Ibid, p.24.
8. *Memoirs*, p.171.
9. Chaney, p.77.
10. *Memoirs*, p. 251.
11. Ibid, p.283.
12. Harrison Salisbury, Footnote, pp. 69–70.
13. *Memoirs*, p.337.
14. Ibid, pp.339–40.
15. Ibid, p.341.
16. Zhukov's own recollection, as told to General Eisenhower after the war. *Memoirs*, p.684.
17. Chaney, p.146.
18. Cited in Chaney, p.171.
19. See Ziemke, *Stalingrad to Berlin: The German Defeat in the East* (New York, Military Heritage Press, 1968) p.500.
20. *Memoirs*, p.684.
21. Ibid, p.352.
22. Ibid, pp.252–3.
23. Ibid, p.377.
24. The classic account is Beevor, *Stalingrad*.
25. *Memoirs*, p.406.
26. Ibid, p.281.
27. Ibid.

28. Ibid.

29. Ibid, p.464.

30. Harrison Salisbury, p.8. The West German military attaché in London in the 1960s, who had served on the Eastern Front, once told me that however much you fired at advancing Soviet troops, however many corpses and wounded accumulated in front of your position, the attacking waves would still keep coming on. You then had the choice of being overwhelmed or retreating in haste.

31. Ziemke, *Stalingrad to Berlin*, p.501.

32. Chaney, p.295.

33. Ibid, p.257.

34. *Memoirs*, p.489.

35. Ibid, p.290.

36. Ibid, pp.592–3.

37. Ibid, p. 607.

38. Cited in Chaney, p.314.

39. Cited in Chaney, p.312.

40. Ibid, p.619.

CHAPTER 19

Adolf Hitler

Spellbinder and Fantasist

Hitler, like Bonaparte, ended up a titanic failure, with all his vast ambitions unrealised and all his conquests undone. But, unlike Bonaparte, he has not been so fortunate as to attract a posthumous myth in which all his political and strategic errors are explained away or blamed on others, and in which he is credited with an enlightened political vision which he never had. The Napoleonic legend was of course readily marketable in the age of nineteenth-century romanticism. Suitably packaged by his admirers, Bonaparte could be made to look like a military genius, even though he ended his career on St Helena and not in Buckingham Palace. He could be made to appear a child of the Enlightenment: a progressive ruler who swept away the ancien régime all over Europe, providing paved footways, street lighting, and constitutions. The intellectuals and poets of Europe, and not just of France, were on his side, or at least on the side of the Napoleon of myth.

In contrast, Hitler's memory is today only celebrated by skin-headed losers in Europe's lower classes. In the history of ideas he stands for the past: for the romantic glorying of the nation and the nation-state, for a belief in a 'master race' destined to rule over all racial inferiors. What could now be more quaintly outmoded than Hitler's folksy claptrap about blood and earth as the essence of tribal identity? In any case, by the time the last shot was fired in Europe in May 1945, the Nazi world-view had been utterly discredited by the revelation of the moral and physical enormity of 'the Final Solution'. The future belonged either to Communism or to western capitalist democracy, or, more than either, to the supermarket and the package holiday. There is yet another reason why Hitler, unlike Bonaparte, has not become a mythical hero: it is that Hitler had the appearance and manners of a waiter, and the personal life and tastes of a lower-middle-class clerk. His table talk exceeded Mr Pooter's for yawn-inducing banality and, whereas Bonaparte had sipped Chambertin and Churchill had relished his brandy and Havana cigars, Hitler had gobbled chocolate cake. These sad characteristics render him in retrospect a misfit in any gallery of national leaders in war.

Nonetheless, he exerted in his lifetime an extraordinary personal spell. An early adherent, Putzi Hanfstaengl, himself an educated, cultured man, describes the effect of Hitler's oratory on a beer-cellar meeting in the 1920s:

I looked round at the audience. Where was the nondescript crowd I had seen only an hour before? What was suddenly holding these people...? The hubbub and the mug-clattering had stopped, and they were drinking in every word. Only a few yards away was a young woman, her eyes fastened on the speaker. Transfixed as though in some devotional ecstasy she had ceased to be herself, and was completely under the spell of Hitler's despotic faith in Germany's future greatness.[1]

Unlike Bonaparte's or Lincoln's oratory, which now lies dead on the page, Hitler at a Nuremberg Rally can be conjured up on film delivering one of his well-rehearsed spontaneous tirades, together with cutaways to the rapt faces of his devout audience. If leadership is at base quite simply the psychological power to persuade other human beings to follow where the leader goes, then Hitler possessed this power in full measure. Albert Speer, Reichsminister for Armaments Production, has testified to this; so too have the generals, including Rommel, who would go to Hitler to warn of impending defeat, and come away believing that victory was still possible.

The tragedy for Germany and Europe lay in the mismatch of such psychological power to a shallow mind and the ideas of an arrested adolescent dreamer.

* * *

During and just after the Second World War it was the widely held belief that Hitler had been implementing step by step a grand design of territorial expansion originally sketched in his early days as a street politician: first the demilitarised Rhineland in 1936; then Austria and the Sudetenland in 1938; Czechoslovakia in March 1939; Poland in September 1939, and finally the Soviet Union in 1941. Yet when Professor A. J. P. Taylor examined the evidence for this supposed programme, such as Hitler's early table talk and a speech to assembled generals in 1937, he concluded that such utterances amounted to no more than rhetoric for a particular political purpose at a particular moment. Moreover, Taylor demonstrated that the occupations of Austria in 1938 and the rump of Czechoslovakia in March 1939, far from being triggered by Hitler, had been actually precipitated by internal political happenings in those countries. Hitler had merely exploited the opportunity.

Yet there is no inherent contradiction between such opportunism and the long-term pursuit of national expansion: the one is tactical, and the other strategic. There is indeed so clear a consistency in Hitler's expressed aspirations from the 1920s onwards as to leave little doubt where he meant to lead German foreign policy when time and opportunity should serve. His 1920s book *Mein Kampf* envisaged a German colonial empire carved out of Soviet Russia. He told the army leaders just after becoming chancellor in 1933 that Germany must solve her economic problems by conquering markets; that this required rearmament; and that thereafter there must be expansion into the East – that is, the Soviet Union – and 'ruthless Germanisation of it'.[2] In 1936 he told Göring that Germany must beat Soviet Russia; and in November 1937 he informed his generals that 'for the solution of the German question, all that remains is the way of force'.[3]

His aims in foreign policy were, then, to restore Germany as a great power, newly re-armed and free of the trammels of the Versailles Treaty; to create a Greater Germany by gathering in German-speaking populations in Austria, Czechoslovakia, and Poland; and eventually to embark on the destruction of the Soviet regime and the Germanic colonisation of Russia west of the Urals.

From 1933 to 1939 his chosen instruments for promoting these aims lay in well-calculated bluff coupled with the psychological leverage of menace. These instruments enabled him to reap the gains of conquest without incurring a burdensomely large defence budget, let alone a war costly in lives and money.

The announcement in 1935 of the re-introduction of conscription and the existence of the Luftwaffe, together with the publication of grossly exaggerated figures of first-line air strength and aircraft production, twanged the nerves of the British and French political leaders, as did the blatant militarism of the Nazi régime, all uniforms, flags, and marching to and fro. In the hope of making a deal with Hitler before he grew too strong, they made ill-advised approaches to him about the settlement of Germany's alleged grievances under the Versailles Treaty, starting in 1934 with a visit by Anthony Eden (then Minister for League of Nations Affairs) and Sir John Simon, the Foreign Secretary; and followed in 1937 by Lord Halifax (Lord President of the Council in Neville Chamberlain's new Cabinet). They all made it clear to Hitler that Britain would not object to German expansion in central and eastern Europe, providing it were carried out in seemly fashion, and not by some embarrassingly obvious smash-and-grab.

Thus Hitler was successfully operating the strongest of all ploys in diplomacy as in war; the strategic offensive coupled with a tactical defensive that compels the enemy to make the forward moves. Clausewitz had pronounced that war is the conduct of policy by another means; in the 1930s Hitler transformed foreign policy into the conduct of war by other means. Thus Germany's rearmament programme, far from amounting to the creation of a war economy as imagined by France and Britain, was designed to produce quickly sufficient aircraft and weaponry to enable the new Wehrmacht to serve as an effective arm-twister behind Hitler's diplomacy.

It was during the crisis in 1938 over the future of the Sudetenland, a German-speaking (formerly Austrian) province of Czechoslovakia, that Hitler achieved the crowning victory in his 'war by other means', even casting his personal spell over the British Prime Minister when Neville Chamberlain twice flew to meet him in an effort to avert war. The Englishman was too decent a man and too much imbued with a strong sense of public responsibility for him to comprehend that Hitler, the leader of a great nation, could be an unprincipled twister. The beguiled Chamberlain reported back to his Cabinet colleagues that Hitler 'would not deliberately deceive a man whom he respected and with whom he had been in negotiation ...'[4] Since Hitler also thoughtfully informed Chamberlain that the German Army was 'a terrific instrument' ready to march at any moment, Chamberlain pressured the French prime minister, Édouard Daladier, into reneging on France's military alliance with Czechoslovakia and joining him in the handover of the Sudetenland (and with it the Czech frontier defences) to Hitler at the Munich Conference on 28 September 1938.

When in March 1939 the rest of Czechoslovakia fell into Hitler's hands, it marked the consummation of an astonishing grand-strategic triumph, decisively tipping the military balance of Europe away from the democracies and towards Hitler's Third Reich. And this was not all: the triumph greatly enhanced Hitler's personal authority vis-a-vis Field Marshal von Brauchitsch (the C-in-C of the German Army) and General Franz Halder (Chief of the General Staff) who had cautioned Hitler during the Munich crisis not to risk a war with the victors of 1918 because Germany was not yet strong enough.

Thus far, therefore, Hitler's 'war by other means' had proved brilliantly successful. But by 1939 the formula was ceasing to work. The bluff that Germany had become a war economy had only spurred the Allies (and Britain in particular) to embark on large-scale rearmament themselves, and by 1940 British output of military aircraft would surpass Germany's. Then again, a diplomacy based on menace and deception finished up by convincing British public opinion that Hitler's word simply could not be trusted, and that he was indeed implementing a systematic plan of bloodless territorial expansion. When Hitler occupied Czechoslovakia in March 1939, proclaiming it 'the Reichsprotectorate of Bohemia and Moravia',[5] even Chamberlain came to believe that Hitler must be stopped from achieving domination over Europe. So Chamberlain issued militarily worthless public guarantees to Romania and Poland that Britain would stand by them if they decided to resist German aggression.

Thus Hitler's game had now been well and truly rumbled. He did not realise this. In the spring and summer of 1939 he tried to repeat his success over the Sudetenland by stoking up a new crisis affecting the Free City of Danzig (administered by a League of Nations Commissioner) and the so-called 'Polish Corridor' to the Baltic Sea which divided East from West Prussia. Both the Free City and the 'Corridor' were creations of the 1919 peace settlement which Hitler was determined to demolish. In Danzig itself, with a Nazi-controlled Senate and a predominantly German-speaking population, the summer months witnessed clamorous demonstrations calling for the city to be returned to the Reich. Hitler meanwhile pursued his usual strategy – increasingly belligerent speeches; blood-curdling threats of forcible intervention to save Poland's Germanic minority from Polish 'oppression'; movement of troops towards the frontier. But the Polish government would not budge. Then on 23 August Hitler regained the diplomatic initiative when Nazi Germany and the Soviet Union, bitter ideological foes, signed a Treaty of Friendship complete with a secret protocol by which they agreed to partition Poland between them in the event of conflict. This Treaty, cynical even by Hitler's standards, freed Hitler from the fear of a war on two fronts. It left Poland isolated from any possible military assistance. In Berlin it therefore seemed clear that Chamberlain's guarantee to Poland must now be, in any practical sense, null and void, even though Chamberlain had re-affirmed it in a speech on 22 August.

As for Hitler himself, he 'was absolutely certain that the Western democracies ... would shrink from a general war.'[6] So he told Count Ciano, the Italian Foreign Minister, on 12 August, while informing him that he meant to attack Poland by the end of the month unless his demands were met. After his face-to-face dealings with Chamberlain during the Munich crisis, he held the British prime minister in contempt as a sanctimonious old busybody who would never resort to arms. Yet in writing off Chamberlain in this way, Hitler made the first of all the calamitous misjudgements that would finally bring him to suicide in a bunker in his own capital city. For Chamberlain was far from weak and craven: on the contrary he was an individual of strong will who dominated his own Cabinet. Certainly he would strive to the last minute and beyond to avert a war that he knew must be ruinous to Europe; and, worst of all, a war that must inevitably bring Great Britain herself to economic collapse. In the spring of 1939 the Cabinet had been warned by the Chiefs of Staff that Britain could only hope to win a long war, while the Treasury had warned that she could only afford a short war: an insoluble puzzle. Nonetheless, Chamberlain was still resolved to honour Britain's pledge to Poland if Hitler refused to compromise.

The British Government therefore made it absolutely clear to the Nazi leadership that the consequence of an attack on Poland must be a war between Britain and Germany. As the days of August ran out, Hitler faced for the first time the choice between cooling a crisis by backing down, or turning his bluff about forcible intervention into the reality of a general war for which Germany was not yet fully prepared industrially or militarily.

On the advice of Reichsmarschall Göring and other close colleagues, Hitler did at least postpone the D-Day for a possible invasion of Poland from 26 August to 1 September. The pressing question now was whether the British – that is,

Chamberlain – would (as went the saying of the time) 'go to war for Danzig'. Hitler, himself a man devoid of principle, could not believe that Chamberlain would fight just because of his pledge to the Poles. He equally could not believe that this 'silly old man' with the umbrella (as Hitler contemptuously characterised him after Munich) would fight this year for Danzig when he had failed to fight for the Sudetenland the year before.

So instead of cooling the crisis by stalling or backing down, he ordered the Wehrmacht to invade Poland on 1 September. When two days later the British ambassador in Berlin presented an ultimatum that if German forces were not withdrawn from Poland by midnight, Britain would be at war with Germany, Hitler was truly flabbergasted, turning to Ribbentrop, his Foreign Minister, to ask 'What now?'

As with Bonaparte, easy success had rendered Hitler over-confident, psychologically blind to the impact of his actions on the minds of his adversaries, and too much in a hurry. Now he was engaged in a general European conflict only twenty years after the last one had ended in Germany's humiliating defeat. The decision to attack Poland must therefore be accounted a catastrophic error of judgement.

That it was indeed catastrophic did not at first become apparent. Although the Wehrmacht's expansion and re-armament were far from complete, it was well capable of dealing in short order with the forces of a second-class power like Poland; and Hitler, the newly-fledged warlord, enjoyed himself watching the panzers roll forward and the Luftwaffe flying overhead on its way to flatten the centre of Warsaw. Meanwhile the French Army on the Western Front, far from launching a grand offensive to relieve the pressure on its Polish ally, hardly stirred from its static defences. Soviet forces invading Poland from the east duly met the Wehrmacht along the agreed line of partition; and on 28 September 1939 Warsaw surrendered to the German besiegers, effectively ending hostilities. A new word was coined to describe this conflict so different from the laborious campaigns of the Great War: *Blitzkrieg*, 'lightning war'.

Throughout the winter of 1939–40, both sides on the Western Front were content to observe each other with hardly a shot fired: the French Army in the Maginot Line, and the Wehrmacht in the Siegfried Line opposite across the Rhine. In fact, both Hitler and Chamberlain thought the conflict might just peter out in a compromise peace – Hitler because he could not see why Britain was fighting on now that Poland was finished; Chamberlain because he could not believe that the combatants would really wish to see the situation degenerate into another great war.

In a speech to the Reichstag on 6 October, Hitler held out vague hopes of a deal if Britain would only accept the new political reality in central and eastern Europe. It seems that he had in mind a peace based on Britain respecting a German sphere of influence in Europe while Germany respected the British Empire (which he apparently much admired). But so utterly mistrusted in Britain was Hitler that Chamberlain did not even bother to comment publically on this speech.

Hitler therefore now faced a grand-strategic dilemma. He had originally opted for rearmament on a limited scale in order not to impact on the German standard of living. By late 1939, however, rearmament by the Allies, and by Britain in particular, was starting to catch up. Hitler was compelled to recognise that within a year or so the allied war machine could be more powerful than his own. Yet if he now began in haste to create a true war economy, the repercussions on the lives of the German people would destroy his political credit as the leader who gave them cream-cakes as well as victory.

He found a characteristic solution to this dilemma in another gamble, the most colossal so far – a grand offensive in the West.

This was first scheduled for November 1939, then for January 1940, and finally for May 1940. The stated objects of this offensive were to conquer territory in the Low Countries and northern France, as in 1914–18, in order to give the Luftwaffe advanced bases for air attacks on England, push the RAF farther away from the Ruhr, and provide the U-boats with forward sally ports along the coasts of the southern North Sea and the English Channel. Yet like Ludendorff's MICHAEL onslaught in 1918, this was a plan with strategic objectives but no ultimate political aim: an offensive in a policy vacuum.

Nonetheless, because the operational planning and execution of this offensive in its final form (*Sichelschnitt*: Sickle Cut) were so brilliant, leading to the fall of France in six weeks, historians have failed to question whether to open up the war in this way constituted wise national strategy. As always with decisive action, the risk lay in the unintended consequences. Why, then, take a chance? After all, it was perfectly plain to Hitler and the German High Command that Britain and France were in no way strong enough to undertake their own grand offensive on the Western Front, let alone break into Germany. It was equally clear that the Allies were in no haste to end the so-called 'phoney war'. Meanwhile, the fighting spirit of the French Army and the French people were gradually decaying. Then again, Germany's supplies of oil and raw materials were assured thanks to the 1939 Treaty with the Soviet Union, so rendering an allied maritime blockade ineffective.

Thus there existed no compelling strategic or economic reason for launching this great offensive in the West.

The compulsion lay in Hitler's own psychology. As a lance corporal and platoon runner he had served on the Western Front in the Great War against the eventually victorious French Army. The humiliation of Germany's defeat, exemplified by the signing of the Armistice in 1918 and the Versailles Treaty in 1919, had reduced him to bitter rage, and bred a lasting resolve for revenge when time should serve. In 1940, with an army and air force at his command that had already proved themselves victorious in war, now was the time.

Yet there were deeper compulsions at work. In Hitler's own eyes, his political life was the expression of a continuing personal struggle against adverse circumstance. Each forward step in the struggle led on inexorably to the next, a process driven by an ultimately insatiable craving for the power and success that would compensate for his dim family origins and humiliating early life as a failed student and odd job man. A similar restless dynamism propelled his political creation, the Nazi Party, or rather, 'movement'. The Party's popularity and his own leadership spell alike depended on bringing home one success after another. A quiet life was no more possible for Hitler and his Third Reich than it had been for Bonaparte and his French Empire.

In the planning and conduct of the great offensive in the West, Hitler's interventions played a significant part. Ever a man for the unorthodox, he gave his decisive support to the proposal by Generals von Manstein and Guderian that the Wehrmacht should strike at the Allied centre on the Meuse between Sedan and Namur, instead of repeating the 1914 Schlieffen Plan and attempt to outflank the enemy's left flank by swinging wide through the Belgian plain. He also backed Guderian's recommendation that after the initial breakthrough on the Meuse, the two panzer corps should drive on all the way to the Channel coast, thus isolating the Allied northern army group from the main body of the French Army.

Yet when Operation SICHELSCHNITT had been successfully accomplished, corralling the allied northern army group into a narrow coastal lodgement round Dunkirk, the panzers were halted for two days, so giving precious time for the British to organise Operation DYNAMO, the successful evacuation from Dunkirk of 338,000 men of the BEF and the First French Army. This decision to halt the panzers robbed the Wehrmacht of the chance to cut the BEF's retreat to the coast and force it to surrender in the open field: a catastrophe that would surely have shaken the will of the British people – and perhaps even of Churchill himself – to fight on after France fell.

For this decision, Hitler and the generals of the high command were equally responsible – the generals because they wanted to give time for the mass of marching infantry divisions with their horse-drawn guns and transport to come up in support of the panzers; Hitler because he wanted to preserve the panzers intact for the second phase of the campaign, the drive south into the heart of France.

This second phase, with the French Army outnumbered one to two, was a foregone conclusion. On 22 June a French military delegation signed an armistice in the very *wagon restaurant* where a German delegation had signed the armistice of 11 November 1918, with Hitler a gloating witness of the event.

In terms of war on the European continent, and measured against the historical record, this was final victory. France, the main enemy, lay helpless under German occupation, with her mass army removed from the strategic board into German prison camps. The little British army was now back in England, having left behind its tanks, guns, and motor transport for want of enough shipping space during Operation DYNAMO.

In Paris, the glum citizenry watched a victory parade by the Wehrmacht up the Champs Élysées and past the Arc de Triomphe: goose-stepping infantry, horse-drawn gun batteries, more infantry in half-tracks, and a proud Führer saluting from a six-wheeled Mercedes open-top tourer. Then followed Hitler's triumphant return to Germany in a train steaming slowly past exultant crowds of hero-worshippers as he waved to them out of the window; and, as the climax of it all, another victory parade on the grandest scale in Berlin.

Now the shops and warehouses of Holland, Belgium, and France were emptied of consumer goods for the gratification of the German people at home.

Victory and plenty! That summer, even the share of military expenditure in the German national economy would shrink. It is no wonder that the vast majority of the *Volk* now attributed to Hitler positively magical powers of leadership.

* * *

Although the campaign in the West had proved such a masterpiece at the operational level, it was to turn out to be a cataclysmic blunder at the level of high national policy: a blunder leading to ramifying ill-consequences.

The victory over France brought Hitler face to face with Britain, an island power led by Winston Churchill, who had become Prime Minister on 10 May (the day the Wehrmacht attacked the Low Countries and France), and who had proclaimed that Britain would fight on until victory was won, no matter what the cost. This would be a contest between a lower-middle-class German upstart on the make and an English aristocrat born and bred to leadership.

For Hitler the obvious strategic answer to the problem of Britain's continuing belligerence was to occupy the country and subject it to German rule. On 16 July 1940, Hitler ordered preparations to begin for Operation SEALION, a large-scale landing on the south-east coast of England.

Neither the German Army nor the *Kriegsmarine* judged SEALION to be a practicable operation of war. The invasion armada would consist of a motley collection of trawlers, tugs, and river-barges brought together in under two months from all over northern Europe. Even on a calm day and without danger of enemy action, it would be a daunting task to get such a maritime rabble to sea in any kind of order, and without the river-barges getting swamped and their cargoes of soldiers drowning. It was clear that it would only take a determined close-quarters attack by a few British destroyers to plunge the entire German operation into irreparable confusion. Furthermore, the *Kriegsmarine* had suffered crippling losses during the Norwegian campaign in April–June 1940, and now had only two cruisers and ten destroyers left fit for sea.

It was clear to the German military leadership (and equally to the British Chiefs of Staff) that only if the Luftwaffe could first obtain air superiority over the Channel and south-eastern England could SEALION be feasible. On 31 July, 'Eagle Day', Hitler ordered 'the air war to begin'. The Luftwaffe was, however, a tactical air force designed to work with the German Army in the field, and in the coming battle it would be operating from forward airfields in France and Belgium much like an air force on the Western Front in the Great War. In sharpest contrast, RAF Fighter Command was the most advanced air-defence organisation in the world. The twenty-one Chain Home radars (with a range of 120 miles) and Observer Corps ground-stations fed intelligence about incoming enemy formations to Fighter Command headquarters at Stanmore, west London, by landlines. As the reports came in, members of the Women's Auxiliary Air Force (Waafs) moved counters across a huge map-table to give the C-in-C, Air Chief Marshal Sir Hugh Dowding, a constantly up-to-the-minute picture of German penetrations and his own defensive deployments, so enabling him to direct the battle.

Neither the Luftwaffe high command nor Hitler had any idea that such an air-defence organisation existed, causing puzzlement as to how it was that time and again the German attackers found the Spitfires and Hurricanes already in place ready to pounce. In what had become an aerial battle of attrition, the Luftwaffe was suffering disproportionate losses in aircraft and aircrews.

Yet the Luftwaffe's own relentless bombing of Fighter Command's sector stations (responsible for the tactical conduct of the defence) was starting seriously to weaken the Command's own combat effectiveness. It was at this critical juncture in the battle that Hitler made an ill-judged personal intervention which gave Fighter Command the relief it so urgently needed. Although he had forbidden attacks on the British capital city in the conviction that Britain was in any case certain to cave in, a few bombs were dropped on central London on the night of 15 August because of errors in navigation. In response, Bomber Command raided Berlin. Though the damage was small, the fact that the capital of the Reich, long proclaimed inviolate, had been bombed at all put Hitler into one of his rages. On 2 September he directed that the Luftwaffe prepare for a mass daylight reprisal raid on London, and on 7 September the Luftwaffe obediently switched its attack to the capital, giving the sector stations the breathing space they needed to restore their combat effectiveness. When, on 15 September, the Luftwaffe launched another daylight mass raid on London, Fighter Command shot down sixty German aircraft, taking the Luftwaffe's cumulative losses since the battle began in July to more than 1,700 aircraft, plus another 640 damaged. This rate of attrition was unsustainable, and it now induced Göring to abandon the daylight offensive in favour of a prolonged campaign of night raids on London and other big cities. The Luftwaffe had lost the Battle of Britain. In consequence of this failure to win air supremacy over southern England and the Channel, Operation SEALION was now dead in the water. On 17 September, Hitler postponed the countdown for its launch for the fourth time, and on 12 October put it off until spring 1941 – in the event, for good.

It remains a puzzle as to whether Hitler ever seriously intended to invade England or merely hoped to cow her into surrender by the threat posed by powerful forces ready to invade – the old ploy tried successfully at Munich in 1938 but unsuccessfully over Danzig in 1939. In those crises, too, he had kept his options open until the last moment. It can only be conjectured what might have been his final decision on SEALION, had the Luftwaffe been victorious in the air battle over Britain.

*   *   *

Now Hitler, like Bonaparte in 1805, turned his back on the stubborn British behind their moat, and prepared to march his main army off eastwards to attack a much more accessible land power: in Hitler's case, the Soviet Union. He had begun to think about this project (codenamed BARBAROSSA) even before the end of the Battle of Britain, and he finally made up his mind in December 1940.

It was his judgement that although Britain would now survive, she was so weak militarily as to be of negligible strategic importance. Here he made another crass error. For the real importance of Britain's continued fight lay in her role as democracy's embattled standard-bearer, to whom the nations of the British Empire had already rallied, and to whom the United States of America could eventually rally. The epic victory of the Royal Air Force in the summer skies of 1940 and the stoicism of British civilians during the long nights of the winter Blitz, as vividly reported in the American press and on radio, was swinging American public opinion away from isolationism and in favour of supporting Britain in her brave fight. Thanks to President Franklin Roosevelt's shrewd leadership, that support took tangible form in the deployment of ships of the US Navy to escort convoys and hunt U-boats in the western Atlantic. But absolutely crucial to British survival was the Lend Lease Act passed by Congress in April 1941, which ensured that Britain would still receive copious supplies of American food, raw materials, oil, machine-tools, weaponry, and aircraft even though her own reserves of dollars and gold were now completely exhausted.

In August 1941 the friendship between the two English-speaking nations was cemented in a summit conference held by Roosevelt and Churchill aboard the USS *Augusta* and HMS *Prince of Wales* in Placentia Bay, Newfoundland. Almost as if America was already in the war as Britain's ally, the two leaders agreed on future grand strategy against Nazi Germany, and, at the end of their meeting, published the 'Atlantic Charter', a resounding statement of democratic values and united purpose.

In contrast, Hitler's own ally, Benito Mussolini, Fascist dictator of Italy, had already proved a liability. In November 1940 he had invaded Greece from Italian-occupied Albania (without consulting Hitler), only for his troops to be humiliatingly repulsed by the Greek Army and driven back into Albania. It fell to Hitler to redeem the failure by launching a blitzkrieg in April 1941 from Bulgaria (a German ally) into Greece and also Yugoslavia. Even though the blitzkrieg was again completely successful, it further widened the war to the shores of the Adriatic, Aegean, and Mediterranean. By this time, moreover, Hitler had also been compelled to send Major General Erwin Rommel and the Afrika Korps to save the Italian army in Tripolitania from final defeat at the hands of the British Western Desert Force. It marked the start of a two-year campaign in North Africa.

Thus Hitler's victory over France, far from bringing the war to an end, had led to its step-by-step widening out. This process puts into even greater question the wisdom of Hitler's decision to attack the Soviet Union: a decision for which there was no rational justification, economic or military.

For Stalin had scrupulously fulfilled every shipment of supplies specified under the Soviet-German pact; and there was nothing to suggest that he might halt them in the future. As for Hitler's argument that he must attack the Soviet Union in order to pre-empt a Soviet aggression against Germany, this was nonsensical, given that Hitler himself reckoned that the Soviet armed forces were so poor that they could be easily defeated in a two-month offensive by the Wehrmacht. Furthermore, his other argument that the Soviet Union was Britain's last hope (and hence must be smashed in order to compel Britain to make peace) was equally nonsensical, given that in the first half of 1941 the Soviet Union was not even in the war, and hence could not constitute Britain's last hope. In any case, as Hitler well knew, it was the United States which was in reality that last hope.

The true motivation for the attack on the Soviet Union, codenamed Operation BARBAROSSA, lay elsewhere. Within the strutting *persona* of the Führer, master of Europe from the North Cape to the Aegean, supreme commander of the mighty Wehrmacht, there still dwelt the lower-middle-class little man who had long dreamed about a vast *Lebensraum* for the German *volk* carved out of Russia; who had long dreamed about a world-changing ideological victory won by National Socialism over Communism. Now Hitler meant to transform these dreams into reality by means of a blitzkrieg against the Soviet Union that he reckoned need not last more than two months.

Yet the purely strategic objective he set for BARBAROSSA was all too vague: after the Wehrmacht had advanced far to the east of Moscow, and reduced the Red Army to impotence, he would establish a permanent military frontier between Germanised Russia and the remainder. The Elder Moltke would have regarded this strategy for a war as unworthy of a first-year cadet at the *Kriegsakademie*, while Bismarck would have judged Hitler's conception of national policy as belonging more to the padded cell than the office of the Reichschancellor.

Hitler's operational plan for BARBAROSSA, as finally thrashed out with his generals, appears impressive enough as arrows on a large-scale map. He envisaged a series of encirclement battles that would eviscerate the Red Army, followed by advances by his three army groups to Leningrad, Moscow, and Rostov. But he failed to take sufficiently into account the ever more acute logistic problems posed by such long advances, especially for an army partly motorised but largely horse-drawn. He also failed to evaluate the delays and difficulties inflicted on German movement by the rudimentary Russian road network, much of it dirt-surfaced and prone to turn to clogging mud in the autumn rains. He even failed to appreciate the strategic implications of Russia's geographical shape and spread, which meant that the further the Wehrmacht advanced from its start-line, the wider its front would become.[7]

He brushed aside the misgivings of his generals, who were all too conscious of the lessons taught by Bonaparte's disastrous Russian campaign, assuring them that they only had to kick the door in and the whole rotten Soviet edifice would collapse. To be fair to Hitler, the British Chiefs of Staff (on the basis of the Red Army's poor performance against the Finns in the winter war of 1939–40) took a similarly dim view of the Red Army's prospects in combat with the Wehrmacht.

And BARBAROSSA, launched on 22 June 1941, did indeed start off brilliantly with week after week of colossal encirclements of the enemy that were made all the easier to achieve because of Stalin's decision to post the Red Army well forward.[8] These encirclements yielded the astonishing total of 1.5 million prisoners. Nevertheless, the operational plan for BARBAROSSA suffered from a fundamental flaw: it called for a broad-front advance by three army groups abreast instead of choosing an overriding thrust-line, or, in the German military jargon, *Schwerpunkt*. The inherent logistic and geographical problems of campaigning in Russia, so underestimated by Hitler, were now compounded by muddled and indecisive German leadership, with Hitler in effect acting as executive chairman of a committee composed of the Commander-in-Chief of the Army (von Brauchitsch), the Chief of the General Staff (Franz Halder) and from time to time the commanders of the three Army Groups (North: von Leeb; Centre: von Bock; South: von Rundstedt). In July Hitler wanted to strip forces from Army Group Centre in order to strengthen offensives by the two wing army groups. Weeks then passed in debate before Hitler on 21 August flatly rejected a proposal by Brauchitsch and Halder to concentrate effort on advancing to Moscow, although the capital city was, after all, vital to the prestige of Stalin and his regime. Instead, Hitler issued a fresh directive:

> Of primary importance before the outbreak of winter is not the capture of Moscow, but rather the occupation of the Crimea, of the industrial and coal-mining area of the Donetz basin, the cutting of Russian supply routes from the Caucasian oil-fields ...[9]

It took until the end of September for Hitler at last to agree to make Moscow the *schwerpunkt* of the whole campaign. This was nearly two months too late, for with the autumn came the rains, turning roads into quagmires in which men and beasts and wagons struggled to move, and which were only readily negotiable by the Wehrmacht's relatively few tracked vehicles. The sheer length of the German lines of communication back to the Fatherland exacerbated the logistic crisis. Although the Wehrmacht battled on, its offensive power was fast ebbing away. By the beginning of December the Wehrmacht had advanced some 400 miles into Russia: to the outskirts of Leningrad, to Mozhaisk (only twenty miles from Moscow), to Rostov on Don. Exhausted, it could go no farther. Yet the Red Army was still in being, and still putting up a dour front-line resistance, and even recaptured Rostov on 29 November in a surprise attack which sent tremors of alarm up the German chain of command.

So Operation BARBAROSSA had now ended in utter failure.

The failure was political as well as military, because, far from bringing down the Soviet state as intended by Hitler, BARBAROSSA had welded the Russian people and Stalin's regime together in waging what Communist propaganda dubbed 'The Great Patriotic War'. And the fundamental cause of BARBAROSSA's failure lay in Hitler's own strategic misjudgements before and during the campaign. Just as his diplomacy by means of deception and threat was bankrupted in 1939, so in 1941 'lightning war' – easy, cheap victories gratifying to the *volk* – ceased to pay a dividend. Henceforward Hitler would be engaged in a real war: a war of attrition; a war of heavier and heavier German casualties; and a war demanding that the German economy be more and more devoted to arms production.

*   *   *

On 5 December 1941, Army Group Centre took the main blow of Zhukov's winter counter-offensive, and reeled back in such disorder that Hitler took personal command of operations, issuing a 'no retreat' order, and sacking army commanders he believed to be fainthearts – and that included Brauchitsch himself, the C-in-C of the Army, dismissed on 9 December. Henceforward, he, Hitler, would be C-in-C.

On 11 December, in the midst of this crisis on the Eastern Front and three days after the Japanese strike on Pearl Harbor, Hitler declared war on the United States. This was another colossal blunder, for it enabled Churchill to persuade Roosevelt to give grand-strategic priority to defeating Germany, rather than Japan, as the US Chief of Naval Operations (Admiral Ernest King) wanted; and this meant that Germany would in time face America's mass military manpower and the overwhelming output of America's war industries. This prospect, coupled with the continuing struggle on the Eastern Front, spelt certain eventual defeat for the Third Reich.

*   *   *

Hitler chose as his principal aim for the 1942 summer campaign in Russia (*Fall Blau*: Case Blue) the seizure of the oilfields of Baku and Grozny in the Caucasus. Their capture would at one and the same time fatally cripple the Soviet war economy while ensuring an abundance of petroleum for the armed forces and industries of the Third Reich. However, Hitler also ordered that the line of the Volga astride Stalingrad must be secured in order to protect the left flank of this southerly advance. He thereby committed the rudimentary error of splitting his offensive forces in two and despatching them on widely divergent axes of advance. It was an error potentially the more dangerous because the Wehrmacht simply lacked the resources to deploy overwhelming strength in two simultaneous major offensives.

Yet to Hitler, poring over the map-table in his advanced headquarters at Vinnitsa or flying over the vast Ukrainian plain to observe the columns of his troops on the march, it all seemed at first to be going well. By early August, the First Panzer Army (von Kleist) had driven southwards deep into the Caucasus to reach the River Terek. On 28 July a spearhead of the Sixth Army (Paulus) on its eastwards march reached the River Don, 350 miles from the start-line and barely forty miles from the Volga at Stalingrad. Although it now took some three weeks to overcome the stout Soviet defence of the Don bend, Hitler was ready by 23 August to launch his onslaught on Stalingrad itself. A month later Paulus's troops had penetrated into the city's industrial district, fighting its way forward factory by factory.

Nevertheless, Halder and the General Staff were already concerned about the long exposed flanks of the Sixth Army, warning Hitler in August that it would not be possible to hold the line of the Don north of Stalingrad as a winter defence. But he would not listen. Instead his headquarters staff at Vinnitsa witnessed Hitler at his gutter nastiest in his arguments with Halder, and on 24 September he sacked him. The capable Halder was the last Chief of the General Staff in the classic mould of the Elder Moltke, but Hitler, unlike Stalin, was too small a man to accept working on equal terms with a senior soldier with strong views of his own. In Halder's place he appointed General Kurt Zeizler, who he hoped would prove more compliant. He was wrong: Zeizler was to do his best to act as the voice of professional wisdom, even though he lacked Halder's personal authority.

As the battle for Stalingrad grew increasingly ferocious, the city ceased to be for Hitler a secondary strategic objective, and instead became an obsession: at all costs he must take Stalin's namesake city. In pursuit of that obsession he poured in more and more resources, upsetting the whole balance of his strategy. In mid-

October he committed his last reserves in an attempt to evict the Red Army from the narrow strip of ruined buildings along the bank of the Volga that it still held. Meanwhile, for want of enough German troops, Hitler was compelled to entrust the security of the Sixth Army's vulnerable flanks north and south of the city to less well-trained and equipped Romanian and Italian divisions: another crass strategic error. It was on these unfortunates that fell Zhukov's double counter-stroke on 19–20 November 1942, cutting off the Sixth Army and turning the besiegers of Stalingrad into the besieged.

Hitler now played into Zhukov's hands by ordering the Sixth Army to stand fast and await a relieving force rather than try to break out before the Red Army could consolidate its encirclement. He was assured by Göring that the Luftwaffe could supply Sixth Army with all the food, munitions and fuel that it needed – a fatuous promise which the Luftwaffe failed to fulfil because of sheer lack of carrying capacity. When, between 12 and 21 December, the rescue attempt by the Fourth Panzer Army failed to break through the Soviet front, the Sixth Army began to suffer a slow, terrible death by frostbite, hunger, disease, and despair. On 30 January 1943 General Paulus signed the instrument of surrender of the remnants of his army. Paulus himself (as seen on a Soviet newsreel) was a wreck of a man, unable to stop his face twitching and his hands shaking – the living epitome of the greatest disaster to befall the German army in the whole of its history so far.

Hitler's response on receiving the report of the surrender was to babble incoherent nonsense in regard to Paulus's failure to commit suicide.[10] This was hardly leadership worthy of the Führer of the German people, the head of the German state, and the supreme commander of the Wehrmacht. When Guderian met Hitler in February 1943 for the first time since 1941, he was shocked by what he saw:

His left hand trembled, his back was bent, his gaze was fixed, his eyes protruded but lacked their former lustre, his cheeks were flecked with red. He was more excitable, easily lost his composure and was prone to angry outbursts and ill-considered decisions.[11]

Just as harmful as ill-considered decisions was Hitler's reluctance to take necessary decisions. Although Army Group A (newly constituted from First Panzer Army and the Seventeenth Army, and commanded by Kleist) far down in the Caucasus now lay in danger of being cut off by the Red Army's advance towards Rostov, Hitler refused to sanction a retreat until perilously late. Only masterful staff-work and manoeuvre by Kleist and Manstein (Fourth Panzer Army) enabled Army Group A to escape the trap.

For the second year running, Hitler had lost the military initiative on the Eastern Front. His attempt to regain it in July 1943 by pinching out the Kursk salient from the north and south with two battering-rams totalling eighteen panzer and panzer-grenadier divisions (virtually all those available on the Eastern Front) foundered in the deep Soviet defence zone; and the enormous losses weakened German resistance to successive Soviet offensives for the rest of the year.

Now Hitler was facing an overwhelming Allied superiority in manpower and firepower across the whole spread of the war from Russia to the Mediterranean, and even to the Fatherland itself under bombardment by Bomber Command and the US 8th Air Force. His response was to defy military reality by issuing 'stand-fast' orders instead of sanctioning timely retreats and withdrawals.

In North Africa this negation of strategy enabled the Anglo-American armies in May 1943 to scoop up some 150,000 men (estimates vary) of Army Group Afrika corralled round Tunis. On the Eastern Front, Hitler's stand-fast orders in 1943–45 again and again condemned divisions, and in one case a complete army group,[12] to be cut off in 'pockets'; there either to die or eventually be taken prisoner. In July 1944 he refused to accept that two months of attrition by the Anglo-American armies had reduced the German front in Normandy to a thin crust which might be smashed at any time; and he rejected the plea by Rundstedt (C-in-C, West) to begin a phased retreat. Hitler was therefore directly responsible for the annihilation in August of the Fifth Panzer Army caught in the Falaise gap between the British 21 Army Group and the American 12 Army Group.

'Stand-fast' must be accounted another product of Hitler's romantic irrationality: in this case, his belief in the triumph of the will over adverse circumstance. Yet this irrationality took other forms that were just as destructive of sound leadership. Hitler loved impressive statistics – of ration-strengths, of inventories of different kinds of weaponry and their rates of production – and enjoyed spouting them at his generals. Yet he never objectively analysed the significance of the figures in terms of the German war effort as a whole. Then again, like a reader of futuristic science-fiction, he was fascinated by the promise of new technologies such as the V-1 flying bomb and the stratospheric V-2 rocket, but failed to relate their small payloads of high explosive to the disproportionately huge investment that they demanded in research and development resources and manufacturing capacity.

In truth, Hitler, being at base a lazy man as well as a fantasist, lacked the personal capacity to make an effective leader of a great industrial country in time of war. Rather than creating a well-organised administration of war production like Lloyd George in the Great War and Churchill in the current conflict, Hitler – ever the little man – set up rival centres of power purely for the sake of preserving his own ascendancy. The result was the administrative chaos of overlapping responsibilities and production programmes, the waste and delay graphically portrayed by Albert Speer in his memoirs. Moreover, Hitler's capricious interference with production programmes for particular weapons systems, such as insisting that the new jet aircraft must be fitted as bombers, caused further delays and confusions.

In his principal role as the supreme commander of the Wehrmacht, Hitler in the years after the Stalingrad debacle more and more holed himself up in remote headquarters like 'The Wolf's Lair' near Rastenburg in East Prussia, where he conducted war off the map-table as if it were a board-game, choosing to occupy his days with tactical detail even down to battalion level rather than with shaping grand strategy, let alone national policy. Unlike Churchill in the Blitz, he did not tour the city centres burned out in 1943–44 by Allied bombing in order to give comfort and hope to the survivors. That grim task was left to Goebbels and Albert Speer. Indeed it was Goebbels who now supplied the visible personal leadership of the Reich: the patriotic oratory, the public relations tours of war factories. And it was Goebbels, not Hitler, who in January 1943 made a powerful speech to assembled gauleiters proclaiming that Germany was now engaged in total war, and the German people must make the efforts and sacrifices needed to win it. It marked an all too rare public appearance for Hitler when in the very last days of the war he emerged from his bunker under the Reichschancellery in Berlin to review a parade of the old and the very young of the *Volksturm*.

Even now, with the Red Army fighting its way into the centre of the city, Hitler in his bunker was still moving armies around the map table, although on the real battlefield those armies were just remnants too weak to do other than fight where they stood against hugely superior Red Army formations.

And yet despite all the calamities on the Eastern and Western Fronts in 1944–45, despite the destruction wreaked on German cities by allied bombers, the German people carried on staunchly, whether in a fox-hole, at a workbench, or an office desk. For Hitler's spell over the *Volk* remained unbroken even while he was leading them to national catastrophe. They continued to believe that the Führer was a 'genius' who would miraculously find a way out of ruin and disaster into victory and peace.

His spell remained unbroken because it had become institutionalised. The Nazi Party was Hitler: the Third Reich was Hitler; the Waffen SS (the Party's own field army) was Hitler. His Party symbol, the swastika, adorned the battle-ensign flown by German warships and the uniforms of German soldiers. The nation's children were indoctrinated in the Führer cult in school and in the militaristic *Hitlerjügend*. The apparatus of Hitlerian rule, as perfected by Heinrich Himmler with ubiquitous surveillance and ruthless punishment of doubters and dissenters, extended down through the gauleiters to the apartment blocks of cities and the remotest rural hamlets. The myth of the Führer as a semi-divine saviour was brilliantly promoted in the press and on radio by Dr Goebbels, Minister for Propaganda and Public Enlightenment. Hitler's victories were trumpeted; Hitler's defeats explained away. Were not the Führer and his *Volk* heroically defending Western civilisation against the Asiatic hordes? It is remarkable that the army officers who in July 1944 vainly plotted to assassinate Hitler and put an end to the war were not widely regarded in Germany as heroes, but as traitors.

Hitler himself, the arch-fantasist, continued to fantasise that victory might yet be his despite all the defeats. In 1944 he fantasised that the V-1s and V-2s would break the spirit of the British people. In the autumn of that year he fantasised that he could repeat the triumph of *Sichelschnitt* in 1940 by driving through the Ardennes, across the Meuse, and on to Antwerp, and so inflict a decisive defeat on the Anglo-American armies now standing on the western frontier of the Reich. He had refused to heed his generals' advice that the available striking force was too small to carry out so grand a project; and the offensive ended in failure and irreplaceable losses.

He even fantasised that he could emulate Frederick the Great in the Seven Years' War who, by prolonging the conflict as long as possible, was rescued from certain defeat by the internal break-up of the enemy coalition. He rightly perceived - as did Goebbels – that the alliance between Communist Russia and the two capitalist democracies, Britain and America, was entirely unnatural, and that their political aims in Europe were in conflict. He therefore correctly deduced that the grand alliance would break down in the end. But, just like Bonaparte in his time, Hitler could not see that it was he himself who was cementing the enemy coalition together; and that so long as he remained German leader, it would remain intact.

For he never comprehended that the allied nations now saw him as a trickster never to be trusted, as a man guilty of perpetrating a war of aggression, and as a criminal guilty of cruel atrocities against the peoples of the countries occupied by his armies. He never comprehended that although the Allies could not know the nature and scale of his secret programme to exterminate the Jews of Europe, they knew enough about the Gestapo, about Himmler's SS and its atrocities in Poland and Czechoslovakia, and about notorious pre-war concentration camps like Dachau, to convince them that Hitler and his entire regime must be utterly destroyed.

In April 1945, with the Red Army closing in on the *Führerbunker*, Hitler could at last fantasise no more. Yet he could still dodge the unbearable reality of his own total failure by putting the muzzle of his pistol to his head and pressing the trigger.

*   *   *

Hitler is exceptional among leaders in that he cared little about the present and future welfare of those he led. Although in pre-war speeches he had pledged his life to the service of the German people, this had been no more than an exercise in successful hypocrisy. For in his eyes the German people's existence was only justified by their usefulness as instruments of his personal ambition. In 1945 the bankruptcy of that ambition rendered them redundant, as he explained to Speer in March that year:

> If the war was lost, the people will be lost also. It is not necessary to worry about what the German people will need for elemental survival. On the contrary, it is best for us to destroy even these things. For the nation has proved to be the weaker, and the future belongs solely to the stronger eastern nation. In any case only those who are inferior will remain after this struggle, for the good have already been killed.[13]

References

1. Cited in Stone, *Hitler*, p.27.
2. Cited in op.cit, pp.91–2.
3. Cited in op.cit., p.103.
4. Cited in Barnett, *The Collapse of British Power*, p.525. See this work, pp.511–47, for an account of the Munich crisis based on Cabinet and Cabinet Committee papers.
5. Slovakia now became a separate political entity, but under the German thumb.
6. Cited in Taylor, *Origins of the Second World War*, p.309.
7. By 1 September, when the Wehrmacht had advanced some 400 miles from its start-line, the German front was twice its original width.
8. See Chapter 18.
9. Cited in Liddell Hart, *History of the Second World War*, pp.166–7.
10. See Walter Warlimont, [Deputy Chief of the OKW Operations Staff], *Inside Hitler's Headquarters 1939–45*, pp.300–07, for a description of Hitler's reaction to Paulus's surrender)
11. Cited in Keegan, *The Second World War*, p.383.
12. Army Group North, cut off in the Baltic states and East Prussia.
13. Speer, *Inside the Third Reich*, p.588.

CHAPTER 20

Winston Churchill

Victory at all Costs

A t 0530 hours (German time) on Friday 10 May 1940, German advanced guards crossed the western frontiers of the Reich and opened the battle for the mastery of Europe. Behind the advanced guards, 137 divisions (eight of them panzer) were on the move.

In London the news of the German onslaught not only caught the British Government utterly by surprise, but also in the midst of a major political crisis. On 7 and 8 May there had taken place in the House of Commons a debate on the disastrous course of the current campaign in Norway, where Anglo-French forces had been ignominiously compelled to evacuate the central part of the country. The debate had transcended the narrow topic of bumbling allied leadership in this secondary theatre, and turned into a general inquest on Neville Chamberlain's conduct of the war as Prime Minister. In the vote on the Labour Opposition's motion of censure, Chamberlain's majority of some 240 sank to only eighty-one, while forty-one government supporters voted with Labour and some sixty abstained. This rendered inevitable Chamberlain's resignation and the creation of a coalition government instead. But under whose leadership?

Because of his record of steadfastly opposing Chamberlain's pre-war policy of appeasement, Winston Churchill (the First Lord of the Admiralty) was the only senior Conservative acceptable to Clement Attlee and the Labour Party: and so Churchill it had to be. At about 1000 hours (British Summer Time) on 10 May (as the French Army and the British Expeditionary Force were advancing to the aid of the Dutch and Belgians) he sent word to King George VI that he was able to form a national coalition of the Conservative, Labour, and Liberal parties.

Thus by a dramatically neat coincidence of a kind rare in history, Winston Churchill became Prime Minister of the United Kingdom on the very day when the Second World War ceased to smoulder on a slow fuse, and exploded.

* * *

You ask, 'What is our aim?' I can answer in one word: 'Victory' – victory at all cost, victory in spite of all terror; victory, however long and hard the road may be; for without victory there is no survival...

In the six weeks that followed this Churchillian trumpet call to the House of Commons the course of events made it brutally clear just how long and how hard must be that road. On the Western Front military disasters crowded one upon another: the surrender of the Dutch army, overwhelmed in five days despite widespread defensive inundations; a German breakthrough of the French front on the Meuse and an advance of the panzer divisions to the Channel coast, so cutting off and destroying the allied Northern Army Group; the hazardous evacuation of the British Expeditionary Force from Dunkirk by the Royal Navy and Merchant Navy; the renewed German offensive into the heart of France by 104 divisions against forty-nine weak French divisions and one British; the entry of Italy into the war on Germany's side; the fall of Paris; the final disintegration of the French army; and then on 25 June the signing of an armistice with Germany by a new French government under the aged Marshal Pétain.

The fall of France plunged Churchill and his countrymen into a truly desperate plight. Britain no longer had a great Continental ally with a mass army, but instead faced the might of Nazi Germany and her ally Fascist Italy alone except for the small forces contributed by the loyal countries of the British Empire.[1] Moreover, that empire was now confronting a triple threat across its global sprawl – not only from Germany and Italy, but also from a third potential enemy, Japan. If Japan were to become a belligerent, neither the United Kingdom nor the rest of the British Empire possessed the military and naval resources to beat off three great enemies simultaneously. And, worst of all, the very island of England was now directly menaced by onslaught by the Luftwaffe from airfields in France and the Low Countries, and even by invasion from across the Channel.

This was the worst storm of war in British history. To steer the nation safely through called for supreme qualities of leadership in the man at the helm: Winston Spencer Churchill.

*　　*　　*

His image - scowling bulldog features ornamented by a cigar like a gun barrel and topped by a square-crowned bowler-hat as worn in the Victorian hunting field – called to mind a traditional English country gentleman standing four-square on his acres, jealous of his independence, and in no way intimidated by trumpery foreign despots. Winston Churchill had indeed been born in Blenheim Palace, the splendid mansion built by his ancestor, John Churchill, First Duke of Marlborough, whose victories had thwarted the ambitions of Louis XIV. It did not matter that the British people of the 1940s were themselves overwhelmingly working-class or lower-middle-class, and dwelling in vast conurbations. Rather, the social and cultural contrasts between the British people and their new leader served to enhance Churchill's mystique as a leader. The families clustering round their wireless sets to listen to his wartime broadcasts relished his orotund language, the fruity cadences of which owed much to Gibbon and Macaulay. They were delighted by his comic mispronunciations of German words, so that 'the Nazis' became 'the Narzees' and the Gestapo (Hitler's dreaded secret police) became 'the Jesta-po'.

Above all, the British nation recognised that Churchill was a born warrior: a pugilist who itched to land the heaviest possible punches on Hitler and his chum Mussolini. And so the nation gave him their trust, believing that his leadership would bring them safely through the storm.

Yet the bulldog public image concealed a very different kind of man: highly emotional, easily moved to tears; the victim of waves of a deep depression that he called 'his black dog'. Churchill was a romantic through and through: a rapt admirer of the great men of history and their heroic deeds. He found inspiration in his own ancestor, the Duke of Marlborough (whose biography he had written in the 1930s), and in Bonaparte (or rather for him 'the great Napoleon'), whose biography too he had been preparing to write when the outbreak of war took him from his study at Chartwell to the boardroom of the Admiralty.

Back in the early 1900s, when Winston's career had hardly started, a government colleague, Charles Masterman, had divined how important were emotion and symbol in his mental workings: 'he is in the Greek sense a Rhetorician, the slave of words which his mind forms about ideas. He sets ideas to Rhetoric as musicians set theirs to music.' Liddell Hart, the military commentator, remarked many years later that it was 'very noticeable that Churchill's mind was apt to focus on a phrase, while Lloyd George seized on a point and followed on to the next point ...'[2] In 1910, when Winston was Home Secretary in the Liberal Government, a perceptive journalist, Charles Gardiner, wrote of him in *The Daily News*:

> He is always unconsciously playing a part – a heroic part. And he is his most astonished spectator. He sees himself moving through the smoke of battle – triumphant, terrible, his brow clothed in thunder, his legions looking to him for victory, and not looking in vain. He thinks of Napoleon; he thinks of his great ancestor. Thus did they bear themselves; thus in this awful and rugged crisis will he bear himself. It is not make-believe; it is not insincerity; it is that in this fervid and picturesque imagination there are always great deeds afoot, with himself cast by destiny in the Agamemnon role.[3]

To this grand sense of history and of his own historic role must be added his sheer force of will – that fundamental quality of a great leader. Force of will sustained him, a man in his late sixties, through five years of huge responsibilities and desperate anxieties; through the batterings of defeat and disappointment; through the crushing strains of work and of world travel in storm-tossed ships or freezing aircraft. Yet in compensation, he also experienced the complete personal fulfilment that came from running Britain's war.

* * *

Yet what the British people could not know was that Churchill was playing a far weaker strategic hand than any of his predecessors in earlier major conflicts. His ancestor the Duke of Marlborough had dominated the alliance against Louis XIV because Britain was the alliance's richest and most commercially successful state. William Pitt (Earl of Chatham) in the Seven Years' War, William Pitt the Younger in the wars of the French Revolution, and even Lloyd George in the Great War, had all been leaders of a Britain economically strong enough to sustain a major conflict out of its own resources or because its creditworthiness enabled it to borrow on the grand scale.

But none of this was the case with Churchill or the Britain which he led.

On 21 August 1940, just when the Battle of Britain was approaching its crisis, the Chancellor of the Exchequer (Sir John Simon) warned the Cabinet that the total cost of munitions, raw materials, and industrial equipment to be bought in North America over the next twelve months would amount to $3,200 million, while our total remaining gold and dollar reserves came to less than $2,000 million.[4] Britain would therefore exhaust her reserves by December 1940, unable any longer to pay for the dollar goods – oil, foodstuffs, raw materials, technology – on which her war effort, indeed her national life itself, depended. So even if Britain could survive the immediate threat of a German invasion she would be unable to carry on the war much beyond New Year 1941.

As Churchill bleakly perceived, Britain's only hope of salvation must lie in rescue by the United States of America, the English-speaking democracy across the Atlantic. While national self-interest played its part in the increasing American support to Britain from 1940 through 1941, it was nonetheless Churchill who convinced Roosevelt that Britain was worth backing. It was Churchill's personal diplomacy that successfully fostered a relationship which a clumsier politician might easily have blighted. From the moment he became prime minister in May 1940 until the Japanese strike at Pearl Harbor in December 1941 finally booted the United States into the war, Churchill set out to draw the United States step by step into a working alliance with Britain. Here he displayed all the patience, the diplomatic skill, the sense of timing, the tenacity in pursuit of a long-term object that had characterised his ancestor, the Duke of Marlborough.

He had begun a personal correspondence with President Roosevelt even while

First Lord of the Admiralty in 1939–40, addressing the President as 'Former Naval Person' in allusion to the President's tour of office as Secretary to the Navy in the 1920s. By the candour of this correspondence, the confiding of problems and hopes, the soliciting of the President's opinion or help, Winston gradually created a relationship of mutual liking and trust; he gradually turned the President into a colleague – an ally in spirit if not yet in fact. In this subtle process he was enormously helped by Roosevelt's personal friend and emissary, Harry Hopkins, who became no less a personal friend of Churchill. Churchill writes of Hopkins' first arrival in England in January 1941 that he immediately sensed 'here was an envoy of supreme importance to our life'.

On 11 March 1941 the passing of the Lend Lease Act by the United States Congress ensured that Great Britain could go on importing the foodstuffs, the oil, the raw materials, the technology and military equipment for which she could no longer pay. From now until the end of the conflict, Lend Lease would cover more than half the United Kingdom's balance-of-payments deficit, signifying that Britain's war effort, indeed her very national life itself, would be underwritten by America's wealth and industrial power. Yet this in turn signified that for the first time since the reign of James II, Britain had ceased to be truly a great power, able to wage war out of her own resources. In judging Churchill's performance as a national leader in war this fact of national weakness and dependency must always be borne in in mind.

*   *   *

Churchill quickly proved a masterful organiser of Britain's governmental machine. By assuming the post of Minister of Defence as well as Prime Minister, he enabled himself to by-pass the cumbersome Committee of Imperial Defence and the political heads of the armed forces (First Lord of the Admiralty, Secretary of State for War, and Secretary of State for Air) as well as the professional service chiefs (First Sea Lord, Chief of the Imperial General Staff, and Chief of Air Staff), and consult directly with any serving officer as he wished. Moreover, as Minister of Defence he could preside over the work both of the main Chiefs of Staff Committee and of any committee set up to solve some particular strategic problem, like the Battle of the Atlantic Committee which masterminded the struggle against the U-boat. His Chief of Staff, General Sir Hastings Ismay, acted as the two-way channel and sifter of paper between Winston and the planning machinery, but never as a source of military advice to the Prime Minister in rivalry to that of the Chiefs of Staff.

This Churchillian system meant that all the top service commanders, and especially General (later Field Marshal) Sir Alan Brooke, Chief of the Imperial General Staff, were really part of the prime-ministerial household. As a result, the military and political leaderships worked together as one team, in stark contrast to the set-piece confrontations between 'brass-hats' and 'frock-coats' during the Great War which had so compromised British policy-making. Now the arguments, though sometimes ferocious, took place within the same family, as it were. And for all Churchill's tenacious advocacy of his own views, there was a genuine meeting of minds between him and the men in uniform. There was free and open debate, which almost always led to genuinely agreed strategic decisions, first taken in the Cabinet Defence Committee or smaller ad-hoc groups, but finally approved by the War Cabinet.

The impact of Churchill's personal leadership was felt throughout the wider machinery of government. The traditional slow-paced civil service methods of transacting business, with long memoranda in opaque mandarin's language, yielded to terse reports on one side of a sheet of paper, as demanded by Churchill. His own orders, peremptorily marked 'Action This Day',

> did much to confirm the feeling [writes Lord Normanbrook] that there was now a strong personal control at the centre. This stream of messages, covering so wide a range of subjects, was like the beam of a searchlight ceaselessly swinging round and penetrating into the remote recesses of the administration – so that everyone, however humble his rank or his function, felt that one day the beam might rest on him and light up what he was doing.[5]

Despite his immense executive authority, Churchill never forgot that he was constitutionally the servant of the King-in-Parliament. He personally briefed King George VI about the war situation at least once a week; he was frequently seen in his place on the Government Front Bench in the House of Commons, even on two occasions (in May 1941 and June 1942) having to defend his conduct of the war in the face of formal motions of censure (crushingly defeated in the eventual votes). Unlike Adolf Hitler, remote from public view in his distant field headquarters, or Stalin behind the walls of the Kremlin, Churchill was a highly visible national leader, filmed by newsreel cameras as he toured bomb-damaged streets in London and other cities, met the workforces of industry, and inspected parades of men and women in uniform.

In his personal dealings with colleagues and subordinates, Churchill was a man of contrasts. Those who served in his close entourage all pay tribute to his kindness and magnanimity. Lord Normanbrook, a deputy Cabinet secretary, writes:

> he would at intervals find time to say or write a few words of appreciation which showed a quite exceptional generosity and kindness. He was essentially a very human man, and no one who worked closely with him can have failed to be affected by the generosity of his temperament.[6]

Sir John Colville, his Personal Private Secretary, pays tribute to 'his charm, his energy, the simplicity of his purpose, his unfailing sense of fun ...'

> he pretended to a ruthlessness which was entirely foreign to his nature and while the thunder and lightning could be terrifying, they could not disguise the humanity and sympathy for those in distress which were the solid basis of his character. I never knew him to be spiteful ...[7]

Yet officers of the armed forces not so fortunately placed as these members of Churchill's prime-ministerial household – and especially those officers who questioned the soundness of Churchill's military judgement – could become the victims of what certainly looks like abiding vindictiveness. There is the mysterious case of Major General Eric Dorman-Smith, Auchinleck's Chief-of-Staff in the field in Egypt in 1942, who, after being sacked by Churchill along with Auchinleck himself, was never able to rebuild his career, and who after the War filed a libel suit against Churchill (settled out of court) because of untrue and unfair references to him in Churchill's war memoirs.

What was Auchinleck's and Dorman-Smith's crime? It was to tell Churchill to his face in Cairo in August 1942 that his demand for an early offensive against Rommel was simply not militarily reasonable, and that the Eighth Army could not be properly re-trained and re-equipped until late September 1942. In the event, Montgomery's famous Second Battle of Alamein was not launched until 23 October 1942.

Naval officers too could find their careers foundering after they had opposed some maritime operation advocated by Churchill.[8] The Director of Plans at the Admiralty lost his job after he strongly criticised Churchill's proposal (as First Lord of the Admiralty) during the winter of 1939–40 to send into the Baltic Sea a task force of obsolete battleships weighted down with extra layers of armour against air attack. This was at a time when Britain's inadequate output of armour-plate was urgently needed for new warships and for the Army's tanks. Moreover, it would have been impossible to maintain a supply line to the old battleships in the Baltic via the Skagerrak and Kattegat in the teeth of the Luftwaffe. In this period, too, the career of the then Director of Anti-Submarine Warfare foundered after daring to doubt Churchill's optimistic estimates at the beginning of 1940 of the total number of U-boats sunk.

Even Churchill's treatment of close colleagues could oscillate between a thoughtful kindness and, on occasion, a curiously brutal insensitivity to their feelings. Lord Normanbrook, though an admirer, later told Lord Moran, Churchill's personal physician:

> He really thinks of those around him only as menials, they do not really count. He is not in the least interested in any of us or in our future. As long

as we are devoted to him, and do not make bad mistakes, Winston will not think of anyone else.[9]

Certainly the almost casual and bluntly unadorned way in which Churchill told General Sir Alan Brooke that he was not going to command the Anglo-American armies in the Normandy invasion displays no awareness of how much this promised command had meant to Brooke and how deeply the disappointment had hurt him.

*   *   *

The key to understanding Churchill as a national leader in war is that he was a romantic through and through. Even his attitude to science and technology had more in common with the science-fiction of H. G. Wells than with the reality of painstaking research and the long lead-time needed to bring a new invention from the drawing-board to the battlefield. Nonetheless, his romantic imagination sometimes conjured up brilliant technological possibilities, as in the case of the Mulberry prefabricated harbours installed on the invasion coast of Normandy in 1944, which stemmed from a memorandum of his written back in 1942. But sometimes his imagination could soar far beyond the bounds of the practicable, as when he espoused the idea of huge floating airbases in mid-Atlantic which, quite apart from the operational and technical problems, would have required impossibly large quantities of steel and scarce items of equipment.

Like a small boy, Churchill was fascinated by ingenious gadgetry, and never more so than in the case of the secret campaign fought between the German electronic enciphering system (Enigma) and the British code-breaking centre at Bletchley Park (Ultra). Here was the excitement of up-to-the-minute technology combined with the romantic allure of the spy yarns of his youth. Yet Churchill fully understood how crucially important it was to the waging of war on land and sea that Britain triumphed in this secret struggle. He personally backed the work of Bletchley Park by making sure that the centre was given all the resources it needed, whether in equipment or human talent. He insisted on seeing the raw decrypts of Enigma signals rather than mere edited reports. In turn, the revelations in these decrypts about German intentions or German operational weaknesses helped to shape his own strategic thinking. Here was one reason (along with this inborn desire to keep on thumping the enemy) why in 1941–42 he nagged Wavell and then Auchinleck to attack Rommel in the Western Desert without delay even though their troops were less well-trained and equipped than the enemy.

It was in the Battle of the Atlantic against the U-boat that teamwork between Churchill and Bletchley Park's code-breakers made its greatest single contribution to the defeat of Nazi Germany. Had the Atlantic lifeline between Britain and North

America been closed down as a result of insupportable losses of shipping (as at times seemed conceivable), it would have become impossible to build up a great American army in the United Kingdom for an eventual invasion of Europe, while Britain herself would have been starved of food, fuel, and raw materials for industry. So Churchill clearly saw that eventual victory over Nazi Germany absolutely depended on mastering the U-boat. As chairman of the War Cabinet's Battle of the Atlantic Committee, he therefore took a leader's role in the joint struggles of Bletchley Park to outwit Enigma and of the allied navies and air forces to outfight the U-boat packs on the high seas. The swaying fortunes of these struggles were closely interlinked. Whenever Ultra could decipher the copious Enigma signals from U-boat Command to submarines at sea, it enabled the Admiralty's Western Approaches Command to route convoys clear of U-boat ambushes and at the same time concentrate air and surface attacks against the lurking enemy. Whenever the enemy changed the Enigma settings, so for a period blinding Ultra, there resulted such colossal losses of merchant ships and tankers (particularly in the first three months of 1943) as to threaten the very ability of the Allies to carry on the struggle against Germany.[10] Churchill himself confesses in his memoirs that that this was his time of greatest anxiety in the war.

Then came sudden deliverance, when Bletchley Park succeeded in breaking the most formidable of all Enigma ciphers (Shark), so enabling allied warships and aircraft to locate and destroy forty-one German submarines in the month of May 1943 alone: a rate of loss so high that it compelled the enemy to admit defeat and withdraw all his U-boats from the Atlantic.

Now the troopships crammed with American soldiers would continue to arrive in British ports; the Royal Air Force and the US 8th Air Force in Britain would continue to be supplied with aviation fuel; British war industry would continue to receive the raw materials it needed to function; and the British nation itself would be sure of its rations of imported foodstuffs, so relieving Churchill of his earlier anxiety about dwindling stocks.

In the Battle of the Atlantic the partnership between Churchill and the code-breakers of Bletchley Park had won its most decisive single victory.

* * *

In his judgements about military commanders, Churchill again reveals himself as a romantic, a man of emotion, rather than a cool appraiser of talent. He responded well to military men who could express themselves with the fluency of a politician; and he wrote off an outstandingly able C-in-C Middle East, General Sir Archibald Wavell, as being like the chairman of a golf club, simply because Wavell was (like Haig and Robertson in the Great War) absolutely tongue-tied. Churchill later also wrote off Wavell's successor, Sir Claude Auchinleck, because he interpreted

Auchinleck's unflinching presentation of military realities as negativism, if not defeatism. He warmed to an outward show of energy, enterprise, and sometimes the unorthodox. This was why he was entirely taken in by Orde Wingate, the eccentric – not to say deranged – leader of the Chindit guerrillas air-landed behind Japanese lines in Burma: operations which, despite their daring, proved highly cost-ineffective in terms of investment of resources balanced against strategic results. Yet Churchill even proposed Wingate as a supreme commander of the British land forces in the south-east-Asian theatre of war.

He was equally misled by his admiration for the very different personality of General (later Field Marshal) Sir Harold Alexander, a handsome, beautifully mannered, elegantly uniformed Guards officer in the shiniest of riding boots, who in truth lacked the brains and the strength of character for the exercise of high command. Nonetheless, Churchill did get it right when he furthered the career of the vain, flashy, and intensely ambitious Lord Louis Mountbatten, for Mountbatten proved a success first as Chief of Combined Operations in 1942 and then in 1943–45 as Supreme Commander South-east Asia Command.

As Churchill's contemporaries had noted many years before, it was his psychological weakness to fall under the spell cast by emotive words or phrases. During the Second World War this weakness could sometimes skew his strategic judgement, most notably in the case of the defence of Malaya and the naval base of Singapore against Japanese attack in 1941. Before the war it had been the plan to despatch the British main battle-fleet to Singapore in time to defend Malaya, the East Indies, and indeed Australia and New Zealand against Japanese aggression. But in 1941, when such aggression appeared to be more and more imminent, Britain had no main fleet to send, for the Royal Navy was now fully committed in the Atlantic, the Mediterranean, and on the Arctic convoys; and had in any case suffered heavy losses in warships sunk or badly damaged in two years of struggle against the Axis navies and air forces.

In the absence of a main fleet, Churchill chose to despatch two capital ships to Singapore, HMS *Prince of Wales* and HMS *Repulse*, in the belief that 'these powerful ships' (his words) could deter or disrupt a Japanese amphibious stroke against Singapore or the East Indies. However, to think that just two capital ships, escorted only by a few destroyers, could deter a Japanese fleet was sheer illusion. He succumbed to this illusion because in May 1941 it had taken the British Home Fleet, plus battleships detached from escorting Atlantic convoys, plus a battle-cruiser and an aircraft-carrier from Force H based on Gibraltar, to hunt down and destroy the single German battleship *Bismarck*. In his belief, the *Prince of Wales* and *Repulse* together would act as the British 'Bismarck' in the Far East. But he failed to take note that the *Bismarck* had been a more formidable fighting machine than even the recently-built battleship *Prince of Wales*, let alone the unmodernised Great-War-vintage battle-cruiser *Repulse*. The German ship's hull had been protected by more than 17,500 tons of armour plate – nearly 39 per cent of displacement, compared with only 30 per cent in the case of *Prince of Wales*. In addition, 6,000 tons of armour had protected the *Bismarck*'s gun turrets, fire-control stations and conning positions.[11] Churchill also failed to bear in mind the crucial fact that the *Bismarck* had not been rendered unmanoeuvrable by the gunfire of British battleships but by a torpedo launched from an obsolescent Swordfish biplane of the Fleet Air Arm, which jammed her twin rudders. He therefore did not appreciate how vulnerable the two British heavy ships would be to attack by modern Japanese torpedo-bombers and their powerful Long-Lance torpedoes.

And then again, Churchill failed to take into account that whereas the *Bismarck* had been a commerce raider free to roam the ocean in search of prey, the *Prince of Wales* and *Repulse* would necessarily be tied to the defence of Malaya. These misjudgements led directly to the sinking of both ships by Japanese aircraft off the Malayan coast on 8 December 1941.

Why did he so lose touch with reality? The likely answer must be that he was deluded by the image of naval might conjured up in his imagination by the words 'these two powerful ships'.

Tragically, Churchill was in similar fashion deluded by references to 'the fortress of Singapore' in Whitehall reports and in the newspapers. For him the word 'fortress' evoked a stronghold designed for all-round defence, formidable in artillery and packed with soldiery. Yet Singapore had never been designed to be such a fortress, but instead solely as a naval base to service the British main fleet when despatched to the Far East under pre-war plans. As a member of the Cabinet Defence Committee in the 1930s and then the wartime Minister of Defence, Churchill ought to have appreciated this. The coastal batteries of 9.5-inch guns on the south of Singapore island had been installed to repel a bombardment by a Japanese fleet; and their armour-piercing shells would be useless against troops in the field.

In any case, it had been assumed by the Chiefs of Staff and the Cabinet Defence Committee from 1937 onwards that the future threat to Singapore lay not in attack from the sea, but in a 'backdoor' assault across the Straits of Johore by a Japanese army which had marched down the length of Malaya from initial landings in the north. The British plan in 1941 for the defence of the base against such an overland attack therefore absolutely depended on holding northern Malaya and its airfields. When in early December this territory was swiftly lost to invading Japanese forces, the base was inevitably doomed. Yet it had in any case become void of purpose now that the *Prince of Wales* and *Repulse* had been sunk, and Britain had no hope of sending out more heavy ships. So there was absolutely no strategic point in fighting on in Malaya.

Yet instead of ordering the timely evacuation of all Imperial forces from Malaya and Singapore island, Churchill impulsively diverted reinforcements in troopships at sea (such as the 18th Division) into Singapore, where they swelled the Japanese bag of prisoners at the time of the British surrender in February 1942.

The word 'fortress' led Churchill into another calamitous error of judgement in June 1942, this time in regard to the port of Tobruk in Libya during Rommel's bold Desert offensive against the Eighth Army. Far from being a 'fortress' fit to withstand a siege, as in 1941, Tobruk's perimeter now consisted of partly-cleared minefields, a dismantled artillery control system, and collapsed slit trenches in the sand. Back in January 1942, Auchinleck had informed London that it was his intention never again to hold on to Tobruk or any other locality in isolation.[12] But now in June Churchill signalled Auchinleck that he presumed that 'there is no question of giving up Tobruk ...'[13] Auchinleck duly obeyed what was effectively an order from the Prime Minister, and committed the 1st South African Division at the last moment to garrisoning the port. On 26 June 1942 Rommel easily overcame the improvised defence, taking prisoner over 20,000 British-Commonwealth (mostly South African) troops. The news of this needless disaster reached Churchill when he was Roosevelt's guest at the White House.

In other ways too, Churchill's mind worked on the basis of broad impressions rather than critical analysis. To him, 'the tank' stood for striking power in modern mobile warfare; and he did not delve into such practical detail as the need in the Desert for sand-filters for the engines, or the mechanical reliability of different models, or the fact that tanks were at first delivered to the Middle East with all their nuts and bolts merely hand-tight. This was why in 1941 he failed to understand the reluctance of Wavell and then Auchinleck to launch straight into battle the tanks shipped out by him at great risk from the United Kingdom.

As a strategist he was prone to grand designs while remaining deeply reluctant to analyse the mundane military factors that make for operational success or failure. Despite the severe lesson afforded by the botched-up Gallipoli landings in 1915, he still appeared to believe during the Second World War that complex large-scale operations – especially amphibious operations – could be improvised at short notice, and that all that was required for success was energetic 'leadership'. His conduct of the Norway campaign in spring 1940 as First Lord of the Admiralty displays this weakness at its worst: he initially failed to make a realistic assessment of the combat-worthiness of the available Anglo-French expeditionary forces compared with that of the better trained, better organised, and better equipped enemy; and then interfered in the conduct of the campaign by ordering opportunist changes of objective.

Equally unsound was his decision in February 1941 to halt the victorious Western Desert Force after its total defeat of the Italian Tenth Army in Libya, and send the best of its formations to Greece in a foredoomed attempt to fight off a German invasion. Again, an enticing grand-strategic concept – here of creating a Balkan alliance and opening a new land front on the Continent of Europe – had blinded him to operational realities. For he counted up the impressive total numbers in the Turkish, Greek, and Yugoslav armies, but failed to take into account their lack of artillery, let alone armour, and their dependence on mule transport, which rendered them quite unfit to take on the panzer divisions and the Luftwaffe. In the event (in April 1941), the Germans, having smashed Yugoslav resistance in short order, easily broke through the Anglo-Greek front, and the British-Commonwealth expeditionary force had to be rescued (with the loss of 8,000 trucks and all its tanks and artillery) by the Royal Navy at heavy cost in ships sunk or damaged by the Luftwaffe.

In 1942 Churchill similarly counted up the ration-strength of the Middle East Command, and was angered that the total did not translate into many more divisions in the field. He simply failed to appreciate that much of the Middle East ration-strength was inevitably and necessarily swallowed up in creating, and then operating, a modern industrial war economy in a backward region: new port facilities, vast workshops and supply depots, roads and railways, telecommunications, hospitals. Nor did he at any time understand that the logistical support of modern mechanised armies necessarily demanded manpower that in earlier times might have fought in the line with rifle and bayonet.

In the autumn of 1943, Churchill was yet again enticed by an apparently splendid strategic opportunity – this time as revealed by the map of the Aegean – when (in a replay of Gallipoli) he attempted to capture the Dodecanese islands with scratch forces hastily cobbled together: a venture which ended in yet another British withdrawal. This amphibious bungle makes a dismal contrast with the carefully prepared and completely successful Anglo-American landings in Sicily and Italy that same year.

Yet Churchill's errors of strategic judgement sprang from the most admirable of motivations – a stubborn resolve never to give up hope in the worst of situations, coupled with an urge to punch the enemy as hard as possible whenever the opportunity presented itself. Such errors are the more understandable in the context of Britain's weakness and peril in 1940–41, when Churchill desperately needed to win military successes somewhere somehow, both in order to hearten his own countrymen and to reassure President Roosevelt that Britain's cause was worth backing. Likewise, it was especially in those years that Churchill yielded to the urge to prod his generals and admirals – very much like Lincoln and his generals in the first three years of the Civil War.

However, from 1942 onwards, with the tide of war running strongly in favour of the allies, and with British commanders he had come to trust, like Alexander, Montgomery, and Mountbatten, or American commanders like Eisenhower not subject to his authority, Churchill became much less prone to interfere in the framing, and conduct, of operations.

*　　*　　*

The relationship between Great Britain and the United States – between the Prime Minister and the President Roosevelt themselves – remained throughout the war the foundation of Churchill's grand strategy. That relationship deepened into true friendship and mutual regard when the two leaders met in person in August 1941 on board HMS *Prince of Wales* during the Atlantic conference in Placentia Bay, Newfoundland. Under Roosevelt's skilful political management a legally neutral America was gradually taking up the military strain: on 1 February 1941 the US Atlantic Fleet was formed; in March and April 1941 American naval bases were opened in Bermuda and the British Caribbean islands; from April American dockyards would re-fit British warships; on 11 April the American Defence Zone was extended to all waters west of 26 degrees East. Finally, in December 1941, just before the Japanese strike at Pearl Harbor, the US Navy was authorised to escort any nation's shipping in the Atlantic: and Roosevelt warned that 'From now on if German or Italian vessels of war enter these waters, they do so at their own peril'.

With America at last booted over the edge into war by the Japanese attack in December 1941, Churchill's primary objective of policy changed: it now lay in enabling Britain to exert an influence over allied grand strategy far greater than her smaller size and her economic dependence strictly warranted.

Here, too, Churchill proved outstandingly successful, partly because in the early years of the alliance, 1941–43, he was backed by a civil and military planning organisation far more able and experienced, and far better integrated, than the one available to Roosevelt, beset by institutional rivalries between the army and navy, and their respective departments of state. At the first Washington Conference [Arcadia] in December 1941, convened at Churchill's suggestion, he persuaded the Americans to adopt a global strategy that put the defeat of Nazi Germany first, and that of Japan second. Given that American foreign policy and grand strategy had traditionally been angled towards the Far East and Pacific, and given too that Admiral Ernest King, the US Chief of Naval Operations, was forcefully arguing that America should concentrate her war effort against Japan, the importance of this decision to take Germany first cannot be over-emphasised.

From now on, it became Churchill's task to persuade President Roosevelt and the US Joint Chiefs of Staff to agree with British grand-strategic proposals for prosecuting the war against Nazi Germany and Fascist Italy. Although Roosevelt as President was constitutionally the national Commander-in-Chief, and although he certainly took the final strategic decisions, he never involved himself in the business of operations as did Churchill, but instead relied heavily on General George Marshall (Chairman of the Joint Chiefs of Staff), a man of imposing personality and outstanding weight of character. All too soon, it became clear that Marshall's concept of what should be allied grand strategy in the European theatre fundamentally diverged from that of Churchill and the CIGS, General Sir Alan Brooke.

It must be remembered that Marshall was the senior military figure of a continental power with a population of 120 million (three times that of Britain), and industrial resources that dwarfed Britain's and even Germany's. So Marshall and his colleagues conceived of grand strategy in classic Clausewitzian terms – the concentration of maximum force on an offensive directed at defeating the enemy's main body and then occupying his country. In March 1942 Marshall strongly urged the President that all available allied strength should be devoted to preparing for, and then launching, an Anglo-American cross-Channel invasion of France in April 1943, there to take on the Wehrmacht in mass battles. He rightly pointed out that a new Western Front with short cross-Channel supply lines would be far more cost-effective than any peripheral theatre with long maritime communications such as (though he did not mention them) the Dardanelles in the Great War, and Britain's current Middle East campaign. Northern France was moreover the country where (thanks to nearby British airfields) the maximum allied airpower could be brought to bear. Nonetheless, in British eyes Marshall's strategy was doubly flawed. In the first place, it would mean that Britain and America would not be opening a major front against Germany for another twelve months, and this when the Red Army was fighting some 200 German divisions on the Eastern Front. In the second place, to launch forty-eight divisions (Marshall's figure) across the Channel in spring 1943 would constitute a colossal and potentially catastrophic gamble. The Anglo-American high commands had as yet no experience of mounting highly complex large-scale amphibious operations. Even supposing that the actual landings went well, and a new Western Front was established, the allied forces would face a German army still near the peak of its formidable combat efficiency. This raised the prospect of sanguinary battles of attrition and a possible stalemate, or even another 'Dunkirk' evacuation.

Such prospects Churchill and Brooke could not face. In the grim accountancy of war, Britain simply could not afford heavy casualties, because the competing demands of the armed forces and of munitions production were now heading her towards a national manpower crisis. Then again, it must be remembered that to Churchill, Brooke, and their countrymen, the battles of the Somme in 1916 and Third Ypres (Passchendaele) in 1917 were still part of living memory. After all, Churchill had himself commanded an infantry battalion in the trenches in 1916 after resigning as First Lord of the Admiralty. For the British nation and its leaders, the Western Front therefore remained a raw psychological wound.

But George Marshall and his contemporaries suffered from no such wound, since Civil War battles like Antietam and Cold Harbor had now receded into history, and the American experience (including Marshall's own) of the Western Front had been limited to local offensives in 1918 against an enemy already on the road to final defeat at the hands of the British and French armies.

When in April 1942 Marshall flew to London to put his grand strategy to the War Cabinet Defence Committee, the Committee agreed in principle that the allies should indeed work towards a large-scale invasion of France in 1943 (Operation ROUNDUP). But what to do in 1942? Marshall suggested that if the situation on the Russian front became desperate, the British and Americans should make a limited landing in France that year (Operation SLEDGEHAMMER). At a meeting on 27 May, Churchill and the Chiefs of Staff dismissed SLEDGEHAMMER on the score that available resources in land forces and assault shipping would be too small.

Now Churchill put forward his own proposal – for an invasion of northern Norway (Operation JUPITER) in order to eliminate the bases from which the German air force and navy were devastating the Arctic supply convoys to Murmansk. As with his Norwegian interventions in 1940, Churchill failed to take account of the logistical or operational problems of either the original landings or of long-term occupation and seaborne supply. The Chiefs of Staff were therefore not enthused when on 1 May 1942 they received a personal minute from Churchill in regard to JUPITER, stating that 'High political and strategic importance must be attached thereto'. Instead they proceeded to kill off JUPITER by well-tried tactics of procrastination and of attrition by sheer volume of detailed facts and figures.

This left as the only alternative for 1942 a project to land joint Anglo-American forces along the coast of Vichy-French North Africa in conjunction with a westward advance into the Italian colony of Tripolitania by the Eighth Army. Codenamed GYMNAST, it had been originally sketched by Churchill back in December 1941 in his cabin in HMS *Duke of York* plunging and rolling across the Atlantic en voyage to the Arcadia conference. GYMNAST could lead to the clearance of the entire North African coast (including Morocco), and open the Mediterranean through-route from Gibraltar to the Suez Canal. But it was the very kind of strategic 'diversion' and dispersal of strength which Marshall had most feared, and which he believed (wrongly) that he had scotched during his April visit to London.

On 18 June 1942 Churchill and Brooke arrived in the US after a gruelling twenty-seven-hour journey by flying-boat, in order to re-forge inter-allied agreement on grand strategy. While the Combined Chiefs of Staff were meeting in Washington, Churchill was staying as a guest at Hyde Park, Roosevelt's neo-Federal mansion on the Hudson River: an American equivalent of Chartwell as a gentleman's country seat of consequence, just as Roosevelt himself, being descended from one of the original seventeenth-century Dutch settler-families along the Hudson, matched Churchill in terms of social class.

Roosevelt now came to agree with Churchill that the allies must carry out some major operation in 1942, and that in this context GYMNAST should be further studied. Meanwhile in Washington the Combined Chiefs of Staff had reached the opposite conclusion: that any major venture in 1942 would have 'some deterring effect upon Continental operations in 1943', and that therefore GYMNAST should not be undertaken. The debate rumbled on into July on both sides of the Atlantic, with Marshall leading the American Joint Chiefs of Staff in a final attempt to convince the President that GYMNAST would be a wasteful diversion in itself and would 'definitely curtail if not make impossible' an invasion of France in 1943. Marshall even came up with the wildly unsound proposal that the Cotentin Peninsula in Britanny should be seized in 1942 as a bridgehead for a later breakout in 1943. After this proposal was rejected by the British Chiefs of Staff, Churchill pressed Roosevelt to decide in favour of GYMNAST without further delay, with a launch-date not later than 30 October. On 30 July Roosevelt told a conference at the White House that 'he as Commander-in-Chief had made the decision that TORCH [as GYMNAST had been renamed] was to be undertaken at the earliest possible date'; and that being 'our principal objective ... it should take precedence over all other operations ...'[14]

The six separate TORCH landings in Morocco and Algeria on 8 November 1942 were successfully accomplished in spite of incidental mishaps and holdups. In contrast to the Dardanelles in 1915, where hastily assembled forces had been rowed ashore in ships' boats, the Anglo-American TORCH armada was the result of two decades of research and development in amphibious warfare. The landings were directed from fully-equipped headquarters ships converted from peacetime liners. Specialised landing-craft with bow ramps enabled troops, tanks, and guns to deploy swiftly on the beaches. The landing forces themselves had been well trained for what they had to do. Here was the tested prototype for future large-scale amphibious operations, including an eventual cross-Channel invasion of France.

The landings marked the start of a hard-fought campaign finally ending in May 1943 with the surrender of some 230,000 men (of which about 100,000 were German) of the enemy's Army Group Afrika. The allies partly owed this crowning triumph to Hitler's folly in ordering that a bridgehead round Tunis should be held to the end. The entire North African shore was now clear of the enemy, and convoys began to steam unscathed from Gibraltar to Malta and Alexandria.

Thus TORCH had completely fulfilled its original purpose of serving as a grand-strategic expedient for 1942. However, Churchill had always seen TORCH as the first stage of ever more ambitious developments of his preferred 'blue-water' strategy in the Mediterranean - whereas George Marshall feared that it would turn out to be the first step into an ever-deeper entanglement in a secondary theatre, to the disservice of a direct thrust in 1943 across the Channel and on towards Berlin.

Churchill's hopes and Marshall's fears sprang alike from the grand-strategic decision taken by the allies back in February 1943 that once North Africa had been conquered, Sicily (just across the Sicilian Narrows from Tunisia) should come next. The successful conquest of Sicily in July and August 1943 in turn brought the Italian mainland temptingly close across the Straits of Messina; and so at the Quadrant summit conference in Quebec in August 1943, Churchill, Roosevelt, and the Combined Chiefs of Staff agreed on an early invasion of Italy, with the limited objective of capturing the cluster of airfields round Foggia, south-east of Rome. It was further agreed that seven allied divisions should later be transferred from Italy to the United Kingdom in good time for a cross-Channel invasion in 1944, along with the bulk of the landing craft now in the Italian theatre.

Yet these decisions masked fresh divergences of grand-strategic judgement between the British and the Americans. For the Americans, and especially Marshall, the cross-Channel invasion must have absolute priority, so ruling out a further advance in Italy to the north of Rome, let alone any wider Balkan venture. But Brooke believed on the contrary that the allies should advance beyond the Apennines in order to capture the airfields of the Po valley, even if this entailed a delay in removing divisions from Italy for the cross-Channel invasion. Above all, however, Brooke saw an Italian campaign as diverting German strength from France.

As for Churchill himself, he still cherished the hope that further major victories in the Mediterranean theatre might render unnecessary a cross-Channel invasion and a bloody encounter with a main body of the German Army on a new Western Front. It was his opinion that Italy represented (in his words) 'the soft underbelly'[15] of Hitler's Europe.

On 3 September 1943 the invasion of Italy began with landings in Calabria by Montgomery's Eighth Army, followed six days later by an assault landing (AVALANCHE) by American and British forces on the Bay of Salerno behind the German front.

All too soon, however, the two allied armies (designated 15 Army Group) discovered that they were not slicing into 'a soft underbelly' but hammering on an armoured carapace consisting of mountainous terrain skilfully defended by first-class troops under an outstandingly able commander, *Generalfeldmarschall* Albert Kesselring. The struggle to break through the Gustav Line south of Rome, with its formidable bastion of Monte Cassino, was to last from autumn 1943 into spring 1944: a bloody attrition battle in rain and mud.

General Marshall's worst fears about Churchill's and Brooke's Mediterranean strategy had thus come to pass.

It is therefore hardly surprising that at the Teheran summit conference in December 1943, Roosevelt (with Stalin's support) simply laid it down that operations in Italy in 1944 must go no farther north than the Pisa-Rimini line, and that thereafter the major Mediterranean effort would be a landing in the South of France in conjunction with Operation OVERLORD, the cross-Channel invasion. Roosevelt and Stalin likewise handed down the decision that OVERLORD must take place no later than May 1944. Nothing that Churchill could say about the virtues of further offensives into northern Italy (with the ultimate objective of reaching Vienna via the so-called 'Ljubljana Gap' through the Slovenian mountains) weighed at all.

What was more, Roosevelt deliberately distanced himself from Churchill at the conference, partly to avoid giving Stalin an impression that the Anglo-Americans were colluding against him.

For not even Churchill's personality, prestige, and diplomatic skill could compensate for the growing disparity between Britain's national weight and that of the United States, now at the peak of her colossal military and industrial mobilisation. As Churchill himself wryly observed of the Teheran Conference, 'there was the little English donkey between the Russian bear and the American buffalo, and only the donkey knew the right way home ...'

But was the Mediterranean theatre and a continued march up the length of Italy the right way?

* * *

In the first place, the Mediterranean theatre was sucking in more allied military and logistic resources than German. In 1944 the Anglo-American military commitment to the Italian campaign (including logistical support) would reach a total of 677,000 men, compared with the German total (in July) of 411,000.[16] And even when the allied forces in Italy were reduced to some 20 divisions by early 1945[17] they still numbered some 536,000 men to Kesselring's 491,000, with twice Kesselring's strength in artillery pieces and treble his strength in armoured fighting vehicles.[18] Two historians of the Italian campaign go so far as to comment: 'It could be said, therefore, that it was not Alexander who was drawing forces that would otherwise be employed against the Allies in north-west Europe, but Kesselring who was containing Alexander.'[19] Furthermore, whereas Kesselring's two armies in Italy could draw supplies from Germany over direct rail and road links only some 600 miles long, the Allied Army Group in Italy was dependent on supplies shipped in by convoys making 8,000-mile round-trips from America and 3,000-mile round trips from Britain. To support a maximum of only twenty-seven allied divisions on the Italian Front demanded an investment of nearly seven million deadweight tons of shipping allotted to the Mediterranean theatre,[20] whereas an average total of one million tons of shipping supported a maximum of ninety divisions on the restored Western Front in 1944–45.

Then again, the course of the fighting in Italy remained throughout a hard and bloody struggle against a skilled and resolute defence. When the Gustav Line was at last broken through during May 1944, Kesselring proceeded to carry out an orderly fighting retreat of his Army Group C to the Gothic Line, a formidable position in front of which the Allied armies became bogged down in another winter stalemate in rain and mud. It was not until 8 April 1945 that the stalemate was broken by an offensive by the Eighth Army that smashed through the Adriatic sector of the German front, and opened up a general pursuit by the Allied armies (now designated 15th Army Group) from the River Po to the foothills of the Alps. On 29 April, Kesselring's successor, General von Vietinghoff-Scheel, signed the unconditional surrender of Army Group C.

So the long march of the allied armies up the length of Italy came to a victorious end, but in the strategic cul-de-sac of the plain of the Po: a cul-de-sac walled in by the towering barrier of the Alps.

*   *   *

There is still dispute among historians as to whether Operation OVERLORD, the Normandy invasion, could have been successfully carried out in 1943, as Marshall had wanted, or whether Churchill and Brooke had been right in judging that the risk of failure was then too great. Nonetheless, that judgement by the two British leaders was surely correct.

The factors making for success grew vastly stronger between 1943 and 1944. In the first place, the Anglo-American naval and military commands had learned much from the operational lessons of TORCH, HUSKY, and AVALANCHE, while the lapse of a further year had allowed major expansion in the output of landing craft of various types. And secondly, and perhaps even more important, by the summer of 1944 the German Army had suffered a series of catastrophic defeats and huge losses on the Eastern Front at the hands of the Red Army. This meant that in Normandy the British and American armies would be fighting an enemy whose combat power had already been severely written down.

On 6 June 1944 George Marshall's long desired strategy of a frontal offensive on Hitler's *Festung Europa* via the English Channel was at last set in motion when, in Operation NEPTUNE, seven allied divisions (plus two back-up divisions) were conveyed across the English Channel by an armada of over 4,000 ships and landed on beaches along the Bay of the Seine in Normandy. These assaults on the German beach defences marked the opening phase of Operation OVERLORD, the engagement and destruction of the main body of the German Army in the West.

*   *   *

297

By the fourth week of August the wreckage of that army had retreated headlong back to the borders of the Fatherland. That left a final campaign to be fought in 1945 within Germany itself. However, the planning of this detonated the last great Anglo-American argument over strategy during the European war. Field Marshal Montgomery (21st Army Group) and Field Marshal Brooke (CIGS) urged (as they had done ever since September 1944) that there should be a single grand offensive thrust across the Rhine and to the north of the Ruhr by 21st Army Group swelled by part of Omar Bradley's 12th Army Group, while the rest of the Western Front was reduced to the defensive. But Eisenhower strongly disagreed. As he wrote to Marshall on 15 January, the fact that this area north of the Ruhr constituted 'an invasion route of the first importance' was 'equally obvious to the German, and if he concentrates in its immediate defense, I may not have the necessary overwhelming superiority to force a satisfactory breakthrough.' He therefore wished to enjoy 'the ability to maneuver' – meaning, for example, 'the ability to advance also on Frankfurt and Kassel, rather than to rely on a single thrust in the north'.[21]

The argument was lifted to the plane of high policy when Churchill chose to intervene in support of Montgomery and Brooke. His intervention was prompted by political considerations as much as by strategic. In order (in Churchill's words) to 'avoid the relegation of His Majesty's Forces to an unexpectedly restricted sphere',[22] he wanted Montgomery's Anglo-Canadian 21st Army Group to remain bolstered in strength by the American Ninth Army. But more importantly, he asked Eisenhower:

> If the enemy's resistance should weaken, as you evidently expect ... why should we not cross the Elbe and advance as far eastward as possible? This has important political bearing, as the Russian Army of the south seems certain to enter Vienna and overrun Austria. If we deliberately leave Berlin to them, even if it should be within our grasp, the double event may strengthen their conviction, already apparent, that they have done everything.[2]

Churchill put this view even more strongly to Roosevelt on 1 April:

> If they also take Berlin, will not their impression that they have been the overwhelming contributor to our common victory be unduly imprinted in their minds. And may this not lead them into a mood which will raise grave and formidable difficulties in the future?[24]

Roosevelt, however, refused for such political reasons to overrule the military judgement of the Supreme Commander.[25] And Eisenhower himself remained convinced that Berlin was no longer a prime military objective, and that the priority now was arranging a tidy junction with the Red Army rather than an untidy encounter. In any case, he was very conscious (as Churchill did not seem to be) that the Red Army already lay within forty-fifty miles of Berlin, while his own armies were still some 250 miles from the city, which did not offer good odds on the Western allies winning the race. So, after a flurry of argument running on into the middle of April, Eisenhower's chosen strategy stood.

But was Churchill's proposal well-judged even on the political plane? The boundaries of the three occupation zones into which Germany was to be partitioned after her defeat had been formally agreed in a Protocol signed at the Yalta summit conference in February 1945, with Berlin designated as a tripartite enclave deep inside the Soviet zone. As it was, the end of the war found Anglo-American forces occupying almost half that part of the Soviet zone lying west of the Oder-Neisse line, from which they then had to withdraw.[26] Just the same, Churchill had proved reluctant so to do, because he wished to retain a bargaining chip in settling outstanding European problems with Stalin, with whom relations were becoming ever more frigid. Yet it must be asked in retrospect whether the immediate aftermath of the war with Nazi Germany was the right moment to bring about an open military confrontation with the Soviet Union.

Churchill's attempted interventions in 1945 in allied strategy in the field and on the plane of high policy were at bottom motivated by a resolve to assert Britain's position as an equal partner with the United States. The failure of those interventions goes to show that in reality Britain had now been relegated to the second rank as a power: a reality which British governments, Labour and Conservative, would go on denying for the rest of the century.

*   *   *

When on 8 May 1945, at Eisenhower's headquarters in Reims, General Alfred Jodl (Chief of the Operations Staff of the *Oberkommando der Wehrmacht*) signed the unconditional surrender of all the German armed forces, it meant that Winston Churchill had achieved the aim which he had set himself on taking office almost exactly five years earlier:

> Victory – victory at all cost, victory in spite of all terror; victory, however long and hard the road may be; for without victory there is no survival ....

References

1. On 1 August 1940, there was a total of just five existing divisions from all the Dominions, as against thirty-four from the United Kingdom. The total naval strength of the Dominions came to just eleven cruisers and twenty destroyers, as against the Royal Navy's twelve capital ships, seven aircraft carriers, fifty cruisers, and ninety-four fleet destroyers. Cited in Barnett, *The Collapse of British Power*, p.11.

2. Both quotations cited in Rhodes James, *Churchill: A Study in Failure, 1900–1939*, pp.26 and 240.

3. Cited in op.cit., p.38.

4. Barnett, *The Collapse of British Power*, pp.14–15.

5. Wheeler-Bennett (Editor), *Action This Day: Working With Churchill*, p.25.

6. Loc. cit.

7. Op.cit., p. 54.

8. See Roskill, *Churchill and the Admirals*, (passim).

9. Wheeler-Bennett, op. cit., p.25.

0. Barnett, *Engage the Enemy More Closely*, Chapter 19, *passim*.

1. Cited in Rhys Jones, *The Loss of the Bismarck: An Avoidable Disaster*, pp. 18–19.

2. Operation Instruction No.110, 19 January 1942, cited in Barnett, *The Desert Generals*, p.155.

3. Barnett, *The Desert Generals*, pp.154–5.

4. For all the Anglo-American debates leading up to the decision for TORCH, and source references, see Barnett, *Engage the Enemy More Closely*, Chapter 17.

5. Cited in Martin Gilbert, *Winston S. Churchill*, Vol. 7, p.253.

6. Barnett, *Engage the Enemy More Closely*, p.689.

7. According to Nigel Nicolson, *Alex: The Life of Field Marshal Earl Alexander of Tunis*, p.274.

8. 1225 tubes to 665; 1320 AFVs to 400. Cf, Nicolson, p.274.

9. Bidwell and Graham, *Tug of War: The Battle for Italy, 1943–1945*, p.382.

20. Even the 'lock-up' element in the Mediterranean total came to nearly 1 million tons. See Behrens, *Merchant Shipping and the Demands of War*, p.391, Footnotes 1 and 2.

2. Chandler, vol cit, p.2431.

22. Signal of 31 March 1945, cited in Chandler, vol. cit., p.2563, Note 2.

23. Ibid.

24. Ibid.

25. See Woodward, *British Foreign Policy in the Second World War*, pp.516–18, and Note 2 on p.518.

26. See Sharp, *The Wartime Alliance and the Zonal Division of Germany*, Chapter V for an analysis of this whole question in its political and military aspects.

Bibliography

Anon, *History of the Ministry of Munitions* (HMSO, London, 1922)
, *Statistics of the Military Effort of the British Empire* (HMSO, London, 1922)
, *Taurus Pursuant: History of 11th Armoured Division* (BAOR Publication, np, 1945)
, *Victory* (HMSO, London, 1961)
Barnett, Correlli, *The Desert Generals* (William Kimber, London, 1960), *The Swordbearers: Supreme Command in the First World War* (Eyre and Spottiswoode, London, 1968)
, *The Great War* (Park Lane Press, London, 1979)
(Ed), *Hitler's Generals* (Weidenfeld and Nicolson, London, 1989),
, *Engage the Enemy More Closely* (Hodder and Stoughton, London, 1991)
, *The Collapse of British Power* (Pan Books, London, 1992)
Beevor, Antony, *Stalingrad* (Viking Press, London, 1998)
, *D-Day: the Battle for Normandy* (Viking, London, 2009)
Behrens, C.B.A., *Merchant Shipping and the Demands of War* (HMSO and Longmans, Green, London, 1955)
Bidwell, Shelford and Graham, Dominick, *Tug of War: The Battle for Italy, 1943–1945* (Hodder and Stoughton, London, 1986)
Carré, Lt Col Henri, *Les Grandes Heures du Général Pétain* (Editions du Conquistador, Paris, 1952)
Catton, Bruce, *Never Call Retreat* (Phoenix Press, London, 2001)
, *Terrible Swift Sword* (Phoenix Press, London, 2001)
, *The Coming Fury*, (Phoenix Press, London, 2011)
Chandler Alfred D., *The Papers of Dwight David Eisenhower; The War Years*: IV (The John Hopkins Press, Baltimore and London, 1970)
Crusius, Major General Baumgarten, *Le Haut Commandement Allemand Pendant La Campagne de la Marne en 1914* (Charles-Lavauzelle, Paris, 1924)
Cunliffe, Marcus, *Soldiers and Civilians: The Martial Spirit in America 1775-1865* (Eyre Methuen, London, 1969)
Danchev Alex and Todman Daniel (Editors), *War Diaries 1939-1945*; Field Marshal Lord Alanbrooke (Phoenix Press, London, 2002)
D'Este, Carlo, *Bitter Victory, The Battle for Sicily 1943* (Collins, London, 1988), *Decision in Normandy: the Unwritten Story of Montgomery and the Allied Campaign* (Collins, London, 1983)
Doherty, Richard, *A Noble Crusade: The History of Eighth Army 1941–45* (Spellmount, Staplehurst, 1999)

Douhet, Giulio, *The Command of the Air*, (London, 1924)

Dowdey, C., *Death of a Nation: The Confederate Army at Gettysburg* (Boston, 1958)

Edmonds, J. E., *Military Operations France and Belgium 1918* (HMSO, London, 1947)

Ehrman John, *Grand Strategy* (HMSO, London, 1956)

Eisenhower, General Dwight D., *Report by the Supreme Commander to the Combined Chiefs of Staff on the Operations in Europe of the Allied Expeditionary Force, 6 June 1944 to 8 May 1945* (HMSO, London, 1946)

Ellis Major L.F., *Victory in the West* (HMSO, London, 1968)

Feldman, Gerald D., *Army, Industry, and Labour in Germany 1914-1918* (Princeton University Press, NJ, 1966)

Foerster, Wolfgang, *Der Feldherr Ludendorff in Ungluck* (Limes Verlag, Berlin, nd)

Fuller, J.F.C., *Grant and Lee*
, *Tanks in the Great War* (London, 1920)

Fussell, Paul, *The Great War and Modern Memory* (Oxford University Press, 1977)

Ganoe, W. A., *The History of the United States Army*, (D. Appleton-Century Company 1942, reprinted by Eric Lundberg, Maryland, 1964)

Gilbert, Martin, *Winston.S.Churchill* (Heinneman, London, 1986)

Goodspeed, D.J., *Ludendorff* (Rupert Hart-Davis, London, 1966)

Grigg John, *The Young Lloyd George* (Eyre Methuen, London)

Guedalla, Philip, *The Two Marshals* (Hodder and Stoughton, London, 1943)

Guinn Paul, *British Strategy and Politics, 1914–1918* (London, 1965)

Harris, Marshal of The Royal Air Force Sir Arthur, *Bomber Offensive* (Collins, London, 1947)

Hart, Basil Liddell, *Strategy: The Indirect Approach* (Faber, London, 1967)

Hart Liddell, Paris, London, Kegan Paul, 1925

Hastings Max, *Bomber Command* (Michael Joseph, London, 1979)
, *Overlord: D-Day and the Battle for Normandy 1944* (Michael Joseph, London, 1984)

Hinsley H, with Thomas E.R, Simkins C.A.G., and Ransome C.F.G., *British Intelligence in the Second World War: Its Influence on Strategy and Operations*, Volume Three, Part II (HMSO, London, 1988)

Howard, Michael, *The Franco-Prussian War* (Rupert Hart-Davis, London, 1961)

Jomini, Henri, *Précis de L'art de la guerre*, 2 vols. (Paris 1838)

Keegan, John, *The Second World War* (Pimlico, London, 1997)

Laure, General, *Le Commandement en chef des Armées Francaises du 15 Mai 1917 á l'Armistice* (Berger-Levrault, Paris, 1937)

BIBLIOGRAPHY

Lehrman, Lewis E, *Lincoln at Peoria: The Turning Point* (Stacpoole Books Mechanicsburg, 2008)

Lewin, Ronald, *Rommel as Military Commander* (Batsford, London, 1968)

Liddell Hart B.H., *History of the Second World War* (Cassell, London, 1970)
, (Ed), *The Rommel Papers* (Hamlyn Paperbacks, London, 1984)

Lloyd George, David, *War Memoirs* (n.d)

Lowe Keith, *Inferno: The Devastation of Hamburg, 1943* (Viking, London, 2007)

Ludendorff, F.W.E., *My War Memoirs, 1914–1918* (Hutchinson, London, 1919)

Marshall-Cornwall, Sir James, *Napoleon as Military Commander* (B.T. Batsford Ltd, London)
, *Haig as Military Commander* (B.T. Batsford Ltd, London, 1973)

Montgomery, Field Marshal The Viscount of Alamein KG, *Memoirs* (Collins, London, 1958)

Nicolson, Nigel, *Alex: The Life of Field Marshal Earl Alexander of Tunis*, London Weidenfeld and Nicolson 1973

Pétain, Marshal Philippe, *La Bataille de Verdun*, Paris, Payot 1919
, *Le Devoir des Élites dans la Défense Nationale*, Paris, Berger-Levrault 1936

Rhodes, James Robert, *Churchill: A Study in Failure, 1900–1939*, London Weidenfeld and Nicholson 1970

Rhys Jones, Graham, *The Loss of the Bismarck: An Avoidable Disaster* (Cassell, London, 1999)

Ritter, Gerhard, *The Schlieffen Plan; Critique of a Myth* (Oswald Wolff, London, 1958)

S.W. Roskill, *Churchill and the Admirals* (Collins, London, 1977)

Serrigny, Général, *Trents Ans avec Pétain* (Plon, Paris, 1959)

Sharp T, *The Wartime Alliance and the Zonal Division of Germany* (Clarendon Press, Oxford, 1975)

Sheffield, Gary, *The Chief: Douglas Haig and the British Army* (Aurum, London, 2011)

Slim, Field Marshal the Viscount, *Defeat into Victory* (Cassell, London, 1956)

Spears, Major General Sir Edward, *Two Men who saved France* (Eyre & Spottiswoode, London, 1968)

Speer Albert, *Inside the Third Reich* (Sphere Books, London, 1970)

Stone Norman, *Hitler* (Coronet Books, London, 1982)

Taylor A.J.P., *Origins of the Second World War* (Harmondsworth Penguin Books, London, 1964)

Terraine John, *The Road to Passchendaele: The Flanders Offensive of 1917; A study in Inevitability* (Leo Cooper, London, 1977)

Terraine, John, *To Win a War: 1918 The Year of Victory* (Sidgwick & Jackson, London, 1978)

, *The Smoke and the Fire: Myths and Anti-Myths of War, 1861–1945* (Sidgwick & Jackson, London, 1980)

Thomas, Benjamin, *Abraham Lincoln* (New York 1952)

Warlimont, Walter (Deputy Chief of the OKW Operations Staff), *Inside Hitler's Headquarters 1939–45* (Weidenfeld and Nicholson, London, 1964)

Webster C. and Frankland N., *The Strategic Air Offensive Against Germany 1939–1945,* 4 vols (HMSO, London, 1961)

Webster, Frankland and Probert, Henry, *Bomber Harris: His Life and Times* (Greenhill Books, London, 2006)

Wheeler-Bennett, J., *Action This Day: Working with Churchill* (Macmillan, London, 1968)

Whitton, Frederick B, *Moltke* (London, 1921)

Williams, T.H., *Lincoln and His Generals* (Knopf, New York, 1958)

Woodward, E.L., *British Foreign Policy in the Second World War* (HMSO, London, 1962)

Zhukov, G.K, *The Memoirs of Marshal Zhukov* (Jonathan Cape, New York, 1971)

Ziemke Earl F, *Stalingrad to Berlin: The German Defeat in the East* (Military Heritage Press, New York, 1968)

Other

National Archives:

ADM 234/363, BS No. 49, *The Campaign in North-west Europe, June 1944- May 1945*

BBC Television series:

The Commanders (1974)

Index

A

admirals xliii, xlvi, liv, 103, 162, 164–5, 168, 185, 205, 208, 217–18, 290, 300

Admiralty 82, 205–6, 278, 280, 282, 284, 286, 289, 292

age 26, 31, 42, 96, 121, 244–5, 258

air xlvii, 152, 155, 158, 164, 171, 182–3, 188–9, 191, 193–4, 202, 206, 212, 217, 227, 229, 236, 264, 267, 282, 286

air attack liii, 192, 264, 284

allied 214

heavy British 154

air battle 268

Air Ministry 191, 193, 196–200

air offensive 189, 227

allied 197

Air Staff 189, 192, 199–201, 282

Airborne Troops 212

aircraft l, lii–lv, 102, 161, 166, 169, 171–2, 190–7, 205, 217, 237, 246, 260, 267–8, 286

freezing 281

new jet 274

reconnaissance liii

spotter liii

tactical lii

aircraft carriers liii, 166, 169, 171, 287, 299

aircrews 187–8, 196, 199, 202, 205, 267

airfields liii, 195, 229, 243, 279, 288, 295

forward 230, 267

airpower liii–lv, 166, 168, 182, 189, 194, 197, 202

Alam el Halfa, Battle of x, 154, 160

Alanbrooke, Field Marshal Lord xlvi, 219, 223, 241, 301

Alexander, General Sir Harold 207, 290, 296

Alexandria 152–3, 294

Allied Air Force lv, 158

allied armies 76, 93, 109, 136–7, 140, 198, 204, 214, 230–2, 295, 297

Allied Army Group in Italy 296

Allied Campaign xlvi, 217, 231

Allied Expeditionary Force x, xlvi, 214–15, 217, 240, 242

allied observers 92

allied offensive, combined 91

Allied superiority 274

Allied victory parade in Berlin 256

allies x, 6, 44–5, 49, 53, 56, 67, 78, 82, 84–5, 89, 92, 96, 102–3, 124, 127–8, 132–3, 159–60, 173, 185, 201, 209, 216, 226, 231, 233–5, 251, 261, 264, 268, 276, 282, 286, 290, 293–6

Alsace 54, 58–60

American

armies lv, 92, 94, 107, 128, 135, 215, 297

command 169, 213

experience 293

divisions 132, 135

fighter aircraft 197

food 268

foreign policy 291

heavy bombers 198

industrial power 163
military power liv
politicians 226
troops 126, 224
American Civil War x, xlviii, 1, 9–10,
    53, 55, 72, 96, 103
American Expeditionary Force 135,
    221, 224
America's military leaders 222
Amiens 131, 135
ammunition 4, 91, 100–1, 197
ANCXF 204, 206, 215, 217
Anglo-American armies 201, 240,
    274, 276, 285
  forces occupying 240, 299
  high commands 233, 292
  invasion 157
  land campaign 215
  landings in Normandy viii, 219
  victory lv
Anglo-French forces 278
anti-tank guns 16, 155–6
Antietam 18, 89, 96
Antwerp 50, 216–17, 231, 276
anxieties 80, 121, 123, 149, 183–4,
    230, 233, 255, 286
Arakan 180–1
Ardennes 74, 216–17, 230–1, 276
area bombing 195, 198–201
armed forces 28, 100, 102, 120, 125,
    240, 251, 269, 272, 282, 284, 292
armistice xlvii, 5, 107, 109, 118–19,
    123, 127, 135, 139–40, 147,
    264–5, 279
Armoured Division 148, 152, 216,
    229, 235, 240
arms 84, 162, 170, 199, 262
army xliii, xlvi, l, liii, 3–7, 10, 12–15,
    17–22, 24, 26, 28–39, 41–4, 46–
    8, 50–3, 57–8, 60–5, 69–70, 72–
    3, 75–80, 82, 87–8, 90, 92, 94–5,

100, 103–5, 109–13, 115, 117–
    19, 121–2, 124–5, 127, 129–30,
    132, 134, 140, 145–6, 151–2,
    155, 158, 162, 164–7, 174, 178–
    80, 188, 197–8, 204, 207, 209,
    214, 217, 219, 222, 224–6, 230,
    236–7, 240, 244–7, 249, 251,
    264, 270–1, 273, 275–6, 291,
    296, 298–9
  field 15, 51, 90, 152, 275
  hostile 51
  invading 80
  new 15, 53, 61, 75, 104, 174
  soviet 247, 254
army command 18, 35, 61, 136
army commanders 29, 35, 47–9, 52,
    65, 76–8, 80, 94, 115, 129, 132,
    137, 184, 228, 238, 246, 254
Army Group liii, 90, 157, 159, 174,
    216, 229–31, 233–40, 273–4,
    295, 297–8
Army Group Afrika 274
Army Group North 277
Army of Italy 5
Army War College 221
Army of Châlons 52, 63–4
Arnhem 216–17, 231, 233, 241
Arras 129–30, 137, 147
artillery liii, 7, 24, 65, 84, 91, 113,
    140, 155, 253–5, 288, 290
Aspern, Battle of 96
Assam 177–8
assault 65, 91, 135, 150–2, 156, 204,
    209–11, 213, 227, 237–8, 295,
    297
  forces 209–11, 213, 246, 252
  troops 146, 211
Atlanta 14, 21–2, 28, 38
Atlantic liii, 92, 126, 281, 285–7, 291,
    293–4
atrocities 276

attack li, liii, 5, 18–19, 24, 31, 34–5,
    38, 47, 50–1, 60, 69–70, 73–4,
    78–9, 83, 91–2, 94, 96, 104–5,
    110–11, 113, 117, 121–3, 126,
    128–31, 137, 139–40, 143–4,
    147, 150, 152–3, 168–71, 180–1,
    187, 189–90, 192, 194, 196,
    198–200, 229, 231, 243, 247,
    252, 255, 262, 267–9, 288
  direct 36, 151
  general 10, 17
  limited 117, 132
  plan of 151, 154, 252
  carriers 166, 171
  France 70
  Poland 262–3
  Rommel 285
attackers 73, 131–2, 177, 194–5,
    235
attrition vii, 23, 38, 96, 155, 194–6,
    234–5, 267, 274, 292–3
  battles 155, 187, 194–5, 217, 230,
    235, 237
  long 110
  murderous 111
Auchinleck 16, 148, 150–1, 153–4,
    284–5, 289
Australia 156, 188, 287
Australian Corps 137
Australian Divisions 148, 154
Australian garrison 144
Australian infantry 143
Austria 3, 7–8, 44–6, 48–50, 56, 70,
    92, 96, 104, 127, 241, 259
  defection 105
  manoeuvre 45
  overrun 239, 298
  supplant 44
Austrian army 44, 47–8, 87
Austrians 4, 6–8, 44–50, 89, 105–6,
    123, 261

authority xlix, 103, 112, 114–15, 130–
    1, 206, 223–4, 226, 232, 245,
    291
  allied 224

B

Baltic 201, 240, 243, 284
Barbarossa, Battle of 269–71
battle viii, x, xlvi, l–li, liii, lvi, 1, 4–6,
    10, 15, 17–19, 21, 24–5, 32–5,
    37–8, 48, 50–2, 59, 62–3, 69,
    73–4, 78–80, 83–4, 86, 88–96,
    104, 112, 116–17, 120–2, 125,
    129, 136, 143, 146–8, 150, 152–
    3, 155–6, 158, 170–2, 177, 179–
    82, 184, 188, 194, 202, 204, 217,
    232–3, 235, 243, 246, 251–2,
    255, 267, 272, 278, 280, 282,
    285–6, 289, 292, 300
  bloody 23, 37, 83
  first 13, 31, 82–3, 126, 135, 180
  frontal 47, 183
  land 180, 204
battle area 13, 158, 246
battlefield l–li, 6, 8, 24, 32, 34, 52,
    57, 79, 83, 90, 95, 128, 139, 152,
    172, 255, 285
  crisis 130
  intended 48
  main 148
  realities 95
  units 113
battleships liii, 165–6, 168–9, 171,
    210, 284, 287
Bavaria 44–6, 138, 140, 220
Bavarian army 46
Bazaine, Marshal Achille 57, 59–65,
    76
beaches 158, 204, 209–15, 294, 297

BEF (British Expeditionary Force) li, 73–5, 79–80, 84, 87, 90, 92–3, 97, 100, 107, 147, 205–6, 265, 278–9

Belgian defences 121

Belgium 69–70, 73–4, 84, 93, 103, 106, 126, 146, 157, 216, 231, 237, 266–7

belief 10, 72, 100, 181, 197, 206, 208, 245, 254, 258–9, 274, 287

Benghazi 143, 148

Berlin x, xlvii, lii, liv, 42, 44, 50, 58, 139–41, 144, 159, 195–6, 199– 201, 231, 233, 237, 239–40, 242, 253–7, 262, 266, 275, 295, 298–9

  raided 267

  surrounding 240

  wreck 195

Bir Hacheim 151

Bismarck xlv, 287–8, 300

Bismarck, Otto von xlv, 41–2, 44–5, 48–9, 51, 53–6, 65, 67–8, 70, 90, 128, 145, 162, 269

  dismissed 68

  facilitated 65

  long negotiations 45

Bletchley Park 285–6

blitzkrieg 146–7, 263, 269

bomb-loads 193

Bomber Command liv, 187–8, 190–6, 198–202, 229, 238, 267, 274

  attacks 200–1

bomber operations 193, 202

bombers liv–lv, 187–90, 192–4, 197– 9, 202, 274

  allied 275

  four-engined 192–3

  hostile 189

  strategic 237

bombing, allied 158, 197, 275

bombs liii, lv, 155, 159, 189, 192–4, 213, 267

Bonaparte, Napoleon vii, xix, xliii, xlv, xlix, 1–8, 14, 41, 44, 48–9, 53, 59–60, 96, 258–9, 263, 265, 268, 270, 276, 280

Boulogne 4, 129, 216

breech-loading guns 1

Bradley, General Omar 215, 236

bridgehead 132, 151, 182–3, 234–6, 238, 294

Britain liv–lv, 15, 70, 83, 85, 87, 90, 93, 96, 98, 100–4, 106, 120, 125–6, 130, 148, 150, 156, 164– 5, 167, 188–9, 191, 193, 195, 204, 207, 226, 260–4, 266–9, 276, 279, 281–2, 284–8, 290–2, 296, 299

  conduct 105

  isolation liv

  losses 96

  position 299

  survival liv

  war effort 282

  weakness 290

British Armies liv, 12, 78, 83, 86–7, 98, 104, 107, 111, 143–4, 174, 190

  in France viii, 85, 136

Britain, Battle of liv, 189, 267–8, 281

British

  battleships 213, 288

  code-breaking centre 285

  forces 16, 137, 173, 180

  front 130

  guns 135

  land forces 287

  offensives 104, 154, 187

  people 188, 265, 276, 279–81

  power 277, 299–300

  soldiers 104, 115, 152, 178

tanks 150, 155
troops 96, 131, 140
British Empire viii, xlvi, 9, 82, 90, 97,
    104, 140, 144, 150, 156, 263,
    268, 279
Brooke, General Sir Alan 89, 149,
    237, 285, 292–3, 295, 297–8
Bull Run, Battle of 13, 15, 17, 20,
    32–3, 40
Burma 177–9, 181–2, 184, 287
  Campaign x, 179–80, 186
  Division 173–5
Byelorussia 244, 253

C

cabinet 17, 41, 88, 93, 99, 102–4,
    106–7, 112, 261–2, 281, 283, 288
Caen 229
Calais 105, 112, 129, 216
calculations vii, li, 43, 45, 50, 74,
    126, 181, 195
campaign viii, xlviii, liv, lvi, 1, 3–4,
    6, 20, 27, 31–4, 36–7, 48, 52, 55,
    58, 60–2, 67, 69, 71, 75, 77, 88,
    95, 122, 126, 141, 144, 147–9,
    175–6, 179–80, 182, 217, 223,
    232–4, 236, 240, 265–6, 271,
    278, 289
  compromised 173
  final liii, 135, 298
  hard-fought 294
  land 192, 206
  plan of 30, 33
  two-year 156, 269
camps 26, 31, 110–11, 115, 179
Canadians 135, 139, 212–13, 235
canteens 102, 111, 115–16
capacity 18, 37, 42, 46, 68, 77, 130,
    178, 194, 219, 222, 224, 226, 273

career xliii, xlvii–xlviii, 1–2, 5, 30,
    68, 85, 98, 100, 145, 162, 181,
    222–3, 245, 258, 284, 287
  civilian 13
  peacetime 98, 221
  political 82–3, 98–9
casualties 63, 104, 110, 116, 188
cavalry 46, 65, 79, 85–6, 110, 136,
    246
Cavalry Division 86–7, 122, 135, 246
cavalryman 85, 91, 245
Châlons 52, 58, 60–4
Chamberlain, Neville 260–4, 278
Chancellorsville, Battle of 18–19, 25,
    32–3
Channel 22, 211, 214, 216, 267, 279,
    292, 295
Chattanooga, Battle of 22, 37
Cherbourg 147, 209, 215–16, 231
China 164, 166, 168
Chinese invasion of Burma 180
Churchill, Winston viii–ix, xliii–xliv,
    xlvi, l, lii, liv–lvi, 2, 4, 6, 8–12,
    14, 16–18, 20, 22, 26, 28, 30, 32,
    34, 36, 38, 40, 42, 44, 46, 48, 50,
    52, 54, 58, 60, 62, 64, 68, 70, 72,
    74, 76, 78, 80, 82–4, 86, 88–90,
    92, 94, 96–7, 100, 102–6, 108,
    110, 112, 114, 116, 118, 122,
    124, 126, 128, 130, 132, 134,
    136, 138, 140, 143–4, 146, 148–
    50, 152, 154, 156, 158, 160, 162,
    164, 166, 168, 170, 172, 174,
    176, 178, 180, 182, 184, 186,
    188–90, 192, 194–6, 198, 200–2,
    206, 208, 210, 212, 214, 216,
    218, 220, 224, 226–8, 230, 232–
    4, 236, 238–40, 242, 244, 246,
    248, 250, 252, 254, 256, 258,
    260, 262, 264–6, 268, 270, 272,
    274–6, 278–300

convinced 192
enabled 271
errors 290
grand strategy 291
interventions 16, 239
mind 280, 289
performance 282
plunged 279
proposal 240, 299
cities 132, 189, 191, 194–5, 198, 201,
    206, 217, 229, 240, 252, 254–5,
    262, 267, 272–3, 275, 283, 299
defenceless 194
well-fortified 255
Civil War vii, xlv, 9, 12–13, 24, 26–7,
    31, 39, 55, 96, 98, 114, 246, 290,
    293
civilians xlv, 23, 120
coalition xliii, xlvii–xlviii, liv, 7, 88,
    90, 98, 100, 103, 125, 135, 149,
    232, 278
coast 129, 148, 153–4, 157–8, 230,
    264–5, 293
  channel 69, 86, 128–30, 199, 265,
    279
  defences 228
Coblenz 77, 199, 236
Cold Harbor, Battle of 38
combat effectiveness 267
command xliii, xlvii, xlix–li, liv, 5,
    13–15, 18, 20–2, 26–7, 30–1,
    35–7, 43, 59–61, 63, 72, 74, 76,
    78, 85, 88, 90, 93, 95, 112–13,
    122, 131, 143, 146–7, 149, 155–
    6, 166–7, 173–4, 177–8, 185,
    189, 191, 193, 202, 207–9, 221,
    223, 232, 235, 245–7, 251, 264,
    267, 271, 285
  allied 158, 223, 239
  direct 153, 171, 219
  mission 32, 48, 76

  temporary 35, 145
commanders vii–viii, xlix, li, 5, 11,
    15, 17–18, 20, 22–3, 26, 28–9,
    31–2, 43, 47, 59–60, 62, 64, 72,
    75–7, 80, 83, 86, 91, 95, 116,
    121, 143–4, 146–7, 159, 176,
    179, 182, 187, 193, 207, 212,
    219, 223–5, 229–30, 232, 236,
    246, 248, 254–5, 270
  allied 224
  decisive 245
  ill-experienced 91
  resolute 184
communications xlix, li–lii, 3, 22, 32,
    36, 39, 44, 47, 50, 53–4, 73, 99,
    115, 151, 156, 171, 178, 180,
    183–4, 229, 233, 271
Communist Party 244–5, 249
compromise 1, 7, 61, 165, 168, 262
Confederate
  armies vii, xlvii, 13, 17, 22, 25, 37–
    8
  capital 16, 21, 29, 31, 37
  forces vii, 13, 16, 29–31
  garrison 35
  heartland 18, 29
  losses 96
  ports 20
  war administration 30
conflicts, major liii–liv, lvi, 8–11, 44,
    48, 53, 55, 96, 103, 107, 168,
    249, 262–3, 274, 276, 281–2
conscription, universal 56–7
conspiracy 105–6
conviction 46, 54, 84, 127, 228, 231,
    238–9, 267, 298
corps 42, 50, 58, 62, 72, 86, 95, 109,
    180, 183, 193, 219, 223, 238,
    257
counter-attacks 96, 133, 158, 235, 248
  launching 248

planned 175
repeated 248
counter-marches 6, 59
counter-offensive 31, 50, 84, 170,
181, 251–2
allied 118, 135
counter-stroke 59, 63, 76, 78, 86, 133,
136, 151, 176, 225, 234, 252–3
decisive 252
first allied 138
soviet 243, 253
courage, moral 89–90, 94, 104, 247
courts martial 114–15
crisis liii, 36, 45, 49, 68, 76, 93, 107,
115–16, 123, 133, 137, 198, 206,
250, 260, 262–3, 268, 271, 281
hour of 120
moral 109, 135
national manpower 292
Cunningham, Admiral 151, 206–7
Cyrenaica 143–4, 148
Czarist Russia 92, 114, 233
Czechoslovakia 259–61, 276

D

D-Day xlvi, 158, 204, 209–14, 217,
227–9, 233, 262
assault forces 210
eve of 207, 229
landings 228
Danish army 41
death xlvii, l, 24, 38, 40, 91, 111, 114,
160, 163, 172, 177
defeat vii–viii, xlv, liv–lv, 6, 15, 17–
18, 25–6, 32–3, 59, 64, 69, 72,
75, 82, 89, 107, 118, 128, 132,
138, 140, 152, 154, 171–3, 175–
7, 179–81, 183, 185–6, 188, 195,
197, 204, 215, 217, 222, 232,
240, 251, 272, 276, 281, 286,
299
catastrophic vii, 297
final 37, 107, 131, 139, 269, 293
national 93, 139
of Nazi Germany 285, 291
tactical 228
total 13, 215, 289
defence lv, 21, 24, 28–9, 37, 63, 77,
96, 113, 117, 125, 129, 131, 137,
143–4, 153–4, 157, 197, 237,
240, 243, 247, 255, 267, 282,
288
allied 147
beach 212
coastal 157
demoralised 247
front-line 129
perimeter 152
well-prepared 154, 255
deployment liv, 50, 70–1, 106, 121,
150, 228, 268
desert 143–4, 148, 150, 154, 156,
237, 289
destroyers 169, 205, 209–10, 266,
287, 299
modern 206
destruction 2, 4–5, 8, 21, 103, 106,
170, 199–201, 227, 231, 234,
238, 243, 253, 260, 275, 297
Devers, General Jacob 236
disasters 4, 12, 97, 139, 168, 176,
181, 187, 247, 275, 279, 289
discipline 31, 93, 110, 224, 244
disembarkations 211, 213
divisions l, 31, 35–6, 42, 72, 84, 95,
110, 116, 118, 122–3, 129, 131–
2, 137, 140, 146–8, 152, 175,
179–82, 209, 219, 223, 230, 238,
249, 278–9, 289–90, 292, 296–7,
299

forward 181
motorised 151
reserve 180
doctrine, tactical 72–3
Don, River 251-2, 272
Dusseldorf 194, 235–6
Dutch army 279

E

E-boats 210–11, 215
East Indies 287
East Prussia 4, 77, 122–3, 159, 233
Eastern Front 69, 92, 106, 122–3,
    156, 200–1, 233, 251–3, 257,
    271–4, 292, 297
Eastern Task Force 207–8, 210
Egypt 3–4, 144, 150, 152–4, 207, 284
Eighteenth Army 130–1
Eighth Army (*British*) 43, 148, 150-4,
    156, 177, 284, 289, 293, 295,
    297
  destroyed 152
  Gazala Line 150
  reinforced 148
Eighth Army (*German*) 121-2
Eisenhower, General Dwight D. ix–x,
    xlvi–xlvii, 52, 95, 206–7, 209,
    212, 216, 219–42, 250, 253, 256,
    290, 298–9
  headquarters 241, 256, 299
  strategy 237, 240
El Alamein, Battle of x, 153–5, 157,
    187, 241, 284
Elbe 44, 47–8, 50, 238–40, 298
enemy xlvi, l, lii, lv, 3–8, 14, 16, 19,
    21, 28–9, 34–6, 38, 47–52, 54–5,
    60, 62, 64, 69, 73, 75, 78, 84–5,
    88–9, 94, 96–8, 103, 105, 117,
    127–8, 132, 135, 137–40, 146,

151–6, 158, 171, 173, 176–7,
    181–2, 187–9, 195–6, 198, 213–
    16, 218, 225, 230, 234–5, 243,
    246–7, 249–50, 252–5, 260, 265,
    270, 285–6, 289–90, 292–4, 297,
    300
  attacks 62, 140
  defences 36, 87
  front 130, 137, 228, 253
  resistance 136, 234, 236
engineers 13, 18, 27, 72, 145, 154
English Channel liv, 14, 146–7, 204,
    264, 297
Enigma lii, 285–6
  errors xlv, 36, 48, 52, 62, 116, 181–
    2, 223–4, 255, 267, 272, 290
  strategic 258, 273
Europe xlvi, lv, 1–2, 4, 7, 10, 14–15,
    41, 49, 53–6, 67, 82, 91, 162,
    167, 192, 194, 242, 247, 258–9,
    261–3, 269, 276, 278, 286
  northern 95, 195, 266
evacuation 147, 205, 265
exploitation 86–7, 163, 234, 238, 245
eyewitness 25, 27, 29, 39, 48, 77, 88,
    116, 175, 215, 250, 255

F

failure xlvi, 19, 30–1, 34–5, 39, 46,
    74, 88, 93, 101, 106, 110, 113,
    127, 131–2, 151, 159, 193, 227,
    229–31, 255, 267, 269, 271, 276,
    289, 297, 299–300
Far East 148, 170, 287–8
Fifteenth Army (*Japanese*) in Burma
    180
Fifth Army (*British*) 129-30
Fifth Army (*French*) 74-6, 78-9
Fifth Army (*US*) 241

INDEX

Fifth Panzer Army 274
Fighter Command liv, 189, 267
fighting viii, li–lii, liv, 7, 16–17, 24,
        28, 79, 82–3, 91–2, 95, 101, 106,
        128, 130, 138–9, 147, 151–3,
        159, 168–9, 175, 177, 201, 213,
        228, 243, 246, 263, 272, 288,
        292, 297
    fitness 109, 114
    powers 44, 79, 136, 167
    troops 83, 107
firepower l, 96, 113, 116–17, 155,
        181, 237, 253, 274
First Army (*British*) 86, 137, 238
First Army (*German*) 47-8, 74, 76,
        78–80
First Army (*Russian*) 122
First Army (*US*) 138, 210, 236,
        238
First Canadian Army 235
First French Army 205, 239, 265
First Guards Tank Army 255
First Panzer Army 272–3
First Parachute Army 235, 240
Flanders liii, 92–3, 107, 129, 132–3
flank 44, 47–8, 50, 52, 58, 74, 128,
        133, 177, 210, 252
    attack 47
    northern 70
    western 132
Foch, General Ferdinand 117, 130
food 4, 60, 64, 111, 116, 125, 131,
        175, 273, 286
foodstuffs 281–2
forces 3, 6, 24, 33, 51, 65, 67, 72, 78,
        104, 112, 117, 126, 139, 144,
        154, 182, 210, 213, 231, 239,
        251–2, 255, 263, 268, 296
    allied 80, 216, 219, 292, 296
    imperial 156, 288
    landing 204, 294

moral xlix, 11, 75
foreign policy 68, 164, 168, 260
formations, large 17, 36–7, 246
Fort Donelson 35–6
Fort Henry 35
fortress 20, 42, 50, 54, 63, 78, 144,
        152, 216, 231, 288–9
Fourteenth Army (*British*) 177, 180–
        2, 184–6
    command of 179, 183
    new 177, 180
    unbalanced 181
Fourth Army (*British*) 91, 133, 137,
        139
Fourth Army (*French*) 138
Fourth Panzer Army 273
France 2, 6–8, 41–2, 44–5, 49–51, 54,
        56–8, 60–3, 65, 67–70, 72–5, 80,
        84–5, 89, 92, 96, 103–4, 106,
        114, 120, 125–7, 130, 137, 145–
        6, 157, 159, 167, 188, 215, 217,
        237, 258, 260, 264–7, 269, 279,
        293–5
    heart of 265, 279
Franco-Prussian War x, xlvi, 55, 65,
        96
Fredericksburg, Battle of 18
French armies vii, 3, 7, 50, 52–3, 58–
        60, 62, 67, 69, 72–5, 79, 84, 91–
        3, 105, 109–11, 114, 117–18,
        128–9, 131, 135, 137, 147, 240,
        263–5, 278–9, 293
French government 54, 56, 76, 85, 90,
        109–10, 147
French offensive 70, 74, 136
frontier 50, 52, 58–9, 77, 96, 243, 262
    defences 69
    natural 2
    western 276, 278
fuel 148–9, 151, 155, 168, 199–200,
        273, 286

G

General Staff lvi, 13, 42, 68, 72, 106,
109, 120–1, 246–8, 253, 261,
270, 272
generals xliii, xlv, liv, 9, 14, 17–18,
20–1, 23, 52, 99, 112, 159, 179,
226, 248, 251, 259–60, 265, 270,
274, 276, 290
assembled 259
subordinate 36
German
armies 73, 78–9, 85, 89, 92–4, 107,
111, 125, 133, 139–40, 157, 216,
273, 292
defences 91, 105, 110, 133, 138,
197, 228, 235, 240
front 80, 94, 136–7, 200, 277, 295,
297
occupation 84–5, 265
offensives x, 74, 86, 91, 150, 251
right wing 70, 73–4, 76–8
German Army 82, 84–5, 88, 127, 136,
152, 204, 240, 251, 256, 261,
266–7, 295, 297
German Empire viii, 67, 82, 120, 124,
140, 145
Germany viii, x, l, 3, 8, 10, 42, 44, 49,
51, 54, 68, 70, 72, 74, 85, 89, 92,
94, 96, 101, 103–5, 120–1, 123,
125–9, 133, 139–40, 144–7, 154,
156–7, 192, 195, 197–8, 201,
216, 230–1, 234, 240, 251, 259–
64, 266, 269, 271, 275–6, 279,
286, 291–2, 296, 298–9
defeat 125, 188, 264
defeating viii, 271
heart of liv
Gestapo 159, 276, 280
Gettysburg, Battle of xlvii, 18, 21, 24,
34, 36, 96

Gibraltar 287, 293–4
Goebbels, Joseph 160, 275–6
Goodwood, Battle of 230
grand strategy xlvi, 20, 27–30, 37, 69,
88, 99, 124–5, 149, 232, 241,
268, 291–3
Grande Armée xlix, 5, 8
Grant, General Ulysses S. vii, xlvii,
lii, 18–19, 21–4, 26–7, 29–30,
35–41, 48, 89, 194, 220
Great Britain 87, 161, 252, 262, 282,
291
Great War 274
Gurkha soldiers 174, 177–8, 182

H

Haig, Field Marshal Sir Douglas viii,
l, 82–99, 105-7, 113, 123, 128-
30, 132-3, 135–41, 194, 220,
224, 233-4, 237, 286
armies l, 94, 128
command 131
critics 84, 95–7, 140
judgement 86, 89, 93
leadership 82, 87, 107
offensive 92, 125, 127
troops 94, 107, 136–7, 139
Hamburg xlvi, 194–5, 201–2, 238, 240
Hamburg, Battle of 194, 202
Harbor, Pearl viii, 161, 169–72, 192,
222, 271, 281, 291
Harris, Air Chief Marshal Sir Arthur
viii, xlvi, 17, 187–203
Hindenburg, Field Marshal von 77,
92, 95, 120, 122, 132–3, 139
Hindenburg Line 92, 125, 139, 154
Hindenburg Programme 124-5, 127
Hitler, Adolf ix, xliv, xlvi, liv, 145–7,
149–50, 152–5, 157–60, 235–7,

243, 247, 251, 253, 255, 258–77, 280, 283
Europe liv, 295
victories 269, 275
horses li, 18, 58, 65, 140, 245
hospitals 87, 104, 154–5, 159, 225, 290

I

Imperial General Staff 89, 94, 98, 106, 185, 216, 219, 232–3, 282
India lii, 86, 156, 175–8, 180, 188
Indian Army 174
Indian Division 173–5, 180
infantry lii, 24, 73, 79, 91, 117, 135, 145, 147, 151, 153, 156, 183, 210, 235, 266
  attacks 73, 253
  divisions 87, 147–8, 151, 214, 243, 255
invasion liv, 3–6, 8, 19, 30, 33, 52, 126, 170, 198, 204, 206, 213, 279, 286, 293–6
  forces 158, 204, 228
  of Vichy-French N. Africa 206, 220
Irrawaddy 176, 183
Ismay, General Sir Hastings 224, 282
Italian army 127, 149, 269
Italian campaign 3, 7, 295–6
Italian formations 153
Italian high commands 149, 152
Italy xlvi, 2–5, 42, 45, 49, 56, 59, 67, 97, 125, 145, 149, 185, 204, 227, 237, 279, 290, 295–7, 300

J

Japan viii, liii, lv, 161, 163–70, 172, 185, 271, 279, 291

Japanese liii, 148, 161, 172–3, 175–7, 180–4, 246, 271, 281, 287, 291
  army 164, 166, 288
  attack 180, 222, 287
  delegation 164–5
  fleet viii, 287–8
  government 164, 167, 169
  Navy 165, 167–8
Jodl, General 159, 256
Joffre, General Joseph 67, 71–2, 74–80, 88, 91, 220
judgement xliv–xlv, lvii, 13, 46, 49, 68, 85, 94, 98, 143, 175, 179–80, 195, 206, 220, 231, 246, 248, 252, 263, 268, 286, 289, 297
Jutland, Battle of liii

K

Kaiser, Wilhelm II 68–71, 77, 129, 136, 139, 141
Kesselring, Generalfeldmarschall 97, 242, 296–7
Kitchener's Army 83, 91
Königgrätz, Battle of 47–8, 53

L

land liv, 15, 20, 26, 150, 152, 158, 188, 204, 206, 209–10, 217, 280, 285, 293
landing craft 209–10, 212–14, 228, 295, 297
landing ships 210–11, 213, 215
landings 16–18, 33, 157, 166, 206, 209–10, 227, 229, 292–6
leadership viii, xliii, xlix–li, lv–lvi, 1, 3, 8–9, 12, 15, 25–6, 30, 32, 34, 43, 52, 57, 61, 63, 67, 76, 82,

87–8, 110, 118, 121, 129, 135,
140, 151, 153, 155–6, 161, 163,
166, 174, 177, 180, 182, 187,
196, 214, 229, 232, 244, 248–9,
259, 266, 268, 273, 278–80, 289
allied 130, 196, 201, 278
France 63

Lee, Robert xlvii, 13, 15, 16–18, 21–
2, 24–40
Leipzig 6, 196, 199
Leningrad 96, 243, 247–8, 250, 253,
270–1
Liège 77, 121–2
Ligny, Battle of 2, 6
Lincoln, President Abraham vii–viii,
xliv–xlvi, l, lii, liv, lvi, 2, 4, 6, 8–
24, 26, 28–30, 32–40, 42, 44, 46,
48, 50, 52, 54–5, 58, 60, 62, 64,
68, 70, 72, 74, 76, 78, 80, 84, 86,
88–90, 92, 94, 96, 98–100, 102,
104, 106–8, 110, 112, 114, 116,
118, 122, 124, 126, 128, 130,
132, 134, 136, 138, 140, 144,
146, 148, 150, 152, 154, 156,
158, 160, 162–4, 166, 168, 170,
172, 174, 176, 178, 180, 182,
184, 186, 188, 190, 192, 194,
196, 198, 200, 202, 206, 208,
210, 212, 214, 216, 218, 220–2,
224, 226, 228, 230, 232, 234,
236, 238, 240, 242, 244, 246,
248, 250, 252, 254, 256, 260,
262, 264, 266, 268, 270, 272,
274, 276, 280, 282, 284, 286,
288, 290, 292, 294, 296, 298, 300
background 23
concept 21
interventions 16
prodding McClellan 16
struggle xliii

Lloyd-George, David viii, xlvii, 9, 16,
83, 88–90, 93–4, 97–108, 120,
128, 130, 141, 274, 280
London xliii, xlv–xlvii, lii, 89, 97,
164–5, 177, 189, 205, 209, 227,
257, 267, 278, 283, 293
Ludendorff, Frau 120–1
Ludendorff, General Erich viii, xlvi,
54, 77, 92, 94, 97, 120–41
offensive 132
soldiers 131
Luftwaffe liv, 189, 200, 243, 248,
260, 264, 267–8, 273, 279, 284,
290
Luxembourg 70, 77–8

M

Mac-Mahon, Marshal 57, 59–60, 63–4
Malaya 148, 168, 170, 185, 287–8
defence of 287–8
Manassas, Battle of 15
manoeuvres 37, 62, 76, 88, 98, 103,
145, 148, 224, 273
manpower lv, 96, 124, 128, 237, 253,
274
march 4, 14, 19, 22, 30, 32–3, 36, 46,
51, 53, 59–60, 70–1, 74, 166,
261, 268, 272, 296
marching 5, 49, 52–3, 64, 78, 130,
260
Marne, River, 132
MacArthur, General Douglas 185, 222
McClellan, General George 13, 15–
22, 24, 29, 31–5, 39
Metz 51, 53–4, 58, 60–5, 69
fortress of 52, 63
Middle East 148–9, 154, 175, 289–90,
292
Midway, Battle of liii

military xliii, lvi, 11–12, 25, 49, 53–4, 57, 64, 106, 130, 170, 174, 201–2, 239, 242, 251, 255, 269, 271, 279, 283, 286, 298, 300
  conservatives 57
  judgements 127
  leaders xlvii–xlviii, 25, 54, 84, 173, 227–8
  system 57, 117
minesweepers 210–11, 213, 217
Mississippi 10, 14, 19–21, 28, 35–7
mobilisation 42–3, 46, 51–2, 55, 57, 71, 121
Moltke, Colonel General Helmuth von vii, 41–61, 64, 67–71, 73–4, 76–81, 90, 121
  forces 53
  top leadership 52
  military sums 45
  mind 44, 46
  peacetime 80
  strategy 51
Moltke, Field Marshal Graf von x, 41, 67–9, 71, 129, 269, 272
Mons, Battle of 74–5, 86
Montenotte, Battle of 4, 6
Montgomery, General Sir Bernard ix, xlvi, 87, 95, 154–6, 158–9, 185–6, 207–9, 215–17, 219, 223, 229–35, 237–42, 284, 290, 295, 298
  army 208
  command 239
  victory 160
morale liv–lvi, 55, 58, 71, 87, 93, 113–14, 116, 127, 133, 138, 140, 173, 177–8, 182, 193–4, 197, 199–200, 202, 228
Mutaguchi, General 180, 182
Moscow 243–4, 246, 248–50, 252, 254–6, 269–71

Munich crisis 261–2, 277
munitions xlvi, 99–102, 108, 125, 157, 237, 273, 281
mutinies viii, 93, 109–11, 113–18

N

Napoleon III 45, 49, 52, 54, 56–61, 63
national policy 49, 125–6, 269, 275
NATO (North Atlantic Treaty Organisation) lv
navy liii, 164–7, 170, 198, 207, 209, 213, 229, 282, 291, 293
  allied 209, 214–15, 286
Nazi Germany lv, 96, 161, 217, 247, 252, 262, 268, 279, 285–6, 291, 299
Netherlands 136, 146, 157, 167, 240
Ninth Army (*French*) 79
Ninth Army (*US*) 235-6, 238-9, 298
Normanbrook, Lord 283–4
Normandy xlvi, liii, 94, 158, 187, 198, 208–9, 211, 215, 217, 227–30, 285, 297
Normandy, Battle of xlvi, liii, 94, 158, 187, 198, 208–9, 215, 217, 228, 230, 285, 297

O

offensive li, 15, 17, 22, 35, 43, 53, 59, 67, 69–70, 75, 85, 91–5, 106, 111, 122, 127–9, 131–3, 137, 150–2, 181, 187, 197, 233–5, 250–3, 255, 264, 276, 292, 296–7
  allied x, 93, 107
  bomber xlvi, 192, 196–7, 202

powers 232, 250, 271
  strategic 36, 260
  victorious 156
officers 12, 26, 64, 86, 109–10, 114,
  116, 118, 145, 149, 162, 164–5,
  174, 176, 182–4, 193, 208, 224–
  5, 282, 284
oil 149, 167–8, 199, 264, 268, 281–2
operation DYNAMO 265–6
operation HUSKY 206–7
operation NEPTUNE x, 204, 297
operation MARKET GARDEN 231,
  241
operation OVERLORD x, 208, 215,
  217, 227–9, 296–7

P

Pacific liii, 9, 168–9, 171
Palestine 4, 86, 152
panzer divisions 146-7, 150–1, 154,
  157–8, 200, 229, 243, 279, 290
Panzerarmee 153, 155
panzers 144, 147–8, 156, 158, 236,
  265, 273, 278
Parachute Army 238
Paris xlvii, lii, 2, 6, 51–4, 58, 60–1,
  64, 69, 75–9, 109–10, 114, 130,
  159, 198, 202, 266, 279
Passchendaele xlvi, 92, 94, 97, 292
Patton, General 225–6, 232, 236
Paulus, General 252, 273
peace lv, 1–2, 6, 12, 53–5, 85, 101,
  103–5, 113–14, 123, 126, 128,
  139–40, 263, 269, 275
  compromise 2, 28, 33, 37, 125,
  263
Peninsula 15–16
Pershing, General John 135, 221
Pétain, Marshal Philippe x, xlvii, 88,

90, 107, 109–19, 130, 132, 135,
  226, 233
Pitt, William 281
plans lii, 5, 14, 19–23, 34, 42–3, 49,
  51, 58, 69–70, 72, 78, 94, 128,
  164, 171, 175, 182, 191–2, 198,
  206–7, 209, 213, 219, 222, 227,
  229, 233–4, 238, 248, 254, 264,
  284, 287
  operational lvi, 20, 58, 63, 93, 161,
  171, 209, 270
Poland 4, 121, 123, 259–63, 276
Polish Army 240
political leaders, allied 106, 196
politicians 2, 9, 18, 55, 71–2, 83, 93,
  99, 120, 189, 286
Prince 170, 287
prisoners vii, 2, 36, 127, 135–6, 138–
  41, 145, 152, 177, 185, 235–8,
  243, 270, 274, 289
Prussia vii, 8, 42, 44–6, 48, 53, 56–9,
  68, 121, 145
Prussian army 44, 46, 49–50, 58–9,
  61, 63

R

raids 33–4, 161, 191–2, 195–7, 267
railways li, 10, 14, 42, 46–7, 52, 72,
  153, 178, 198, 290
Ramsay, Admiral Sir Bertram viii,
  204–18
Rangoon 173, 184
Red Army liv, 156, 192, 197, 200–1,
  233–4, 239–40, 243–7, 249–50,
  255, 269–71, 273, 276, 292,
  297–9
  fighting 275
  newly-created 245
Remagen 236

Repulse 170, 287

reserves 50, 86–7, 90, 99, 106–7, 128, 131–2, 136, 140, 148, 158, 166, 191, 209–10, 226, 281

reservists 51, 58

Rezonville, Battle of 62

Rhine 2, 45, 50, 52–3, 62, 72, 191, 217, 230–1, 234–9, 263, 298

Richmond 14–18, 20–1, 28–32, 37–8, 89

Rommel, Generalfeldmarschall Erwin viii, xlv, 7, 143–60, 225, 284, 289

  armour 148, 155

  defence x, 155

  fighting 275

  offensive 154

  papers xlvi, 160

  plan 151, 154

  saved 148

Roosevelt, President 9, 152, 194, 239, 268, 271, 281–2, 290–1, 293–6, 298

Royal Air Force viii, liii–liv, 135, 159, 187, 189, 191, 242, 268, 286

Ruhr 194, 197, 216, 230–4, 236, 238–9, 264, 298

Russia 1, 3, 5, 7–8, 14, 42, 45, 67–71, 92, 114, 123, 125, 127, 129, 247, 269–72, 274

Russian Army 69, 92, 105, 239, 298

Russian Front 95, 157, 192, 293

Russian offensive 77, 123

Russians 5–6, 8, 42, 77, 92–3, 106, 122, 157, 296

S

Schlemm, General 235

Schlieffen, Graf von 68–70, 74, 76, 81

Schlieffen Plan vii, x, xlvi, 50, 73, 77–8, 81, 84, 121–2, 265

Second Army (*British*) 210, 238

Second Army (*German*) 80, 121–2, 130

Second Army (*Russian*) 47-8

Second World War xlv–xlviii, li–liii, lvi, 7, 16, 19, 83, 87, 89, 95, 97, 103–4, 106, 109, 146, 161, 167, 175, 177, 187–8, 190, 193, 202, 220, 242, 251, 259, 277–8, 287, 289, 300

Seven Days Battle 17, 31–2

Seventeenth Army (*German*) 130, 236, 273

Seventh Army (*German*) 236

Seventh Army (*US*) 236, 239, 241

shells li, 100–1, 104, 125

Sherman, General William 22, 29

Sicily 204, 206, 225–7, 290, 295

siege 36, 38, 54–5, 63, 65, 96, 148, 152, 251, 289

signals lii, 17, 25, 76, 78, 139, 150, 207, 233, 240–2, 300

Singapore 148, 185, 287–9

sinkings 51, 93, 126, 161, 170, 173, 202, 288

Sixth Army (*French*) 78-9

Sixth Army (*German*) 251-2, 272-3

Sixty-second Army 252

slavery 10, 13, 25, 28

sleep 60, 146, 244, 249–50, 254

Slim, General Sir William viii, 173–86

  army 178

  command 180

  leadership 176, 180

  soldiers 185

  stunning victory 184

soldiers xlv, xlix, 2, 15, 23, 25–6, 31–2, 38–9, 41–2, 44, 53–5, 58, 65,

69, 73, 75–6, 78, 82–3, 85, 87,
98, 106, 109–16, 120, 125–7,
139–40, 144–6, 151–3, 156–7,
175, 177–80, 183–5, 205–6, 208,
210, 213–15, 220, 225–6, 228,
233, 237, 245, 249, 251, 254
educated 61, 84
front-line 145, 251
intellectual 21, 41
soldier's wellbeing 111, 115
Somme x, 82–3, 86, 88–9, 91–2, 95–
6, 101, 104, 120, 125, 129, 133,
135–7, 147, 292
Soviet Union liv–lv, 96, 149, 161,
175, 192, 233, 240, 243–4, 247,
251–2, 254–6, 259–60, 262, 264,
268–9, 299
Spain 3, 8, 56, 61, 222
Speer, Albert xlvi, 195, 197, 259,
274–5, 277
Spotsylvania, Battle of 37
Stalin, Joseph 233, 240, 243–4, 246–
8, 250–4, 269–70, 272, 283, 296,
299
Stalingrad, Battle of viii, xlvi–xlvii,
96, 234, 242, 251–2, 256–7,
272–3
Strasbourg 49–52, 54, 58
strategic air offensive xlvi, lv, 191,
196, 198, 201–2, 242
strategy xlvi, 4–6, 13, 15, 21–2, 29–
30, 40, 42, 44, 47, 52, 54, 59, 64,
78, 82, 89–90, 122, 129, 137,
149, 152, 158, 195, 207, 216,
221, 230, 236, 239, 242, 262,
269, 272, 274, 295, 297–9
allied 216, 299
defensive 72, 168
narrow-front 216, 230–1
supreme commander, allied 88, 130,
135, 137, 222–3, 226, 230

surrender 20, 53–5, 65, 121, 140, 147,
160, 177, 195, 206, 265, 268,
273, 279, 294

T

tactics 41–2, 91, 145, 227
tanks xlvii, lii, 16, 83, 88, 97, 133,
136, 139, 146–7, 151–2, 155,
190, 197, 202, 210–15, 235, 243,
245–6, 255, 266, 289–90, 294
Tannenberg, Battle of 77, 122
territories x, 9–10, 14, 25, 121, 149,
157, 182, 288
Tenth Army (*Italian*) 143, 289
Third Army (*British*) 129, 137, 238
Third Army (*US*) 236, 241
Third Reich xlvi, 160, 204, 261, 265,
272, 275, 277
Tokyo 164–5, 168
traitors 109, 276
trenches li, 24, 37, 73, 82, 87, 96,
110–11, 114–15, 235, 292
Tripoli 143–4, 155
troops vii, li, liii–liv, 4–5, 15, 26, 30–
1, 46, 57–9, 62–4, 73, 75–7, 86,
90, 92, 95, 97, 107, 110–11, 113,
117, 122, 127, 129–33, 137–40,
143–4, 146–7, 153–5, 157, 159,
176, 179, 182–3, 214, 228–9,
231, 237–8, 248, 250, 252, 254,
262, 269, 272, 285, 288–9
green 35, 224, 243
soviet 175, 255, 257
troopships li, 286, 289
Tshushima, Battle of 162

U

U-boats liii, 126–7, 210–11, 215, 264,
282, 285–6

United States liii–lv, 9–10, 21, 28, 33, 39, 92, 100, 126–7, 161, 163, 166–7, 170, 191–2, 220, 222, 224, 254, 269, 271, 281, 291, 296, 299

V

vehicles 159, 210, 213–15, 235, 253–4
Verdun xlvii, li, 62, 75, 77–9, 89, 91–2, 109–10, 112, 117–18, 120, 123, 128–9, 138, 181, 251
Versailles 54, 106
Versailles Treaty 145–6, 260, 264
veterans 7, 235, 241, 247
victory xliii–xlvi, liv, 3–9, 21, 32, 34, 36, 39, 41, 44, 49–50, 55, 57, 63, 75, 78–9, 89, 103–5, 107, 110, 116, 120, 122–4, 141, 149, 152–3, 164, 170, 173, 176–7, 180, 182, 185–6, 198, 215, 220, 228, 230, 240, 242, 248–9, 252, 259, 264, 266, 275–6, 278–80, 286, 299
  allied 100, 107
  cheap 96, 271
  common 239, 298
  decisive liv, 17, 48, 63, 112, 130
  final liv, 93, 136, 153, 265
  parade 266

W

War Cabinet 93–4, 102, 107, 126, 188, 200, 283

War Ministry 124–5
war office 99–101, 224
Washington 13–15, 17–19, 22, 27, 33, 35, 150, 163–4, 169, 209, 222, 293–4
Waterloo, Battle of 1, 2, 6, 8, 32, 34
Wavell, Field Marshal 16, 143–4, 177, 286, 289
weapons 100, 124–5, 157, 204
Wehrmacht liv, 95, 188, 192, 197, 200–1, 233, 241, 243, 249–50, 253, 263, 265–6, 269–73, 275, 277, 292, 299
Western Desert Force 143
Western Front viii, xlix–li, liii, 37–8, 67, 82–5, 87, 89–96, 98, 104–5, 107, 109, 111, 117, 124, 127–9, 135, 140, 150, 187, 189, 194, 201, 204, 215, 217, 233, 236, 238, 251, 263–4, 267, 279, 292–3, 295, 298
Wilson, General Sir Henry 106

Y

Yamamoto, Admiral Isoruku viii, 161–172
Ypres, Battle of 86, 92, 94–6, 106, 127–9, 137–8, 235, 292

Z

Zhukov, Marshal Georgi, viii, xlvii, 243–56, 271, 273